Taking Off
Teacher's Edition

Second Edition

Susan Hancock Fesler   Christy M. Newman

Teacher's Edition by Kristin Sherman

 **McGraw-Hill**

Taking Off Beginning English Teacher's Edition, 2nd Edition

Published by McGraw-Hill ESL/ELT, a business unit of The McGraw-Hill Companies, Inc. 1221 Avenue of the Americas, New York, NY 10020. Copyright © 2008 by The McGraw-Hill Companies, Inc. All rights reserved. No part of this publication may be reproduced or distributed in any form or by any means, or stored in a database or retrieval system, without the prior written consent of The McGraw-Hill Companies, Inc., including, but not limited to, in any network or other electronic storage or transmission, or broadcast for distance learning.

ISBN 10: 0-07-331436-6
ISBN 13: 978-0-07-331436-5
 2 3 4 5 6 7 8 9 QPD 11 10 09

Project manager: Linda O'Roke
Developmental editor: Amy Lawler
Cover designer: Wanda Espana
Interior designer: Aptara
Artists: Anna Divito, Nancy Carpenter, Roberta Rieple

www.esl-elt.mcgraw-hill.com

Cover image by Anna Divito

Table of Contents

To the Teacher

The *Taking Off* Teacher's Edition provides support to teachers using the *Taking Off* Student Book. Each unit of the Teacher's Edition begins with a table listing the unit's lesson title, the objectives of each lesson, and the corresponding Student Book page number. Below that, there are suggestions for how and where to use the unit-opening big picture illustration to present new language from the unit. Finally, the page lists the focus, title, and page number of the reproducible worksheets provided in the Teacher Edition. There are four worksheets for each unit.

Each lesson lists the objective along with any new vocabulary. It also provides page references to the corresponding lesson in the *Taking Off* Workbook and Literacy Workbook. Teaching instructions, new language, and learning points are provided for each lesson. Seasoned teachers can use the teaching instructions as a quick refresher, while newer teachers, or substitute teachers, can use the step-by-step instructions as a helpful guide. A variety of notes highlighting grammar, culture, and pronunciation are called out separately to make them easy to find. Literacy Development and Extra Challenge activities appear in special easy-to-find boxes. Listening scripts and Student Book answers are conveniently located within the teaching instructions for each activity.

Taking Off Teacher's Edition Features

- **NEW 300 expansion activities** including Literacy Development activities and Challenge activities for more advanced students

- **NEW 48 reproducible worksheets** many of which offer creative tasks tied to the "big picture" unit openers

- **NEW "Unit Opener" Expansion Activities** that focus on speaking, reading, grammar, and writing

- **NEW Culture, Grammar, and Pronunciation Notes**

- **Two-page unit tests** (*Note:* Listening passages for the tests are available on the Student Book audio program.)

- **Listening scripts** for Student Book audio program

- **Answer keys** for Student Book and Workbook (Note: Literacy Workbook answer key is located in the back of the Literacy Workbook)

Taking Off Second Edition is a four-skills, standards-based program for beginning students of English. Picture dictionary art pages teach life-skills vocabulary in a clear and visual way. The gradually accelerating pace of the book instills confidence in students as they establish a solid foundation in the basics of English.

Taking Off Second Edition Features

- **NEW** *Grammar* lessons summarize and provide practice on central grammar points in each unit.

- **NEW** *Read* lessons reuse and recycle vocabulary and grammar in new contexts as students practice finding the main idea and other comprehension skills.

- **NEW** *Write* lessons provide structured writing experiences that encourage students to personalize the vocabulary and grammar they have learned in the unit.

- **NEW** *My Life* activity boxes offer students the opportunity to personalize new vocabulary and concepts while participating in communicative activities.

- **NEW** *Our Cultures* sections with photos and graphic organizers help student discuss and compare their native cultures with their new culture.

- **Four-skills foundation course** prepares students for Book 1 in a variety of popular series, such as *All Star* and *Excellent English*.

- **Activities correlated to CASAS, EFF, LAUSD Course Outlines, and Florida Adult ESOL Syllabi** prepare students to master a broad range of critical competencies.

- **Picture dictionary art pages** highlight life-skills vocabulary in engaging contexts.

- **Listening activities** help students develop speaking, reading, and writing skills in a low-anxiety environment.

- *Numbers* **pages** in each unit help students build numeracy skills for basic math work.

- *Community* **pages** in each unit introduce students to critical civics topics.

Components

- **Student Book** has twelve 16-page units with a wealth of individual, pair-, and group-work activities. In four special sections throughout the book, students and teachers will also find new *Review* lessons for additional study and practice. Listening scripts are found at the back of the Student Book and in the Teacher's Edition.

- **Student Book with Audio Highlights** provides students with audio recordings of all the vocabulary in the Student Book. This CD also includes recordings of all the *Read* lessons in the units.

- **Workbook** includes supplementary practice activities correlated to the Student Book. A flexible set of activities correlated to each unit builds vocabulary, listening, reading, writing, and test-taking skills. As a bonus feature, the Workbook also includes online activities for students to do in a computer lab or at home.

- **Literacy Workbook with Audio CD** incorporates phonics activities, letter and number practice activities, and "on-ramp" activities for emerging literacy students. This component is designed for students who do not have foundational literacy skills in their first language. The Literacy Workbook offers supplementary activities for each unit in the Student Book.

- **Teacher's Edition with Tests** provides:
  - Step-by-step teaching instructions
  - Over 300 expansion activities including Literacy Development activities and Extra Challenge activities
  - 48 reproducible worksheets, many of which offer creative tasks tied to the "big picture" unit openers
  - Culture, Literacy, and Pronunciation Notes
  - Two-page test for each unit
  - Audio scripts for audio program
  - Answer keys for Student Book, Workbook, and test materials.

- **Post-Testing Study Guide** provides reproducible worksheets to help students create performance portfolios that document post-testing readiness.

- **NEW Character Cards** stimulate conversation in the classroom with lively visual and conversation cues for the teacher to use. Durable, full-color cards provide ideal teacher presentation tools.

- **Color Overhead Transparencies** encourage teachers to present new vocabulary and concepts in fun and meaningful ways. This component provides a full-color overhead transparency for each of the "big picture" unit openers.

- **Audio Program** contains recordings for all listening activities in the Student Book. Listening passages for each unit test are provided at the end of the audio section for that unit.

Program Overview

Consult *Welcome to Taking Off* on pages xviii-xxiii. This guide offers teachers and program directors a visual tour of one Student Book unit.

Predictable lesson format

Student Book lessons are one page in length and contain three to five activities. This one-page format allows teachers to "chunk" their instruction into short, manageable sessions that give students a sense of accomplishment in their swift completion of each lesson. The first activity usually asks students to listen to and repeat new vocabulary and language. These listen and repeat activities help students prepare for speaking, reading, and writing skills in a low-anxiety environment. At the low beginning level, it is critical that students have a chance to listen to and repeat all new vocabulary and language before being asked to speak, read, or write.

Unit-opening illustrations

Each unit opens with a dynamic, full-page color illustration, providing context for the key vocabulary items and language presented in the unit. This illustration sets the scene for the unit, activating students' background knowledge and encouraging them to share words they can say in English. Teachers can present the unit-opening illustrations on an overhead projector with the Color Transparencies.

CASAS, EFF, LAUSD Course Outlines, and Florida Adult ESOL Syllabi

Program directors and teachers are often asked to benchmark student progress against national, state, or district standards. With this in mind, *Taking Off* carefully integrates instructional elements from a wide range of standards. Here is a brief overview of our approach to meeting these standards:

- **CASAS** Many states in the U.S. tie funding for adult education programs to student performances on the Comprehensive Adult Student Assessment System (CASAS). The CASAS (www.casas.org) competencies identify more than 300 essential skills that adults need in order to succeed in the classroom, workplace, and community. Examples of these skills include: identifying or using appropriate non-verbal behavior in a variety of settings, responding appropriately to common personal information questions, and comparing price or quality to determine the best buys. *Taking Off* carefully integrates CASAS competencies that are appropriate for low beginning students.

- **EFF** Equipped for the Future (EFF) is a set of standards for adult literacy and lifelong learning, developed by the National Institute for Literacy (www.nifl.gov). The organizing principle of EFF is that adults assume responsibilities in three major areas of life—as parents, citizens, and workers. These three areas of focus are called "role maps" in the EFF documentation. In the parent role map, for example, EFF addresses these and other responsibilities: participating in children's formal education and forming and maintaining supportive family relationships. Each *Taking Off* unit addresses one or more of the EFF role maps. The focus on the student as community citizen is particularly strong in Lesson 9 of each unit, which is devoted to *Community* activities.

- **LAUSD Course Outlines** were developed to guide teachers in lesson planning and to inform students about what they will be able to do after successful completion of their course. The LAUSD course outlines focus on acquiring skills in listening, speaking, reading, and writing in the context of everyday life. *Taking Off* addresses all four language skills in the contexts of home, community, and work, with appropriately targeted vocabulary for Beginning Low adult ESL students.

- **Florida Adult ESOL Syllabi** provide the curriculum frameworks for all six levels of instruction; Foundations, Low Beginning, High Beginning, Low Intermediate, High Intermediate, and Advanced. The syllabi were developed by the State of Florida as a guide to include the following areas of adult literacy standards: workplace, communication (listen, speak, read, and write), technology, interpersonal communication, health and nutrition, government and community resources, consumer education, family and parenting, concepts of time and money, safety and security, and language development (grammar and pronunciation). Each *Taking Off* unit carefully integrates these standards.

Number of hours of instruction

The *Taking Off* program has been designed to accommodate the needs of adult classes with 70–216 hours of classroom instruction. Here are three recommended ways in which various components in the *Taking Off* program can be combined to meet student and teacher needs.

- **70–120 hours** Teachers are encouraged to work through all of the Student Book materials, incorporating the *Review* and *Our Cultures* lessons as time permits. The Color Transparencies and Character Cards can be used to introduce and/or review materials in each unit. Teachers should also look to the Teacher's Edition for teaching suggestions and testing materials as necessary. *Time per unit: 7–10 hours.*

- **120–168 hours** In addition to working through all of the Student Book materials, teachers are encouraged to incorporate the Workbook and/or Literacy Workbook for supplementary practice. *Time per unit: 10–14 hours.*

- **168–216 hours** Teachers and students working in an intensive instructional setting can take advantage of the wealth of expansion activities threaded through the Teacher's Edition to supplement their use of the Student Book and Workbook materials. *Time per unit: 14–18 hours.*

Assessment

Some teachers prefer to evaluate their students informally by monitoring their students' listening and speaking abilities during pair-work or group-work activities. These teachers may also maintain portfolios of student writing to show the progress students are making in writing skill development.

For teachers who need or want formal assessments of their students, the Teacher's Edition provides two-page, reproducible tests for each Student Book unit. Each test takes approximately 30 minutes to administer, and these tests are designed to assess vocabulary, grammar, writing, listening, and reading comprehension skills, as well as grammar and writing development. There is a listening activity on each test, and the recorded passages for these sections are found on the Student Book Audio Program. Audio scripts for the tests appear in the Teacher's Edition.

SPECIAL FEATURES

Grammar Pages

Fundamental grammar points, such as nouns, pronouns, and adjectives, basic past and present tenses, and simple question forms are newly incorporated into each unit. These two-page descriptive *Grammar* spreads provide summary charts or visual explanation of important grammar points covered in each unit followed by activities that progress from highly to less structured.

Read and *Write* Pages

Simple but exciting readings about the lives and adventures of characters in *Taking Off* can be found in Lesson 12 of each unit. These readings use the vocabulary of the unit to expand reading and comprehension skills, including the critical skill of understanding the main idea. The complexity of the readings develops from basic realia-based readings to three-paragraph challenging, engaging stories. Each reading rests on a foundation of state and national standards, such as positive parental involvement or understanding bank forms.

Lesson 13, the *Write* page, provides a model of an important, standards-based writing skill, such as completing a form, writing a letter to the landlord requesting a repair, or preparing a health plan. Following the model, students are given the opportunity to complete a form with personalized information. These activities progress from highly structured to more and more independent writing choices as students move through the units.

Numbers pages

Learning basic math skills is critically important for success in school, on the job, and at home. Accordingly, most national and state-level standards for adult education mandate instruction in basic math skills. With this in mind, Lesson 8 in each Student Book unit is dedicated to helping students develop numeracy skills they need for basic math work. In Unit 1, for example, students learn the numerals 1–10 and the English words for these numbers. Labeled *Numbers*, these lessons enable students to complete activities on working with American money, reading temperatures, and understanding numbers on a paycheck.

Community pages

Many institutions focus direct attention on the importance of civics instruction for English language learners. This type of instruction is often referred to as *EL/Civics* and is designed to help students become active and informed community members. Lesson 9 in each Student Book unit explores a community- or work-related topic. Labeled *Community*, these lessons have areas of focus like learning about reading safety signs, writing a check, using an ATM, learning about health insurance, having a potluck dinner, and going to garage sales.

Classes with literacy and low beginning students

A special *Taking Off Literacy Workbook* has been designed for literacy students enrolled in low beginning classes. Most low beginning students are true beginners in English who are literate in their first language. Literacy students, on the other hand, usually do not have fundamental first-language literacy skills. Literacy students often need specific instruction in letter formation, phonics, and other fundamental reading, listening, and writing skills.

As teachers who have worked with mixed groups of literacy and low beginning students know, dealing simultaneously with the needs of each of these groups of learners is a great challenge. The Literacy Workbook offers a unique resource for teachers in such multi-level classes. Each Literacy Workbook unit provides essential support for key elements of the Student Book. Working with or without a teacher's aide, literacy students can tackle basic reading, listening, and writing activities in the Literacy Workbook while their low beginning classmates tackle tasks at their ability level.

The *Taking Off* Cast of Characters

Taking Off features an engaging cast of characters enrolled in a beginning English class. The authors developed the book around these characters to help students learn new language from familiar faces.

Carlos Avila
Waiter, *Brazilian*

Maria Cruz
Salesclerk, *Mexican*

Leo Danov
Taxi driver, *Russian*

Sandy Johnson
Teacher, *American*

Tien Lam
Delivery person, *Vietnamese*

Ben Lee
Construction worker, *Chinese*

Grace Lee
Homemaker, *Chinese*

Paul Lemat
Computer programmer, *Haitian*

Isabel Lopez
Office worker, *Colombian*

Nadira Shaheed
Health aide, *Somali*

Scope and Sequence

Unit	Topics	Listening & Speaking Skills	Reading & Writing Skills	Grammar
1 **Welcome to the classroom.** *Page 2*	• Meeting new people • The alphabet • Greetings • Countries • Classroom language • Classroom objects • Emergency form • Homework • Learning log	• Introduce yourself • Say the name of the country you come from • Listen and identify classroom objects • Say your telephone number, address, and email address • Ask for and give the spelling of words • Listen to and practice simple dialogs • Follow classroom directions	• Read & write alphabet letters • Interpret basic sight words • Write proper names, countries, and classroom words • Examine classroom commands/directions • Write and read personal information • Check new vocabulary in a learning log	• *I'm, It's* • *What's*
2 **Where are you from?** *Page 18*	• Native language • Country of origin • Marital status • Physical appearance • Address • U.S. map • Identification form	• Collect information from classmates • Ask and answer about country of origin • Ask and answer about the language you speak • Recognize differences in marital status • Discuss height and color of eyes and hair	• Fill in information on a chart • Write personal information statements • Use writing to describe height • Identify vocabulary that describes physical appearance • Read and write words for select countries and languages • Read a map of the USA • Write about your teacher • Write about new students	• *Am, Is, Are* • *Has/Have*
3 **This is my family.** *Page 34*	• Relatives • Name titles *(Mr., Mrs., Ms., and Miss)* • Family tree • Ages • Family form • Children	• Ask questions about family • Discuss family members with classmates • Ask about someone's age • Listen to information about family members • Say name titles *(Mr., Mrs., Ms., Miss)* • Recognize numbers 20-100	• Write family position words to complete a sentence • Read names using titles *(Mr., Mrs., Ms., Miss)* • Make your own family tree • Read a paragraph about a family member • Identify the topic of a story • Complete a family form	• *Yes, I do. / No, I don't.* • *My, His, Her, Your, Their*

Review for Units 1–3 *Page 50*
• Matching Activity: personal information
• Listening Activity: marital status
• Grammar: present tense of *Be* and *Have*

Our Cultures: Greetings *Page 52*
• Identify different types of greetings
• Complete a Venn Diagram to compare greetings in different countries
• Discuss forms of greetings in groups

Numeracy	Community Awareness	Florida Standards	CASAS	EFF	LAUSD Beginning Low
• Learn numbers 1–10 • Identify numbers used in context • Say and write telephone numbers with area code • Say and write addresses and email addresses	• Complete an emergency form • Identify your emergency contact person • Learn 911 for police and fire emergencies	**1:** 1.05.01 **2:** 1.17.02 **3:** 1.17.02 **4:** 1.15.02 1.15.03 **6:** 1.09.03 **7:** 1.09.03 **8:** 1.09.03 **9:** 1.09.03 **12:** 1.16.11 **13:** 1.15.05	**1:** 0.1.1, 0.1.4 **4:** 0.1.6 **6:** 0.1.5 **8:** 0.1.1 **9:** 0.1.1, 0.1.5 **10:** 6.0.1 **13:** 0.2.1 **13:** 0.2.2 **13:** 2.1.2	• Speak So Others Can Understand • Listen Actively • Cooperate With Others • Take Responsibility for Learning	LIFE SKILLS • 1 • 5 • 9a, b • 18 • 16 • 17 • 15 • 58a GRAMMAR • 13a • 16c (i)
• Learn numbers 11–19 • Say and write numbers in an address • Say and write zip codes	• Complete a detailed identification form • Learn to write your name as follows: last name, first name, middle initial • Learn the components of an address	**1:** 1.05.02 **2:** 1.05.02 **3:** 1.05.02 **6:** 1.15.06 **8:** 1.15.05 **9:** 1.15.05 **10:** 1.16.02 **11:** 1.16.02 **12:** 1.13.03 1.13.04	**1:** 2.7.2 **2, 3:** 0.1.3 **4:** 0.1.2 **5:** 1.1.4, 1.1.9 **6:** 0.2.1 **8:** 2.4.1, 6.0.1 **9:** 0.2.2 **12:** 2.2.5	• Read with understanding • Convey Ideas in Writing • Cooperate With Others • Reflect and Evaluate	LIFE SKILLS • 2 • 4 • 5 • 6 • 7 • 23b GRAMMAR • 1 • 20
• Learn numbers 20-100 • Say your age • Recognize number words • Write the ages of family members • Write the number of people in your family	• Complete a form about your family • Politely decline to answer a question	**1:** 1.14.01 **2:** 1.14.01 **3:** 1.14.01 **4:** 1.14.01 **8:** 1.08.01 **9:** 1.08.01 1.14.01 **11:** 1.16.10 **13:** 1.15.06	**1:** 7.5.5 **2, 3:** 7.4.8 **6:** 2.7.3 **7:** 0.1.6 **8:** 6.0.2 **9:** 5.3.1, 0.2.2 **12, 13:** 0.2.3	• Convey Ideas in Writing • Resolve Conflict and Negotiate • Use Math to Solve Problems and Communicate • Learn Through Research	LIFE SKILLS • 4 • 6 • 7 • 9c • 60 • 10c • 17 GRAMMAR • 16a, b

Scope and Sequence

Unit	Topics	Listening & Speaking Skills	Reading & Writing Skills	Grammar
4 **Welcome to our house.** *Page 54*	• Rooms in a house • Items in a house • Types of houses • Household needs • Your dream house • Garage sales	• Listen to and recognize the rooms in a house • Discuss household items • Learn the names of different types of housing • Speak with a partner about household items and needs • Differentiate between numbers that sound alike (18 vs. 80).	• Write the names of the rooms in a house • Review a paragraph about a new apartment • Write and read about a dream house • Read a paragraph about garage sales • Write a note about a household problem	• Singular and Plural Nouns • *a* and *an*
5 **I talk on the phone.** *Page 70*	• Daily activities • Days of the week • Months and dates • Time • Appointments • Medical form • Birthdays	• Discuss your daily activities • Listen to and say the days of the week • Listen to and say the months of the year • Listen to and say times • Talk about birthdays • Use the telephone to make appointments • Listen to ordinal numbers	• Read the time on analog and digital clocks • Recognize abbreviations for months • Write times on a calendar • Write and read ordinal numbers • Read about a birthday • Write about what you see in a picture • Write an email	• Simple Present Tense
6 **Let's go shopping.** *Page 86*	• Clothes • Colors • Clothing sizes • Problems with clothing • Money • Paying by check	• Listen to and identify articles of clothing • Ask for what you need in a store • Ask about clothing size • Say that clothing is too large or small • Say color words • Ask about favorite colors • Play a spoken guessing game with classmates	• Read and write clothing words • Write sentences about clothing size • Write about problems with clothes • Learn words for American coins and bills • Write a check • Read a catalog • Write a shopping list • Write about favorite clothes	• Adjectives and Nouns

Review for Units 4–6 *Page 102*
- Matching activity: answers to *Wh-* questions
- Reading activity: interpret an internet page
- Grammar: singular/plural nouns, simple present tense

Our Cultures: Homes *Page 104*
- Identify types of houses from different cultures
- Compare your house to your house in your native country
- Discuss types of housing in groups

Numeracy	Community Awareness	Florida Standards	CASAS	EFF	LAUSD Beginning Low
• Differentiate between numbers with similar digits • Complete sentences using numbers • Associate numbers above one with plural forms	• Learn that garage sales are community activities • Recognize the different types of houses in a community • Ask a landlord for household repairs	**4:** 1.11.06 **11:** 1.16.06 **12:** 1.11.06	**1:** 1.4.2 **2, 3:** 7.4.3 **4:** 1.4.1 **7:** 7.1.1 **8:** 6.0.1 **9:** 8.3.2 **13:** 1.4.7	• Advocate and Influence • Solve Problems and Make Decisions • Plan • Use Information and Communications Technology	LIFE SKILLS • 4 • 14a • 38 • 39 • 60 GRAMMAR • 9a, b
• Practice ordinal numbers • Recognize the days and dates on a calendar • Write your date of birth on a form • Write month, date, and year in numerical form (MM/DD/YY)	• Complete a medical form • Learn about the following services: dental cleaning, car tune-up, and haircut • Keep community appointments on a calendar	**2:** 1.08.03 **3:** 1.08.03 **4:** 1.08.02 **5:** 1.08.02 **6:** 1.06.01 **8:** 1.08.04 **9:** 1.15.05 **10:** 1.16.02 **11:** 1.16.02	**1:** 0.2.4 **2, 3:** 2.3.2 **4, 5:** 2.3.1 **6:** 2.1.8, 7.1.4 **7:** 7.1.2 **8:** 0.2.1, 6.0.1 6.0.2 **9:** 3.2.1 **12:** 2.7.1 **13:** 4.6.2	• Listen Actively • Solve Problems and Make Decisions • Plan • Use Math to Solve Problems and Communicate	LIFE SKILLS • 3 • 12 • 25 • 26 • 27 • 60 GRAMMAR • 1a, b
• Write a check • Recognize American coin and bill denominations • Match coins and bills to monetary values • Recognize page references	• Ask for assistance in a store • Buy clothes in a store • Buy clothes from a catalog • Recognize and use American money	**3:** 1.15.01 **4:** 1.15.01 **5:** 1.15.01 **6:** 1.11.02 1.11.04 **7:** 1.11.02 1.11.04 **8:** 1.11.03 **9:** 1.08.07 1.11.01 **10:** 1.16.06 1.16.07 **11:** 1.16.06 1.16.07 **R:** 1.11.02	**1:** 0.1.3, 1.3.9 **2:** 1.3.3 **3:** 0.2.4, 8.1.2 **4:** 1.2.5 **5:** 1.3.4, 7.5.1 **6:** 1.1.9, 1.2.1 **7:** 1.2.1, 1.2.2 **8:** 1.1.6, 1.2.2 6.0.2 **9:** 1.2.4, 1.8.2 **12:** 1.3.4 **13:** 1.2.1	• Read with understanding • Observe Critically • Advocate and Influence • Use Math to Solve Problems and Communicate	LIFE SKILLS • 11b • 14a • 30a, b • 31 • 32 • 33 • 34 • 60 GRAMMAR • 12a, b

Scope and Sequence

Unit	Topics	Listening & Speaking Skills	Reading & Writing Skills	Grammar
7 **I'm so hungry!** *Page 106*	• Grocery shopping • Food • Food groups • Containers for food • Meals • Supermarket coupons • Potluck dinner	• Listen for the names of food items • Talk about what food items you need • Discuss breakfast, lunch, and dinner foods • Order in a restaurant • Ask and answer questions about foods you eat • Discuss frequency of activities	• Make a shopping list • Read the names of food items • Complete a chart about location of foods in a supermarket • Read a paragraph about potluck dinners • Read supermarket coupons • Identify true and false statements about a reading	• Count Nouns • Non-count Nouns
8 **How's the weather?** *Page 122*	• Weather • Seasons • Leisure activities • Temperature (Fahrenheit and Celsius) • U.S. map • Weather Map	• Discuss different types of weather • Listen to and discuss leisure activities • Discuss activities you like to do in different seasons • Listen to a weather report • Talk about temperature in a city	• Read and write about the seasons • Recognize weather-related vocabulary • Write sentences about weather • Interpret a weather map • Make a chart about weather in your country • Read an email • Write a letter to a friend	• Present Continuous Tense • Contractions
9 **Where's the post office?** *Page 138*	• Neighborhood map • Places in the community/ neighborhood • Banking • ATM (Automated Teller Machine)	• Talk about places you see in your neighborhood • Ask and answer questions about the location of neighborhood places • Ask your classmates what places they live near • Ask your classmates where they do things	• Read a neighborhood map • Write sentences about the location of neighborhood places • Read about depositing money into a savings account • Read about how to use an ATM • Read about cashing a check • Complete a supermarket card club application	• Prepositions of place

Review for Units 7–9 *Page 154*
• Group discussion: "What are you doing now"?
• Writing activity: containers
• Listening activity: identify words in a short dialog
• Grammar: contractions with *be*, present continuous tense

Our Cultures: Marketplaces *Page 156*
• Talk about marketplaces in other countries
• Complete a chart on food shopping
• Discuss food shopping in groups

Numeracy	Community Awareness	Florida Standards	CASAS	EFF	LAUSD Beginning Low
• Write times of the day for meals • Use times of the day in sentences • Use container words to talk about food (a bunch of grapes) • Identify what you can afford with an amount of money	• Explore a supermarket • Learn about a potluck dinner • Practice ordering food in a restaurant • Use supermarket coupons • Make a shopping budget	**1:** 1.07.06 **2:** 1.07.06 **3:** 1.07.06 **4:** 1.07.07 **5:** 1.07.07 **6:** 1.07.08 **8:** 1.11.02 **10:** 1.16.06 **11:** 1.16.06 **12:** 1.08.05 **R:** 1.07.06	**1:** 1.3.8 **2:** 1.3.8 **3:** 0.1.2, 1.3.7 **4:** 3.5.2, 8.2.1 **5:** 8.2.1 **6:** 2.6.4, 8.1.3 **7:** 3.5.9, 8.2.1 **8:** 1.1.4, 1.1.7 **9:** 2.7.2, 2.7.3 **12:** 1.2.3, 1.3.5 **13:** 1.3.4 **14:** 0.1.3 **R:** 7.4.3, 7.4.7	• Speak So Others Can Understand • Guide Others • Take Responsibility for Learning • Reflect and Evaluate	LIFE SKILLS • 12 • 13 • 14a • 31 • 32 • 35 • 36 • 37 GRAMMAR • 9d
• Interpret a thermometer in degrees Fahrenheit and Celsius • Write numbers using degrees Fahrenheit and Celsius	• Read a weather map • Practice personal correspondence • Talk about the weather in your community • Discuss community related leisure activities	**1:** 1.13.01 **2:** 1.13.01 **3:** 1.13.01 **6:** 1.13.01 **7:** 1.13.01 **9:** 1.13.01	**1:** 2.3.3, 5.7.3 **2:** 1.1.5, 2.3.3 **3:** 5.7.3 **4:** 0.2.4 **5:** 0.1.6 **6:** 0.2.4, 7.5.6 **7:** 2.63, 2.3.3 **8:** 1.1.5, 6.6.4 **9:** 1.1.3, 2.3.3, 6.6.5 **12:** 4.6.2 **13:** 7.4.2 **R:** 7.4.2, 7.4.8	• Convey Ideas in Writing • Observe Critically • Learn Through Research • Use Information and Communications Technology	LIFE SKILLS • 14a • 13 • 28 • 29 • 60 GRAMMAR • 2 • 3
• Read dates and money amounts on a bank deposit slip • Find information on a deposit slip • Complete a bank withdrawal • Use an ATM PIN number • Read about subtraction of a fee from a check	• Interpret a neighborhood map • Recognize business in your community • Practice banking procedures • Understand check cashing fees • Fill out an application form	**1:** 1.12.02 **2:** 1.09.02 1.09.03 **3:** 1.12.02 **4:** 1.08.06 **7:** 1.12.02 **8:** 1.08.06 **10:** 1.16.08 **11:** 1.16.08 **12:** 1.08.07 **13:** 1.08.07	**1:** 5.6.2 **2:** 2.2.1, 2.2.5 **3:** 2.5.4, 2.6.1 **4, 5:** 2.2.1 **6:** 0.1.6 **7:** 0.2.4, 2.4.2 **8:** 1.8.2 **9:** 1.8.1 **12:** 1.8.2 **13:** 0.2.2	• Read with understanding • Listen Actively • Guide Others • Use Information and Communications Technology	LIFE SKILLS • 7 • 11a, b • 13 • 22 • 23a, b • 30a, b GRAMMAR • 14a, b • 14c, d

Scope and Sequence   xvii

Scope and Sequence

Unit	Topics	Listening & Speaking Skills	Reading & Writing Skills	Grammar
10 **You need to see a doctor.** *Page 158*	• Health problems • Body parts • Medicine • Healthy food • Exercise • Health insurance	• Discuss health problems and remedies • Listen and identify health information in dialogs • Express physical pain • Make a doctor's appointment for your relative • Discuss medicines e • Listen to information about health insurance	• Recognize words for physical ailments • Read about staying fit and healthy • Write a phone conversation • Read a health insurance card • Fill in an insurance information form • Complete a Venn diagram to compare healthy habits • Write a health plan	• Action Verbs • Negatives
11 **What's your job?** *Page 174*	• Jobs • Workplaces • Driving • Want ads • Safety signs • Paychecks • Job applications • Job items • Work Skills	• Talk about jobs • Say what job conditions you like (indoors, with people) • Say what work-related skills you can do (fix things) • Ask and answer questions with affirmative and negative responses • Ask classmates about their past occupations	• Examine the tools different jobs require • Complete sentences about what you and others can do • Read want ads • Read safety signs • Fill in a form about what your job was before • Complete sentences about paychecks • Read and fill out a job application	• Simple Past of *Be* • *Can / Can't*
12 **How do you get to school?** *Page 190*	• Transportation • Directions to places in the community • Public transportation • Learner's permit • Road signs • Bus schedule	• Practice dialogs about methods of transportation • Differentiate among left, right, and straight ahead • Follow directions in the community • Listen to dialogs about time phrases • Ask about train and bus schedules	• Use a community map to give directions • Analyze a bus schedule • Complete sentences about a learner's permit • Read and respond to road signs • Read a story and answer question about driving with a new baby • Read and write about how to get to school	• Questions with *Be* • Questions with *Do / Does*

Review for Units 10–12 *Page 206*
• Group discussion about personal skills
• Matching activity: questions and answers
• Listening activity: identify health problems and times in dialogs
• Grammar: simple past tense of *Be, Can / Can't*

Our Cultures: Transportation *Page 208*
• Identify forms of transportation in other countries
• Complete a chart comparing transportation and lifestyle
• Discuss transportation in groups

Numeracy	Community Awareness	Florida Standards	CASAS	EFF	LAUSD Beginning Low

• Learn about health insurance co-payments
 	
• Say medicine dosages and frequency words
	• Complete health insurance forms
	
	• Understand a doctor's role in the community
	
	• Read medicine labes from a community pharmacy
	
	• Learn about healthy habits
	
	• Make a plan to stay healthy
		1: 1.07.01
		    1.07.02
		2: 1.07.01
		    1.07.02
		4: 1.07.03
		6: 1.07.07
		8: 1.07.04
		9: 1.01.06
		10: 1.16.02
		11: 1.16.02
		13: 1.07.04
			1, 2: 3.1.1
			3: 3.1.2, 3.1.3
			4: 3.3.1
			5: 3.4.3
			6: 3.4.5, 3.5.9, 7.5.4
			7: 3.3.3, 3.5.9
			8: 3.3.2
			9: 3.2.3
			12: 3.5.2
			13: 3.5.2
			R: 8.3.1
				• Observe Critically
				
				• Guide Others
				
				• Advocate and Influence
				
				• Solve Problems and Make Decisions
					<u>LIFE SKILLS</u>
					• 7
					• 19
					• 43
					• 44
					• 45
					• 46
					• 60
					
					<u>GRAMMAR</u>
					• 5
					• 19

• Understand paycheck deductions
 	
• Learn about hourly wages
 	
• Review concept of depositing money in bank account
	• Examine various jobs in the community
	
	• Recognize want ads as a community resource
	
	• Learn about safety signs
	
	• Gain information about the job application process
	
	• Complete an application form
		1: 1.01.01
		    1.03.02
		2: 1.01.01
		    1.03.02
		3: 1.01.01
		    1.03.02
		5: 1.01.04
		6: 1.01.07
		    1.02.01
		7: 1.01.04
		8: 1.02.05
		9: 1.02.03
		10: 1.16.02
		12: 1.01.03
		13: 1.06.02
		    1.06.03
			1: 4.1.6, 4.1.8
			2: 4.1.6, 4.1.8
			3: 4.1.9
			4: 4.4.2
			5: 4.4.2
			6: 4.1.3
			7: 4.1.2, 4.4.7
			8: 4.2.1
			9: 4.3.1
			12: 4.1.1
			13: 4.4.3
			R: 4.1.3
				• Speak So Others Can Understand
				
				• Cooperate With Others
				
				• Resolve Conflict and Negotiate
				
				• Reflect and Evaluate
					<u>LIFE SKILLS</u>
					• 19
					• 48, 49
					• 50, 51
					• 52, 53
					• 54, 55
					• 56a, b
					
					<u>GRAMMAR</u>
					• 4a, b, c
					• 6
					• 7

• Read times related to public transportation
 	
• Practice time phrases
	• Read schedule for community transportation
	
	• Review various forms of transportation (bus, train, subway)
	
	• Read about car safety equipment
	
	• Get around your community
		1: 1.09.01
		2: 1.09.03
		3: 1.09.03
		4: 1.09.03
		6: 1.09.02
		    1.09.04
		7: 1.09.02
		    1.09.04
		9: 1.08.02
		10: 1.16.02
		11: 1.16.02
		12: 1.14.05
		R: 1.09.01
		    1.09.02
			1: 2.2.3
			2, 3: 1.9.4, 2.2.1, 2.2.5
			4: 0.1.2, 2.2.2
			5: 2.2.4
			6: 1.9.2, 2.5.7
			7: 1.9.1, 2.2.2
			8: 2.2.4, 4.2.1, 6.6.6
			9: 2.2.4, 4.2.1
			12: 3.5.7, 3.5.9
			13: 2.2.5
				• Resolve Conflict and Negotiate
				
				• Solve Problems and Make Decisions
				
				• Take Responsibility for Learning
				
				• Learn Through Research
					<u>LIFE SKILLS</u>
					• 7, 13
					• 11a, b, c
					• 14a, b
					• 23a, b
					• 24a, b
					• 42, 60
					
					<u>GRAMMAR</u>
					• 17

Unit 1 — Welcome to the classroom.

UNIT OVERVIEW

Lesson	Objective	Student Book Page
1. Welcome!	Introducing yourself	p. 3
2. The Alphabet: A–M	Saying and writing the letters A–M	p. 4
3. The Alphabet: N–Z	Saying and writing the letters N–Z	p. 5
4. How do you spell that?	Spelling names	p. 6
5. What's in the classroom?	Identifying classroom objects and people	p. 7
6. Follow directions.	Following classroom directions	p. 8
7. Practice directions.	Following classroom directions	p. 9
8. Open the book.	Understanding classroom instructions	p. 10
9. Point to the book.	Reading and writing classroom directions	p. 11
10. My phone number is (981) 555-2305.	Saying and writing numbers	p. 12
11. Nestor's Homework	Reading about homework	p. 13
12. Grammar: *I'm, It's, What's*	Using contractions	p. 14
13. Read and Write: An Emergency Form	Completing emergency forms	p. 15
What do you know?	Review and assessment	p. 16

Big Picture Expansion Activities

Focus	Activity	Suggested Use
Listening/ Speaking	*Yes* or *No*	**Lesson 11**
Reading	Recognizing Character Names	**Unit Opener**
Grammar	*I'm, It's, What's*	**Lesson 12**
Writing	Grace Lee	**Lesson 10**
Conversation/ Vocabulary	Review and Tally of Classroom Objects	**What do you know?**

Worksheets

Worksheet #/ Focus	Title	Teacher's Edition Page
1. Writing	Grace Lee	**p. 327**
2. Grammar	*I'm, It's, What's*	**p. 328**
3. Speaking	Interview	**p. 329**
4. Review and assessment	Count the objects.	**p. 330**

Unit Opener

- Put the transparency for Unit 1 on the overhead projector (OHP) or have students look at the big picture on page 2.

- Point to the picture as you ask the questions at the bottom of the page: *Where are the students? What do you see?*

- Elicit any vocabulary words the students know and write the words on the board.

Expansion Activity:
Reading: Recognizing Character Names

- This can be used here or in Lesson 3.

- **Before class:** Create index cards with the names of the characters on the transparency. You will need one card for each student in your class. Make a set of character names with each name written on a piece of paper large enough for students to read. You will also need the character cards created for *Taking Off*.

- Greet the students. Introduce yourself. Gesture to one student and ask *What is your name?* Repeat until all the students have answered. Next, say *Welcome to the classroom*, and gesture to your classroom.

- Put the transparency for Unit 1 on the OHP or have students look at the big picture on page 2 in their books. Use a circle motion on the transparency and repeat *Welcome to the classroom.* Point to a character on the transparency, hold up the corresponding character card, and say the name. Repeat the name, and gesture to students to repeat after you. Do the same with the other characters in the picture.

- In random order, point to the characters on the transparency and have your students say the names.

- Pass out the index cards with the names of the people on the transparency. Hold up one of the character cards. Say the name. Have students stand if their card has that name.

- Have students walk around and find other students with the same name on their card.

Objective
Introducing yourself

Literacy Workbook pages 68–73
Workbook page 2

  A CD 1, TRACK 2 **Listen.**

- Have students open their books and look at the picture of Isabel and Paul. Point to both characters and read their names.

- Play the audio or read the conversation.

- Play the audio or read the conversation again. Pause after each line and ask the students to repeat.

Expansion Activity: **Choral Practice**

- Gesture to yourself and say *Paul*. Gesture to the class and say *Isabel*. Read Paul's lines. Cue students to read Isabel's lines with you. Respond with Paul's line. Repeat.

- Change characters so you now read Isabel's lines and students read Paul's lines. Repeat.

- Divide the class in half. Gesture to one half and say *Paul*. Gesture to the other half and say *Isabel*.

- Cue the Paul side to read Paul's lines. Then cue the Isabel side to read Isabel's lines. Switch roles and repeat.

B Talk with a partner.

- Model the activity with a more advanced student. Greet the student and say *Hello. I'm _____*, and give your name. Cue the student to read the next line, making the appropriate substitutions. Respond with the last line.

- Call on two advanced students to demonstrate the activity again. Cue each student to make the appropriate substitutions.

- Put students in pairs. Pair a more advanced student with a less advanced student if possible.

- Have students practice the conversation in pairs.

- Walk around the room to monitor the activity and provide help as needed.

  C CD 1, TRACK 3 **Listen.**

- Have students look at the conversation.

- Play the audio or read the conversation. Play the audio or read the conversation again and have students repeat after each pause.

- Divide the class into two sides. Have one side read Carlos's lines. Have the other side read Tien's lines. Move in front of each group to cue them to read.

Expansion Activity: **Pair Work**

- Put students in pairs. Designate one partner to be Carlos and the other to be Tien.

- Have students practice the conversation in pairs at least three times; then switch roles.

- Walk around the room to monitor the activity and provide help as needed.

D Talk with 5 classmates.

- Write the conversation on the board.

- Have students stand and walk around the room introducing themselves to five classmates.

Expansion Activity:
Introduction Lines 1

- Divide the students into two groups. Have each group form a line facing the other group.

- Designate one line as A, the other as B.

- Have the students in Line A introduce themselves with A's line from the conversation to the students opposite them. Cue the B students to respond appropriately.

- Have the first student in Line A go to the end of the line. Each student is now facing a new partner from Line B. Have students repeat the conversations.

- Continue until students have talked to at least five partners; then have them switch roles.

E   Read and write.

- Point to the nametag and say *nametag*. Elicit the name (*Sandy*) and have students repeat it.

- Have students write their own names on the blank name tags.

Expansion Activity: **Name Cards**

- Bring in index cards.

- Have students fold the cards in half to make "tents."

- Have students write their names on one side of the tent.

- Have students put the name cards in front of them on the desks, until you and the students know everyone's name.

Objective
Saying and writing the letters A–M

Literacy Workbook pages 68–74
Workbook page 3

  A CD 1, TRACK 4 **Listen.**

- Direct students' attention to the letters.

- Play the audio or read the letters.

- Play the audio or read the letters again and have students repeat.

- Read the letters in random order and have students point to them. Check for accuracy.

Expansion Activity: Pair Work

- Put students in pairs.

- Have students take turns reading the letters in random order as their partners point.

- Walk around to monitor the activity and provide help as needed.

B Say and write.

- Write an upper and lowercase *A* on the board. Point to the uppercase *A*. Extend your hands and say *uppercase A*. Point to the lowercase *a*. Put your hands close together and say *lowercase a*.

- Point to the line of capital letters in the book. Say each letter: *uppercase A, uppercase B,* etc. Have students repeat as they write the letters.

- Point to the line of lowercase letters in the book. Say each letter: *lowercase a, lowercase b,* etc. Have students repeat as they write the letters.

LITERACY DEVELOPMENT Notes

- Distinguishing between upper and lowercase letters can be difficult for literacy students. It means they have to remember 52 symbols.

- Whenever you spell something for the class, say *uppercase* before each capitalized letter.

C Match.

- Write the upper and lowercase letters from the first item on the board. Draw a line from the uppercase *A* to the lowercase *a*.

- Elicit the match for the uppercase *B*, and draw the line on the board, or have a student draw the line.

- Have students complete the activity.

- Put students in pairs to compare answers. Each pair should have a more advanced and a less advanced student if possible.

PRONUNCIATION Notes

- Students may have difficulty with the pronunciation of letters, especially the long vowels *a, e,* and *i*. Say the letter names of the vowels in isolation and exaggerate the position of your mouth. Students should see the lips stretched wide in both the *a* and the *e*, but notice that for *e*, the mouth is just open slightly.

- Say the three letters and have students repeat. Make sure their mouths are in the correct position.

 **D**   **CD 1, TRACK 5**   **Listen and write.**

- Direct students' attention to the picture. Ask: *Name?* Elicit *Nadira.* Point to the activity in the book; then say *Listen and write* as you make listening and writing gestures.

- Point to the line of lowercase letters and then to the lowercase *a* in the example.

- Play the audio or read the letters in the listening script. Make sure students are looking at the book and writing.

...... Listening Script

D. LISTEN AND WRITE.

1. a-b-c
2. d-e-f
3. g-h-i
4. j-k-l
5. m

> **Answer Key**   **1.** a-b-c; **2.** d-e-f;
> **3.** g-h-i; **4.** j-k-l; **5.** m

Expansion Activity: **Dictation**

- Dictate words that use letters from *A* to *M*. Use names of your students if possible (e.g., *Jaime, Diego, Lam*), or use words from Unit 1 (e.g., *am, check*). If you use names, say *uppercase* in front of the first letter.

- Say the letters in each word three times (*L-a-m, L-a-m, L-a-m*).

- Have students compare their answers in pairs.

- Go over the answers with the class. NOTE: it's not important that students know the words or names. Point out that the letters form names or words.

Expansion Activity: **Pair Work**

- Put students in pairs.

- Have students take turns dictating letters from this lesson to each other and writing them down.

Extra Challenge
Create words.

- Put more advanced students in pairs.

- Ask students to create as many words as they can, beginning only with the letters *A* through *M*. They may look through the book for ideas.

- Check students' work.

- Have students write words on the board.

- Read each word and have the class repeat.

Objective
Saying and writing the letters N–Z

Vocabulary

Brazil	Haiti	Somalia
China	Mexico	U.S.A.
Colombia	Russia	Vietnam

Literacy Workbook pages 68–74
Workbook page 4

  A CD 1, TRACK 6 **Listen.**

• Direct students' attention to the letters.

• Play the audio or read the letters.

• Play the audio or read the letters again and have students repeat.

• Read the letters in random order and have students point to them.

B **Say and write.**

• Write an upper and lowercase *N* on the board. Point to the uppercase *N*. Extend your hands and say *uppercase N*. Point to the lowercase *n*. Put your hands close together and say *lowercase n*.

• Point to the line of capital letters in the book. Read each letter. Have students repeat as they write the letter.

• Point to the line of lowercase letters in the book. Read each letter. Have students repeat as they write the letter.

Expansion Activity: **Match Game**

• Give each pair 12 index cards. Have the pairs choose six letters and write an uppercase or lowercase letter on each card to form six pairs.

• Show students how to shuffle the cards and place them face down on the desk.

• Have students practice matching pairs of upper and lowercase letters.

  C CD 1, TRACK 7 **Listen and say the letters.**

• Direct students' attention to the picture. Say *students.* Ask: *What letters?* Elicit the letters *U, S, A.* Point out that U.S.A. is an abbreviation, so students should just read the letters. There is a map of the U.S. on the back cover of the student book. Point to the map and repeat *u, s, a.*

• Play the audio or read the listening script and have students repeat.

Expansion Activity: **More with Countries**

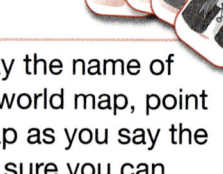

• Point to each word and say the name of the country. If you have a world map, point to each country on the map as you say the name. Before class, make sure you can locate each country on the map.

• Say *U.S.A.* and point to yourself if you are from there. Say each country and elicit or point to students from that country if possible. Hold up each character card and say the country for that character. The character's name and country are listed on the character cards and in the Expansion Activity on the next page.

Listening Script

C. LISTEN AND SAY THE LETTERS.

1. USA U-S-A
2. China C-H-I-N-A
3. Haiti H-A-I-T-I
4. Russia R-U-S-S-I-A
5. Brazil B-R-A-Z-I-L
6. Mexico M-E-X-I-C-O
7. Colombia C-O-L-O-M-B-I-A
8. Somalia S-O-M-A-L-I-A
9. Vietnam V-I-E-T-N-A-M

Expansion Activity: Character Introduction

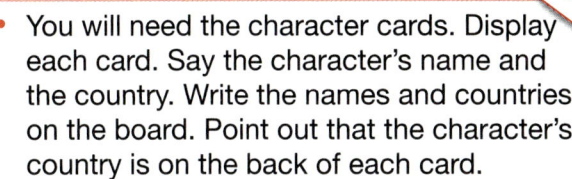

- You will need the character cards. Display each card. Say the character's name and the country. Write the names and countries on the board. Point out that the character's country is on the back of each card.

Sandy	U.S.A.
Carlos	Brazil
Maria	Mexico
Leo	Russia
Tien	Vietnam
Grace	China
Ben	China
Paul	Haiti
Isabel	Colombia
Nadira	Somalia

- Model the activity. Hold up a character card (e.g., *Nadira*) and say *My name is Nadira. I'm from Somalia.*

- Have volunteers come to the front of the room. Give each a card and have them introduce themselves as the character, giving their countries using the model.

- After all the characters and countries have been introduced, hold up each card and elicit the name and country.

D   CD 1, TRACK 8   Listen and write.

- Play the audio for the first item or read it in the listening script. Point out the completed example. Point out that each line is for one letter.

- Play the audio or read the listening script below. Make sure students are looking at the book and writing.

- Put students in pairs to compare answers.

- Play the audio or read the letters again and have students check their answers.

- Go over the answers with the class.

Listening Script

D. LISTEN AND WRITE.

1. h-i
2. y-o-u
3. n-a-m-e
4. f-r-o-m
5. w-r-i-t-e
6. h-e-l-l-o

Expansion Activity: Name Dictation

- Dictate names of your students by spelling them out. Dictate the letters three times.

- As you finish each name, elicit who it is.

Literacy Development Activity: Alphabet Practice

- Write the alphabet on the board.

- Point to letters in random order and elicit the name of the letter.

- Increase speed after eliciting a few letters.

- For greater challenge, call on individual students and/or elicit whether it is uppercase or lowercase.

Objective
Spelling names

Literacy Workbook pages 68–74
Workbook page 4

  A   CD 1, TRACK 9   **Listen.**

- Have students look at the picture. Point to each person, say the name, and have students repeat.

- Play the audio or read the conversation as students look at the conversation.

- Play the audio or read the conversation a second time. Pause after each line and ask the students to repeat.

- Read Maria's lines and have students respond with Tien's lines.

- Divide the class in half. Designate half as Maria and half as Tien. Cue the students to read the appropriate lines.

- Put students in pairs to practice the conversation. Have them switch partners and read it again.

Expansion Activity:
Conversation Shuffle

- Write the sentences from Activity A on strips of paper. Make enough copies so that each group of four students has a set.

- Put students in groups of four. Give each a strip of paper.

- Have students arrange themselves in the order of the conversation.

- Have students in each group read their lines in order.

- In a variation, write each word of the conversation on a card (26 cards, or 31 if you write each letter of Tien's name on a separate card).

- Give one card to each student and have them put themselves in order to recreate the conversation.

B   **Talk with 5 classmates.**

- Make sure students understand the terms *first name* and *last name*. Model the activity with a more advanced student.

> I'm _____. What's your name?
>
> My name is _____.

Read A's lines and cue the student to respond with B's lines. Make sure the student responds with his or her first and last name. Switch roles.

- Have students stand and walk around the room to practice the conversation with five classmates. Remind students to practice both roles.

- Walk around to monitor the activity and provide help as needed.

Expansion Activity:
Introduction Lines 2

- Divide the students into two groups. Have each group form a line facing the other group.

- Designate one line as A, the other as B.

- Have the students in Line A introduce themselves with A's line from the conversation to the students opposite them. Cue the B students to respond appropriately.

- Have students switch roles.

- Have the first student in Line A go to the end of the line. Each student is now facing a new partner from Line B. Have students repeat the conversations.

- Continue until students have talked to at least five partners, then have them switch roles.

My Life

- Direct students' attention to the picture. Elicit the name of the person (*Isabel*) and what she is doing (*writing*).

- Copy the information from the form on the board or make a transparency of the information and put it on the OHP.

- Model the activity. Write your first and last names. Circle each letter in your first name as you point to it on the board. Circle each letter in your last name.

- Have students complete the form.

- Put students in pairs to share the information on the form. Pair a more advanced student with a less advanced student to check the information.

Expansion Activity: Circle for the Characters

- Write the alphabet on the board.

```
A B C D E F G H I J K L M
N O P Q R S T U V W X Y Z
```

Model the activity. Show the students all the character cards. Then begin to circle the letters of a character's name. Encourage students to read the letter as you circle it, and name the character as soon as they can.

- Have volunteers come to the board and choose a character without indicating the choice to the class. Have the student circle the letters and elicit the name from the class. Have the student erase the circles and rewrite the letters when the class has correctly guessed.

- Continue with other students and characters. Have the volunteer erase and rewrite the letter each time after the character's name has been elicited.

Extra Challenge
Spell from Memory

- Have more advanced students write the characters' names from memory, and for added challenge, the characters' country names, too.

- Put students in pairs to compare answers.

- For added challenge, have students alphabetize character names and country names. You may need to explain how to alphabetize a list first.

Objective
Identifying classroom objects and people

Vocabulary

backpack	computer	paper
board	desk	pen
book	door	student
chair	notebook	teacher

Literacy Workbook pages 68–74
Workbook page 5

  A   CD 1, TRACK 10   **Listen.**

- Have students look at the pictures.

- Play the audio or read the words.

- Play the audio or read the words again and have students repeat.

PRONUNCIATION Notes

- Activity A includes words with both the *b* and *p* sounds (*book, board, backpack, paper, pen*).

- Point out that both sounds are made with lips closed and then puffs of air. The *p* sound is voiceless (the vocal cords don't move), the *b* sound is voiced (the vocal cords do move). Have students put their hands on their throats to make both sounds and feel the difference.

Literacy Development Activity: *b*, *d*, and *p*

- Write *b*, *d,* and *p* on the board.

- Have students write the words from Activity A for each letter.

- Go over the answers with the class.

Extra Challenge
Alphabetize

- Have more advanced students alphabetize the words in Activity A. Make sure students know to look at the second or even third letter when they alphabetize words with the same initial letter.

- Have students compare lists in pairs or small groups.

Expansion Activity: Syllable Claps

- Say *student* in syllables and clap on each syllable.

- Repeat with the other words.

- Call on students and point to the word. Have the student say the word and clap on each syllable.

  B   CD 1, TRACK 11   **Listen.**

- Direct students' attention to the picture. Elicit the name of the character (*Sandy*) and the vocabulary word (*backpack*).

- Play the audio or read the conversation.

- Play the audio or read the conversation again and have students repeat.

Expansion Activity: Flashcards

- Put students in pairs.
- Distribute index cards. Have students write each word from Activity A (e.g., *student*) on a card.
- Model the activity with a more advanced student. Hold up a card and ask *What's this?*

  What's this?   **student**

  Elicit the word from the student.
- Have students work with partners, taking turns asking and answering questions with the flashcards.
- For extra spelling practice, after students read the words, have them spell them without looking at the card.

Expansion Activity: Draw it.

- Model the activity. Draw one of the objects from Activity A on the board. Elicit its name.
- Divide the class into two teams.
- Call a student from each team to the board. Whisper or show the students one of the words.
- Have the "artists" draw the object on the board.
- The student who first guesses the object correctly earns a point for his or her team.

C Talk with a classmate.

- Model the activity with a student. Point to one of the pictures in Activity A and ask *What's this?* Elicit the answer. Cue that student to point to a different object and ask you *What's this?*
- Encourage students to ask and answer questions about all of the objects in Activity A.

Objective
Following classroom directions

Vocabulary

check	complete	match
circle	fill in	

Literacy Workbook pages 68–74
Workbook page 6

  A CD 1, TRACK 12 **Listen.**

- Point to the picture and elicit the object (*pen*).

- Point to the word *circle* and pantomime the motion of circling.

- Play the audio or say *pen*. Then point to the circled pen.

- Play the audio or read the words as you point to the other words. Then point to the completed task on the page.

B Circle.

- Point to each word in the activity and read it. Have students repeat.

- Point to the picture of a pen. Elicit its name (*pen*). Point to the words and ask *pen?* Make sure students see that the word pen is circled because that is what is in the picture.

- Point to the picture of the backpack. Elicit the name and have students circle it.

- Repeat with the third item.

Answer Key pen; backpack; chair

Expansion Activity: **Circle it.**

- Create a 3 x 3 grid on the board. Write the words from Activity B in the same places on the grid.

- Have students copy the 3 x 3 grid on a piece of paper, or copy and distribute Worksheet 5 in Unit 2, *Three in a Row,* with the words written in.

- Read the words in random order and have students circle them. Walk around to monitor the activity and provide help as needed.

- Put students in pairs to take turns reading the words and circling them again.

C Check.

- Point to the picture of a student. Elicit the word *student* and point to the check next to the word *student*.

- Have students complete the other two items.

- Go over the answers with the class.

Answer Key student; board; computer

Expansion Activity: **Mixed Pairs**

- Model the activity with a more advanced student. Write words from the unit on the board.

computer   backpack
book   board

Say the words in random order and have the student circle them as you say them.

- Put students in pairs of mixed levels.

- Have the more advanced partner write nine words on a piece of paper and then give the paper to the less advanced partner.

- Have the more advanced student read the words in random order as the less advanced student circles the words.

Objective
Following classroom directions

Literacy Workbook pages 68–74
Workbook page 6

A Complete.

- Point to the directions for Activity A and say *Complete*.

- Go over the example. Have students review the vocabulary in Lessons 1 and 4 if they need help completing the activity.

- Have students complete the conversation.

- Put students in pairs to compare answers.

- Go over the answers with the class.

Answer Key 1. meet; 2. name; 3. first; 4. last

Expansion Activity: Letter Scramble

- Choose words from the conversation (*nice, first, hello, your, name, meet*).

- Write the letters from each word in random order on the board (*cine, mane, olhel, strif, rouy, etem*), keeping the letters in word groups.

- Have students unscramble the letters to form the words.

- For added challenge, have more advanced students use any of the letters on the board to form new words or names (*me, Matt, time*). They may work together or use a dictionary.

B Fill in.

- Draw a circle on the board. Say *fill in* as you color it in.

- Point to the picture and elicit that it is *paper*. Point out that the bubble next to the word *paper* is filled in.

- Have students complete the next two items. If necessary, point to the picture and elicit the name; then have students fill in the correct bubbles.

Answer Key 1. paper; 2. chair; 3. pen

Expansion Activity: Fill in Practice

- Distribute copies of bubble-in answer sheets to students.

- For each number, say a letter (*a–d*) and have students fill in the appropriate bubble.

- Have students compare answers in pairs.

- Go over the answers with the class.

C **Match.**

- Point to the word *door* in number one and
  ask, *What's this?*

  What's this?   **Door**

  Then point to the three pictures on the right
  and ask, *door?* Elicit that *b* is the picture of a
  door. Point out that *b* is written on the line
  next to *door*.

- Have students complete the other two items.

- Go over the answers with the class.

Answer Key **1.** b; **2.** a; **3.** c

Objective
Understanding classroom instructions

Vocabulary

close	open	put away
go to	point to	take out

**Literacy Workbook pages 68–74
Workbook page 7**

  A **CD 1, TRACK 13** **Listen.**

- Have students look at the pictures and words.

- Play the first part of the audio or read the first part of the listening script as students read the words in their books.

- Play the rest of the audio or read the list of words and have students repeat.

····· **Listening Script**

A. LISTEN.

1. Open. Open the book.
2. Close. Close the book.
3. Take out. Take out the pen.
4. Put away. Put away the book.
5. Go to. Go to the board.
6. Point to. Point to the computer.

LISTEN AND REPEAT.

1. Open.
2. Close.
3. Take out.
4. Put away.
5. Go to.
6. Point to.

Expansion Activity: TPR

- Say *Open the book* and have students open their books.

- Continue with other directions (*close the book, take out a pen, put away the pen, go to the board, point to the teacher*) and have students follow each one.

- Call on volunteers and give directions (*Open the door, take out paper, close the door, put away the book, point to the board, go to the door*).

- Put students in pairs to practice giving and following directions.

 B **CD 1, TRACK 14** **Listen and circle.**

- Point to each picture and elicit the verb (e.g., *take out, go to*).

- Play the audio for the first item or read number 1 in the listening script. Stop and elicit the verb (*take out*). Point out that the picture for *take out* is circled.

- Play the audio or read the words. Have students circle the correct picture.

- For added practice, call on students to pantomime the meaning of the incorrect answer.

····· **Listening Script**

B. LISTEN AND CIRCLE.

1. Take out the paper. **2.** Put away the book.
3. Open the book. **4.** Close the door.

Answer Key **1.** Illustration on the left;
2. Illustration on the right; **3.** Illustration on the right; **4.** Illustration on the left

GRAMMAR Notes

- Students don't need to understand phrasal verbs, but you should point out that four of the new vocabulary items have two parts (verb + preposition).

- Say *take* and cue students to respond with *out*. Continue with the other verb + preposition combinations (*take out, put away, point to, go to*).

- Call on individual students, say a verb, and elicit the appropriate preposition.

Expansion Activity: **Say and check.**

- Draw a checkmark on the board and say, *check*.

- Model the activity with a more advanced student. Say a verb (*go to*) and have the student check the corresponding picture or pictures from Activity B.

- Put students in pairs to take turns saying and checking the verbs in the pictures.

Objective
Reading and writing classroom directions

Literacy Workbook pages 68–74
Workbook page 7

  A   CD 1, TRACK 15   **Listen and fill in.**

- Read each sentence aloud and have students repeat.

- Play the first sentence of the audio or read the first sentence in the script. Point out that *B* is the correct answer, so bubble B is filled.

- Play the rest of the audio or read the sentences. Have students fill in the correct bubble as they listen.

- Put students in pairs to compare answers.

- Play the audio or read the sentences again if necessary to confirm answers.

- Go over the answers with the class.

········ **Listening Script**

A. LISTEN AND FILL IN.

1. Open the door.
2. Go to the board.
3. Take out the pen.
4. Put away the notebook.
5. Open the door.
6. Put away the paper.
7. Point to the desk.
8. Take out the book.

Answer Key   **1.** B; **2.** A; **3.** A; **4.** A;
5. B; **6.** B; **7.** A; **8.** B

Expansion Activity: **TPR**

- Read each direction in Activity A and have the class act it out.

- Call on individual students and give a direction. Have the student follow the direction.

- Put students in pairs to take turns giving and following the directions in Activity A.

B   **Write.**

- Write *Open the* on the board.

Open the _____.

- Elicit words that can complete the sentence. Point out that *door* is written on the line.

- Brainstorm words that can complete each sentence. Have students choose one and write it on the line.

- **Note:** More advanced students may know other words to complete the sentences. Acknowledge that other options are correct (e.g., *window*), but don't expect all students to use these words in their answers.

Answer Key   Answers will vary but may include: **1.** door, book, notebook, backpack; **2.** board, door, teacher, student, computer, desk, chair; **3.** pen, book, notebook, paper; **4.** pen, book, notebook, paper; **5.** door, book, notebook, backpack; **6.** chair, desk, notebook, book, pen, student, teacher

Expansion Activity:
Two Rights and a Wrong

- Write *Close the* _____ three times on the board. Write three different words to complete the sentence, two of which are appropriate (*door, book*), one which is not (*student*).

- Read your sentences aloud. After the correct sentences say *right*, and after the incorrect sentence say *wrong*. Indicate the meaning of right and wrong by nodding for *right*, and shaking your head for *wrong*.

- Say three variations of each sentence and elicit if it is right or wrong. Alternatively, dictate sentences and have students put a check or an *X* next to each.

- In a variation, have students write three sentences (two rights and one wrong) and exchange them with a partner to make checkmarks or *X*s. Have them read the sentences as they work for pronunciation practice.

- Walk around to monitor the variations and provide help as needed.

My Life

- Have students copy five directions from Activity B on the lines.

- Put students in groups and have them take turns reading the directions. Have students follow the direction, too.

- Provide help as needed.

Expansion Activity: **Pair Dictation**

- Model the activity with a more advanced student. Dictate a classroom direction from this lesson (*close the door, open the book*) and have the student write it on the board.

- Put students in pairs to take turns dictating and writing directions.

- Walk around and provide help as needed.

Expansion Activity: **Card Sort**

- Write each noun from Lesson 5 on an index card or piece of paper. Make sure the word is big enough to read from across the room.

- Give each card to a student.

- Have the students with cards come to the front of the room.

- Say *Open the* and point to one side of the room. Cue the students with nouns that can be opened to move to the area of the room. If necessary, read or have the student read the word on the card. Elicit from the class if the word on the card is something that can be opened. Physically move the students.

- Cue the other students, with nouns that can't be opened, to move to the other side of the room.

- Continue with the other verbs and have students move. Involve the whole class in sorting out the nouns.

Objective
Saying and writing numbers

Vocabulary

zero	four	eight
one	five	nine
two	six	ten
three	seven	

Literacy Workbook pages 68–74
Workbook page 8

 A CD 1, TRACK 16 **Listen.**

- Have students look at the numbers.
- Play the audio or read the numbers.
- Play the audio or read the numbers again and have students repeat.

Expansion Activity: Listen and point.

- Say the numbers in random order and have students point to the correct numbers.
- Put students in pairs to take turns saying the numbers and pointing.

B Write the number.

- Go over the directions and the example.
- Have students write the number next to each word.
- Put students in pairs to compare answers.
- Go over the answers with the class.

Answer Key
1. 6; **2.** 4; **3.** 7; **4.** 3; **5.** 0; **6.** 10; **7.** 2; **8.** 9; **9.** 5; **10.** 1; **11.** 8

Expansion Activity: Write the word.

- Write numerals on the board in random order.
- Have students write the words for each numeral. Literacy students can refer to the book. Have more advanced students close their books.
- Call volunteers to the board to write the word next to the numeral.

Expansion Activity: 3 x 3 Grids

- Have students create 3 x 3 grids on a piece of paper, or photocopy and distribute Worksheet 5 in Unit 2 (Teacher's Edition page 331).
- Have students write the number words (one through nine) in random order in the boxes on the grid.
- Hold up numeral cards, or write numerals on the board, and have students circle the word on their grids.
- Remind students to call out *three in a row* when they have three circled number words in a row.

Expansion Activity: Writing: Grace Lee

- Put the transparency for Unit 1 on the OHP or have students look at page 2 in their books.
- Photocopy and distribute Worksheet 1: *Grace Lee* (Teacher's Edition page 327).
- Have students read the information and complete the form.
- Put students in pairs to compare forms.
- Copy the form on the board and have students fill in the information.

Answer Key First name: Grace; Last name: Lee; First name: Ben; Last name: Lee; Phone Number: (831) 555-9021.

 C CD 1, TRACK 17 **Listen.**

- Go over the information in the yellow note.
- Play the audio or read the conversation. Tell them to listen for the pronunciation of 'oh' in the phone number.
- Play the audio or read the conversation again.

D **Write about you. Tell 5 classmates.**

- Model the activity. Write the sentence starters on the board. Complete a sentence with real or pretend information.
- Have students complete the sentences for themselves. If they don't have an email

address, either help them make one up or tell them to skip that item.

- Have students stand and walk around the room to say the sentences to five classmates.

CULTURE Notes

- Students may not want to share actual personal information with their classmates. Point out that they are not writing this information down.
- Point out that email addresses are relatively safe to share, but they don't have to share phone numbers or addresses.

 E CD 1, TRACK 18 **Listen and circle.**

- Play the audio for the first item or read the first item in the listening script. Point out that *six* is circled.
- Play the audio or read the rest of the items in the listening script and have students circle what they hear.
- Put students in pairs to compare answers.
- Go over the answers with the class.

········· **Listening Script**

E. LISTEN AND CIRCLE.

1. Six
2. Five
3. Ten
4. 5 Pen Avenue
5. 555-5050
6. 781-555-9876

Answer Key 1. Six; 2. Five; 3. 10; 4. 5 Pen Avenue; 5. 555-5050; 6. 781-555-9876

Objective
Reading about homework

Literacy Workbook pages 68–74
Workbook page 9

 A CD 1, TRACK 19 **Listen and read.**

- Have students look at the picture. Elicit vocabulary students know (e.g., *paper, backpack, book,* and numerals).

- Play the audio or read the sentences as students read along silently.

- Ask comprehension questions: *What is the homework? Nestor writes…?*

- Play the audio or read each sentence again. Pause after each sentence and have students repeat.

- Put students in pairs to take turns reading sentences aloud.

Expansion Activity: Sentence Strips

- Photocopy the sentences and cut them into strips. Make enough copies so each pair of students will have a set.

- Have students recreate the story.

- To extend the activity, cut one set of strips into single words (there are 28 words).

- Give each student one word.

- Have students recreate the story by standing in order.

- Call on students to say their words and thus, say the story aloud.

Literacy Development Variation: Sentence Strips

- Rewrite the sentences on long strips of paper.

- Put the sentences in the correct order in a pocket chart, or tape them to the board.

- Take the strips down and mix them up.

- Call on volunteers to recreate the story in the pocket chart or taped to the board.

- Read the complete story chorally. Point out each word as students read.

B Look at Activity A. Check what you see.

- Have students look at the pictures in Activity A.

- Ask: *alphabet?* Point out that there is an alphabet, so *yes* is checked in the chart.

- Have students look at the pictures and check *yes* or *no.*

- Put students in pairs to compare answers.

- Go over the answers with the class.

Answer Key alphabet—yes; backpack—yes; board—no; book—no; computer—no; desk—no; homework—yes; nine numbers—no; paper—yes

Extra Challenge

Personalize

- Point to the picture of Nestor doing his homework at home. Say *Nestor and Maria's home.*

- Model the activity. Say *my home* and list things in your home (e.g., *computer, paper, pen, books*). Say things you don't have in your home (e.g., *zero boards, zero students*).

- Have students list four things they have in their homes and four things they don't.

- Put students in pairs to compare ideas.

Expansion Activity:
Listening/Speaking: *Yes* or *No*?

- Have students look at the big picture on page 2 in their books, or put the transparency for Unit 1 on the OHP.

- Model the activity. Say a number and a classroom object (e.g., *two teachers*) and elicit a *yes* or *no* (*no*).

- Put students in pairs to list as many things as they can from the picture. Have students write a number from 1 to 10 next to each item on their list.

- Have each pair join another pair.

- Have the pairs take turns saying a number and object and responding with *yes* or *no*.

- Walk around the room to monitor the activity and provide help as needed.

Objective
Using contractions

Literacy Workbook pages 68–74
Workbook page 10

 A CD 1, TRACK 20 **Listen and circle.**

- Have students look at the first picture. Read each sentence in the speech bubbles, or call on more advanced students to read each bubble.

- Point out the contractions in the yellow note and make sure students understand them.

- Personalize the activity. Point to yourself and say, *I'm from* _____. Point to something and say, *It's a* _____.

- Call on students and prompt them: *I'm from* _____. Elicit the correct sentence (e.g., *I'm from Mexico*).

- Play the first conversation of the audio or read the conversation for the first item in the listening script. Point out that *What's* is circled. Play the audio or read the conversation again so students can hear the correct answer again.

- Play the rest of the audio or read the rest of the conversations as students complete the activity.

- Have them check their answers with a partner.

- Elicit or provide answers as a class. Provide or elicit corrections as needed.

Listening Script

A. LISTEN AND CIRCLE.

1. **Sandy:** What's this?
   Isabel: A chair.
2. **Isabel:** What is this?
   Sandy: A desk.
3. **Leo:** Hi, I'm Leo.
4. **Ben:** Hello. I am Ben.
5. **Tien:** My name is Tien. I am from Vietnam.
6. **Paul:** My name is Paul. I'm from Haiti.
7. **Nestor:** It's my homework.
8. **Maria:** It is complete.

Answer Key 1. What's; 2. What is; 3. I'm; 4. I am; 5. I am; 6. I'm; 7. It's; 8. It is

LITERACY/GRAMMAR Notes

- Some students may not be familiar with either contractions or the apostrophe. Explain that contractions are short forms and that the apostrophe replaces one or more letters.

- Write *I am* on the board.

Cross out the *a* and replace it with an apostrophe and close up the space to show how a contraction is formed. Repeat for *It is* and *What is*.

B Circle.

- Copy the first item on the board.
- Elicit the answer (*I'm*). Point out that *I'm* is circled.
- Have students circle the correct word or phrase.
- Put students in pairs to compare answers.
- Go over the answers with the class.

Answer Key 1. I'm; 2. I am; 3. What is; 4. It is; 5. What's; 6. It's

C Write.

- Model the activity. Copy the sentence starters on the board. Say a sentence about yourself (e.g., *I'm Imelda Zuelke. I'm from the Philippines*). Say sentences that begin with *It's* (e.g., *It's a computer*) and *What's* (*What's this?*).
- Have students complete the sentences.
- Put students in pairs to compare ideas.

Expansion Activity:
Practicing contractions

- Model a short conversation using contractions, e.g., *What's your name? It's Maria.*
- In pairs, have students practice asking and answering questions using contractions.

BIG PICTURE

Expansion Activity:
Grammar: *I'm, It's, What's*

- Photocopy and distribute Worksheet 2: *I'm, It's, What's* (Teacher's Edition page 328).
- Put the transparency for Unit 1 on the OHP or have students look at the big picture on page 2.
- Go over the directions and the example.
- Have students complete the worksheet.
- Elicit answers from class members.

Answer Key 1. I'm/Nadira; 2. What's/Isabel; 3. It's/Maria; 4. I'm/Sandy; 5. It's/Tien; 6. What's/Paul; 7. It's/Carlos

Objective
Completing emergency forms

Literacy Workbook pages 68–74
Workbook page 11

 **Read.**

- Have students read the form.

- Ask comprehension questions: *What is her first name? What is her last name? What is the phone number? What is an emergency?*

- Have students look at the yellow note. Explain that in an emergency, they should call 911, but that a school or workplace will call 911 and then a contact person if there is an emergency at school or work.

- Point out also that it is important to put all phone numbers down if students have, for example, a home, work, and/or cell phone number.

B **Complete.**

- Model the activity. Copy the form on the board or make a transparency and put it on the OHP. Complete it for yourself.

- Have students complete the form.

- Walk around the room to monitor the activity and provide help as needed.

Expansion Activity: Pair Share

- Put students in pairs to share the information on the forms.

- Call on students to tell the class about their partner.

Expansion Activity: Interview

- Photocopy and distribute Worksheet 3: *Interview* (Teacher's Edition page 329).

- Put students in pairs.

- Have students complete the emergency form for their partners. Remind students that they do not have to give their real phone numbers in the interview.

Objective
Review and assessment

  A CD 1, TRACK 21 **Listen and write.**

- Go over the directions.

- Play the first sentence of the audio or read the first sentence in the listening script. Point out that *What's* is written on the line.

- Play the rest of the audio or read the rest of the sentences as students write the words. Stop after each sentence so students have time to write.

- Put students in pairs to compare answers.

- Play the audio or read the sentences again and have students check their answers.

- Elicit the answers and write them on the board.

Listening Script

A. LISTEN AND WRITE.

Sandy: Hello. I'm Sandy. What's your name?
Ben: My name is Ben.
Sandy: Nice to meet you, Ben.
Ben: Nice to meet you too, Sandy.

Answer Key   name; Nice; meet

  B CD 1, TRACK 22 **Listen and circle.**

- Go over the directions.

- Play the first sentence of the audio or read the first sentence. Stop and elicit that the picture on the left is correct. Point out that it is circled.

- Play the rest of the audio or read the sentences. Have students complete the conversation.

- Put students in pairs to compare answers.

- Go over the answers with the class.

Listening Script

B. LISTEN AND CIRCLE.

1. Go to the board.
2. Close the book.
3. My first name is Leo.
4. I-S-A-B-E-L
5. I live at 2039 Board Street.

Answer Key   1. go to the board;
2. close the book; 3. Leo; 4. I-S-A-B-E-L;
5. 2039 Board Street

  C CD 1, TRACK 23 **Listen and complete.**

- Play the first sentence of the audio or read the first sentence in the listening script. Point out the answer *I'm* is written on the line, and crossed out in the list of words.

- Play the rest of the audio or read the rest of the listening script. Have students complete the conversation with the words from the box.

- Put students in pairs to compare answers.

- Play the audio or read the conversation again and have students check their answers.

- Go over the answers with the class.

⋯⋯ **Listening Script**

C. COMPLETE.

Sandy: Hi. I'm Sandy. What's your name?
Grace: My name is Grace Lee.
Sandy: How do you spell that?
Grace: My first name is G-R-A-C-E. My last name is L-E-E.

Answer Key   I'm; name; How; first; last

 D CD 1, TRACK 24 **Listen and write.**

• Go over the example.

• Play the audio for the first item or read and spell out the first item in the listening script.

• Play the audio or read and spell out the words in the listening script and have students write the words—one letter on each line, as in the example.

• Put students in pairs to compare answers.

• Play the audio or read and spell out the words again and have students check their answers.

• Elicit the answers and write them on the board.

⋯⋯ **Listening Script**

D. LISTEN AND WRITE.

1. name   n-a-m-e
2. close   c-l-o-s-e
3. board   b-o-a-r-d
4. book   b-o-o-k
5. ten   t-e-n
6. seven   s-e-v-e-n

Answer Key   **1.** name; **2.** close; **3.** board; **4.** book; **5.** ten; **6.** seven

E **Learning Log**

• Read each word aloud. Have students check the words they know.

Expansion Activity: Charades

• Model the activity. Act out one of the words from the list. Have students guess the word.

• Call a volunteer to the front of the room. Whisper or point to a word on the list (not country names). Have the student act it out.

• Continue with other students and words until everyone has had a chance to participate.

🔍 **LOOKING BACK**

• Go over the directions.

• Put students in pairs to talk about the big picture on page 2.

• Walk around to monitor the activity.

• Call on students to talk about the picture.

Expansion Activity:
Conversation/Vocabulary:
Count the objects.

- **Before class:** Make copies of Worksheet 4: *Count the objects* (Teacher's Edition page 330).

- Put the transparency for Unit 1 on the OHP, or have students look at the big picture on page 2. Distribute Worksheet 4. Read each item in the column on the left and have students repeat. Read Item 1 again (*student*). Point to Leo and begin counting (*one*); point to Carlos and say *two*. Gesture to students to continue counting the students with you. **Note:** There are nine students in addition to Sandy, the teacher.

- Say *There are nine students.* Count to nine on your fingers. As you hold up each finger, make a tally mark on the board. Show students the tally marks next to student on the worksheet.

- Tell them to count the other objects on the list that they see on the transparency and make tally marks on the worksheet.

- **Option:** Tally the objects in your classroom.

Answer Key student: 9; chair: 10; book: 5; door: 1; backpack: 2; notebook: 4; board: 1; computer: 1

UNIT OVERVIEW

Lesson	Objective	Student Book Page
1. Where are you from?	Saying where you are from	p. 19
2. What do you speak?	Saying languages	p. 20
3. What does he speak?	Saying countries and languages	p. 21
4. Grace is married.	Saying marital status	p. 22
5. I am average height.	Describing height	p. 23
6. We have brown eyes.	Describing eye and hair color	p. 24
7. He has brown hair.	Describing people	p. 25
8. What's your address?	Saying and writing addresses; practicing numbers 11–19	p. 26
9. An Identification Form	Understanding and filling out an identification form	p. 27
10. Grammar: *Am, Is, Are*	Using *am/are/is*	p. 28
11. Grammar: *Have/Has*	Using *have/has*	p. 29
12. Read: A Map of the United States	Reading maps	p. 30
13. Write: Welcome New Students	Writing descriptions using *is, are, has, have*	p. 31
What do you know?	Review and assessment	p. 32

Big Picture Expansion Activities

Focus	Activity	Suggested Use
Listening/ Speaking	Characters	**Lesson 6**
Reading	Using a Bar Graph	**What do you know?**
Grammar	*Be* or *Have?*	**Lesson 11**
Writing	Guess who.	**Lesson 6**
Conversation/ Vocabulary	Identifying National Flags	**Unit Opener**

Worksheets

Worksheet #/ Focus	Title	Teacher's Edition Page
5. Listening/ Speaking	*Yes/No* Cards	**p. 331**
6. Writing	Three in a Row	**p. 332**
7. Grammar	*Be* or *Have?*	**p. 333**
8. Reading	Using a Bar Graph	**p. 334**

Unit Opener

- Put the transparency for Unit 2 on the overhead projector (OHP) or have students look at the big picture on page 18.

- Ask the questions at the bottom of the page: *Where are the students? What do you see?*

Expansion Activity:
Conversation/Vocabulary: Identifying National Flags

- **Before class:** Bring an index card or piece of white paper for each student and enough crayons or colored pencils for the class.

- Write *flag* on the board. Put the transparency for Unit 2 on the OHP or have students look at page 18 in their books. Point to several of the flags, saying *flag* as you point to each.

- Point to the American flag on Sandy's shirt and say, *U.S. flag.* Point to other flags on shirts and elicit the names of the countries.

- On an index card, a transparency, or the board, draw one of the flags. Show it to the students and say the name of the country.

- Pass out an index card (or piece of paper) to each student. As you walk around, tell each student the name of a country in the picture.

- Ask the students to look at the big picture in their book on page 18, find the flag of the country you said to them, and draw it on their card. Collect the flags.

- Divide the class into teams for a game. Give each team some index card flags. Tell them to write the name of the country on each card. The first team to finish wins.

- **Option:** If you have a world map in your classroom, give each student a flag and ask him or her to find that country on the map.

Expansion Activity:
Character Cards

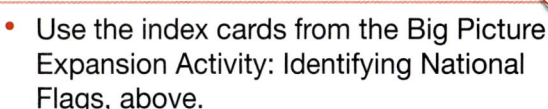

- Use the index cards from the Big Picture Expansion Activity: Identifying National Flags, above.

- Call students to the front of the room. Give each student a character card.

- Have the students find the appropriate flag for the character.

Objective
Saying where you are from

Vocabulary

Brazil	Mexico
China	Russia

Literacy Workbook pages 74–79
Workbook page 14

  A   CD 1, TRACK 26   **Listen.**

- Have students look at the conversation. Point out the countries (*Russia* and *China*) in bold type.
- Play the audio or read the conversation.
- Play the audio or read the conversation again and have students repeat.
- Ask: *Where is Leo from? Where is Ben from?*

PRONUNCIATION Notes

- Point out that the *si* sound in *Russia* is pronounced as *sh*.
- The intonation in the first line is easy to describe: BUMbumBUMbum. BUMbumBUMbum. Have students clap loud then soft to mimic the pattern.

Expansion Activity: **Chant it.**

- Divide the class in half.
- Work with one half of the class to say, *I'm from Russia. Where are you from?* Then work with the other half to respond, *I'm from China. Where are you from?*

- Lead students through several rounds of the chant, until they have mastered the intonation.

B   **Talk with a partner.**

- Model the activity with a more advanced student. Say, *I'm from the U.S.A. (or another country). Where are you from?* Elicit the correct country from the student.
- Put students in pairs to practice the conversation.

CULTURE Note

- Point out that there are several ways to say *United States: United States, USA, and U.S.*

  C   CD 1, TRACK 27   **Listen.**

- Direct students' attention to the picture next to the conversation. Ask: *Who do you see?*
- Play the audio or read the conversation as students read the conversation silently.
- Play the audio or read the conversation again and have students repeat.
- Ask comprehension questions: *Where is Carlos from? Where is Isabel from? Who is talking?*

GRAMMAR Notes

- Point out that *he* is used for a male and *she* for a female. Point to several male students and say *he* each time. Repeat with female students and *she*.
- Point out that *'s* is a contraction for *is: She is = She's; He is = He's.* Practice forming the contraction and check for understanding.

Expansion Activity: Pair Work

- Put students in pairs. Designate one partner to be Grace and the other to be Maria.
- Have students practice the conversation in pairs; then switch roles.
- Walk around the room to monitor the activity and provide help as needed.

D Talk with a partner.

- Write the conversation on the board.
- Model the activity with a student. Have the student read A's line. Cue the student to ask about one of the people in the box (e.g., *Grace*). Respond with the appropriate pronoun and country (e.g., *She's from China.*).
- Put students in pairs to practice the conversation. Tell students to take turns asking and answering questions about all the people listed in the box.
- Walk around the room to monitor the activity and provide help as needed.
- Ask volunteers to practice their conversations in front of the class.

Expansion Activity: Character Beanbag Toss

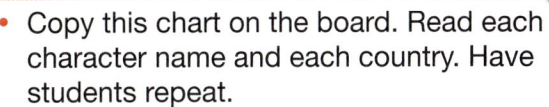

- Copy this chart on the board. Read each character name and each country. Have students repeat.

Character	Country
Sandy Johnson	USA
Carlos Avila	Brazil
Maria Cruz	Mexico
Leo Danov	Russia
Tien Lam	Vietnam
Ben Lee	China
Grace Lee	China
Paul Lemat	Haiti
Isabel Lopez	Colombia
Nadira Shaheed	Somalia

- Show a character card to the class. Call on a student, toss a beanbag or ball, and ask about the character (e.g., *Paul*). Elicit the appropriate response *(He's from Haiti.)*.
- Continue with other students and characters. With more advanced students, have the students call on classmates and ask about the characters. Show the character card as the student asks the question.
- If you have the room in your classroom, you may want to have students stand in a circle for this activity. Otherwise, make sure students are paying attention if classmates are tossing the beanbag.

CIVICS Note

- Find the countries above on a map.

Extra Challenge
Write the sentences

- Have more advanced students write sentences about each of the characters (e.g., *Paul is from Haiti.*).

Objective
Saying languages

Vocabulary

Portuguese	Somalia
Somali	Spanish

Literacy Workbook pages 74–79
Workbook page 15

  A CD 1, TRACK 28 **Listen.**

- Write *What do you speak?* on the board. Under the heading, write, *Spanish* and *Portuguese*.

- Have students look at the picture. Ask: *What do you see? Where is Isabel from? Where is Carlos from?*

- Play the audio or read the conversation as students read the conversation silently.

- Play the audio or read the conversation again and have students repeat.

- Ask comprehension questions about the languages that Isabel and Carlos speak.

B **Talk with 3 classmates.**

- Elicit or provide the names of all the languages spoken in your classroom and write them on the board under *What do you speak?*

- Model the activity with a more advanced student. Say *I speak English. What do you speak?* Cue the student to respond with his or her language.

> **I speak English. What do you speak?**
> **I speak Spanish.**

- Repeat with several more students.

- Have students walk around and talk to three classmates.

- Walk around to monitor the activity and provide help as needed.

- Call on students to tell the class about someone they talked to.

Expansion Activity: Character Conversations

- Make sure all the languages for the character cards are listed on the board.

- Model the activity with a more advanced student. Give the student a character card (*Carlos*). Hold up a card in front of yourself (*Nadira*) and say: *I speak Somali. What do you speak?* Elicit the correct response (*I speak Spanish.*).

> **I speak Somali. What do you speak?**
> **I speak Spanish.**

- Call two volunteers to the front of the room. Have the students perform the conversation as two different characters.

- Repeat with other students.

VOCABULARY Note

- Elicit or point out the common endings for languages (*-ese, -ish, -ic, -i, -an*) and point to or elicit examples of each. Explain that these endings are used for nationalities, too.

Expansion Activity: **Suffix Match**

- Write the languages in your classroom on index cards so that the suffix is separated from the stem. For example, Spanish would be on two cards: *Span* on one, *ish* on the other. Make enough cards so that everyone in the class will get one. If your class is made up of people from one language group, use these languages: *Russian, Chinese, Korean, Somali, Vietnamese, Spanish, Arabic, Polish, Hindi.*

- Give each student a card. Have students stand and walk around the room to find the correct ending and then stand with their partner. Point out that if someone is already standing with a suffix, they must find another.

- Call on pairs to say what language they form.

- Have students sort their languages by suffix.

- Have students talk to seven classmates and complete the chart.

- Walk around the room to monitor the activity and provide help as needed.

- Call on students to tell the class about someone on their charts.

C Write about you.

- Write the sentence starters on the board.

- Model the activity. Complete the sentences with information about yourself.

- Have students complete the sentences about themselves.

- Put students in groups to read their sentences.

D Talk with 7 classmates. Complete the chart.

- Copy the chart on the board.

- Go over the chart and the example.

- Model the activity with a more advanced student. Ask the questions and write the information on the chart.

Objective
Saying countries and languages

Vocabulary

Chinese　　Vietnamese

Literacy Workbook pages 74–79
Workbook page 16

  A CD 1, TRACK 29 **Listen and read.**

- Have students look at the pictures. Elicit the names of the characters.

- Play the audio or read the name, country, and language in each row of the chart as the students read along silently.

- Play the audio or read the words in the chart again and have students repeat.

- Ask comprehension questions: *What country is Carlos from? What does Ben speak?*

PRONUNCIATION Notes

- Point out that the *–ese* ending has a *z* sound.

- Point out that the *x* in *Mexico* is pronounced as *ks*.

Expansion Activity: Card Match

- Write the names of all the countries the characters come from on index cards. Include countries your students come from.

- Write the languages spoken in all those countries on different index cards.

- Show an index card with a country name. Ask a student to come to the front of the class and find the index card that shows the language spoken there.

- As a variation, distribute the country and language cards to students in the class. (You will need to duplicate the language cards if you have multiple countries that speak that language). Give each student a card. Have students find their match.

  B CD 1, TRACK 30 **Listen.**

- Play the audio or read the conversation as the students read the conversation silently.

- Play the audio or read the conversation again and have students repeat.

- Put the students in pairs to practice the conversation.

- Walk around the room to monitor the activity and provide help as needed.

C **Look at Activity A. Talk with a classmate about Carlos, Tien, Ben, and Maria.**

- Model the activity with a more advanced student. Read A's line and complete it with information about Ben and Maria. Cue the student to respond appropriately about Maria.

- Put students in pairs to practice talking about the people in the chart.

- Walk around to monitor the activity and provide help as needed.

Expansion Activity:
Talk about your classmates.

- Put students in pairs.
- Have students use the chart from Activity D on page 20, to practice talking about their classmates. Remind students to use the same sentence starters as in Activity C.

Expansion Activity:
Conversation/Vocabulary: Say the countries and the languages.

- Have students look at the big picture on page 18 or put the overhead transparency for Unit 2 on the OHP.
- Model the activity. Point to a character and say the name *(Leo)*. Say the country and the language *(Leo is from Russia. He speaks Russian.)*.
- Put students in pairs to take turns talking about the people in the picture.
- Call on students and say a name. Elicit the sentence about the country and language.

Objective
Saying marital status

Vocabulary

divorced	single
married	widowed

**Literacy Workbook pages 74–79
Workbook page 17**

  A CD 1, TRACK 31 **Listen.**

- Have students look at the pictures.
- Play the first part of the audio or read the sentences in the listening script as students follow along silently.
- Play the rest of the audio or read the sentences and have students repeat the words, focusing on the pronunciation. Stress final *d*.
- Explain the new vocabulary as needed.

⋯⋯ Listening Script

A. LISTEN

1. Married. Grace is married.
2. Single. Paul is single.
3. Divorced. Leo is divorced.
4. Widowed. Maria is widowed.

LISTEN AND REPEAT.

1. married
2. single
3. divorced
4. widowed

Extra Challenge
Dictation

- Play the audio or read the sentences. Have more advanced students write the sentences they hear.
- Write the sentences on the board.
- Ask how you would write the sentences using contractions.

Expansion Activity: **And you?**

- Write *I am* _____. on the board.
- Complete the sentence about you (e.g., *I am married.*).
- Have students write a sentence about themselves.
- Call on volunteers to read their sentences.

  B CD 1, TRACK 32 **Listen and circle.**

- Have students look at the first picture. Ask: *Who is that?* Elicit that it is Sandy.
- Play the audio or read the sentences in the listening script. Have students circle the correct picture.
- Put students in pairs to compare answers.
- Go over the answers with the class.

⋯⋯ Listening Script

B. LISTEN AND CIRCLE

1. They are married.   3. They are single.
2. He's widowed.   4. They are divorced.

Objective
Describing height

Vocabulary

average	short
height	tall

Literacy Workbook pages 74–79
Workbook page 18

  A CD 1, TRACK 33 **Listen.**

- Have students look at the pictures. Elicit the names.

- Play the first part of the audio or read the sentences in the listening script while students follow along silently.

- Play the rest of the audio or read the second part of the listening script and have students repeat.

- Call on students. Read one of the words and have students repeat.

- Have students work in pairs and take turns saying the words in random order as their partner points to the picture.

Listening Script

A. LISTEN

Paul: I am average height. Leo is tall. Tien is short.
Tien: Paul and Carlos are average height.

LISTEN AND REPEAT.

average height
tall
short

GRAMMAR Note *is* vs. *are*

- Point out that *am* is used with *I, is* with one other person (e.g., *Leo*), and *are* with two or more (e.g., *Paul and Carlos*). Students don't need to focus on the grammar now as they will practice it later in the unit.

Literacy Development Activity: Pronunciation Practice

- Write the three new vocabulary phrases on the board. Point out that *average height* is two words.

- Say the words, stressing the beginning sounds. Point to the *sh* in *short* and say *sh*.

- Write the sentences from Activity A on the board but leave a blank for the last word.

> I am _____.
> Leo is _____.
> Tien is _____.
> Paul and Carlos are _____.

- Read each sentence and elicit the missing word. You can either write the word on the line or have volunteers write the words.

B **Talk with a partner.**

- Have students look at the picture.

- Go over the directions.

- Read the first sentence and elicit the completion.

- Put students in pairs to complete the other sentences.

- Go over the answers with the class.

Answer Key

Tien and Maria are <u>short</u>.

Grace is <u>tall</u>.

Sandy is <u>average height</u>.

Expansion Activity: Measure Up

- Bring in a tape measure or use a yardstick if there is one in your classroom.

- On the board, mark off lines to indicate short (men 5'6", women 5'2"), average height (men 5'7"–5'11", women 5'3"–5'6"), and tall (men 6'+, women 5'7"+). Point out that these standards are for American culture.

- Have students stand next to the marks and note which adjective describes their height.

C Write about classmates.

- Go over the example.

- Model the activity. Say sentences about students in the classroom.

- Have students complete the sentences.

- Walk around the room to monitor the activity and provide help as needed.

- Put students in small groups to compare their sentences.

- Call on students to read their sentences to the class or to write their sentences on the board.

Expansion Activity: Lineups by Height

- Have students stand.

- Point to one side of the room and say *short.* Point to the other side and say *tall.* Help students begin to line up by height order. Once students understand the task, let them do it themselves.

- Call on students at different places in the line and ask, *short, average height, or tall?*

- Point to students in the line and elicit the name and height (e.g., *Maria is tall.*).

- Have students make general statements about the class's height, e.g., *Five women are tall. Two men are short.*

Extra Challenge
Challenge Dictation

- Put more advanced students in pairs to take turns dictating sentences about classmates.

Literacy Development Activity: Missing Letters

- Write on the board: __ h o __ t, __ a __ l, a __ e __ __ g __.

- Have literacy students look at the words on page 23 and write the missing letters.

Objective
Describing eye and hair color

Vocabulary

black	eyes	hair
blond	glasses	red
blue	gray	
brown	green	

Literacy Workbook pages 74–79
Workbook page 18

  A   CD 1, TRACK 34   **Listen.**

- Direct students' attention to the picture. Ask questions: *Who is that? What's his name? (Carlos). What color eyes does he have?*

- Play the audio or read the sentences as students look at the pictures.

- Play the audio or read the sentences again and have students repeat.

GRAMMAR Notes

- Point out that we use *have/has* with eye and hair color and glasses. Remind students we use *am/is/are* with other describing words.

- Point out that *eye* and *I* are two different words but pronounced the same.

PRONUNCIATION Note

- The two *s* sounds in *glasses* may be overlooked by students. Make sure they pronounce both *s* sounds.

B   Talk about your classmates.

- Model the activity. Have a student stand in front of the class. Look at his or her eyes and say, _____ *has* _____ *eyes.*

- If possible, have two students with glasses come to the front of the room. Say, _____ *and* _____ *have glasses.*

- Put students in pairs to talk about three classmates.

- Call on students and say another student's name (or names). Elicit the correct sentence about eye color.

  C   CD 1, TRACK 35   **Listen.**

- Have students look at the picture. Ask: *Who do you see? What are their names?*

- Play the audio or read the conversation.

- Play the audio or read the conversation again and have students repeat.

Expansion Activity: Listening/Speaking: Characters

- Put the transparency for Unit 2 on the OHP or have students look at the big picture on page 18.

- Call on students and point to a character on the transparency or say a character's name and show the card *(Leo)*. Elicit the correct sentence about hair color *(Leo has gray hair.)*.

- Continue until everyone has had a chance to participate.

- Repeat with eye color.

D **Write.**

- Copy the sentence starters on the board.

- Model the activity. Complete the sentences about you and about students in the class.

- Have students complete the sentences.

- Put students in groups to read their sentences.

- Call on volunteers to read their sentences to the class.

Extra Challenge
Write sentences.

- For more advanced students, write five character names on the board.

- Have students write sentences to describe the five characters.

- Put students in pairs to read their sentences.

Expansion Activity: Writing: Guess who.

- Put the transparency for Unit 2 on the OHP or have students look at the big picture on page 18.

- Put students in pairs to write descriptions of a character in the big picture. Tell students to write each sentence with *I (I have gray hair. I have green eyes.)*.

- Have students read the descriptions aloud. Elicit the character's name from the other students.

- As a variation, put the character cards on the tray under the OHP. After a student reads a description, have another student come and pick up the correct character card.

Objective
Describing people

Literacy Workbook pages 74–79
Workbook page 18

 **A** **Write.**

- Have students look at the pictures and the words in the box.

- For each item, have students write the word or phrase from the box that matches the picture above each line. Have them cross out each words or phrases as they complete the items.

- Do the first item together.

- Put students in pairs to compare answers.

- Go over the answers with the class.

Answer Key **1.** gray hair; **2.** married; **3.** blue eyes; **4.** glasses

Expansion Activity:
Characters *Yes* or *No*?

- Give each student two index cards or photocopy Worksheet 5: *Yes/No Cards* (Teacher's Edition page 331) and cut the cards up.

- If using index cards, have students write *yes* on one card and *no* on the other.

- Hold up one of the character cards and say *glasses.* Cue students to hold up the correct card—*yes* or *no*—for that character.

- Continue with other descriptors (*tall, short, brown hair, blue eyes*) and different characters. When students are comfortable with the task, increase the speed.

Literacy Development Activity:
Characters *Yes* or *No*?

- Write the descriptors on a card or piece of paper *(gray hair)* and hold it up with a character card. Don't say anything.

- Have students hold up a *yes* or a *no* card.

  B **CD 1, TRACK 36** **Listen. Write the number.**

- Have students look at the pictures.

- Play the first item of the audio or read the first sentence. Ask: *Who is it?* Point out that *1* is written next to *Carlos.*

- Play the rest of the audio or read the descriptions and have students write the number next to the person being described. If necessary, hold up the correct number of fingers to indicate the item number as students are listening and writing.

- Have students compare their answers with a partner.

- Go over the answers with the class.

········· **Listening Script**

B. LISTEN. WRITE THE NUMBER.

1. He has brown hair and brown eyes. He's from Brazil.
2. He has gray hair. He's divorced.
3. She is tall. She's from Somalia.
4. She has red hair. She's from the USA.

Answer Key **1.** Carlos; **2.** Leo; **3.** Nadira; **4.** Sandy

Expansion Activity: **Guess who.**

- Write a description of yourself on the board. Follow the models in Activity B.

> She is married. She has brown hair and green eyes. She's from the USA.

- Ask: *Who is it?* Elicit that the description is of you.

- Have students write descriptions of themselves. If you have a mixed level class, pair a more advanced student with a less advanced student. The less advanced student can dictate to the more advanced student.

- Collect the descriptions. Read them aloud and elicit which student is described.

My Life

- Have students bring in a picture of a friend or member of their family.

- Have students look at their picture. Ask: *Who do you see? Who is in the picture?*

- Model the activity. Hold up a photo of a friend or a photo from a magazine. Describe the person and write the sentences on the board.

- Put students in small groups. Have students describe their friends or family.

- Call on students to tell the class about their own friends or the friend of a classmate.

Expansion Activity: **Category Sort**

- Have students stand. Say *height* and cue students to form groups according to height (*tall, average height, short*).

- Say *eyes* and have students sort themselves by eye color. Provide help if necessary. Ask someone in each group to say the color.

- Continue the activity with hair color and marital status.

CULTURE Note

- Some students may come from cultures that don't allow the taking of photographs or from cultures where cameras are not typically owned. Tell students that for the *My Life* activity, they can draw a picture of a friend, or find a photo in a magazine that is similar. Bring in magazines if you use this option.

Objective
Saying and writing addresses; practicing numbers 11–19

Answer Key
1. 11; **2.** 17; **3.** 12; **4.** 15; **5.** 16; **6.** 13; **7.** 18; **8.** 14

Vocabulary/Numeracy

address	fourteen	thirteen
eighteen	nineteen	twelve
eleven	seventeen	zip code
fifteen	sixteen	

Literacy Workbook pages 74–79
Workbook page 19

A CD 1, TRACK 37 **Listen.**

- Have students look at the numbers as you play the audio or read the numbers.
- Play the audio or read the numbers again and have students repeat.
- Say the numbers in random order and have students point.

B **Write the numbers.**

- Have students write the numbers in order. Remind students to look at the numbers above if they need help.

C **Write the numbers.**

- Have students read the written numbers and write the actual numbers. Review the example.
- Put students in pairs to compare answers.
- Go over the answers with the class. Have students write the answers on the board.

Expansion Activity: Three in a Row

- Photocopy and distribute Worksheet 6: *Three in a Row* (Teacher's Edition page 332).
- Have students write the numbers 11–19 in the nine squares of the worksheet. The numbers should be randomly ordered.
- Tell students to circle the numbers on their worksheet when you say those numbers.
- Tell students that they should say *three in a row* when they circle three numbers in a row. Point to the three squares vertically, diagonally, and horizontally.
- Call out the numbers 11–19 in random order. When a student calls out *three in a row*, have the student say the numbers to the class for confirmation.

Expansion Activity: Dictation

- Put students in pairs to take turns dictating and writing numbers. Pair a more advanced student with a less advanced student to help literacy skills.
- Have the literacy student write the numeral and the advanced student write both the numeral and the word.

D CD 1, TRACK 38 **Listen.**

- Have students listen and follow along as you play the audio or read the conversation.

- Play the audio or read the conversation again as students repeat.

- Explain or elicit what a zip code is.

- Put students in pairs to practice the conversation.

PRONUNCIATION Notes

- Explain that we usually say four digit numbers as two pairs of two-digit numbers (*seventeen fourteen*). We usually say zip codes as single digits (*zero one three one three*).

- Numbers higher than 19 are taught in Unit 3.

E **Write about you.**

- Copy the sentence starters on the board.

- Model the activity.

My name is

_____.

My address is

_____.

- Complete the sentences with your real or pretend information.

- Have students complete the sentences. If they don't know their zip code, give them the one for your school.

- Have them share their information in small groups.

CULTURE Note

- Students may not feel comfortable giving their addresses to their classmates. Point out that they can change their addresses or use the address of the school in this activity if they are uncomfortable. However, stress that students must give the correct information on work, school, or other real-life forms.

Expansion Activity: **Keep a record.**

- Write three headings on the board: *Name, Address, Zip code.*

Name   Address   Zip code

- Have students copy the headings on a piece of paper.

- Have students record the information about themselves and their classmates from Activity E under the correct headings. Remind students that they don't have to give real information if they are uncomfortable, or have students only record name and zip code.

Objective
Understanding and filling out an identification form

Vocabulary

identification form

Literacy Workbook pages 74–79
Workbook page 20

 **Read.**

- Direct students' attention to the form.

- Ask comprehension questions: *What is his name? What is his address? Marital status? Eye color? Hair color?* Elicit the meaning of *marital status.*

- Go over the yellow note.

Expansion Activity: *Yes/No* Cards

- Have students use the *Yes/No* cards from the expansion activity in Lesson 7 or photocopy, cut up, and distribute Worksheet 5 (Teacher's Edition page 331).

- Say sentences about the form (e.g., *Leo is single.*) and have students hold up a card (e.g., *no*). Keep the activity fast-paced so you can see how well students understand the form and you.

- As a variation, have students say sentences about the form as their classmates hold up cards.

B **Complete.**

- Copy the form on the board or make an overhead transparency.

- Model the activity. Complete the form for yourself. Say the information as you write (e.g., *My last name is Turner.*).

- Have students complete the forms with their information.

- Put students in pairs or small groups to talk about the information on their forms.

Extra Challenge
Pair Interview

- With more advanced students, you can continue the activity as an interview. Have students copy the form onto a piece of paper.

- Put students in pairs to ask questions and complete the form about their partner. Point out that students can share real information or make up information.

- Call on students to tell the class about their partner.

Objective
Using *am/is/are*

Literacy Workbook pages 74–79
Workbook page 21

  A   CD 1, TRACK 39   **Listen and read.**

- Have students look at the picture. Point to Nadira and ask: *Who is it?*

- Have students listen and follow along as you play the audio or read the words in the chart.

- Play the audio or read the information in the chart again and have students repeat.

GRAMMAR Note

- Reinforce students' understanding of the pronouns. Point to yourself and say *I*, point to the class and say *you*. Continue pointing and saying the pronouns until students understand. Then add the correct form of *be* (e.g., *I am*).

  B   CD 1, TRACK 40   **Listen.**

- Have students look at the pictures.

- Have students listen and follow along as you play the audio or read the sentences.

- Play the audio or read the sentences again and have students repeat.

- Call on volunteers to read sentences aloud.

Expansion Activity: **Beanbag Toss**

- Call on a student, toss a beanbag or a small ball, and say a pronoun. Elicit the correct form of *be*.

- Continue with other students and pronouns until everyone has had a chance to participate.

- Remember: If this is hard logistically, have students stand, or eliminate the beanbag and just have students call on classmates.

C   **Write.**

- Have students complete the sentences. You will need to tell them the country you are from.

- Put students in pairs to compare sentences.

- Call on students to read their sentences to the class.

Expansion Activity: **Category Sort**

- Have students stand and group themselves by country of origin. If everyone is from the same country, you can have them sort by town or city.

- When students are standing in their groups, call on a representative from each group and elicit where they are from.

> **Where are you from?**   **We are from Mexico.**

- Then call on a student and point to a student in another group and elicit where he or she is from (*He is from Colombia.*).

- Continue until everyone has had a chance to participate and you have used most if not all of the pronouns.

Extra Challenge
Write sentences.

- Have advanced students write three sentences about people in the class from the above expansion activity (e.g., *We are from Mexico. He is from Colombia. You are from the USA.*).

Objective
Using *have/has*

Literacy Workbook pages 74–79
Workbook page 21

  A CD 1, TRACK 41 **Listen.**

- Have students look at the picture next to the verb chart. Point to Carlos and ask: *Who is it?*

- Have students listen and follow along as you play the audio or read the sentences in the chart.

- Play the audio or read the sentences again and have students repeat.

GRAMMAR Note

- Make sure students understand that we use *have* for all the pronouns except *he/she/it*.

  B CD 1, TRACK 42 **Listen.**

- Have students look at the pictures.

- Have students listen and follow along as you play the audio or read the sentences.

- Play the audio or read the sentences again and have students repeat.

- Call on volunteers to read sentences aloud.

Expansion Activity: Add-on

- Call on a student and say, *eye color.* Elicit a sentence about the student's eye color (*I have brown eyes*).

- Say a sentence about your eye color (*I have green eyes.*) and repeat the information from the student (*He has brown eyes.*).

> I have green eyes.   He has brown eyes.

- Call on a second student and elicit a sentence about the student's eye color. Then prompt the student to say a sentence about your eye color (*She has green eyes.*).

- Continue with other students, prompting a sentence about themselves and restating information about the previous student. Cue the student by pointing to the previous student.

C **Write.**

- Put students in pairs to compare sentences.

- Call on students to read their sentences to the class.

BIG PICTURE Expansion Activity: Grammar: *Be* or *Have*?

- Photocopy and distribute Worksheet 7: *Be* or *Have?* (Teacher's Edition page 333)

- Put the transparency for Unit 2 on the OHP or have students look at page 18 in their books.

- Have students complete the worksheet.

- Put students in pairs to compare answers.

Answer Key 1. has/Sandy; 2. are/Ben and Grace; 3. has/Leo; 4. has/Tien; 5. has/is/Paul; 6. has/Carlos; 7. has/Isabel

Objective
Reading maps

Literacy Workbook pages 74–79
Workbook page 22

A Circle.

- Have students look at the map of the United States.

- Elicit or point out that it shows the United States. Elicit or point out the state where you are.

- Point to each named state on the map and say the name. Have students repeat.

- Read the first sentence. Point to Sandy and elicit the state. Point out that *California* is circled.

- Have students look at the map and circle the correct state in each sentence.

- Put students in pairs to compare answers.

- Go over the answers with the class.

CULTURE/CIVICS Notes

- Point out that Hawaii and Alaska are not on the map. They are not physically connected to the other 48 states. Point these two states out on another map.

- Point out that we often say *the United States*, rather than *the United States of America*.

PRONUNCIATION Note

- Read each of the states listed in Activity A. Point out the *ch* sound in *Michigan* (like *sh*).

Answer Key
1. California;
2. Minnesota; **3.** Florida; **4.** New York;
5. Oregon; **6.** Texas; **7.** Illinois; **8.** Colorado

B Write about you.

- Write the name of your state on the board.

- Have students complete the sentence.

LITERACY DEVELOPMENT Note

- Point out that state names are capitalized.

Expansion Activity: States Near You

- Have students write the name of your state on the map if it's not already labeled.

- Write the names of neighboring states on the board.

- Point to these states on the map and have students label them in the book.

- As a variation, have students find and point out the other states listed in Activity A.

Literacy Development Activity: State Dictation

- Pair an advanced student with a literacy student. Have the advanced student dictate the letters of the states (e.g., *T-E-X-A-S*). Have the literacy student write the letters then say the name.

Objective

Writing descriptions using *is, are, has, have*

**Literacy Workbook pages 74–79
Workbook page 23**

A   Write *is, are, has,* or *have.*

- Direct students' attention to the picture. Ask questions: *Who are they? Is Tien tall or short? Who has glasses? Who has brown hair? Who has brown eyes?*

> **Who has glasses?**   **Tien.**

- Go over the example, then have students complete the story. Remind students to use *is* or *are* with countries and height and adjectives, e.g., *happy,* and *has* or *have* with eye color, hair color, and glasses.

- Put students in pairs to compare answers.

- Go over the answers with the class.

Answer Key   are; is; is; is; is; have; has; has; has; are

Expansion Activity: Sentence Strips

- Photocopy the version of the story below and cut into strips, or copy the story on to sentence strips. (The highlighting is for use in the next Expansion Activity.)

  Two new students are in Sandy Johnson's class.

  Nadira Shaheed is from Somalia.

  Tien Lam is from Vietnam.

  Nadira is average height.

  Tien is short.

They both have brown eyes.

Tien has glasses.

Tien has brown hair, but Nadira has black hair.

Both students are happy in their new class.

- Scramble the order of the sentences.

- Give each pair of students a set of strips and have them reconstruct the story.

Expansion Activity: Class Story

- Copy the story on the board. Leave blanks for the highlighted words in the box.

- Have two students come to the front, preferably one with glasses.

- Elicit the words from the class to complete the class story. For added difficulty, have students close their books and have them complete the story from memory.

- Read the story aloud and have students repeat. Call on individual students to read the story.

- Repeat if helpful with two different students.

B   Write about your teacher.

- Direct students' attention to the box. Read each word and have students repeat.

- Write your name, country, and language on the board.

- Have students complete the story. Point out that your name can go in the first blank.

- Call on volunteers to read their stories to the class.

Objective
Review and assessment

  A CD 1, TRACK 43 **Listen and write.**

- Go over the directions.

- Play the first sentence of the audio or read the first sentence in the listening script. Point out that *tall* is written on the line.

- Play the rest of the audio or read the sentences and have students write the words they hear. Pause after each line if necessary to give students time to write their answers.

- Play the audio or read the sentences again if necessary so students can confirm answers.

- Call on students to read the sentences to the class.

⋯⋯ Listening Script

A. LISTEN AND WRITE.

Grace: I am tall.
Leo: I speak Russian.
Tien: I have glasses.
Isabel: I have blond hair. I have blue eyes.
Sandy: He has brown hair.
Paul: You are from Somalia.
Ben: We have brown eyes.

Answer Key tall; speak; glasses; blond; blue; has; are; have

  B CD 1, TRACK 44 **Listen and fill in.**

- Have students read the sentences.

- Play the first sentence of the audio or read the first sentence and elicit that the answer is B. Point out that B is filled in.

- Play the rest of the audio or read the sentences and have students bubble in the correct answer.

- Put students in pairs to compare answers.

- Go over the answers with the class.

⋯⋯ Listening Script

B. LISTEN AND FILL IN.

1. I speak Vietnamese.
2. Leo is divorced.
3. Maria speaks Spanish.
4. What is your address?

Answer Key **1.** B; **2.** A; **3.** B; **4.** B

C **Talk about a classmate. Say, "Guess who."**

- Go over the directions and the example.

- Have students complete the sentences.

- Call on students to read their sentences to the class. Elicit the name of the student from the class.

D **Complete.**

- Read the words in the box aloud and have students repeat.

- Direct students' attention to the picture. Make sure students know that Pete is the boy and Linda is the girl.

- Go over the example. Have students complete the sentences.

- Go over the answers with the class.

> **Answer Key** **1.** green; **2.** red; **3.** short; **4.** brown; **5.** glasses; **6.** tall

E Learning Log

- Have students put a checkmark by words they know.

- Elicit words students are unsure of and write them on the board. Elicit the meanings.

Expansion Activity: Vocabulary Practice

- Assign or have students pick a certain number of words from the log and have them write or say sentences using them.

- **Challenge:** Have students use several words in one sentence.

BIG PICTURE
Expansion Activity: Reading: Using a Bar Graph

- Make student copies of Worksheet 8: *Using a Bar Graph* (Teacher's Edition page 334).

- Review the numbers 1 through 19 by having students count aloud. Cue them by holding up one finger and counting *one*. Continue cuing by holding up additional fingers.

- Tell the students what color hair you have (e.g., *I have brown hair.*). Write *Brown hair* on the board. Repeat the sentence and gesture to students to stand if they have brown hair. Count the students with brown hair, cuing the class to count with you. Put tally marks on the board next to *brown hair*.

- Repeat with *black hair, blond hair, gray hair,* and *red hair.*

- Copy the graph from the worksheet on the board or make a transparency of it. In the column labeled *brown hair,* color in the number of boxes that equal the tally marks on the board, pointing to each tally mark as you color each square. Ask volunteers to color in the other columns.

- Pass out Worksheet 8.

- Ask students to look at the big picture on page 18 and count the number of students pictured with gray hair (one student). Have them color in one block in the *gray hair* column on their graphs.

- Tell the students to continue counting the hair color of the people in the big picture. Have students work in pairs to complete their bar graphs.

🔍 LOOKING BACK

- Go over the directions.

- Put students in pairs to talk about the big picture on page 18. Walk around to monitor the activity.

- Call on students to talk about the picture.

UNIT OVERVIEW

Lesson	Objective	Student Book Page
1. Sandy Johnson's Family	Saying the names of family members	p. 35
2. Sandy's Family Tree	Identifying family members	p. 36
3. Who is that?	Asking and answering questions about family members	p. 37
4. Carlos's Relatives	Identifying family members by name	p. 38
5. She is young.	Understanding and writing personal descriptions	p. 39
6. *Mr., Mrs., Ms.,* and *Miss*	Recognizing and writing titles	p. 40
7. Do you have children?	Asking and answering questions about family members	p. 41
8. How old are you?	Practicing numbers 20–100 and saying your age	p. 42
9. A Family Form	Understanding and filling out a family form	p. 43
10. Grammar: *Yes, I do. / No, I don't.*	Asking and answering *yes/no* questions	p. 44
11. Grammar: *My, His, Her, Your, Their*	Using possessive adjectives	p. 45
12. Read: Nadira's Favorite Relative	Understanding a family story	p. 46
13. Write: My Family	Writing about families	p. 47
What do you know?	Review and assessment	p. 48

Big Picture Expansion Activities

Focus	Activity	Suggested Use
Speaking	Say the words.	**Lesson 2**
Reading	Using Adjectives	**Lesson 5**
Grammar	Possessive Adjectives	**Lesson 11**
Numeracy	Practicing Numbers	**Lesson 8**
Writing	Sandy's Family	**Lesson 13**
Vocabulary	Vocabulary Review	**Lesson 13**

Worksheets

Worksheet #/ Focus	Title	Teacher's Edition Page
9. Writing	Sandy's Form	**p. 335**
10. Grammar	Possessives	**p. 336**
11. Reading	Sandy's Family	**p. 337**
12. Vocabulary	Vocabulary Review	**p. 338**

Unit Opener

- Put the transparency for Unit 3 on the overhead projector (OHP) or have students look at the big picture on page 34.

- Point to each word of the question at the bottom of the page as you ask: *Who do you see?*

- If necessary, prompt the students by pointing to Sandy and asking: *What is her name?* Say, *This is Sandy's family.*

- Review the vocabulary learned in Units 1 and 2. Point to different people in the picture and ask questions such as, *What color hair does he have? Is he tall? Is she married? Does she wear glasses?*

- Begin a story by pointing to Sandy and saying, *She has red hair.* Point to a student, and have him or her say a new sentence.

- Continue around the room, with each student adding a new sentence.

- Point to different people in the picture and elicit words related to family that they already know and write them on the board.

- Point to the words on the board and say the words. Have students repeat.

Objective

Saying the names of family members

Vocabulary

brother	father	sister
daughter	mother	son

Literacy Workbook pages 80–88
Workbook page 26

  A CD 1, TRACK 46 **Listen.**

- Have students open their books and look at the pictures. Ask: *What do you see?*

> **What do you see?**

Write all the words the students know on the board (e.g., *mother, father, husband*).

> **mother, father, husband**

- Have students look at the pictures and listen while you play the audio or read the words in the listening script.

- Play the audio or read the words again. Pause after each word and ask the students to repeat the word and point to the person.

- Call on students. Say one of the words and have students repeat.

- Have students work in pairs and take turns saying the name as their partner points to the person.

⋯⋯ Listening Script

A. LISTEN.

1. **Sandy:** Father. This is my father.
2. **Sandy:** Mother. This is my mother.
3. **Sandy:** Brother. This is my brother.

4. **John:** Sister. This is my sister.
5. **Sandy:** Daughter. This is my daughter.
6. **Sandy:** Son. This is my son.

LISTEN AND REPEAT.

1. father	4. sister
2. mother	5. daughter
3. brother	6. son

Expansion Activity: **Spell it.**

- Model the activity. Say one of the words and then spell it (*father, f-a-t-h-e-r*).

- Call on students and say a word. Have students spell it.

- For a challenge activity, give students two minutes to review the words.

- Have students close their books. Ask volunteers to spell the words. Or, put students in pairs. Have one student look at the words in Activity A and say them as the partner spells them.

  B CD 1, TRACK 47 **Listen.**

- Have students look at the conversation.

- Play the audio or read the conversation as students follow along silently.

- Play the audio or read the conversation again and have students repeat after each line.

- Divide the class into two sides. Have one side read Carlos's lines. Have the other side read Sandy's lines. Point to each group to cue them to read.

- Then have them switch roles.

Expansion Activity: **Pair Work**

- Put students in pairs. Designate one partner to be Carlos and the other to be Sandy.

- Have students practice the conversation in pairs, then switch roles.

- Walk around the room to monitor the activity and provide help as needed.

C   Ask 4 classmates.

- Write the conversation on the board or on a transparency. You may want to write it in speech bubbles to show it's a dialogue.

- Fill in the first and third blank with words from the box (e.g., *What's your brother's name?* and *What's your sister's name?*). Point out or elicit that *father, son,* or *brother* goes in the first line, and *mother, daughter,* or *sister* in the second because of the possessive pronoun in the response. Circle or underline *his* in the second line and *her* in the fourth line.

- Model the activity with a student. Demonstrate how to substitute a male family member in the question. Elicit the answer from the student

> **What's your brother's name?**

> **His name is Hugo.**

Then ask the question about a female family member.

- Have students walk around the room to practice asking and answering the questions.

- Write a new word in the blanks of the first and third lines and have students practice again. As a variation, write a wrong answer and ask for a correction.

- Walk around the room to monitor the activity and provide help as needed.

- Ask volunteers to practice their conversations in front of the class.

- Call on students and ask them about their family members (e.g., *What is your mother's name?*).

GRAMMAR Note

- Point out that *What's = What is,* and that both are correct.

Expansion Activity: **Question Whip**

- For this activity, ask students to stand in a line, put students in small groups to form a circle, or just go up and down the rows of seats.

- Model the activity. Ask the first student a question (*What is your mother's name?*). Elicit the answer and then cue the student to ask the next student a new question (*What is your father's name?*).

> **What is your mother's name?**

> **What is your father's name?**

Continue until every student has had a chance to ask and answer a question.

Extra Challenge
Write the conversation.

- Have more advanced students write all the questions for Activity C (e.g., *What is your brother's name? What is your son's name?*) on a piece of paper.

- Put the advanced students in pairs to exchange papers and write answers.

Objective
Identifying family members

Vocabulary
children   husband   wife

Literacy Workbook pages 80–88
Workbook page 26

  A CD 1, TRACK 48 **Listen.**

- Have students look at the family tree. Show students the family tree in your book. Say *Sandy?* in a questioning voice. Then point to Sandy. Continue saying names and have students point to the person on the family tree.

- Have students look at the pictures and listen while you play the audio or read the sentences in the listening script.

- Play the audio or read the sentences again. Pause after each sentence and ask the students to repeat and point to the person.

- Have students work in pairs and take turns reading each name as their partner points to the person.

······ **Listening Script**

A. LISTEN

Arthur is Sandy's father.
Ann is Sandy's mother.
Tomiko is John's wife.
John is Tomiko's husband.
Sandy is Will's wife.
Will is Sandy's husband.
Sara is Tomiko and John's daughter.

Miles is Tomiko and John's son.
Andy, Justin, and Jane are Sandy and Will's children.

  B CD 1, TRACK 49 **Listen and write.**

- Write the first item on the board:
Sandy: Arthur is my _____.

- Play the first part of the audio or read the first sentence. Write *father* on the line on the board. (See the Literacy Development Note below.)

- Point to sentence 1 in the book.

- Play the rest of the audio or read the sentences as students fill in the blanks with the correct word.

- Put students in groups to compare answers.

- Give the answers and answer any questions.

- Note that students may want to talk about the names of other family members. These will be taught in Lesson 4 of this unit.

LITERACY DEVELOPMENT Notes

- For literacy students, write the words on the board: *father, mother, husband, wife, son, daughter.*

> ### father, mother, husband, wife, son, daughter

- Underline the first letter of each word. Then say each word, stressing the beginning sound.

60 Unit 3

Listening Script

A. LISTEN.

1. **Sandy:** Arthur is my father.
2. **John:** Ann is my mother.
3. **Will:** Sandy is my wife.
4. **Tomiko:** John is my husband.
5. **Sandy:** Justin is my son.
6. **Will:** Jane is my daughter.
7. **John:** Sara and Miles are my children.

Answer Key
1. father; 2. mother; 3. wife; 4. husband; 5. son; 6. daughter; 7. children

Expansion Activity: Assumed Identities

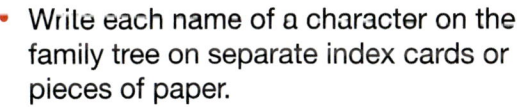

- Write each name of a character on the family tree on separate index cards or pieces of paper.

- Model the activity. Hold up a character card (e.g., *Arthur*) and say *I am Arthur.* Give another name card to a student (e.g., Ann). Say *Ann is my wife.* Elicit a sentence from the student about you (*Arthur is my husband*).

  | Ann is my wife. | Arthur is my husband. |

  Try to give female name cards to female students and male name cards to males.

- Call a group of students to the board (11 or fewer). Give each student a character name to hold. Try to give each student a card with the same gender as the character.

- Pull two students out and elicit sentences from them about each other. Have the class correct the sentences if they are wrong.

- Continue with other pairs of students.

Expansion Activity: **Pair up.**

- This is an extension of Assumed Identities.

- Call another group of students to the board and distribute cards.

- Say a pair of words that expresses a single relationship (e.g, *husband and wife*). Elicit the combinations that fit from the students with cards or from the class (e.g., *Arthur and Ann, Will and Sandy, John and Tomiko*).

- After the students are paired, point to each student (e.g., *Arthur*) and elicit the name of the family relationship (e.g., *husband*). Point out that everyone is more than one type. By giving each student a character name, you can continue to make new pairs and elicit relationships to clarify for students.

BIG PICTURE

Expansion Activity: Speaking: Say the words.

- Have students look at the big picture on page 34 or put the transparency for Unit 3 on the OHP.

- Model. Point to a character and say the name (*Justin*). Point to another character and say the name (*Sandy*). Then say the relationship (*son/mother*).

- Put students in pairs to take turns saying the names and relationships.

- Call on students and say two names (*Justin and Sandy*). Elicit the relationships. Make sure the names you say are relationships the students know.

Extra Challenge
Write the story.

- Give more advanced students a character card from the Assumed Identities activity.

- Model the activity. Choose one of the characters in Sandy's family (*Arthur*). Write a story on the board: *Ann is my wife. Sandy is my daughter.* Elicit the name of the person speaking (*Arthur*).

- Have advanced students write a story modeled after the example from their character's point of view.

- Pair these students with less advanced students and have them read their stories and elicit the names.

Literacy Development Activity:
Write the words.

- Write the first letter of each vocabulary word on the board followed by the correct number of lines to indicate the letters.

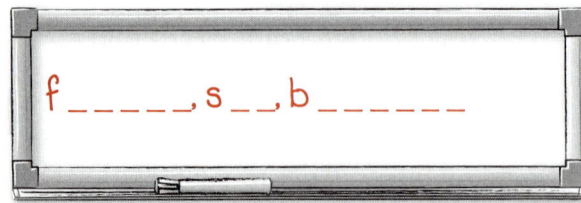

f _ _ _ _ _ , s _ _ , b _ _ _ _ _ _

Objective
Asking and answering questions about
family members

Literacy Workbook pages 80–88
Workbook page 27

  A CD 1, TRACK 50 **Listen.**

- Have students look at the picture.

- Play the audio or read the conversation in the
listening script.

- Play the audio or read the conversation again
and have students repeat.

PRONUNCIATION Note

- Students from some language backgrounds
may have difficulty with the ending sibilant
sounds like *s, sh,* and *z* sounds. Have students
exaggerate the possessive *s* of *Sandy's.* Point
out the possessive *s* is actually a /z/ sound.

GRAMMAR Note

- Students may not be familiar with the word
who to ask questions about people. Put this
in context for students. Students have used
what to refer to things (Unit 1, *What's this?*).
Pick up a book and ask: *What's this?* Point to
a student and ask: *Who's this?* Again, through
gestures repeat the word *what* as you refer to
the book, and *who* as you refer to a person.

Expansion Activity: **Possessives**

- Students will learn about the possessive
pronouns *my, his, her, your,* and *their*
in Lesson 11. However, students may
ask about the *'s* after Sandy. If so, you
can do an activity to demonstrate its
function. Students do not need a complete
grammatical explanation.

- Walk around the room and pick up a
student's book. Gesture to the student
and ask: *Who is this?* Elicit the name (e.g.,
Hugo), then point to the student's book
and say the possessive and book (*Hugo's
book*).

- Continue modeling the activity by walking
around the room and picking up books.
Elicit the student's name and then the
possessive.

B **Look at Sandy's family tree. Ask
your partner.**

- Direct students' attention to the box. Say
each word and have students repeat.

- Model the activity with a student. Hold up
the book and point to someone on page 36.
Ask: *Who is that?* Elicit the answer.

- Put students in pairs to practice asking and
answering questions about the people on
page 36. Tell them to ask a question about
each person in the box. Circulate around the
room and assist as needed.

Expansion Activity: **Family Photos**

- Have students bring in pictures of their
own families or distribute pictures from
magazines that show families and have
students pretend one of the magazine
families is their own.

This is my family. 63

- Model the activity. Show a picture of your family or your pretend family to the class. Cue a student to ask: *Who is that?* Answer with the relationship (e.g., *my brother*).

- Put students in pairs to practice asking and answering questions about their families.

- Walk around to monitor the activity and provide help as needed. You may want to point to someone in a picture and ask, *Who is that?* to check their comprehension.

C Fill in.

- Read the first question (*Who is Will?*).

- Read both responses and point out that the correct answer (*A*) is filled in.

- Have students read and fill in the bubbles next to the correct answers.

- Put students in pairs to compare answers.

- Go over the answers with the class.

Answer Key   1. A; 2. A; 3. A; 4. A

My Life

- Explain that students will draw their own family trees.

- Point out that each family tree may have a different arrangement. They don't have to include maternal and paternal grandparents if there isn't room, but they should try to include three generations like Sandy's tree. Encourage students to include those relatives they think are important. If they have 15 aunts, or 12 nieces, they do not have to include them all.

- Model the activity. Draw your own family tree or a fictitious tree on the board.

- Walk around the room to monitor the activity and provide help as needed.

- Ask volunteers to draw their trees on the board.

- Have students keep their trees to use in a later lesson.

Expansion Activity: Scribe

- Model the activity. Call on a student to show his or her family tree to the class and talk about it (e.g., *Grace is my sister.*). As the student talks, write phrases or short sentences on the board (*Grace is my sister.*).

- For mixed level classes, pair a more advanced student with a less advanced student.

- Have the less advanced student talk about his or her family trees as the more advanced partner writes the sentences or phrases.

- Have less advanced students write down several of their sentences or the phrases as an out-of-class assignment.

Objective

Identifying family members by name

Vocabulary

aunt	parents
cousin	relatives
grandfather	uncle
grandmother	

Literacy Workbook pages 80–88
Workbook page 28

 A CD 1, TRACK 51 **Listen and read.**

- Have students look at the picture. Point to each person, say the names and have students repeat. Have students look at the pictures and listen while you play the first part of the audio or read the sentences in the listening script below.

- Play the rest of the audio or read the list of words. Have students repeat the word and point to the picture of that person.

- Read the yellow note together.

Listening Script

A. LISTEN AND READ.

Grandfather. This is Carlos's grandfather.
Grandmother. This is Carlos's grandmother.
Uncle. This is Carlos's uncle.
Aunt. This is Carlos's aunt.
Cousin. This is Carlos's cousin.
Parents. These are Carlos's parents.

LISTEN AND REPEAT.

grandfather
grandmother
uncle
aunt
cousin
parents

 B CD 1, TRACK 52 **Listen and circle.**

- Have students look at the first picture. Ask: *Who is that?* Elicit that it is Carlos's relatives, Ricardo and Celina.

- Play the audio or read the sentences in the listening script. Have students circle the correct pictures. The first one is done for them.

- Play the audio or read the sentences again if needed. Put students in pairs to compare answers.

- Go over the answers with the class.

This is my family. 65

Listening Script

B. LISTEN AND CIRCLE.

1. My name is Carlos. These are my relatives.

2. This is my grandfather. His name is Umberto.

3. This is my grandmother. Her name is Vera.

4. This is my uncle. His name is Ricardo.

5. This is my aunt. Her name is Celina.

6. This is my cousin. His name is Alfredo.

7. These are my parents. Their names are Magda and Rudolfo.

Answer Key **1.** Ricardo and Celina;
2. Umberto; **3.** Vera; **4.** Ricardo; **5.** Celina;
6. Alfredo; **7.** Magda and Rudolfo

Expansion Activity: **Beanbag Toss**

- Write *husband* on the board. If possible, point to a married male student in the class and say *husband*. Point to a married female student and elicit *wife*. Write *wife* next to husband. If no one in your class is married, point to a married couple in the book.

- Elicit other male-female matched pairs and write them on the board (*son-daughter, aunt-uncle, grandmother-grandfather, brother-sister, mother-father*).

- Call on a student and toss a beanbag or small ball as you say one half of a matched pair (e.g., *father*). Elicit the match (e.g., *mother*) and have the student toss the beanbag back.

- Continue until all students have had a chance to participate.

Extra Challenge
Toss to a classmate.

- For more advanced classes, continue with the Beanbag Toss, but have the students call on classmates and provide the cues.

- If you have the room in your classroom, you may want to have students stand in a circle for this activity. Otherwise, make sure students are paying attention if classmates are tossing the beanbag.

Expansion Activity: **Riddles**

- Write and say a riddle sentence: *My grandmother is my mother's _____.* Elicit the correct word (e.g., *mother*).

- Put students in pairs to write two riddles using the words in the lessons.

- Collect the riddles and say them aloud, or have the students write them on the board.

- Elicit the answers.

Objective

Understanding and writing personal descriptions

Vocabulary

middle-aged   young
old

**Literacy Workbook pages 80–88
Workbook page 28**

 A   CD 1, TRACK 53   **Listen and read.**

- As a warmup to this activity, have students look at the pictures. Point to Ben's grandfather. Say: *Ben's grandfather. He has* _____ *hair?* Elicit *gray*. Point to other people in the picture and elicit words to describe their hair color.

- Have students look at the pictures as you play the audio or read the sentences.

Literacy Development Activity: Speaking Practice

- Write the three new vocabulary words on the board (*old, middle-aged, young*).

- Say the words, stressing the beginning sounds. Point to the first letter of each word and elicit the sound.

- Write the sentences from Activity A on the board but leave a blank for the last word.

1. Ben's grandfather is _____.
2. His parents are _____.
3. His sister is _____.

- Read each sentence and elicit the missing word. You can either write the word on the line or have volunteers write the words. Point out the hyphen in *middle-aged*.

B **Complete.**

- Go over the directions.

- Point to the first picture. Ask: *old, middle-aged, young?* Elicit that she is old.

- Have students complete the other sentences.

- Go over the answers with the class.

Answer Key   **1.** old; **2.** young;
3. middle-aged; **4.** old

C **Write about you.**

- Go over the example.

- Model the activity. Say sentences about people in your family: *My mother is old. My daughter is young.*

- Have students complete the sentences. You may want to have students look at their family trees that they prepared in the Lesson 2 expansion activity, or other pictures of families you provide.

- Walk around the room to monitor the activity and provide help as needed.

- Put students in pairs or small groups to compare their sentences.

- Call on students to read sentences to the class or to write their sentences on the board.

- Call on students to talk about their partner's families (e.g., *Fiona's mother is middle-aged.*).

This is my family.   67

Expansion Activity: Find the match./Character Cards

- Put students in pairs.

- Distribute index cards. Have students write each adjective from Activity A (e.g., *old*) on a card and each relationship name (e.g., *sister*) on a card.

- Model the activity. Choose a family member card and show the students (e.g., *sister*). Choose the adjective card that matches the family member you chose and show the students (e.g., *middle-aged*). Form a sentence using the two cards. Say, *My sister is middle-aged.*

- Have students work with their partner, taking turns and matching cards. Point out that students are using the cards to describe their own family members.

- **Character card version:** Hold up each character card and have students hold up the adjective they think describes that character's age. It's okay if they have different opinions.

Expansion Activity: Challenge Dictation

- Dictate three sentences to the class (e.g., *My grandmother is old. My sister is middle-aged. My daughter is young.*). Read each sentence three times.

- Have volunteers write the sentences on the board.

- Put students in pairs. Have students dictate their sentences from Activity C in random order to their partners.

- Have students correct their partners' sentences.

Literacy Development Activity: Sentence Cards

- Write each word for three or more sentences on a separate index card. For example, the sentence *My grandmother is old* would take four index cards.

- Put students in groups according to the sentences. Give each student a card.

- Have students form the sentence from the cards.

- Call on groups to read their sentences aloud.

BIG PICTURE
Expansion Activity: Reading: Using Adjectives

- Each student or pair of students will need the adjective cards *old, middle-aged,* and *young* from the Find the Match expansion activity on this page.

- Put the color transparency for Unit 3 on the OHP or have students look at the big picture on page 34 in their books.

- Explain the activity: when you point to a character, the students should hold up the correct card.

- Model the activity. Point to Sandy and signal to students to hold up the *middle-aged* card.

- Continue pointing to other people and have students hold up appropriate cards. This is a fast-paced activity. For additional challenge, you can add other cards (e.g., *red hair, gray hair, blue eyes*).

Objective
Recognizing and writing titles

Vocabulary

Miss	Mrs.	Ms.
Mr.		

Literacy Workbook pages 80–88
Workbook page 29

 A CD 1, TRACK 54 **Listen.**

- Direct students' attention to the picture at the top of the page. Ask questions: *Who is that? What's his name? Who is that? What's her name?*

- Read the words in the speech bubbles aloud. Point out that *Who is she?* is similar to *Who is that?*

- Read the yellow note. Answer any questions students may have about it. Point out or elicit that *Mrs., Ms.,* and *Miss* refer to women. *Mrs.* or *Ms.* can be used with married women, and *Ms.* or *Miss* with single women. Draw stick figures of a man and a woman to convey this idea.

- Have students look at the pictures. Elicit or point out that the two people in the first picture are married. Point out we often use *Mr.* and *Mrs.* to talk about two people who are married.

- Play the audio or read the words as students look at the pictures.

- Play the audio or read the words again and have students repeat.

CULTURE Notes

- Students may not understand the differences among the titles.

- Students may wonder about the use of *sir* and *ma'am*. If so, explain that we use *sir* to show politeness in addressing an adult man, and *ma'am* to show politeness to an adult woman. We sometimes use *miss* to show politeness to a younger woman. They are not followed by the last name of the person, whereas the other titles are.

PRONUNCIATION Notes

- Stress the ending sounds of *Mrs., Ms.,* and *Miss.* Students should hear the two distinct sibilant sounds in *Mrs.* Point out that the *r* is not pronounced.

- Point out that *Ms.* ends in /z/, while *Miss* ends in /s/.

Listening Script

A. LISTEN.

1. Mr. and Mrs. or Ms. Hancock
2. Mr. Hancock and Mrs. or Ms.. Tanaka
3. Miss or Ms. Lopez

B Write *Mr., Ms., Mrs., or Miss.*

- Say *Leo Danov.* Ask *Man? Woman?*. Elicit that Leo is a man. Ask: *Mr.? Mrs.?* Elicit that the answer is *Mr. Danov.* Point out that *Mr.* is written on the line.

- Have students write the titles on the lines. If necessary, prompt students by asking questions (e.g., *Is Isabel Lopez a woman? Is she married?*).

- Put students in pairs to compare answers.

- Go over the answers with the class.

Answer Key 1. Mr.; 2. Mrs./Ms.;
3. Miss/Ms.; 4. Mr.

**Expansion Activity:
Character Titles**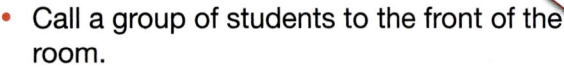

- Call a group of students to the front of the room.

- Give each student a character card.

- Elicit an appropriate title for each character from the student holding the card (e.g., *Mr. Danov*).

- Model the activity. Say a sentence about a character using a title (*Mr. Danov is old*).

- Call on students and point to a character. Elicit a sentence.

**Extra Challenge
Write sentences.**

- For extra practice, have students take turns writing their sentences on the board.

Objective

Asking and answering questions about family members

Vocabulary

children   daughter   son

Literacy Workbook pages 80–88
Workbook page 30

  A CD 1, TRACK 55 **Listen.**

- Direct students' attention to the picture. Point to each character and elicit the name.

- Have students listen and follow along in the book as you play the audio or read the conversation.

- Play the audio or read the conversation a second time and have students repeat.

Expansion Activity: Conversation Practice

- Model the activity. Ask two students to read the lines for Leo and Tien while you play the part of Paul. Ask: *Do you have children?* Cue the two students to read the appropriate line.

- Put students in groups of three. Assign each a role.

- Have students practice the conversation, then switch roles so they can play all roles.

- Walk around to monitor the activity and provide help as needed.

B **Ask 5 classmates.**

- Go over the words in the box.

- Model the activity. Cue a student to ask: *Do you have children?* Answer about yourself (e.g., *Yes, I do. I have one son and one daughter.*).

- Have students circulate around the room asking and answering the question. They should keep track of the responses by writing down the names of their classmates and their answers.

- Alternatively, put students in groups of six and have them take turns asking and answering the question. As a variation, put students in mixed groups according to language background.

- Call on students to tell about their classmates.

Expansion Activity: Two Lines

- Have students stand in two lines facing each other.

- Gesture to one line and say: *ask.* Gesture to the other line and say: *answer.*

- Model the activity. Have the first student from the ask line ask the question: *Do you have any children?* The person facing the student should answer about himself or herself. Then have the *answer* person go to the end of the line.

- Cue the students in the *ask* line to ask their new partners. After partners answer, cue the head student to go to the end of the line. This will ensure that students are always facing a new partner.

- After several rounds, have the lines switch roles. Remember to cue students to ask, answer, and shift positions when necessary.

C Complete.

- Read the first sentence. Point out that *son* is written on the line and crossed off in the box.

- Have students complete the sentences.

- Put students in pairs to compare answers.

- Go over the answers with the class.

Answer Key **1.** son; **2.** have; **3.** don't; **4.** do; **5.** children

Objective
Practicing numbers 20–100 and saying your age

Vocabulary

twenty	twenty-nine
twenty-one	thirty
twenty-two	forty
twenty-three	fifty
twenty-four	sixty
twenty-five	seventy
twenty-six	eighty
twenty-seven	ninety
twenty-eight	one hundred

  A CD 1, TRACK 56 **Listen.**

- Have students look at the numbers as you play the audio or read them.
- Play the audio or read the numbers again and have students repeat.
- Say the numbers in random order and have students point.
- Say other examples of numbers between 30 and 100 (e.g., *33, 46, 62*) so that students can understand the pattern.

  B CD 1, TRACK 57 **Listen and write.**

- Go over the example.
- Have students write the numbers as you play the audio or read them.
- Put students in pairs to compare answers.
- Go over the answers with the class. Have students write the answers on the board.

PRONUNCIATION Note

- Students may have difficulty distinguishing between numbers like 30 and 13. Point out that numbers ending in 0 (30, 40, 50, 60, 70, 80, 90), have the stress on the first syllable. The /t/ in the middle of the word is also pronounced more like /d/. Model this pronunciation. The numbers beginning with 1 (13, 14, 15, 16, 17, 18, 19) have stress on both syllables and the medial /t/ sounds like /t/. Model this pronunciation.

Answer Key
1. 28; **2.** 30; **3.** 90; **4.** 60; **5.** 50; **6.** 40; **7.** 80; **8.** 70; **9.** 100

Expansion Activity: Three in a Row

- Draw a three-by-three grid on the board. Have students draw their own grids.
- Write the numbers from the Pronunciation Note above on the board.
- Have students choose nine of the numbers. Have students write one number in each square of their three-by-three grids. The numbers should be randomly ordered.
- Explain that you will call out numbers and that they should say *three in a row* when they get three numbers in a row vertically, diagonally, or horizontally. Point to the three squares vertically, diagonally, and horizontally.
- Begin the game. Call out the numbers in random order. When a student calls out *three in a row*, have the student say the numbers to the class for confirmation.

This is my family. 73

Expansion Activity:
Say and write the number.

- Write the numbers 20-100 on the board. Randomly point to a number and prompt the students to say it.

- Continue with additional random numbers.

- Call on individual students to say numbers and point to the numbers they say.

Expansion Activity: Dictation

- Put students in pairs to take turns dictating and writing numbers. Pair a more advanced student with a less advanced student to help with literacy skills.

- Have the literacy student say the number as the advanced student writes it.

- Have students check the answers in the book.

  C   CD 1, TRACK 58 **Listen.**

- Go over the yellow note.

- Have students listen and follow along as you play the audio or read the conversation.

- Play the audio or read the conversation again as students repeat.

D   **Ask 5 classmates.**

- Model the activity. Cue a student to ask: *How old are you?* You can answer with your correct age, or an obviously wrong age (e.g., *I'm twenty-one years old*). If you use a wrong age, you may want to make a comic expression so students understand you are pretending.

- Put students in groups of six to practice asking and answering the question about age.

- Call on students and ask questions: *How old are you? How old are your children?*

CULTURE Notes

- Students may come from cultures where talking about age is not considered polite. Point out in some cultures including American culture older people may not like to tell their ages.

- Make sure students understand that they need to tell the correct age on documents like registrations, applications, and driver's licenses.

BIG PICTURE

Expansion Activity:
Numeracy: Practicing Numbers

- Put the transparency for Unit 3 on the OHP or have students look at the big picture on page 34.

- Point to Sandy and ask: *Is Sandy 20?* Elicit a more realistic guess.

- Continue with other characters in the picture.

- This activity can be done with character cards, too.

Objective
Understanding and filling out a family form

Literacy Workbook pages 80–88
Workbook page 32

 A   CD 1, TRACK 59   **Listen and read.**

- Direct students' attention to the form. Have students follow along as you say the information or play the audio.

- Ask comprehension questions: *Who is the grandfather? How old is he?*

CULTURE/ACADEMIC Notes

- Point out or elicit that we complete forms for many things—to register for school, to get a driver's license, to apply for a job.

- Provide or elicit the type of information that is usually included on forms (name, address, date of birth, etc.).

B   **Complete.**

- Make an overhead transparency of the blank form or copy it on the board.

- Model the activity. Complete the form for yourself. Talk about the people on your form (e.g., *Mr. Jack Warner is my father. He is 70 years old.*).

- Have students complete the form with information about their family members.

- Put students in pairs or small groups to talk about the information on their forms.

Expansion Activity: **Sandy's Form**

- Photocopy and distribute Worksheet 9: *Sandy's Form* (Teacher's Edition page 335).

- Put the Unit 3 transparency on the OHP or have students look at the big picture on page 34. Point out that the names and relationships are in Lessons 1 and 2.

- Have students complete Sandy's form.

- Go over the answers with the class.

Answer Key

Family Form   Your name: _Sandy Johnson_

Mr./Mrs./Ms. First and Last Name	Relative
Mr. Will Johnson	husband
Mr. Andy Johnson	son
Mr. Justin Johnson	son
Miss/Ms. Jane Johnson	daughter
Mr. Arthur Hancock	father
Mrs./Ms. Ann Hancock	mother
Mr. John Hancock	brother

Extra Challenge

Interview

- With more advanced students, you can continue Activity B as an interview. Have students use Worksheet 9.

- Put students in pairs to ask questions and complete the form about their partner's family. Students can share real information or make it up.

- Call on students to tell the class about their partner's family.

Objective

Asking and answering *yes/no* questions

Literacy Workbook pages 80–88
Workbook page 33

  A CD 1, TRACK 60 **Listen and read.**

- Have students look at the pictures. Point to each picture and ask: *Who is it?*

- Have students listen and follow along as you play the audio or read the conversation.

- Play the audio or read the conversation again and have students repeat.

GRAMMAR Note

- Point out that *don't* is the short form of *do not*, and that we use the negative contraction more often than the full form.

  B CD 1, TRACK 61 **Listen and circle.**

- Write *Yes, I do.* and *No, I don't.* on the board.

- Model the activity. Ask a question (e.g., *Do you have a brother?*)

> Do you have a brother?

and call on individual students to answer. As students answer, point to the answer on the board.

- Ask a volunteer to come to the board. Ask a question (*Do you have a sister?*). Have the student circle the answer on the board.

- Have students circle the answers they hear as you play the audio or read the conversations in the listening script. If necessary, play the audio or read the conversations again so that students can check their work.

Listening Script

B. LISTEN AND CIRCLE.

1. **Sandy:** Do you have a sister?
   Leo: Yes, I do.
2. **Ben:** Do you have two brothers?
   Tien: No, I don't.
3. **Paul:** Do you have a young daughter?
   Sandy: Yes, I do.
4. **Nadira:** Do you have a tall uncle?
   Carlos: Yes, I do.

Answer Key **1.** Yes, I do.; **2.** No, I don't.; **3.** Yes, I do.; **4.** Yes, I do.

Expansion Activity: Answer Cards

- Give each student two index cards.

- Have students write *Yes, I do.* on one card, and *No, I don't.* on the other.

- Ask questions of the class (e.g., *Do you have two sisters?*) and have students show the card that expresses their answers.

- Call on students to ask the class questions.

C **Ask 8 classmates. Complete the chart.**

- Write *a tall uncle* on the board.

- Model the activity with two students. Have one student be Paul and the other be Carlos. Have "Carlos" write his name the board.

- Point out that Carlos's name is written on the chart because he has a tall uncle, so he could answer, *Yes, I do.* Tell students that a classmate can only write his or her name on a line if the answer to the corresponding question is *Yes, I do.*

- Have students stand and walk around asking their classmates questions and completing the chart.

- Monitor the activity and provide help as needed.

- When students are finished, call on individual students and ask questions: *Who has a middle-aged uncle? Who has two cousins?*, etc.

Expansion Activity:
Vote with your feet!

- Write *Yes, I do.* on one side of the board and *No, I don't.* on the other.

- Have the students stand and come to the front of the room.

- Ask questions from the chart and others (e.g., *Do you have a short aunt?*) and have students move to the side of the room that expresses their answers.

- When students have moved, call on individual students and repeat the question. Elicit the answer.

- As a variation, have a student stand at the board and tally answers. After the activity, review how many people have answered *yes* to the different questions. Point out or elicit the most and least popular answers, as well as other interesting results.

Objective
Using possessive adjectives

Vocabulary

her	my	your
his	their	

Literacy Workbook pages 80–88
Workbook page 33

  A CD 1, TRACK 62 **Listen and read.**

- Have students look at the pictures and follow along as you play the audio or read the sentences.

- Play the audio or read the sentences again and have students repeat.

- Call on individual students to read the sentences.

- Write the subject pronouns on the board (*I, you, he/she/it, we, they*).

- Point to each and elicit the possessive. Write it on the board next to the subject pronoun.

- Point out the list of possessive adjectives next to this activity.

  B CD 1, TRACK 63 **Listen and circle.**

- Have students look at Activity B in their books as you play the audio or read the sentences in the listening script. Have students circle the correct possessive.

- Play the audio or read the sentences again if needed so students can check their answers.

- Put students in pairs to compare answers.

- Go over the answers with the class.

········ **Listening Script**

B. LISTEN AND CIRCLE.

1. Her name is Ann.
2. His name is Will.
3. Your name is Tomiko.
4. Her name is Jane.

Answer Key   1. Her; 2. His; 3. Your;
4. Her

Expansion Activity: Beanbag Toss

- Call on a student. Toss a beanbag or small ball and say a subject pronoun (e.g., *you*). Elicit the corresponding possessive (e.g., *your*). Have the student throw the beanbag to a classmate and say a subject pronoun.

- Continue until everyone has had a chance to participate.

- Remember, if this is hard logistically, have students stand, or eliminate the beanbag and just have students call on classmates.

C **Complete.**

- Direct students' attention to the picture. Ask: *Who is that?* (Paul).

- Read each word in the box and have students repeat. Point out that *my* is written on the first line so it is crossed out in the box.

- Have students write the other words on the lines. Remind them to cross words out as they go to help them keep track of what words are left to use.

- Put students in pairs to take turns reading the story.

- Call on students to read sentences to the class.

CULTURE/CIVICS Notes

- Students may not know where Haiti is. Point to Haiti on a map or have a student do it.

- Have students point to their countries on a map.

Answer Key My; His; Her; Their

BIG PICTURE

Expansion Activity: Grammar: Possessives

- Photocopy and distribute Worksheet 10: *Possessives* (Teacher's Edition page 336).

- Have students complete the worksheet in pairs.

- Put students in groups to compare answers.

- Go over the answers with the class.

Answer Key **1.** My; **2.** your; **3.** His; **4.** My; His; **5.** your; **6.** Their; **7.** Her; Her; **8.** Your

Extra Challenge
Personalize

- Have more advanced students rewrite the sentences in Activity C, substituting information about their own families. This will prepare them for the writing activity in Lesson 13.

- As a variation, pair advanced students with less advanced students. Have the less advanced students dictate the information as the advanced students rewrite the sentences about their partner's family.

This is my family. 79

Objective
Understanding a family story

Literacy Workbook pages 80–88
Workbook page 34

 A CD 1, TRACK 64 **Listen and read.**

- Direct students' attention to the picture of Nadira and Ubah. Point to Nadira and ask: *Who is this?* Point to Ubah and ask: *Who is this? Nadira's mother? Sister? Grandmother?* Elicit ideas.

- Have students listen and read along silently as you play the audio or read the story aloud.

- Play the audio or read the story aloud again and have students repeat.

- Put students in pairs to take turns reading the story aloud.

- Call on volunteers to read to the class.

- Ask comprehension questions such as: *Who is Ubah? How old is she? Where is she from?*

CULTURE Note

- Point out or elicit where Somalia is on a map.

Literacy Development Activity: Strip Story

- Rewrite the story on long strips of paper. Write one sentence on each strip. Make sure to leave a large space between each word.

- Put the first strip in a pocket chart or tape it to the wall or board.

- Read the first strip aloud and have students repeat.

- Continue with the other sentence strips.

- Take the strips out of the chart or off the board and mix them up.

- Call a volunteer to the front of the class and have him or her put the strips in order. Have the class approve or correct the sentence order. Reread.

- Continue with other volunteers.

- For very low level literacy students, have them practice counting the words in each sentence to reinforce word discrimination and focus on beginning sounds.

B   Check. What is the story about?

- Read the question aloud.

- Point out or elicit that a topic is the big (or main) idea, not the little details. Use gestures to convey the ideas of big and little.

- Model the concept. Tell a story about someone in your family (e.g., *My sister is my favorite person. She is 35 years old. She is a mother. She is….*). Ask: *What is the story about? What is the topic?* Elicit who it is about (e.g., *sister*).

- Read the answers aloud. Have students put a checkmark next to the answer.

Answer Key
2. Ubah is Nadira's favorite relative.

C   Circle.

- For lower level students, see the activity on the next page.

- Read the first sentence aloud with both choices (e.g., *Ubah is tall?* with hand high to show tall; *Ubah is short?* with hand low to show short). Elicit the answer (*short*). Point out that *short* is circled.

- Have students circle the correct words to complete the rest of the sentences.

- Put students in pairs to compare answers.

- Go over the answers with the class.

Answer Key
1. short; **2.** white; **3.** the United States; **4.** grandchildren; **5.** grandmother

Literacy Development Activity:
Key Words

- Copy the sentences from Activity C on the board. Write the choices in different colors from the other words in the sentence. Remember to leave spaces between the words.

- Point to each word in the first sentence as you read it. Use gestures to remind students of the meaning of *tall* and *short*. Point to the beginning letter in each word. Say the words again exaggerating the beginning sound. Elicit the answer. Have a volunteer circle the correct word on the board. Have students circle the correct word in their books.

- Continue with the other sentences.

- For extra practice, have students study then spell the correct answer, then check their work with a partner.

Expansion Activity:
Write two more.

- Have students write two more sentences about the story (e.g., *Ubah is old.*).

- Call on students to read the sentences aloud. Elicit the answers.

Extra Challenge
Your Favorite Relative

- Have more advanced students write sentences to describe their favorite relatives.

- Put advanced students in pairs to share their information.

- As a variation, pair an advanced student with a less advanced student. Have the students talk about their favorite relatives. Have the advanced students write the sentences for the less advanced students to copy in their notebooks.

Objective
Writing about families

Literacy Workbook pages 80–88
Workbook page 35

A Complete.

- Read each word in the box and have students repeat. Point out that each box goes with each section of the story. Point out that *my* is crossed out in the list and written on the first line.

- Have students complete the story. Remind students to use words with uppercase letters to start a sentence.

- Put students in pairs to compare answers. Have them take turns reading sentences.

- Go over the answers with the class.

CULTURE Note

- Direct students' attention to the map of the United States and Mexico on the inside back cover. Elicit or point out where Mexico is on a world map.

Answer Key My, I, family, children, son, daughters, Their, young, four

Expansion Activity: Read it aloud.

- Have students read the corrected story aloud and record it.

- Have students listen to their recorded story. Point out or elicit words that were problematic and correct the pronunciation.

B Write about you.

- Model the activity. Write about yourself on the board or OHP. Follow the template provided. Read it aloud to the students.

- Have students complete the story with information about their own families. Provide help as needed. Students may need help with the middle paragraph since there are no helping words provided.

- Put students in pairs to read their stories.

- Call on volunteers to read their stories to the class.

BIG PICTURE
Expansion Activity: Writing: Sandy's family

- Photocopy and distribute Worksheet 11: *Sandy's Family* (Teacher's Edition page 337).

- Put the transparency for Unit 3 on the OHP or have students look at the big picture on page 34 in their books.

- Have students complete the story. Remind students to look at Activity A for a model.

- Put students in pairs to compare answers and read the story aloud to each other.

- Go over the answers with the class.

Answer Key Her name is <u>Sandy Johnson</u>. She is from <u>the USA</u>. She has three <u>children</u>. She has one <u>daughter</u> and two <u>sons</u>. Their names are <u>Andy, Justin,</u> and <u>Jane</u>. Her children are <u>young</u>. She has <u>eleven</u> people in her family.

BIG PICTURE

Expansion Activity: Vocabulary: Vocabulary Review

- **Before class:** Make student copies of Worksheet 12: *Vocabulary Review* (Teacher's Edition page 338).

- Copy Worksheet 12 on the board. Put the transparency for Unit 3 on the OHP.

- Demonstrate the concept of *same* by pointing to the hair of two people in your room or on the transparency who have the same hair color. Pointing to one person, ask: *What color is his/her hair?* Pointing to the other person, ask: *What color is his/her hair?* Repeat the color as you point to each (e.g., *brown, brown*) and say *same*. Repeat with other qualities.

- Demonstrate *different* by pointing to two people in your room or on the transparency who have different hair colors. Pointing to one person, ask: *What color is his/her hair?* Pointing to the other person ask: *What color is his/her hair?* Repeat the different colors as you point to each (e.g., *gray, blond*) and say *different*. Repeat with other qualities.

- Point to Sandy and her husband. Write *Sandy* next to Person A on the board; write *Will* next to Person B. Ask about

hair color. Elicit that Sandy has red hair, and Will has white hair. Write *red hair* under Sandy and *white hair* under Will.

- Ask if Sandy is married. Ask if Will is married. Point to Sandy and say *married*. Point to Will and say *married*. Write *married* under *A and B*.

- Pass out Worksheet 12. Tell the students to choose any two people on the transparency for Person A and Person B. Have students work in pairs to complete the chart.

- **Option:** Have the students work with a partner to complete the chart about themselves. Share with the class.

This is my family. 83

Objective
Review and assessment

  A CD 1, TRACK 65 **Listen and fill in.**

- Go over the directions.

- Play the first sentence of the audio or read the first sentence in the listening script. Point out that B is filled in.

- Play the rest of the audio or read the sentences as students mark the answers. Stop after each sentence so students have time to mark their answers.

- Put students in pairs to compare answers.

- Play the audio or read the sentences again and have students check their answers.

- Elicit the answers and write them on the board.

Listening Script

A. LISTEN AND FILL IN.

1. My name is Ms. Tanaka.
2. I live at 60 Brown Road.
3. I am married.
4. My husband's name is John.
5. We have two children.
6. My brother has five children.

Answer Key 1. B; 2. A; 3. B; 4. A; 5. A; 6. B

  B CD 1, TRACK 66 **Listen and fill in.**

- Go over the directions.

- Play the first sentence of the audio or read the first sentence in the listening script. Point out that the B bubble is filled in.

- Have students look at each pair of answers.

- Play the rest of the audio or read the sentences as students fill in the answers. Stop after each sentence so students have time to fill in their answers.

- Put students in pairs to compare answers.

- Play the audio or read the sentences again and have students check their answers.

- Elicit the answers and write them on the board.

Listening Script

B. LISTEN AND FILL IN.

1. Tien's grandmother is 60 years old.
2. Mr. Avila is Carlos's grandfather.
3. Her name is Ms. Tanaka.
4. Sandy is your teacher.
5. Their names are Paul, Jessie, and Marie.

Answer Key 1. B; 2. B; 3. A; 4. B; 5. B

  C CD 1, TRACK 67 **Listen and circle.**

- Go over the directions and example.

- Have students circle the number as you play the audio or read the numbers in the listening script.

- Put students in pairs to compare answers.

- Play the audio or read the numbers again and have students check their answers.

- Elicit the answers and write them on the board. Check for understanding.

········ **Listening Script**

C. LISTEN AND CIRCLE.

1. eighty
2. sixty
3. nineteen
4. twenty-five
5. seventeen
6. twelve
7. fourteen
8. fifty

Answer Key **1.** 80; **2.** 60; **3.** 19; **4.** 25;
5. 17; **6.** 12; **7.** 14; **8.** 50

D **Write *Mr., Ms., Miss,* or *Mrs.***
• Go over the example.
• Have students complete the sentences.
• Put students in pairs to compare answers.
• Read the sentences and have students check their answers.
• Elicit the answers and write them on the board.

Answer Key **1.** Mrs.; **2.** Mr.; **3.** Miss/
Ms.

E **Complete the chart. Write about your family.**
• Go over the directions.
• Have students complete the chart.
• Walk around to monitor the activity and provide help as needed.

• Put students in pairs to talk about their charts.
• Call on students to tell the class about the information in their charts.

F **Learning Log**
• Go over the directions.
• Have students check the words they know.
• Put students in pairs to compare lists and review the words.
• Elicit words that students do not know and review their meanings.

LOOKING BACK

• Go over the directions.
• Brainstorm a list of things students can now say about people and write the ideas on the board (*relatives, hair color, eye color, age, country*).
• Put students in pairs to talk and list ideas about the picture on page 34. Encourage students to write sentences about what they see.
• Walk around to monitor the activity.
• Call on students to talk about the picture. Elicit sentences about the relationships and descriptions of the people.

Objective
Review of *be* and *have*

A Write *am, is,* or *are.*
- Review the information in the chart.
- Read the sentences and have students repeat them after you.
- Go over the directions and the example.
- Have students write *am, is,* or *are* on the lines.
- Put students in pairs to compare answers.
- Call on pairs of students to write the completed sentences on the board or read them aloud.

Answer Key **1.** is; **2.** are; **3.** are; **4.** is; **5.** are; **6.** am; **7.** are; **8.** are; **9.** are; **10.** am

B Write *have* or *has.*
- Review the information in the chart.
- Read the sentences and have students repeat them after you.
- Go over the directions and the example.
- Have students write *have* or *has* on the lines.
- Put students in pairs to compare answers.
- Go over the answers with the class.

Answer Key **1.** have; **2.** has; **3.** have; **4.** has; **5.** has; **6.** have; **7.** has; **8.** have; **9.** has; **10.** have

C Write about you.
- Write the first sentence on the board with your full name. Ask why *is* is the correct form.
- Point out that students need to choose between a form of the verb *be* and *have* when completing the sentences.
- Have students complete the sentences.
- Walk around the room to monitor the activity and provide help as needed.
- Put students in pairs to read their sentences aloud.
- Call on students to read sentences to the class.

Answer Key Answers will vary. Correct verb forms are: **1.** is; **2.** have; **3.** have; **4.** am

D Match.
- Go over the directions and the example. Point out that *g* is written on the line and crossed out in the right column.
- Have students write the letters on the line to match the answers to the questions.
- Put students in pairs to compare answers.
- Elicit answers from the pairs. Elicit or provide corrections as needed.

Answer Key **1.** g; **2.** b; **3.** f; **4.** h; **5.** a; **6.** c; **7.** d; **8.** e; **9.** j. **10.** i

E CD 1, TRACK 68 **Listen and circle.**

- Direct students' attention to the pictures.

- Play the audio or read the sentences in the listening script and have students circle the picture that corresponds to what they hear.

- Play the audio or read the sentences again so students can check their answers.

- Put students in pairs to compare answers.

- Call on different students to share their answers with the class.

Listening Script

E. LISTEN AND CIRCLE.

1. Mary is young. She has red hair. She is single.
2. Peter is old. He has gray hair. He is single.
3. Ellen is young. She has black hair. She is married.
4. Mario is middle-aged. He has brown hair. Hc is single.

Answer Key **1.** illustration on the left; **2.** illustration on the left; **3.** illustration on the right; **4.** illustration on the right

Our Cultures
Greetings

A Write the words under the pictures.

- Tell students that this culture topic is about greetings.

- Act out greeting a new student. Smile and shake hands. Ask students to point to the picture illustrating this greeting.

- Say each word or phrase and have students repeat.

- Say the words in random order and have students point to the picture.

- Call on students as you say a type of greeting. Have the student mime the word or phrase.

- Ask about greetings in your students' countries: *In Korea, shake hands? In Brazil, hug?*

- Put students in pairs to talk about and point to what they do in their countries.

Answer Key left to right, top to bottom: shake hands; hug; kiss; bow; wave; say hello

B Think about it. Complete the chart. How do people greet each other?

- Go over the words in the box.

- Copy the diagram on the board.

- Go over the example in the Venn diagram.

- Have students add at least one thing to each part of the diagram.

- Elicit student answers and add them to the diagram on the board.

C Talk in groups.

- Direct students' attention to the picture and ask: *Who do you see? What is he doing? What do people do in Leo's country?*

- Put students in small groups to talk about their countries. Tell them to refer to what they wrote in their Venn diagram in Activity B.

- Call on students to tell the class about greetings in their countries and in other countries.

UNIT OVERVIEW

Lesson	Objective	Student Book Page
1. He's in the kitchen.	Identifying rooms in a house	p. 55
2. Is there a lamp in the bedroom?	Identifying furniture	p. 56
3. There's a shower in the bathroom.	Identifying appliances and furnishings	p. 57
4. Where do you live?	Identifying types of housing	p. 58
5. I need a refrigerator.	Talking about what you need for a home	p. 59
6. Where do you study?	Talking about activities and places	p. 60
7. My Dream House	Talking about a dream house	p. 61
8. 18 or 80?	Distinguishing numbers	p. 62
9. A Garage Sale	Talking about garage sales	p. 63
10. Grammar: Singular and Plural Nouns	Understanding singular and plural nouns	p. 64
11. Grammar: Singular and Plural Nouns	Using singular and plural nouns	p. 65
12. Read: Tien's Apartment	Reading about a home	p. 66
13. Write: A Note	Writing a note about a housing problem	p. 67
What do you know?	Review and assessment	p. 68

Big Picture Expansion Activities

Focus	Activity	Suggested Use
Listening/ Speaking	Ask and answer.	Lesson 3
Reading	John's House	Lesson 12
Grammar	What does Sandy have?	Lesson 11
Writing	Rooms in a House	Unit Opener
Conversation/ Vocabulary	Answering Questions about a House; Word Map	What do you know?

Worksheets

Worksheet #/ Focus	Title	Teacher's Edition Page
13. Writing	Rooms in a House	p. 339
14. Grammar	What does Sandy have?	p. 340
15. Reading	John's House	p. 341
16. Vocabulary	Word Map	p. 342

Unit Opener

- Put the transparency for Unit 4 on the overhead projector (OHP) or have students look at the big picture on page 54.

- Point to each word as you ask the questions at the bottom of the page: *Where are the people? Where is Sandy?*

- Review the vocabulary learned in Units 1–3. Point to different people in the picture and ask questions such as, *Is he tall?*

- Point to different people and places and elicit words related to family or homes. Write them on the board. Point to the words on the board and say them. Have students repeat.

Expansion Activity:
Writing: Rooms in a House

- Make and distribute student copies of Worksheet 13 (Teacher's Edition page 339).

- Put the Unit 4 transparency on the OHP or have students look at the big picture on page 54.

- Tell students that you are going to dictate some words. They should write the words on their worksheet. Dictate the words from Units 1 and 3: *grandmother, grandfather, son, teacher, husband, door, book*. Pause after each and repeat three times. If necessary, dictate the letters (*b-o-o-k*).

- Using the transparency, point to each room and say its name: *bathroom, bedroom, kitchen, dining room, backyard*.

- Hold up the worksheet and repeat the words as you point to each place in the diagram. Point out that the rooms are in the same place on both the transparency and worksheet.

- Put the students in pairs. Tell them to look at the transparency or page 54 and write each of the words from Part A in the correct place on the diagram. Point out the example.

Answer Key bathroom: son; bedroom: book, door; kitchen: teacher, husband, door; dining room: son; yard: grandmother, grandfather.

Objective
Identifying rooms in a house

Vocabulary

backyard	dining	living
bathroom	room	room
bedroom	kitchen	

Literacy Workbook pages 86–91
Workbook page 38

  A CD 2, TRACK 2 **Listen.**

- Have students open their books and look at the pictures. Ask: *What do you see?* Write all the words the students know on the board.

- Have students look at the pictures and listen while you play the first part of the audio or read the sentences in the listening script.

- Play the rest of the audio or read the list of words. Ask the students to repeat the words and point to the correct room.

- Call on students. Say one of the words and have students repeat.

- Working in pairs, have one partner say the words in a random order while the other partner points to the correct room.

········ **Listening Script**

A. LISTEN.

1. Kitchen. It's in the kitchen.
2. Living room. It's in the living room.
3. Bedroom. It's in the bedroom.
4. Dining room. It's in the dining room.
5. Bathroom. It's in the bathroom.
6. Backyard. It's in the backyard.

LISTEN AND REPEAT.

1. kitchen	**4.** dining room
2. living room	**5.** bathroom
3. bedroom	**6.** backyard

VOCABULARY Note

- Point out that most of the words are formed by two words joined together. In some cases, the two words are still separate words (*living room*), and in other cases, the two words combine to form one word (*bedroom*).

PRONUNCIATION Notes

- Point out that all the words and phrases have the stress on the first syllable.

- Practice saying the words and phrases, emphasizing the first syllable stress.

Expansion Activity: Spell it.

- Model the activity. Say one of the words and then spell it (*kitchen, k-i-t-c-h-e-n*).

- Call on students and say a word. Have students spell it.

- For a challenge activity, give students two minutes to review the words.

- Have students close their books. Ask volunteers to spell the words. Or, put students in pairs. Have one student look at the words in the book and say them as the partner spells them.

B CD 2, TRACK 3 **Listen.**

- Have students look at the conversation.

- Play the audio or read the conversation. Pause and have students repeat.

- Divide the class into two sides. Have one side read Will's lines. Have the other side read Sandy's lines. Move in front of each group to cue them to read.

GRAMMAR Note

- Point out that *he's* is the short form of *he is,* and *they're* is the short form of *they are.*

Expansion Activity: Pair Work

- Put students in pairs. Designate one partner to be Will and the other to be Sandy.

- Have students practice the conversation in pairs, then switch roles.

- Walk around the room to monitor the activity and provide help as needed.

Expansion Activity:
Conversation Cards

- Write each word of the conversation on an index card (17 cards needed).

- Mix the cards up and give one to each student.

- Have students arrange themselves in order of the conversation.

- Have students read their words to form the conversation.

C Look at page 54. Talk with a partner.

- Write the conversation on the board.

- Fill in the first two blanks with words from the box (e.g., *Where is Andy? He's in the bathroom*).

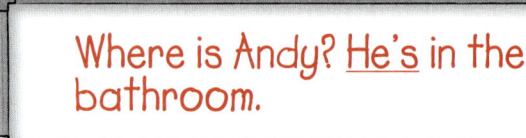

Where is Andy? <u>He's</u> in the bathroom.

Point out or elicit that *he* goes with Andy and Justin, and *she* goes with Jane, and *they're* goes with Sandy and Will.

- Model the activity with a student. Have the student read A's line and name one of the students in the box. Answer the question and ask the student another question. Elicit the answer.

- Put students in pairs to practice the conversation.

Expansion Activity:
Draw your home.

- Model the activity. Draw your home on the board. Draw the people who live with you in the room in which they spend a lot of their time. Tell the class about your home (*This is my kitchen. My father is in the kitchen.*).

- Have the students draw their homes and the people in them.

- Put students in pairs to talk about their homes.

- Call on students to tell the class about someone in their family.

Objective
Identifying furniture

Vocabulary

air conditioner	lamp
bed	rug
dresser	sofa
fireplace	table

Literacy Workbook pages 86–91
Workbook page 39

  A CD 2, TRACK 4 **Listen.**

- Have students look at the pictures and listen while you play the first part of the audio or read the sentences in the script.

- Play the rest of the audio or read the list of words. Have students repeat the words as they point to the pictures.

- Have students work in pairs and take turns saying the name as their partner points to the object.

GRAMMAR Notes

- This lesson uses the structures *Is there* and *There is*. Write the two expressions on the board.

> Is there...? There is...

- Point out that we use these words to ask about and tell what things are in certain places.

······ Listening Script

A. LISTEN.

1. Table. Is there a table in the dining room?
2. Sofa. Is there a sofa in the living room?
3. Bed. Is there a bed in the bedroom?
4. Lamp. Is there a lamp in the bedroom?
5. Air conditioner. Is there an air conditioner in the living room?
6. Fireplace. Is there a fireplace in the living room?
7. Dresser. Is there a dresser in the bedroom?
8. Rug. Is there a rug in the bedroom?

LISTEN AND REPEAT.

1. table	5. air conditioner
2. sofa	6. fireplace
3. bed	7. dresser
4. lamp	8. rug

  B CD 2, TRACK 5 **Listen.**

- Have students look at the picture. Elicit the objects they see.

- Have students look at the picture as you play the audio or read the conversation.

- Play the audio or read the conversation again and have students repeat.

- Put students in pairs to practice the conversation.

Welcome to our house. 93

Literacy Development Activity: Beginning Sounds

- For literacy students, write the words on the board: *table, sofa, bed, lamp, air conditioner, fireplace, dresser, rug.*

table, sofa, bed, lamp, air conditioner, fireplace, dresser, rug

- Underline the first letter of each word. Then say each word, stressing the beginning sound.

Extra Challenge
Alphabetize.

- Have more advanced students write the words from this activity in alphabetical order.

C　Talk with a partner.

- Go over the words in the box.
- Model the activity with a more advanced student. Ask: *Is there a lamp in the living room?* Elicit the answer (*Yes, there is.*).

> **Is there a lamp in the living room?**
>
> **Yes, there is.**

- Put students in pairs to practice asking and answering questions about the items in the word list.
- Walk around to monitor the activity and provide help as needed.

Expansion Activity: Ask and answer.

- Call on a student and ask a question about the picture (*Is there a lamp in the bedroom?*). Elicit the answer (*No, there isn't.*).
- Continue the activity until all students have had a chance to participate.
- With more advanced students, have the students ask questions of their classmates.

Extra Challenge
Write sentences.

- Write, *There is a _____ in the _____.* on the board.
- Have more advanced students write sentences using the vocabulary words from Lessons 1 and 2.
- Put students in pairs to read their sentences.
- Call on students to read their sentences to the class.

Literacy Development Activity: Write the words.

- For less advanced students, write the first letter of each vocabulary word on the board followed by the correct number of lines to indicate the letters.

Objective
Identifying appliances and furnishings

Vocabulary

closet	shower	tub
microwave	sink	window
refrigerator	stove	

Literacy Workbook pages 86–91
Workbook page 40

 A CD 2, TRACK 6 **Listen.**

- Have students look at the pictures as you play the first part of the audio or read the sentences in the listening script below.
- Play the rest of the audio or read the list of words and have students repeat and point to the correct word.
- If helpful, play the audio or read the words again and have students repeat.
- Read the words in random order and have students point to the picture.
- Put students in pairs to take turns reading the words as their partner points.

······· Listening Script

A. LISTEN.

1. Shower. This is a shower.
2. Sink. This is a sink.
3. Stove. This is a stove.
4. Window. This is a window.
5. Microwave. This is a microwave.
6. Closet. This is a closet.
7. Refrigerator. This is a refrigerator.
8. Tub. This is a tub.

LISTEN AND REPEAT.

1. shower	**5.** microwave
2. sink	**6.** closet
3. stove	**7.** refrigerator
4. window	**8.** tub

PRONUNCIATION Notes

- Write the three vocabulary words beginning with *s* on the board.

shower, sink, stove

- Say each word. Point out the different sounds. Students may have trouble with the *st* combination. Have students elongate the beginning *s* sound before they add the *t*.
- All the vocabulary words except *window* end in a consonant sound. Have students say the words, exaggerating the ending consonant.

 B CD 2, TRACK 7 **Listen and circle.**

- Read the words and have students repeat.
- Play the first sentence of the audio or read the first sentence in the listening script. Pause and point out that *refrigerator* is circled.
- Play the rest of the audio or read the sentences and have students circle the words they hear.
- Put students in pairs to compare answers.
- Elicit answers from the class.

LITERACY DEVELOPMENT Note

- Focus on the initial letter/sound of each word to help literacy students with this activity. Number 2 is the most difficult for literacy students because the initial sounds of the two answer choices (*sink, sofa*) are the same. Make sure students also notice the vowel sound in these words.

Listening Script

B. LISTEN AND CIRCLE.

1. There's a refrigerator in the kitchen.
2. There's a sink in the kitchen.
3. There's a tub in the bathroom.
4. There's a window in the dining room.
5. There's a closet in the bedroom.
6. There's a microwave in the kitchen.

Answer Key **1.** refrigerator; **2.** sink; **3.** tub; **4.** window; **5.** closet; **6.** microwave

Expansion Activity: Listening/Speaking: Ask and answer.

- Have students look at the big picture on page 54 or put the transparency for Unit 4 on the OHP.

- Model the activity. Call on a student and ask: *Is there a lamp in the kitchen?* Elicit the answer (*No, there isn't.*).

> **Is there a lamp in the kitchen?**
>
> **No, there isn't.**

- Put students in two teams to write questions using the vocabulary words from Lessons 1 and 2.

- Call on a student from Team A to ask a question of someone on Team B. Continue, alternating teams until everyone has had a chance to ask and answer questions.

- For added challenge, have students study the picture and then turn the OHP off and have students close their books. Award a point to each team that answers a question correctly.

My Life

- Copy the chart on the board.

- Elicit ideas from the students of things in each column. Write one example under each heading.

- Have students complete the chart.

- Have students write words to complete the sentence.

- Put students in groups to compare charts and read their sentences.

- Call on students to tell the class what is in their home.

Answer Key Answers will vary but may include:

Things in my kitchen	Things in my living room	Things in my bathroom
window refrigerator sink table microwave	sofa window lamp table rug fireplace	sink tub shower window

Expansion Activity: Picture Match

- Bring in magazines or have students bring them in.
- Have students cut out objects representing the new words in Lessons 1-3.
- Have students write the words on index cards.
- Put students in pairs to practice matching pictures to words.
- As a variation, have one partner read and show the word as the other partner finds the correct picture.

Expansion Activity: Same and Different

- Copy the chart below on the board.

	Partner A has …	Partner B has …
In the kitchen		
In the living room		
In the bathroom		

- Have students copy the chart on a piece of paper.
- Put students in pairs to complete the chart.
- Have students circle the things on the chart that are not the same for A and B.

Objective
Identifying types of housing

Vocabulary

an apartment   a rented room
a house

Literacy Workbook pages 86–91
Workbook page 40

 A   CD 2, TRACK 8   **Listen.**

- Direct students' attention to the pictures and ask: *Who do you see?*

- Have students look at the pictures and listen while you play the audio or read the sentences in the listening script.

- Play the audio or read the sentences a second time. Pause after each item and ask the students to repeat the word and point to the picture.

- Read the words in random order and have the students point to the pictures.

.... Listening Script

A. LISTEN.

1. **Paul:** A house. I live in a house.
2. **Isabel:** A rented room. I live in a rented room.
3. **Tien:** An apartment. I live in an apartment.

LISTEN AND REPEAT.

1. a house
2. a rented room
3. an apartment

CULTURE Notes

- Types of housing may differ in parts of the country. For example, more people in cities live in apartments than in houses. Mobile homes are popular in some parts of the country. Elicit the types of housing your students live in.

- Point out or elicit that a *rented room* is a single room, usually in a house, but it could be in an apartment or larger building. The renter pays for the room and has access to a bathroom and sometimes other common areas such as the kitchen.

B   **Talk with 5 classmates.**

- Model the activity with a more advanced student. Cue the student to ask the question. Answer with your type of home.

- Have students stand and walk around the room to ask five classmates where they live.

- Call on students to tell about a classmate.

Literacy Development Activity: Point and tally.

- Model the activity. Display the lesson in the book. Ask a student where he or she lives. Put a tally mark under the appropriate picture. Repeat with another student.

- Have students put tally marks under each picture to represent their classmates' answers in Activity B.

- If they live in a type of home not shown, such as a mobile home, have them draw a picture of it in the margin and include it in their tally.

- Call on students and elicit the number for each category.

Extra Challenge

Write sentences.

- Have more advanced students write sentences about their five classmates (e.g., *Marcos lives in a rented room.*).

Marcos lives in a rented room.

C   Complete. Work with a partner.

- Have students look at the first picture. Ask: *an apartment, a house, or a rented room?* Elicit that it is an apartment. Point out *an apartment* is written on the line.

- Put students in pairs to complete the activity.

- Go over the answers with the class.

Answer Key   **1.** an apartment; **2.** a house; **3.** an apartment; **4.** a rented room

Objective
Talking about what you need for a home

Vocabulary

| happy | have | need |

Literacy Workbook pages 86–91
Workbook page 41

VOCABULARY Note

- Students may be unfamiliar with three words in this lesson: *happy, have, need.* If necessary, explain these words to the class. Otherwise, have students practice guessing meaning from context as they read, and elicit the definitions.

A   CD 2, TRACK 9 Listen and read.

- Have students look at the pictures. Ask: *What do you see? Who do you see?* Elicit words they know.

- Have students read along silently as you play the audio or read the story. Repeat if necessary.

- Ask comprehension questions: *Is there a bed in Carlos's new apartment? Is there a table in Carlos's new apartment? Is there a table in Paul's garage?*

> **Is there a bed in Carlos's new apartment?**
> **Yes, there is.**

Extra Challenge
What else?

- Put more advanced students in pairs to write three sentences to add to the story.

- Have students look at the picture in Activity A. Write these sentence starters on the board:
  Carlos has _____.
  Carlos needs _____.
  Paul has _____.

- Elicit ideas for the first sentence (e.g., *a TV*). Make sure it is not something already written in Activity A.

- Have students write the sentences.

- Call on students to read their sentences to the class.

Literacy Development Activity: Sentence Strips

- Photocopy the story below and cut into strips. Make a set for each pair of students doing the expansion activity. Mix the strips up.

- Put students in pairs. Give each pair a set of strips.

- Have students recreate the story by putting the strips in order. Remind literacy students to use the initial letters of each sentence for help. For example, the first sentence of the story begins with *C.* Have students find the sentence that begins with *C* to start the strip story.

- Read each strip aloud one at a time and have students repeat.

Carlos is happy with his new apartment.

There is a bed and a dresser.

There are four kitchen chairs.

But Carlos needs a table.

He needs other furniture, too.

Paul has furniture for Carlos.

The furniture is in Paul's garage.

  **B** CD 2, TRACK 10 **Listen.**

- Have students read along silently as you play the audio or read the conversation.

- Play the audio or read the conversation a second time and have students repeat.

- Divide the class in half. Have one side say A's lines and the other side say B's lines, then switch roles.

- Put students in pairs to practice the conversation.

Expansion Activity: **Have or need?**

- Write two headings on the board: *Has* and *Needs*

- Elicit one thing Carlos has (*rug*) and one thing he needs (*table*) and write the examples under the headings.

- Have students complete the lists.

- Put students in pairs to compare lists.

- Call on students to read one thing in each column and write the ideas on the board.

C **Look at Activity A. Talk with a partner.**

- Go over the words in the box.

- Model the activity with a more advanced student. Have the student read Paul's question. Respond with a word from the list. Cue the student to ask about another word on the list.

- Put students in pairs to practice asking and answering questions. Remind students to use their lists from the Expansion Activity above.

Expansion Activity: **Personalize.**

- Model the activity. Have a student ask the first question in the conversation and answer with one thing you need

    What do you need?   I need a microwave.

- Write, *Do you need a _____?* on the board. Elicit the words students know about things in a home. Remind students to look at Lessons 1–4 for ideas.

- Put students in pairs to practice the conversation, asking and answering questions about themselves.

- For literacy or less advanced students, provide more help by writing the vocabulary words on the board that students elicit.

Expansion Activity: **Magazine Photos**

- Bring in magazine photos of different houses and rooms.

- Have students talk about what the house/room has and what it needs.

Objective
Talking about activities and places

Vocabulary

cook	shower	study
eat	sleep	

Literacy Workbook pages 86–91
Workbook page 42

A Check.

- Have students look at the chart. Ask: *Where do you eat?* Elicit answers. After someone answers *kitchen*, point out that there is a checkmark next to *kitchen* and under *eat*.

- Have students complete the chart for themselves.

- Walk around to monitor the activity and provide help as needed. Some students may be confused by the chart.

Answer Key Answers may vary but may include:

eat: kitchen or dining room;
cook: kitchen;
shower: bathroom;
sleep: bedroom;
study: living room, dining room, kitchen, bedroom

B CD 2, TRACK 11 Listen and circle.

- Point to each picture and elicit the name of the room.

- Have students look at the pictured activities in Activity B. Make sure students understand the meanings of *eat, sleep, shower, cook, study*.

- Play the audio or read the questions in the listening script and have students circle the room for the activity they hear.

- Play the audio or read the questions again and have students confirm their answers.

- Go over the answers with the class.

Listening Script

B. LISTEN AND CIRCLE.

1. Where do you eat?
2. Where do you sleep?
3. Where do you shower?
4. Where do you cook?

CULTURE Note

- Students may do some activities in different places from what is typical for most people. For example, students who share housing may sleep and eat in the living room. Point out that people may use different rooms for different things.

GRAMMAR Note

- Elicit or remind students that *where* questions are asking about a place.

Answer Key 1. illustration on the left;
2. illustration on the right; 3. illustration on the left; 4. illustration on the left

Expansion Activity: Acting Out

- Read one of the vocabulary words and elicit its meaning. Act out the word as you say it again.

- Continue with the other words.

- Call on a student and read one of the actions and have the student act it out. Have that student call on a classmate and read an action.

- Continue until everyone has had a chance to participate.

C **Talk to a partner. Talk about your chart in Activity A.**

- Go over the conversation model.

- Model the activity with a more advanced student. Ask a different question.

- Put students in pairs to talk about their charts in Activity B.

- Call on students and ask questions from the chart.

VOCABULARY Note

- For more advanced classes, you can point out other phrases that mean the same thing as the phrase *What about you?*, e.g., *And you? How about you?*

Expansion Activity: Category Sort

- Have students stand. Ask: *Where do you eat?*

  Where do you eat?

  Indicate different areas of the classroom for different answers (*kitchen, living room, dining room*). Cue students to move to the appropriate area for their answer.

- Ask all the questions on the chart and cue students to move. This is a fast-paced activity.

Expansion Activity: Write sentences.

- Write, *I _____ in the _____.*

- Have students write sentences about all of the actions using this sentence format.

- Put students in pairs to read their sentences.

- Call on students to read their sentences to the class.

- In a variation, pair advanced students with less proficient students. Have the less proficient students dictate their sentences to their partners.

Welcome to our house. 103

Objective
Talking about a dream house

Vocabulary

beach   country   suburbs

**Literacy Workbook pages 86–91
Workbook page 42**

  A CD 2, TRACK 12 **Listen.**

- Direct students' attention to the pictures. Point to each character and elicit the name.

- Have students listen and follow along in the book as you play the first part of the audio or read the sentences in the listening script.

- Play the rest of the audio or read the phrases and have students repeat.

Listening Script

A. LISTEN.

1. In the city. Leo's dream house is in the city.
2. In the country. Isabel's dream house is in the country.
3. At the beach. Paul's dream house is at the beach.
4. In the suburbs. Nadira's dream house is in the suburbs.

LISTEN AND REPEAT.

1. in the city
2. in the country
3. at the beach
4. in the suburbs

  B CD 2, TRACK 13 **Listen and read.**

- Have students read silently as you play the audio or read the sentences.

- Ask comprehension questions: *Where is Leo's dream house? What rooms are in his house?*

Expansion Activity: Character Stories

- Show the character cards.

- Have students choose a character and write about the character's dream house. Point out that they already know where Leo's, Isabel's, Paul's, and Ben's dream houses are, but that they can decide where the other characters want to live.

- Call on students to read their stories.

My Life

- Model the activity. Write on the board and say your sentences to the class.

- Have students complete the sentences.

- Put students in groups to read their sentences.

Expansion Activity: Category Sort

- Have students stand. Ask questions and have students sort themselves according to their answers. Create your own questions or use these:

  Where is your dream house?

  Is there a dining room?

  How many bedrooms are there?

  How many bathrooms are there?

- When you ask a question, students should find other students who have the same answers. They can do this by repeating the question. Once they have found students with the same answer, they should stand in a group.

Objective
Distinguishing numbers

Vocabulary/Numeracy

12/20	15/50	18/80
13/30	16/60	19/90
14/40	17/70	

Literacy Workbook pages 86–91
Workbook page 43

  A CD 2, TRACK 14 **Listen.**

- Have students look at the numbers as you play the audio or read the numbers.

- Play the audio or read the numbers again and have students repeat.

- Read the numbers in random order and have students point.

PRONUNCIATION Note

- Remind students that numbers ending in 0 (30, 40, 50, 60, 70, 80, 90) have the stress on the first syllable. The *t* sound in the middle of the word is also pronounced more like a *d*. The numbers beginning with 1 (13, 14, 15, 16, 17, 18, 19) have stress on both syllables and the medial *t* sounds like a *t*.

  B CD 2, TRACK 15 **Listen and circle.**

- Have students circle the numbers as you play the audio or read the numbers.

- Put students in pairs to compare answers.

- Go over the answers with the class. Have students write the answers on the board.

.... **Listening Script**

B. LISTEN AND CIRCLE.

1. sixty
2. nineteen
3. forty
4. eighteen
5. thirteen
6. seventy
7. twelve
8. fifty

Answer Key   **1.** 60; **2.** 19; **3.** 40; **4.** 18; **5.** 13; **6.** 70; **7.** 12; **8.** 50

Extra Challenge
Exaggerate.

- Write on the board:
  A: *That's* _____.
  B: *Did you say* _____?
  A: *No,* _____.

> A: That's _____.
> B: Did you say _____?
> A: No, _____.

- Model the activity with a student. Have the students say *That's* and a number (e.g., *That's thirteen*). You respond *Did you say 30?* The student will say *No, thirteen.* and really exaggerate the pronunciation.

- Put students in pairs to practice the conversation. Encourage students to say at least five numbers.

C CD 2, TRACK 16 **Listen and write.**

- Play the first sentence of the audio or read the first sentence in the listening script. Pause and elicit the number. Point out that *50* is written on the line.

- Play the rest of the audio or read the sentences and have students write the words they hear.

- Put students in pairs to check their answers.

- Play the audio or read the sentences again if necessary.

- Have students volunteer answers. Provide correction as needed.

Listening Script

C. LISTEN AND WRITE.

1. My address is 50 Beach Street.
2. The house is 70 years old.
3. The rented room is at 20 Green Street.
4. There are 13 apartments.
5. There are 19 windows.
6. I have 12 tables.
7. We need 40 chairs in the dining room.
8. Ben has 14 pens.
9. The house has 18 rooms.
10. There are 17 lamps in the garage.

Answer Key **1.** 50; **2.** 70; **3.** 20; **4.** 13; **5.** 19; **6.** 12; **7.** 40; **8.** 14; **9.** 18; **10.** 17

Expansion Activity:
How many... Scavenger Hunt

- Write *Days in June* on the board. Elicit the number (*30*).

- List other things students can count on the board (*months in a year, days in August, days in February, students in the class, desks in the classroom, classrooms in the building, cell phones in the class, married people in the class, computers in the computer lab, chairs in the library*, etc.). Tailor the list to your school environment.

- Put students in pairs.

- Have students think of or find out the correct numbers for these items. Note that this activity may take students out of the classroom if appropriate.

- Call on students to tell the class about one of the categories.

Objective
Talking about garage sales

Vocabulary

backpack	fan	seller
bike	pan	toaster
CD	sale	

Literacy Workbook pages 86–91
Workbook page 44

  A   CD 2, TRACK 17   **Listen and read.**

- Direct students' attention to the picture. Ask questions: *What do you see? How much is the bike?*

- Have students follow along as you play the audio or read the sentences.

- Ask comprehension questions: *What is a garage sale? What things are at a garage sale?*

> **What things are at a garage sale?**
>
> **books and furniture**

VOCABULARY Note

- Some words may be unfamiliar to students (*new, good, love, fun*). Elicit or explain their meanings.

CULTURE Notes

- *Garage sales* and *yard sales* are common in the United States. They mean the same thing. Point out that people sell their old stuff outside of their homes, usually on weekends. These sales are often advertised in the newspaper or on signs posted around the neighborhood.

- Point out that people can bargain at yard sales.

  B   CD 2, TRACK 18   **Listen and match.**

- Have students look at the words in Activity B. Ask if there are any words they don't understand (e.g., *bike, CDs*). Elicit or explain the meanings.

- Go over the directions.

- Play the first sentence of the audio or read the first sentence in the listening script. Ask: *What does Isabel need?* Point out that the letter *b* is written on the line.

- Play the rest of the audio or read the sentences and have students match the person and thing.

- Put students in pairs to compare answers.

- Go over the answers with the class.

⋯⋯ Listening Script

B. LISTEN AND MATCH.

Sandy's students are at a garage sale. What do they need?

1. Isabel needs a lamp.
2. Carlos needs a backpack.
3. Ben needs some CDs.
4. Grace needs a bike.

Answer Key   **1.** b; **2.** d; **3.** c; **4.** a

Extra Challenge

Dictation

- Have more advanced students write the sentences they hear as you play the audio or read the script for Activity B.

- Put students in pairs to compare sentences.

- Have students write the sentences on the board.

 C CD 2, TRACK 19 **Listen.**

- Point out the word *seller*—one of the speakers in the conversation. Make sure students understand what it means.

- Have students follow along silently as you play the audio or read the conversation.

- Play the audio or read the conversation again and have students repeat.

- Put students in pairs to practice the conversation.

D Talk with a partner.

- Go over the words in the box.

- Model the activity with a more advanced student. Have the student read A's lines.

  What do you need?   **I need a fan.**

- Put students in pairs to practice asking and answering questions about the things listed in the box.

Expansion Activity:
Garage Sale Ads

- Bring in some garage sale ads. Photocopy the ads so that each pair of students has a set.

- Put students in pairs. Have students read the ads to find something they need. Help students with any abbreviations or unfamiliar vocabulary.

- Call on students to tell the class about the ad and what they need.

Extra Challenge

Write an ad.

- Brainstorm the information in a garage sale ad (e.g., *address, things for sale, time, date*).

- Pair more advanced students with less proficient students.

- Have each pair write an ad including an address, the things they want to sell, the time and the date of the sale. Suggest students include four things in their ad.

- Have students read or post their ads.

Objective
Understanding singular and plural nouns

Literacy Workbook pages 86–91
Workbook page 45

  A CD 2, TRACK 20 **Listen and read.**

- Have students look at the pictures. Point to each picture and ask: *What is it? How many?*

- Have students listen and follow along as you play the audio or read the words.

- Play the audio or read the words again and have students repeat.

PRONUNCIATION Note

- Make sure students see and pronounce the ending *s* sounds on each plural word.

GRAMMAR Note

- Go over the Post-it Note. Explain that many nouns ending in *y* follow the pattern shown.

Expansion Activity:
Write the plurals.

- The words students know already that follow the pattern in the Post-it Note are *family, city, country,* and the number words ending in *-ty.*

- Elicit and write the plurals on the board.

family	families
city	cities
country	countries

B CD 2, TRACK 21 **Listen and check.**

- Play the audio or read the sentences and have students check the word they hear.

- Play the audio or read the sentences again if necessary. Put students in pairs to compare answers. Play the audio or read the sentences a third time if there is still some confusion.

- Go over the answers with the class.

······· **Listening Script**

B. LISTEN AND CHECK.

1. Apartment. I live in an apartment.
2. Rooms. My apartment has two rooms.
3. Kitchen. There is one kitchen.
4. Bedroom. There is one bedroom.
5. Closets. There are four closets.
6. Shower. There is a shower in the bathroom.
7. Families. Five families live in the building.
8. Seventies. My grandmother is in her seventies.

Answer Key 1. apartment; 2. rooms; 3. kitchen; 4. bedroom; 5. closets; 6. shower; 7. families; 8. seventies

C **Write a singular or plural noun.**

- Go over the directions and the example. Point out that students can write their own ideas in number 5.

- Have students write the missing singular and plural forms.

- Put students in pairs to compare answers.

- Go over the answers with the class.

Answer Key **1.** dining rooms; **2.** closets; **3.** dresser; **4.** cities; **5.** Answers will vary.

Literacy Development Activity:
Letter Scramble

- Write the following sets of letters on the board.

  t, c, y, i

  r, d, s, e, e, s, r, s

  s, t, c, o, l, e, s

- Have students order the letters into words from Activity C.

- If time permits, scramble more of the words from Activity C and have students unscramble them.

Objective
Using singular and plural nouns

Literacy Workbook pages 86–91
Workbook page 45

A   Circle the plural nouns.

- Have students read the story, or read the story aloud and have students follow along silently. Have students circle the plural nouns as they read. Point out that the first one has been done for them.

- Put students in pairs to compare answers.

- Have students read it again. Ask comprehension questions: *Who is this about? What does Isabel like? Where does she live?*

GRAMMAR Notes

- Students may be confused by the third person *s* ending and the plural *s* ending. Remind students that plurals are formed by adding an *s* to nouns (things), not to verbs (action words).

- Elicit the verbs with *s* endings and write them on the board (*likes, lives, has*).

PRONUNCIATION Note

- Students may notice or you can point out that the *s* ending can have different pronunciations. If helpful, point out that it is pronounced as an *s* after the consonants *c, k, f, p, t* (voiceless) and as *z* after other consonant and vowel sounds (voiced).

Answer Key   plural nouns: buildings; cities; chairs; pens; books; parents; brothers; rooms; bedrooms

Extra Challenge
Underline singular nouns.

- Have more advanced students underline the singular nouns.

- Put students in pairs to compare answers.

- Have students write the singular nouns on the board.

Expansion Activity:
Write answers.

- Write the questions listed in the procedural steps above for Activity A on the board.

> Who is this about? What does Isabel like?

- Have students write answers.

- Put students in pairs to compare answers.

B   Write singular or plural nouns.

- Direct students' attention to the first picture. Elicit that there are three tables. Point out that *tables* is written in the box.

- Have students write singular or plural nouns and then compare answers with a partner.

- Go over the answers with the class.

Answer Key   **1.** tables; **2.** beds; **3.** fireplace; **4.** lamps

C **Write *a* or *an*.**

- Go over the information in the box. Check comprehension by asking: *When do we use* a? *When do we use* an? *Do we use* a *or* an *before* bed?

> **Do we use *a* or *an* before *bed*?** *a*

- Elicit the list of vowels.

- Read the first sentence. Ask: *Do we use* a *or* an *before* rented room? Point out that *a* is written on the line.

- Have students write *a* or *an* on the lines.

- Put students in pairs to compare their answers.

- Go over the answers with the class.

Answer Key

I live in ___a___ rented room. I want to live in ___an___ apartment. I need ___a___ kitchen, a living room, two bedrooms, and ___a___ bathroom. I need ___an___ apartment building with ___a___ backyard, too.

BIG PICTURE

Expansion Activity: Grammar: What does Sandy have?

- Photocopy and distribute Worksheet 14: *What does Sandy have?* (Teacher's Edition page 340).

- Have students complete the worksheet.

- Put students in pairs to compare answers.

- Go over the answers with the class. Put students in pairs to compare answers.

- Go over the answers with the class.

Answer Key

1. a table; **2.** two chairs; **3.** five chairs; **4.** a refrigerator; **5.** a sofa; **6.** a tub; **7.** three lamps; **8.** a dresser; **9.** a fireplace; **10.** a closet

Extra Challenge

Personalize.

- Have more advanced students rewrite the sentences in Activity C, substituting information about themselves.

- As a variation, pair advanced students with less advanced students. Have the advanced students rewrite the sentences to tell about their partner's home. Have the less advanced students focus on writing the singular and plural nouns correctly.

Literacy Development Activity: Write the nouns.

- Write two headings on the board: *singular (1)* and *plural (2+)*.

- Put students in pairs. Have students write a list of the singular nouns in this lesson, and a list of the plural nouns.

- If possible, have a more advanced student check their lists.

- Call students to the board to write nouns under each heading.

Objective
Reading about a home

Vocabulary

balcony

Literacy Workbook pages 86–91
Workbook page 46

 A CD 2, TRACK 22 **Listen and read.**

- Direct students' attention to the picture. Ask: *Who do you see? Where does she live? What do you see?*

- Have students listen and read along silently as you play the audio or read the story aloud.

- Play the audio or read the story aloud again and have students repeat.

- Put students in pairs to take turns reading the story aloud.

- Call on volunteers to read to the class.

- Ask comprehension questions: *How many floors are in the building? How many apartments are on a floor? What is the number of Tien's apartment? Does it have a balcony? What does Tien have in her apartment?*

Literacy Development Activity:
Strip Story

- Rewrite the story on long strips of paper. Write one sentence on each strip. Make sure to leave a large space between each word.

- Put the first strip in a pocket chart or tape it to the wall or board.

- Read the first strip aloud and have students repeat.

- Continue with the other sentence strips.

- Take the strips out of the chart or off the board and mix them up.

- Call a volunteer to the front of the class and have him or her put the strips in order. Have the class approve or correct the sentence order. Reread.

- Continue with other volunteers.

- **Low-level literacy option:** Practice counting the words in each sentence to reinforce word discrimination and focus on beginning sounds.

B Check.

- Read the question aloud.

- Point out or elicit that a topic is the big idea, not the little details. Use gestures to convey the ideas of big and little.

- Read the answers aloud. Have students put a check mark next to the answer.

Answer Key 2. Tien's apartment

C Check *Yes* or *No*.

- Read the first sentence in a questioning tone and ask *yes* or *no*. Elicit that the answer is *no*, that Tien lives in an apartment. Point out that *no* is checked.

- Have students read the sentences and check *yes* or *no*.

- Put students in pairs to compare answers.

- Go over the answers with the class.

Answer Key **1.** No; **2.** No; **3.** No; **4.** Yes; **5.** Yes

Expansion Activity: **Make it true.**

- Have students rewrite the *no* sentences to make them correct.

- Have volunteers write the sentences on the board.

Literacy Development Activity: Key Words

- Copy the sentences from Activity C on the board. Write the key words (*a house, 18 floors, apartment 503, small, flowers/ balcony*) in different colors from the other words in the sentences. Remember to leave spaces between the words.

- Point to each word in the first sentence as you read it. Point to the key word and say *a house*. Ask: *Tien lives in a house?* Elicit the answer (*no*). Point out that *no* is checked.

- Continue with the other sentences.

Extra Challenge
More *Yes/No* Sentences

- Have more advanced students write four new sentences about the story, two with correct information and two with incorrect information. For example, a correct sentence might be, *Tien has one bedroom.* An incorrect sentence might be, *Her apartment building has 10 floors.*

- Have students exchange sentences with a partner and write *yes* or *no* for each of their partner's sentences. Have students confirm their answers with their partners.

- As a variation, collect the sentences. Give each student a *yes* index card and a *no* index card. Read the sentences and have students hold up the correct card.

BIG PICTURE

Expansion Activity: Reading: John's House

- Put the transparency for the big picture for Unit 4 on the OHP or have students look at the big picture on page 54 in their books.

- Photocopy and distribute Worksheet 15: *John's House* (Teacher's Edition page 341).

- Go over the directions.

- Have students read about John's house and check the things each house has.

- Put students in pairs to compare answers.

- Go over the answers with the class.

Answer Key **John's house:** a bathroom, a kitchen, a living room, a bedroom, a balcony
Sandy's house: a bathroom, a kitchen, a living room, a yard, a garage, a dining room, a bedroom

Objective

Writing a note about a housing problem

Literacy Workbook pages 86–91
Workbook page 47

  A CD 2, TRACK 23 **Listen and read.**

- Read the sentences above the note. Point to the note as you say, *She writes a note to Mr. Green.*

- Have students follow along silently as you play the audio or read the note.

- Ask comprehension questions: *What is Tien's address? What is the problem? What does she want? What is her telephone number?*

| What is Tien's address? | 16 Beach Street |

CULTURE Notes

- Point out or remind students that the *area code* is the first three numbers of a 10-digit phone number, and it is often written inside parentheses.

- Point out that we usually write *Dear* before the name of the person we are writing to. We also write a closing (e.g., *Thank you,* or *Sincerely,*) before our own names at the end.

Expansion Activity: **Taking Notes**

- Point out that it is a good idea to take notes about the important information in phone calls. Write the comprehension questions from the procedural notes for Activity A on the board, or elicit the type of information that is important in this call.

- Tell students to pretend they are Mr. Green taking notes on the phone call.

- With books closed, have students write important information in their notebooks as you play the audio or read the note. Play the audio or read the note several times so students can write the information.

- Put students in pairs or small groups to compare notes.

- Elicit the information and write it on the board.

B **Write about a problem.**

- Brainstorm problems, or things that can break in homes. Write the ideas on the board.

> window, door,
> air conditioner, fan,
> refrigerator

- Model the activity. Write about your home on the board. Follow the template.

- Have students complete the story with information about their own problems. Suggest they use one of the ideas on the board after *broken* _____ and *fix the* _____. They can use their own addresses and telephone numbers or make the information up.

- Put students in pairs to read their notes.

- Call on volunteers to read their notes to the class.

-

CULTURE/CIVICS Note

- Point out that it often takes a while before someone comes to fix things in a house or apartment. Often the building manager, landlord, or repairperson will set an appointment time, or block of time during which they will come to make the repair.

Expansion Activity:
Telephone Call

- Write this conversation model on the board:

  A: Hello. This is _____Tien Lam_____. I live at ___16 Beach Street___. I have a problem.

  B: What's the problem?

  A: There is a broken _____window_____ in the _____kitchen_____. Please fix the _____window_____.

  B: Sure.

  A: Thank you.

- Model the activity with a more advanced student. Have the student read B's lines. Substitute your information for Tien's.

- Put students in pairs to practice the conversation using the information in their notes.

Objective
Review and assessment

  A CD 2, TRACK 24 **Listen and circle.**

- Go over the directions.
- Play the first sentence of the audio or read the first sentence in the listening script. Point out that *bathroom* is circled.
- Play the rest of the audio or read the sentences as students circle the answers. Stop after each sentence so students have time to circle their answers.
- Put students in pairs to compare answers.
- Play the audio or read the sentences again and have students check their answers.
- Elicit the answers.

Listening Script

A. LISTEN AND CIRCLE.

1. There is a sink in the bathroom.
2. There are books in the bedroom.
3. Paul lives in the city.
4. Nadira is 30.

Answer Key **1.** bathroom; **2.** bedroom; **3.** suburbs; **4.** 30

  B CD 2, TRACK 25 **Listen and fill in.**

- Go over the directions.
- Play the first sentence of the audio or read the first sentence in the listening script. Point out that A is filled in.

- Have students look at each pair of answers.
- Play the rest of the audio or read the sentences as students mark the answers. Stop after each sentence so students have time to mark their answers.
- Put students in pairs to compare answers.
- Play the audio or read the sentences again and have students check their answers.
- Elicit the answers and write them on the board.

Listening Script

B. LISTEN AND FILL IN.

1. Maria is in the dining room.
2. Is there a lamp in the living room?
3. Do you need a rug?
4. Do you need two dressers?

Answer Key **1.** A; **2.** B; **3.** B; **4.** B

C **Look at page 54. Complete the chart. Work with classmates.**

- Direct students' attention to the chart. Ask: *What is in the bathroom?* Point out the answers already filled in, elicit more answers, and have students write them in the chart.
- Put students in pairs or small groups to complete the chart with their own ideas.
- Go over the answers with the class.

Answer Key Answers may vary but will likely include:

bathroom: window, tub, sink, toilet, rug
living room: lamp, sofa, fireplace
kitchen: table, chairs, refrigerator, microwave, sink, stove, computer

D Look at the picture. Complete.

- Go over the directions and point out that the first item has been done.

- Have students complete the sentences.

- Put students in pairs to compare answers.

- Read the sentences or call on a student volunteer to do so and have students check their answers.

- Elicit the answers and write them on the board.

Answer Key kitchen; stove; chairs; table

E Learning Log

- Go over the directions.

- Have students check the words they know.

- Put students in pairs to compare lists and review the words.

- Elicit words that students do not know and review their meanings.

LOOKING BACK

- Go over the directions.

- Put students in pairs to talk about the big picture on page 54.

- Call on students to talk about the picture using vocabulary from the unit.

BIG PICTURE

Expansion Activity:
Conversation/Vocabulary: Answering Questions about a House

- Put the transparency for Unit 4 on the OHP or have the students look at the big picture on page 54 in their books. Divide the students into teams.

- Tell students to look at the transparency or the big picture and try to remember what they see. Tell them they have one minute to look at the picture.

- Give them one minute. Turn off the OHP or have them close their books.

- Tell the students that you are going to ask questions. Each student can only answer one question, but can confer with their teammates before answering. Begin by asking Student 1 on Team A a question; then ask Student 1 on Team B another question. Next, ask Student 2 on Team A the third question, and so on, giving each team the same number of turns.

- Ask the teams questions about the picture. (e.g., *Where is Sandy? Where is the microwave/stove/bed/sofa/tub/refrigerator/ barbecue/dresser? Where are Sandy's sons?*). For every correct answer, the team earns a point.

Expansion Activity:
Vocabulary: Word Map

- Photocopy and distribute Worksheet 16: *Word Map* (Teacher's Edition page 342).

- Put the transparency for Unit 4 on the OHP or have students look at the big picture on page 54 in their books.

- Go over the directions and the example.

- Put students in pairs to complete the graphic organizer.

- Call on students to share their ideas with the class.

Answer Key Answers will vary but may include:
Bedroom: bed, dresser, chair, lamp, table
Bathroom: tub, sink, window, rug
Kitchen: refrigerator, sink, microwave oven, stove, table, chairs
Dining Room: table, chairs, fireplace, sofa, lamp

Unit 5 — I talk on the phone.

UNIT OVERVIEW

Lesson	Objective	Student Book Page
1. What do you do every day?	Talking about everyday activities	p. 71
2. Days of the Week	Saying the days of the week	p. 72
3. Months	Saying the months of the year	p. 73
4. What time is it?	Telling time	p. 74
5. It's 5:45.	Saying times	p. 75
6. Making an Appointment	Making an appointment	p. 76
7. How often do you study?	Talking about frequency of activities	p. 77
8. Ordinal Numbers	Practicing ordinal numbers and saying dates	p. 78
9. A Medical Form	Understanding and filling out a medical history form	p. 79
10. Grammar: Simple Present Tense	Understanding the simple present tense	p. 80
11. Grammar: Simple Present Tense	Using the simple present tense	p. 81
12. Read: Happy Birthday	Reading about birthdays	p. 82
13. Write: An Email	Understanding an email	p. 83
What do you know?	Review and assessment	p. 84

Big Picture Expansion Activities

Focus	Activity	Suggested Use
Speaking	Answering Questions About Location	Unit Opener
Reading	Whose birthday is it?	Lesson 12
Grammar	Who does what?	Lesson 11
Writing	How often do you ...?	Lesson 7
Conversation/ Vocabulary	Review with a Timeline	Lesson 13

Worksheets

Worksheet #/ Focus	Title	Teacher's Edition Page
17. Speaking/ Writing	Medical History Form	p. 343
18. Grammar	Who does what?	p. 344
19. Reading	Whose birthday is it?	p. 345
20. Conversation/ Vocabulary	What time do you ...?	p. 346

Unit Opener

- Put the transparency for Unit 5 on the overhead projector (OHP) or have students look at the big picture on page 70 in their books.

- Point to each word as you ask the questions at the bottom of the page: *Where are the people? What do they do every day?*

Expansion Activity:
Speaking: Answering Questions about Location

- Put the transparency for Unit 5 on the OHP or have students look at the big picture on page 70 in their books. With a marker, number the six pictures, moving from top to bottom. Point to each picture and have students say the number.

- Divide the class into teams. Tell the students that you will call on one person on a team and name an object or person in one of the pictures. The team member called on must say the number of the picture where that object or person can be found. For example, if you say *Sandy*, the student says *3*. Set a time limit of 10 seconds for each answer.

- Every correct answer earns the team a point.

- Use your own words or the following list to prompt the students: *Sandy, table, computer, papers, window, chair, Justin, Paul, living room.*

Objective
Talking about everyday activities

Vocabulary

brush my teeth	**read the newspaper**
comb my hair	
eat breakfast	**talk on the phone**
listen to music	**work on my computer**

**Literacy Workbook pages 92–97
Workbook page 50**

  A CD 2, TRACK 27 **Listen.**

• Have students open their books and look at the big picture on page 70. Ask: *What do you see?*

> **What do you see?**

Write all the words the students know on the board (e.g., *lamp, computer, kitchen, chair, desk,* etc.).

> **lamp, computer, kitchen, chair, desk**

• Have students look at the pictures and listen while you play the audio or read the sentences.

• Play the audio or read the sentences again. Pause after each sentence and have the students repeat.

• Call on students. Read one of the sentences and have a student repeat.

• Have students work in pairs and take turns reading the sentences in random order.

Expansion Activity: **Match**

• Write *read* on the board and elicit the completion (*the newspaper*). Write *the newspaper* on the board some distance away from *read*. Box both.

• Write the verbs and objects on separate cards, with enough sets so that each student gets a card.

• Give each student a card. Have students walk around the room to find their match. When students have a match they should stand with their partners.

• Call on students to say their matches (*read the newspaper*).

• In a variation, give 14 index cards to each pair of students. Have students write the verbs and objects on separate cards, shuffle the cards, and make matches.

 B CD 2, TRACK 28 **Listen and circle.**

• Have students look at the pictures in the first item. Ask: *What do you see?* Elicit that the first picture is *read the newspaper* and the second is *work on the computer.* Elicit the activities for the other pictures.

• Play the audio for the first item or read the first conversation in the listening script. Pause and elicit that the answer is *read the newspaper.* Point out that *read the newspaper* is circled.

• Play the rest of the audio or read the rest of the conversations. Have students circle what they hear.

• Go over the answers with the class.

Listening Script

B. LISTEN AND CIRCLE.

1. **Sandy:** What do you do every day, Leo?
   Leo: I read the newspaper.
2. **Sandy:** What do you do every day, Paul?
   Paul: I brush my teeth.
3. **Sandy:** What do you do every day, Carlos?
   Carlos: I listen to music.
4. **Sandy:** What do you do every day, Maria?
   Maria: I eat breakfast.

> **Answer Key** **1.** Illustration on the left;
> **2.** Illustration on the left; **3.** Illustration on
> the left; **4.** Illustration on the right

Extra Challenge
Write sentences.

- Have more advanced students write
  sentences for the other activities
  pictured in 1-4 of Activity B.

- Have students write them on the board.

> **Answer Key** **1.** I use my computer.
> **2.** I comb my hair. **3.** I watch TV. **4.** I talk
> on the phone.

 C CD 2, TRACK 29 **Listen.**

- Play the audio or read the conversation with a
  student volunteer as students listen.

- Play the audio or read the conversation again
  and have students repeat.

- Put students in pairs. Designate one partner
  to be Sandy and the other to be Leo.

- Have students practice the conversation in
  pairs, then switch roles.

D **Talk with 5 classmates.**

- Direct students' attention to the box. Say
  each phrase and have students repeat.

- Model the activity with a student. Have the
  student read A's line. Answer the question.
  Then ask the student the same question.
  Elicit the answer.

> **What do you do every day?**   **I eat breakfast.**

- Have students stand and walk around the
  room to talk to five classmates. Encourage
  students to vary their answers.

Expansion Activity:
Inside/Outside Circles

- Divide the class in half. Have one group
  form a circle facing out. Have the other
  group form a circle outside the first circle
  facing in. Each student should be standing
  in front of a classmate.

- Have the students practice the
  conversation with the students facing
  them. Make sure each partner asks and
  answers the question. Then have the
  outside circle rotate counterclockwise, or
  one place to the right. Now everyone is
  facing a new partner.

- Have students practice the conversation
  with the new partner. After 20 or
  30 seconds, have the circle rotate again.
  Repeat three more times.

Objective
Saying the days of the week

Vocabulary

Sunday	Thursday
Monday	Friday
Tuesday	Saturday
Wednesday	

Literacy Workbook pages 92–97
Workbook page 51

  A   CD 2, TRACK 30   **Listen.**

- Have students look at the calendar and listen while you play the audio or read the words. If you wish, use a large calendar or draw one on the board or OHP.

- Play the audio or read the words again. Pause after each word and ask the students to repeat the word and point to the word.

- Have students work in pairs and take turns reading the day as their partner points to the word.

GRAMMAR Note

- Point out that days of the week are always capitalized.

CULTURE Note

- In some cultures (including Europe) the week begins on Monday rather than on Sunday as it does in the United States.

Literacy Development Activity: Put in order.

- Write each day of the week on an index card or strip of paper.

- Have literacy students practice putting the cards in order, starting with Sunday.

 B   CD 2, TRACK 31   **Listen and circle.**

- Play the audio and stop after the first sentence or read the first sentence in the listening script. Elicit the day Ben and Grace study (*on Monday*). Point out that *Monday* is circled.

- Play the rest of the audio or read the sentences and have students circle the day of the week they hear.

- Play the audio or read the sentences again so students can confirm answers.

- Go over the answers with the class.

GRAMMAR/PRONUNCIATION Note

- Students may notice the *s* ending in the second sentence. Explain that when we talk about one other person, we add an *s* to the verb. Students will practice this grammar in Lessons 10 and 11.

Listening Script

B. LISTEN AND CIRCLE.

1. Ben and Grace study on Monday.
2. Leo cooks dinner on Thursday.
3. Maria and Carlos go to garage sales on Sunday.
4. Nadira and Sandy watch TV on Saturday.

Answer Key   1. Monday; 2. Thursday;
3. Sunday; 4. Saturday

 C CD 2, TRACK 32 **Listen and complete.**

- Write *Paul plays soccer on _____.* on the board.

Paul plays soccer on
_____.

- Play the audio and stop after the first sentence or read the first sentence in the listening script. Write *Thursday* on the line on the board. (See the Literacy Development Notes on this page.)

- Point to Sentence 1 in the book. Point out that *Thursday* is written on the line.

- Play the rest of the audio or read the sentences as students fill in the correct days.

- Go over the answers with the class.

Listening Script

C. LISTEN AND COMPLETE.

1. Paul plays soccer on Thursday.
2. Carlos and Ben go to school on Friday.
3. Isabel and Grace go to garage sales on Saturday.
4. Leo and Maria go to class on Monday.
5. Nadira cooks dinner on Tuesday.

Answer Key   1. Thursday; 2. Friday;
3. Saturday; 4. Monday; 5. Tuesday

LITERACY DEVELOPMENT Notes

- For literacy students, write the days of the week on the board.

- Underline the first letter or digraph (*th-*) of each word. Then say each word, stressing the beginning sound.

- Point out that the days of the week always start with an uppercase letter.

D **Ask 5 classmates.**

- Model the activity with a more advanced student. Have the student read A's lines. Demonstrate how to complete each sentence with a day of the week.

- Have students stand and walk around the classroom to practice the conversation with five classmates.

- Call on students to tell the class about a classmate.

Expansion Activity: Category Sort

- Explain the activity. You will ask a question (e.g., *When do you play soccer?*). Students should stand with classmates who answer in the same way. For example, all students who play soccer on Saturday would form a group.

- Have students stand. Ask a question (*When do you go to the store?*). Prompt the students to form groups by answer. Point out that students should repeat the question to find people with the same answer.

- Continue with other questions about activities. Keep the activity fast-paced.

Objective
Saying the months of the year

Vocabulary

January	July
February	August
March	September
April	October
May	November
June	December

Literacy Workbook pages 92–97
Workbook page 51

  A   CD 2, TRACK 33   **Listen and read.**

- Have students look at the words, including the lesson title. Bring in a calendar and point to the different months. Introduce the term *year: There are 12 months in a year.*

- Play the audio or read the words.

- Play the audio or read the words again and have students repeat.

Literacy Development Activity: Order cards.

- Have students with emerging literacy skills write one month on each of 12 index cards.

- Have students shuffle the cards, then practice putting the months in order.

- Walk around to monitor the activity and provide help as needed.

- When students have the cards in order, say each month and have students clap out the syllables.

Extra Challenge
Alphabetize.

- Have more advanced students write the months in alphabetical order.

  B   CD 2, TRACK 34   **Listen.**

- Play the audio or read the conversation as students listen.

- Play the audio or read the conversation again and have students repeat.

- Put students in pairs. Designate one partner to be Paul and the other to be Isabel.

- Have students practice the conversation in pairs, then switch roles.

Expansion Activity: Birthday Tally

- Before students do Activity C, have them write each month in order in a column on a piece of paper.

- Have students put a tally mark next to each month as they talk to classmates and complete Activity C.

- Call on students and ask questions: *How many of your classmates have birthdays in January? In August? This month?*

- As a variation, have an advanced student do the tally on the board and discuss the results. You may want to give the students index cards to create a bar graph of the results, with one card indicating each person.

C   **Talk with 7 classmates.**

- Model the activity with a more advanced student. Have the student read A's lines.

- Demonstrate how to complete each sentence with a month of the year.

  When is your birthday?   **It's in May.**

- Have students stand and walk around the classroom to practice the conversation with seven classmates.

- Call on students to tell the class about a classmate.

Expansion Activity: Draw it.

- Have students draw activities that they typically do on birthdays.

- Put students in groups to talk about their pictures.

- Provide help with unknown vocabulary as needed.

D Write.

- Explain to students that abbreviations are short forms that end in a period (*Mr., Feb., Dr.*).

- Read the first item (*January*). Point out that the abbreviation for *January* is *Jan.* and that *Jan.* is crossed out in the box and written on the line.

- Have students write the abbreviations on the lines next to the appropriate months. Point out or elicit that there is no abbreviation for *May.*

- Call on individual students to provide the answers.

Answer Key **1.** Jan.; **2.** Feb.; **3.** Mar.; **4.** Apr.; **5.** May; **6.** Jun.; **7.** Jul.; **8.** Aug.; **9.** Sept.; **10.** Oct.; **11.** Nov.; **12.** Dec.

Objective
Telling time

Literacy Workbook pages 92–97
Workbook page 52

  A   CD 2, TRACK 35   **Listen.**

- Have students look at the pictures and listen while you play the first part of the audio or read the words and the sentences.

- Play the rest of the audio or read the list of words. Pause after each word and ask the students to repeat the word and point to the picture.

- Read the words in random order and have the students point to the pictures.

⋯⋯ **Listening Script**

A. LISTEN.

1. Ten o'clock. It's ten o'clock.
2. Seven fifteen. It's seven fifteen.
3. One forty-five. It's one forty-five.
4. Three thirty. It's three thirty.
5. Two o'clock. It's two o'clock.
6. Four forty-five. It's four forty-five.
7. Twelve thirty. It's twelve thirty.
8. Eight fifteen. It's eight fifteen.
9. Nine twenty. It's nine twenty.

LISTEN AND REPEAT.

1. ten o'clock   **6.** four forty-five
2. seven fifteen   **7.** twelve thirty
3. one forty-five   **8.** eight fifteen
4. three thirty   **9.** nine twenty
5. two o'clock

  B   CD 2, TRACK 36   **Listen.**

- Play the audio or read the conversation with a student as students follow along silently.

- Play the audio or read the conversation again and have students repeat.

- Point to the times in Activity A in random order and have students give the time, saying *It's _____.*

GRAMMAR Note

- Point out the information on the yellow note. Tell students that we use *It's* to say the time.

VOCABULARY Notes

- Students may have heard other ways to say the time (10:15 = a quarter past 10, 10:45 = a quarter to 11, 3:30 = half past 3. Mention this last one is British English). Acknowledge that these are also correct if students mention them, but you don't need to introduce this vocabulary at this level.

- Point out that P.M. refers to the times between noon and midnight (post-meridian) and A.M. refers to the times from midnight until noon (ante-meridian). Meridian refers to noon, or the time when the sun is the highest in the sky.

C **Look at the clocks. Talk with a partner.**

- Model the activity with a more advanced student. Point to one of the clocks and ask: *What time is it?* Elicit the answer.

- Put students in pairs to take turns asking the time and answering appropriately.

- Walk around the room to monitor the activity and provide help as needed.

Expansion Activity:
Set your clocks.

- Buy cardboard clock faces (Judy clocks) at a teacher store, or bring in paper plates, construction paper, and clasps. Show students how to cut out hands and attach them to paper plates with the clasps.

- Display a clock and say a time. Set the hands of the clock to the time you say. Have students set their clocks.

- Continue saying times and having students set the time on their clocks and repeat the time you say (*It's 10:30.*). Have students display their clock faces so you can check.

- Put students in pairs to practice saying times as their partners set their clocks.

Objective
Saying times

Literacy Workbook pages 92–97
Workbook page 52

  A CD 2, TRACK 37 **Listen.**

- Have students look at the pictures as you play the first part of the audio or read the sentences.

- Play the rest of the audio or read the list of times and have students repeat.

⋯⋯ **Listening Script**

A. LISTEN.

1. Six o'clock. It's six o'clock.
2. Eight fifteen. It's eight fifteen.
3. Three thirty. It's three thirty.
4. Five forty-five. It's five forty-five.

LISTEN AND REPEAT.
1. six o'clock
2. eight fifteen
3. three thirty
4. five forty-five

Expansion Activity:
Dictate and order.

- Dictate 10 clock times (*1:15*) and have students write the times on a piece of paper. Say each clock time three times.

- Have students rewrite the times in chronological order.

- Have students write the times on the board.

  B CD 2, TRACK 38 **Listen and circle.**

- Direct students' attention to the first item. Play the audio and stop after the first item or read the first sentence in the listening script. Point out that *6:30* is circled.

> What time is it?   6:30.

- Play the audio or read the sentences in the listening script and have students circle the times they hear.

- Put students in pairs to compare answers. Play the audio or read the sentences again if necessary.

- Go over the answers with the class.

⋯⋯ **Listening Script**

B. LISTEN AND CIRCLE.

1. It's six thirty.
2. She eats breakfast at eight thirty.
3. She goes to school at twelve forty-five.
4. They study at two fifteen.
5. Carlos reads the newspaper at four o'clock.
6. He goes to sleep at nine fifteen.

Answer Key **1.** 6:30; **2.** 8:30; **3.** 12:45; **4.** 2:15; **5.** 4:00; **6.** 9:15

Extra Challenge
Write what you hear.

- With more advanced classes, play the audio or read the sentences again. Pause after each sentence and have students write the sentence down.

- Play the audio or read the sentences again so students can check their answers.

- Have volunteers write the sentences on the board.

Expansion Activity: Act it out.

- Model the activity. Say a time and act out what you do at that time. For example, if you say *6:00 A.M.*, you might act out getting up and stretching.

- Call some volunteers to the front of the room.

- Say a time. Remember to say *A.M.* or *P.M.* (or *in the morning, in the evening*). Remind students to act out what they do at that time. Elicit the actions from the class.

- Continue to say times. Have other volunteers come to the front of the class to act out their activities.

C Write about you. Read your sentences in groups.

- Model the activity. Tell the class what time you get up, go to school, and eat lunch. Write the sentences on the board to show students what you are actually modeling.

- Have students complete the sentences with information about themselves.

- Put students in groups of three or four to talk about their answers.

- Call on students to share their answers with the class.

Objective
Making an appointment

Vocabulary

appointment	a haircut
a checkup	a tune-up

Literacy Workbook pages 92–97
Workbook page 53

  A CD 2, TRACK 39 **Listen.**

- Direct students' attention to the picture at the top of the page. Ask questions: *Who is that? What's her name? What is she doing?* Make sure students understand what an appointment is.

- Play the audio or read the conversation as students follow along silently.

- Play the audio or read the conversation again and have students repeat.

- Put students in pairs to practice the conversation. Have students switch roles.

GRAMMAR Note

- Explain that we use *would like* or *'d like* to make polite requests.

B **Talk with a partner.**

- Direct students' attention to the pictures. Say each phrase and have students repeat. Make sure students understand the words.

- Model the activity with a more advanced student.

- Put students in pairs to complete the activity.

- Walk around to monitor the activity and provide help as needed.

Expansion Activity:
I'm sorry, I can't.

- Copy the first two lines of the conversation on the board.

> A: I'd like to make an
>   appointment for _____.
> B: Can you come on Friday at
>   _____?

- Add these lines: A: *I'm sorry, I can't.* B: *What about Friday at _____?* A: *Friday at _____? That's fine.*

- Point out that sometimes we can't make an appointment time, so we have to get another time.

- Model the activity with a more advanced student. Have the student read B's lines. Propose a second time.

- Put students in pairs to practice refusing the first time and accepting the second.

  C CD 2, TRACK 40 **Listen and write the times.**

- Direct students' attention to the calendar.

- Play the audio for the first conversation or read the first conversation in the listening script. Point out that the answer, *5:30*, is written on the line under Monday the 13th.

- Play the audio or read the conversations in the listening script and have students write the times.

- Play the audio or read the conversations again so students can check their answers.

- Elicit the answers from the class.

Listening Script

C. LISTEN AND WRITE THE TIMES.

Grace: I'd like to make an appointment for a haircut.

Man: Can you come on Monday at five thirty?

Grace: Monday at five thirty? That's fine.

Grace: I'd like to make an appointment for a tune-up.

Woman: Can you come on Wednesday at three o'clock?

Grace: Wednesday at three o'clock? That's fine.

Grace: I'd like to make an appointment for a checkup.

Man: Can you come on Friday at one fifteen?

Grace: Friday at one fifteen? That's fine.

CULTURE Note

- Point out that it is polite to call and cancel an appointment if you can't make it. Most offices would like people to call the day before.

Answer Key   haircut—5:30; tune-up—3:00; checkup—1:15

NOVEMBER						
Sunday	Monday	Tuesday	Wednesday	Thursday	Friday	Saturday
12	13 haircut 5:30	14	15 tune-up 3:00	16	17 checkup 1:15	18

Expansion Activity: Role Play

- Have students create a calendar for the next week, including days Sunday through Saturday as in the calendar for Activity C.

- Put students in pairs to take turns making appointments for different activities. Remind students to write the appointments on the calendar.

- Walk around the room to monitor the activity and provide help as needed.

Objective
Talking about frequency of activities

Literacy Workbook pages 92–97
Workbook page 54

  A   CD 2, TRACK 41   **Listen and read.**

- Direct students' attention to the pictures.

- Have students listen and follow along in the book as you play the audio or read the sentences.

- Play the audio or read the sentences a second time and have students repeat.

VOCABULARY Notes

- Point out that some people say *go grocery shopping* instead of *shop for food.*

- Point out that *every day* and *once a day* are similar, but may be slightly different. For example, we eat every day, but we probably eat more than once a day. However, most people only shower once a day.

Expansion Activity:
Every day or once a day?

- Put students in pairs to list activities they do every day, but perhaps more than once a day (e.g., *eat, brush teeth, comb hair, study, watch TV*). Then have students create a list of things they do once a day (e.g., *shower, read the newspaper, eat breakfast*).

- Call on students to share one idea from each list.

  B   CD 2, TRACK 42   **Listen.**

- Have students follow along silently as you play the audio or read the conversation.

- Play the audio or read the conversation again and have students repeat.

Expansion Activity:
Choral Reading

- Divide the class into four groups.

- Designate the first group to read Sandy's line, the second to read Will's, the third to read Tien's, and the fourth to read Carlos's line.

- Cue each group to read their lines.

- Switch roles, so that each group reads the next person's line (the Sandy group now reads Will's line).

- Continue switching but at a faster pace each time.

My Life

- Copy the sentences on the board.

- Model the activity by completing the sentences with information about yourself and telling the class.

- Have students complete the sentences.

- Put students in small groups to read their sentences.

- Call on students to read one of their sentences to the class.

Expansion Activity: Category Sort

- Write *How often do you* _____? on the board.

How often do you _____?

- Point out that the sentences in *My Life* are answers to the question *How often do you…*

- Have students stand. If your class is large, call a group of students to the front of the class. Ask: *How often do you get a haircut?* Have students stand by classmates who have the same answer. Remind students to ask the question in order to find classmates in their category.

- Repeat with other questions about activities (*eat breakfast, study, take a shower, comb your hair, shop for food, get a tune-up, get a checkup*).

Expansion Activity: Character Schedules

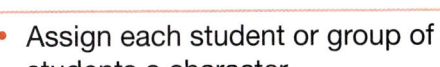

- Assign each student or group of students a character.

- Have students look at Lessons 1, 2, and 7 (pages 71, 72, and 77) to find out information about the characters' activities and schedules. Give students a minute or two to remember the information.

- Have students stand and tell the class about their character from memory (e.g., *Leo reads the newspaper every day*).

BIG PICTURE

Expansion Activity: Writing: How often do you …?

- Put the color transparency for Unit 5 on the OHP or have students look at the big picture on page 70 in their books.

- Write these expressions on the board: *once a day, twice a day, three times a day, four times a day.*

- Point to a picture on the transparency (e.g., *Sandy talking on the phone.*). Ask: *How often do you talk on the phone?* Elicit how often they do this. Write an example sentence on the board (*I comb my hair once a day.* or *I comb my hair three times a day.*).

- Have students write sentences for each of the pictures following the model on the board. Suggest that they make up an answer if they don't do the activity at all.

- Put students in pairs to read their sentences.

- Call on students to read their sentences to the class.

I talk on the phone. 135

Objective
Practicing ordinal numbers and saying dates

Vocabulary

first	sixth	eleventh
second	seventh	twelfth
third	eighth	thirteenth
fourth	ninth	fourteenth
fifth	tenth	

Literacy Workbook pages 92–97
Workbook page 55

  A **CD 2, TRACK 43** **Listen.**

- Have students look at the numbers as you play the audio or read the numbers.

- Play the audio or read the numbers again and have students repeat.

- Read the numbers in random order and have students point to the correct number.

PRONUNCIATION Notes

- Point out that the ordinal numbers for 1, 2, 3, and 5 change more than other numbers. The ordinal numbers for 1 and 2 are completely different, while those for 3 and 5 have the same beginning sounds as their cardinal partners, but then change. Practice distinguishing these sounds.

- Point out or elicit how ordinal numbers 6 and on are different from their cardinal partners (final /th/ is added to make an ordinal number). Because they are so similar, point out that it is important to pronounce the final *th* in ordinal numbers to distinguish them.

- Model the pronunciation and have students repeat. Make sure students know to put their tongue between their teeth as they make the sound.

B **Write the number.**

- Point out the example.

- Have students write the numbers.

- Go over the answers with the class. Have students write the answers on the board, saying them as they write them.

Answer Key
1. 14th; **2.** 12th; **3.** 5th; **4.** 7th; **5.** 3rd; **6.** 1st; **7.** 2nd; **8.** 9th

  C **CD 2, TRACK 44** **Listen and circle.**

- Play the audio and stop after item 1 or read the first sentence in the listening script. Ask *What number?* Point out that *5th* is circled.

- Play the audio or read the sentences and have students circle the ordinal numbers they hear.

- Have students compare answers with classmates.

- Go over the answers with the class.

Listening Script

C. LISTEN AND CIRCLE.

1. Paul lives on Fifth Street.
2. Tien lives on Third Avenue.
3. Go to Twelfth Street.
4. The garage sale is on Fourteenth Street.
5. I live on Thirteenth Street.
6. Grace lives on First Avenue.

Answer Key **1.** 5th; **2.** 3rd; **3.** 12th;
4. 14th; **5.** 13th; **6.** 1st

Expansion Activity:
Three in a Row

- Draw a three-by-three grid on the board. Have students draw their own grids or photocopy and distribute Worksheet 5 (Teacher's Edition page 332).

- Have students write one number (1–9) in each square of their three-by-three grids. The numbers should be randomly ordered.

- Tell students that they should say *Three in a row* when they get three numbers in a row. Point to the three squares vertically, diagonally, and horizontally.

- Call out ordinal numbers in random order (e.g., *third, ninth, first*) and have students cross out the corresponding number on their grid.

- When a student calls out *three in a row*, have the student read the numbers to the class for confirmation.

  D   CD 2, TRACK 45   **Listen.**

- Go over the yellow note and practice saying different years.

- Have students listen and follow along as you play the audio or read the conversation.

- Play the audio or read the conversation again as students repeat.

CULTURE Notes

- Students may come from cultures in which their birthdays were not recorded (e.g., Somali Bantus, Montagnards, Hmong).

When students from these cultures arrive in the United States, they are often assigned birthdays for paperwork purposes. Many students may be assigned the birthday January 1st, for example.

- In some cultures that use a lunar calendar, people may have two birthdays, one based on the calendar year, one based on the lunar calendar.

- If people are uncomfortable giving their year of birth, suggest they use any year.

E   **Ask 7 classmates.**

- Model the activity. Ask *What is your date of birth?* Elicit the answer.

- Have students stand and walk around the room to talk to seven classmates.

Expansion Activity:
Birthday Lineup

- Have students line up in chronological order by birthday (not birth year, but day in the year). Point to one side of the room and say *January 1st*. Point to the other side and say *December 31st*.

- Help students as necessary.

- When students are lined up, have them say their birthdays, e.g., *February 29, May 1, September 12*, etc.

Objective
Understanding and filling out a medical history form

Literacy Workbook pages 92–97
Workbook page 56

A Read.

- Go over the information on the yellow note. Point out that in some cultures the month and day are reversed, so students might be used to seeing, e.g., *16/3/80* for March 16, 1980, for example.

- Direct students' attention to the form.

- Ask comprehension questions: *Who is it for? What is her date of birth? What kind of form is it?*

B Complete the form.

- Copy the form on the board or make a transparency of Worksheet 17: *Medical History Form* (Teacher's Edition page 343) and put it on the OHP.

- Model the activity. Complete the form for yourself.

- Have students complete the forms with their own information. Remind them that MI = middle initial.

- Put students in pairs or small groups to talk about the information on their forms.

CULTURE Note

- Not every culture uses middle names (or even last names). Although for official purposes everyone in the United States must have a last name, even if it is assigned, it is not necessary to have or use a middle name. If students do not have a middle name, they should put a line in the space.

Extra Challenge
Interview

- Photocopy and distribute Worksheet 17: *Medical History Form.*

- Put students in pairs to ask questions and complete the form with their partner's information. For this activity, pair two advanced students together while less advanced students are completing their own forms. Or have an advanced student conduct the interview with a less advanced student.

My Life

- Model the activity. Write the date of birth for five of your relatives on the board. Point out that for dates between 2000–2009, they need to include a zero, e.g., *daughter: 2/29/00; son: 12/4/03.*

- Have students write the dates of birth for five of their relatives. Point out that students can refer to Unit 3 for family relationship vocabulary.

- Put students in groups to share their information.

- Call on students to tell the class about one of their relatives.

Expansion Activity: Write the date of birth of your classmates.

- As a variation or extension of the My Life activity, have students write the date of birth of five of their classmates. Remind students they can give any year for this activity.

Objective
Understanding the simple present tense

Vocabulary

call on the phone	**say "Happy Birthday"**
eat cake	
open presents	**take photos**

Literacy Workbook pages 92–97
Workbook page 57

  A CD 2, TRACK 46 **Listen and read.**

- Have students look at the picture. Point to each person and ask: *Who is it?*

- Have students listen and follow along as you play the audio or read the sentences.

- Play the audio or read the sentences again and have students repeat.

- Make sure students see the *s* ending on *take* for *he, she,* and *it.*

  B CD 2, TRACK 47 **Listen and circle.**

- Play the audio and stop after item 1 or read the first sentence and ask: *take or takes?* Elicit that *takes* is the answer. Point out that *takes* is circled.

- Have students circle the form they hear as you play the audio or read the sentences.

Listening Script

B. LISTEN AND CIRCLE.

1. She takes photos.
2. It eats cake.
3. We say, "Happy Birthday."
4. I open my presents.
5. Paul calls Isabel on the phone.

Answer Key 1. takes; 2. eats; 3. say; 4. open; 5. calls

Expansion Activity: Beanbag Toss

- In the first round, call on a student, toss a beanbag or small ball, and start a sentence (*I eat* _____). Elicit the completion from the student who catches the beanbag or ball.

- Have the student throw the beanbag back to you or call on a classmate, start the next sentence, and toss the beanbag to him or her.

- Continue with subjects and verbs (e.g., *she takes, we open, they call, he says*) until everyone has had a chance to participate.

- In the second round, say a subject and then both forms of the verb (e.g., *I take or takes*) and elicit the correct form and the object and have them complete a sentence (*I take photos.*).

  I take or takes   I take photos.

- Continue until everyone has had a chance to participate.

Extra Challenge
Write sentences.

- Have more advanced students write each of the sentences from Activity B, items 2–5, using all the subject pronouns.

- Put students in pairs to compare sentences.

- Go over the sentences with the students.

Objective

Using the simple present tense

Literacy Workbook pages 92–97
Workbook page 57

A Complete.

- Go over the example.

- Have students complete the sentences. Remind students to add an *s* if necessary to the verb.

- Go over the answers with the class.

Answer Key   **1.** have; **2.** combs; **3.** gets; **4.** work; **5.** reads; **6.** talk; **7.** eats

B Write *am, is,* or *are.*

- Review the information in the box.

- Go over the example.

- Have students complete the sentences.

- Elicit the answers from the class.

- Put students in pairs to read the conversations.

- Have students switch roles and read the conversations again.

Answer Key   **1.** are/am/is; **2.** is; **3.** are; **4.** is/are

C Write.

- Have students complete the sentences. Point out that they can use any activity they want for the last sentence. If they need some ideas, tell them to look at the activities in Activity A.

- Put students in pairs to read their sentences.

- Call on students to read their sentences to the class.

Expansion Activity: Write more sentences.

- Have students write more sentences about themselves and their family.

- Encourage them to use the verb *be* and the third person singular form.

BIG PICTURE Expansion Activity: Grammar: Who does what?

- Photocopy and distribute Worksheet 18: *Who does what?* (Teacher's Edition page 334)

- Put the transparency for Unit 5 on the OHP or have students look at the picture on page 70 in their books.

- Have students complete the worksheet.

- Have students check their answers with a partner.

- Go over the answers with the class.

Answer Key   **1.** eats breakfast/ reads the newspaper; **2.** listens to music; **3.** works on the computer; **4.** comb their hair/brush their teeth; **5.** eat breakfast; **6.** are/talk on the phone

Objective
Reading about birthdays

**Literacy Workbook pages 92–97
Workbook page 58**

  A   **CD 2, TRACK 48**   **Listen and read.**

- Direct students' attention to the picture and ask questions: *Who do you see? What do you see? Who has a birthday today?*

- Have students listen and read along silently as you play the audio or read the story aloud.

- Play the audio or read the story aloud again and have students repeat.

- Put students in pairs to take turns reading the story aloud.

- Call on volunteers to read to the class. Elicit or point out the *s* ending for *takes, opens,* and *says.*

- Ask comprehension questions: *What is the date of Isabel's birthday? How old is she? Who is at her house? What time is it? What do they do?*

Expansion Activity: **Strip Story**

- Rewrite the story on long strips of paper. Write one sentence on each strip. Make sure to leave a large space between each word.

- Put the first strip in a pocket chart or tape it to the wall or board.

- Read the first strip aloud and have students repeat.

- Continue with the other sentence strips.

- Take the strips out of the chart or off the board and mix them up.

- Call a volunteer to the front of the class and have him or her put the strips in order. Have the class approve or correct the sentence order. Reread.

- Continue with other volunteers.

- **Literacy option:** Practice counting the words in each sentence to reinforce word discrimination and focus on beginning sounds.

CULTURE Notes

- Point out that Isabel's friends may also sing "Happy Birthday" to her.

- Sing the song and ask if it is the same in your students' countries. If not, elicit the songs they sing for birthdays.

B   **Circle.**

- Read the pair of sentences. Elicit which one is correct. Point out that *May 10* is circled.

- Have students circle the correct information.

- Go over the answers with the class.

> **Answer Key**   **1.** May 10; **2.** 21;
> **3.** Isabel's; **4.** eat cake; **5.** "Thank you."
> **6.** party

Literacy Development Activity: Key Information

- Copy the sentences from Activity B on the board. Write the choices in different colors from the other words in the sentence. Remember to leave spaces between the words.

- Have a volunteer circle the correct word on the board. Have students circle the correct word in their books.

- Continue with the other sentences.

Expansion Activity: Reading: Whose birthday is it?

- Photocopy and distribute Worksheet 19: *Whose birthday is it?* (Teacher's Edition page 345)

- Put the transparency for Unit 5 on the OHP or have students look at page 70 in their books.

- Have students read the information. You may want to read each sentence aloud and have students repeat.

- Have students complete the sentences.

- Put students in pairs to read their sentences to each other.

- Go over the answers with the class.

Answer Key **1.** Maria; **2.** daughters/ son; **3.** "Happy Birthday"; **4.** eat; **5.** 35

Objective
Understanding an email

**Literacy Workbook pages 92–97
Workbook page 59**

A   **Complete.**

- Read each word in the box and have students repeat. Point out that each word goes on one of the blanks in the story.

- Go over the example. Point out that *are* is written on the line and crossed out in the box.

- Have students complete the email. Remind students to use words with capital letters to start a sentence.

- Put students in pairs to read their emails aloud.

- Go over the answers with the class.

> **Answer Key**   are, Birthday, are, give, eat, say

B   **Write about Isabel. What does Isabel do at the party?**

- Read the question. Point to the pictures and elicit the activities.

- Have students complete the sentences.

- Go over the answers with the class.

> **Answer Key**   **1.** eats cake; **2.** opens presents; **3.** takes photos

Expansion Activity:
Write more about birthdays.

- Have students rewrite the email in Activity A with true information about birthdays in their country. Provide help as needed.

- If you have several students from one country in your class, have them work together on the email.

- Ask volunteers to read their emails to the class.

BIG PICTURE

Expansion Activity:
Conversation/Vocabulary: Review with a Timeline

- Before class, make student copies of Worksheet 20: *What time do you… ?* (Teacher's Edition page 346)

- Put the transparency for Unit 5 on the OHP or have students look at the big picture on page 70 in their books. Point to each picture on the transparency and ask students to name the activity (e.g., *listen to music, work on the computer,* etc.).

- Pass out Worksheet 20.

- Point to yourself and say, *I listen to music at seven o'clock.* Write the sentence on the board (*I listen to music at 7:00.*). Have the students complete Section A by writing sentences about when they do the activities pictured.

- Copy the timeline on the board or make an overhead transparency of Worksheet 20 and put it on the OHP. Next to the appropriate times on the timeline, write when you do the activities. For example, write *I read the newspaper* next to 7:00 A.M.

- Ask the students to complete Section B on Worksheet 20.

- **Option:** Put students in pairs. Student A asks B, *What time do you listen to music?* B answers, *I listen to music at* _____, and says the time on the timeline.

Objective
Review and assessment

 A CD 2, TRACK 49 **Listen and write.**

- Go over the directions.
- Play the audio and stop after the first sentence or read the first sentence. Point out that *October* is written on the line.
- Continue to play the audio or read the sentences as students write the missing information on the lines. Pause after each sentence so students have time to write their answers.
- Have students check their answers in a small group.
- Play the audio or read the sentences again and have students correct any wrong answers.
- Elicit the answers and write them on the board.

CULTURE Note

- Point out that birthdates are pronounced as ordinal numbers even though they are written as cardinal numbers.

······· Listening Script

A. LISTEN AND WRITE.

1. My birthday is October twelfth.
2. Paul's birthday is July fourth.
3. My class is at four thirty.
4. I study on Tuesday.

Answer Key **1.** October; **2.** July; **3.** 4:30 or four thirty; **4.** Tuesday

 B CD 2, TRACK 50 **Listen and fill in.**

- Go over the directions.
- Play the audio and stop after the first sentence or read the first sentence in the listening script. Point out that A is filled in.
- Have students look at each pair of answers.
- Continue to play the audio or read the sentences as students mark the answers. Stop after each sentence so students have time to mark their answers.
- Play the audio or read the sentences again and have students check their answers.
- Elicit the answers and write them on the board.

······· Listening Script

B. LISTEN AND FILL IN.

1. Ben is Chinese.
2. Leo reads the newspaper.
3. We talk on the phone.
4. They eat breakfast every day.
5. Jane cooks dinner.
6. It's 10 o'clock.
7. Leo's birthday is September third.
8. Nadira has class on Thursday.

Answer Key **1.** A; **2.** B; **3.** A; **4.** B; **5.** B; **6.** A; **7.** A; **8.** B

C CD 2, TRACK 51 **Listen and circle.**

- Go over the directions.

- Have students circle the number as you play the audio or read the sentences.

- Play the audio or read the sentences again and have students check their answers.

- Elicit the answers and write them on the board.

Listening Script

C. LISTEN AND CIRCLE.

1. Can you come at seven o'clock?
2. He lives on Sixth Street.
3. The house is on Eleventh Street.
4. I go to school at two thirty.
5. My birthday is May thirteenth.
6. I go to school at nine forty-five.
7. He always wakes up at eight o'clock.
8. This is my third English class.
9. Linda's address is 50 G Street.
10. She lives on the 13th floor.

Answer Key **1.** 7:00; **2.** 6th; **3.** 11th; **4.** 2:30; **5.** 13th; **6.** 9:45; **7.** 8:00; **8.** 3rd; **9.** 50; **10.** 13th

D **Ask 5 classmates.**

- Read the questions and have students repeat.

- Have students ask five classmates each question. For added challenge, have students record the answers in a chart format that you help them prepare.

- Call on students to tell the class something about a classmate.

E CD 2, TRACK 52 **Listen and write.**

- Play the audio or read the information in the listening script and have students write the information on the cards.

- Play the audio or read the information again so students can finish or check their work.

- Go over the answers with the class.

Listening Script

E. LISTEN AND WRITE.

Checkup Appointment
On: Monday, April 21st at eight a.m.
Edward J. Weiss, D.D.S.
517 Old Road

Jane's Haircuts
Tuesday to Saturday
nine thirty a.m. to six p.m.
310 Cook Road

Answer Key

Checkup Appointment On: Monday, April 21, at 8:00 A.M. Edward J. Weiss, D.D.S. 517 Old Road	Jane's Haircuts Tuesday to Saturday 9:30 A.M. to 6:00 P.M. 310 Cook Road

F **Learning Log**

- Have students check the words they know.

- Put students in pairs to review the words.

- Elicit words that students do not know and review their meanings.

LOOKING BACK

- Go over the directions.

- Put students in pairs to talk about the big picture on page 70.

- Call on students to talk about the picture.

UNIT OVERVIEW

Lesson	Objective	Student Book Page
1. I'm looking for a coat.	Asking for merchandise in a store	p. 87
2. May I help you?	Asking for help in a store	p. 88
3. What color is your jacket?	Identifying colors	p. 89
4. What are you wearing?	Talking about what people are wearing	p. 90
5. What's your favorite color?	Talking about clothing and favorite colors	p. 91
6. What size are you?	Identifying clothing sizes	p. 92
7. The jacket is too small.	Talking about clothing problems	p. 93
8. Money	Recognizing denominations of American money	p. 94
9. A Check	Writing checks	p. 95
10. Grammar: Adjectives and Nouns	Understanding nouns and adjectives	p. 96
11. Grammar: Adjectives and Nouns	Using nouns and adjectives	p. 97
12. Read: A Catalog	Reading a catalog	p. 98
13. Write: Sandy's Shopping List	Understanding a shopping list	p. 99
What do you know?	Review and assessment	p. 100

Big Picture Expansion Activities

Focus	Activity	Suggested Use
Listening/ Speaking	Confirming Information About People's Clothes	What do you know?
Reading	How much is it?	Lesson 11
Grammar	What are they wearing?	Lesson 10
Writing	Sentences about Clothes	Lesson 4
Vocabulary/ Numeracy	Taking Inventory	Lesson 1

Worksheets

Worksheet #/ Focus	Title	Teacher's Edition Page
21. Vocabulary	Taking Inventory	p. 347
22. Writing	Blank Checks	p. 348
23. Grammar	What are they wearing?	p. 349
24. Reading	How much is it?	p. 350

Unit Opener

- Put the transparency for Unit 6 on the Overhead Projector (OHP) or have students look at the big picture on page 86 in their books.

- Point to each word as you ask the questions at the bottom of the page: *Where are the students? What do you see?*

- Elicit the words the students know and write them on the board.

Objective
Asking for merchandise in a store

Vocabulary

a coat	pants	a sweater
a dress	a shirt	a suit
follow	shoes	a watch

Literacy Workbook pages 98–103
Workbook page 62

  A CD 2, TRACK 54 **Listen.**

- Have students look at the pictures and listen while you play the first part of the audio or read the sentences in the script.

- Play the rest of the audio or read the word list and have the students repeat.

- Call on individual students. Read one of the words and have the student repeat.

- Have students work in pairs and take turns reading the words in random order as their partner points to the picture.

Listening Script

A. LISTEN.

1. A shirt. Paul is looking for a shirt.
2. A coat. Tien is looking for a coat.
3. A sweater. Isabel is looking for a sweater.
4. Shoes. Grace is looking for shoes.
5. A watch. Leo is looking for a watch.
6. A dress. Maria is looking for a dress.
7. Pants. Ben is looking for pants.
8. A suit. Carlos is looking for a suit.

LISTEN AND REPEAT.

1. a shirt
2. a coat
3. a sweater
4. shoes
5. a watch
6. a dress
7. pants
8. a suit

VOCABULARY Note

- Point out or elicit that two of the words are in plural form (*pants* and *shoes*). Explain that although pants are just one thing, they have two legs and are always plural.

PRONUNCIATION Notes

- Write the words beginning with *s* on the board.

> shirt, sweater, shoes, suit

- Say each word stressing the beginning sound. Students should understand that *sh* is a very different single sound from *s*, and that *sw* is blended together.

Expansion Activity: Character Cards

- Write _____ *is looking for* _____. on the board.

- Play the first part of the audio or read the sentences. Have students listen for which character wants which clothing item.

- Hold up a character card (Paul, Maria, Carlos, Grace, Isabel, Leo). Elicit what each character is looking for (e.g., *Paul is looking for a shirt and pants.*).

B CD 2, TRACK 55 **Listen.**

- Play the audio or read the conversation.

- Play the audio or read the conversation again and have students repeat.

- Put students in pairs. Designate one partner to be Isabel and the other to be the clerk.

- Have students practice the conversation in pairs, then switch roles.

VOCABULARY Note

- Make sure students understand what a *clerk* is. Elicit or provide alternative terms, e.g., *salesperson, salesclerk*.

C **Talk with a partner.**

- Review the words in the box.

- Divide students into pairs and have them take turns playing the two roles.

BIG PICTURE Expansion Activity: Vocabulary/Numeracy: Taking Inventory

- Copy and distribute Worksheet 21: *Taking Inventory* (Teacher's Edition page 347).

- Copy Worksheet 21 on the board, or make a transparency and put it on the OHP.

- Tell the students that they work in a store. Customers go to the store and buy many things. The workers have to know how many items are left at the end of the day.

- Point to the example, *Sweaters*. Put the transparency for Unit 6 on the OHP or have students look at the big picture on page 86. Point to the sweater that Isabel is holding. Ask *How many sweaters do you see?* Elicit *four*. Tell the students that Isabel buys one. Ask *How many will be left?* If necessary, write *4 − 1 =* on the board. Write *3* in the fourth column labeled *Number left*.

- Point to each picture on the worksheet. Say the name and have students repeat.

- Point to the men's suits on the transparency. Ask students *How many men's suits are in the picture?* If necessary, cue the students by pointing to each suit and counting. Elicit that there are 13. Write *13* in the second column on the board. Have students write it on their worksheet. Ask *How many suits does Paul buy?* Point to the third column. Have students say *5*. Ask them how many are left. Tell them to write this number in the column labeled *Number left*.

- Have them work in pairs to finish the worksheet.

- As a variation, put students in groups and have them decide what the group will buy. Have them subtract their purchases from the totals.

Answer Key Men's suits: 13 − 5 = 8
Women's coats: 18 − 3 = 15
Men's shirts: 9 − 4 = 5

Objective

Asking for help in a store

Vocabulary

a bathing suit	a blouse	a scarf
a belt	a cap	a skirt
	a jacket	socks

**Literacy Workbook pages 98–103
Workbook page 62**

  A CD 2, TRACK 56 **Listen.**

- Have students look at the pictures and listen while you play the first part of the audio or read the sentences in the script.

- Play the rest of the audio or read the list of words. Have students repeat the words as they point to the picture.

- Working in pairs, have one partner read the words in a random order while the other partner points to the correct picture.

⋯⋯ Listening Script

A. LISTEN.

1. A blouse. Isabel needs a blouse.
2. A bathing suit. Carlos needs a bathing suit.
3. A skirt. Grace needs a skirt.
4. A belt. Tien needs a belt.
5. A jacket. Paul needs a jacket.
6. A cap. Leo needs a cap.
7. Socks. Maria needs socks.
8. A scarf. Nadira needs a scarf.

LISTEN AND REPEAT.

1. a blouse	**5.** a jacket
2. a bathing suit	**6.** a cap
3. a skirt	**7.** socks
4. a belt	**8.** a scarf

VOCABULARY Notes

- Point out that *socks* is plural just as *pants* is. We usually speak of socks in the plural because we wear two at a time. *Pants* is plural because they have two legs.

- A *blouse* is a shirt worn by a woman, while a *shirt* can be worn by either a man or a woman.

Literacy Development Activity: Count the letters.

- Write the first letter of each word on the board followed by the appropriate number of blank lines to indicate each letter.

- Have students write the words in their notebooks.

- Call volunteers to the front of the room to complete the words.

B CD 2, TRACK 57 **Listen.**

- Play the audio or read the conversation alone or with a student as students listen.

- Play the audio or read the conversation again and have students repeat.

- Put students in pairs. Designate one partner to be Carlos and the other to be the clerk.

- Have students practice the conversation in pairs, then switch roles.

Expansion Activity: **Venn Diagram**

- Draw a Venn diagram on the board.

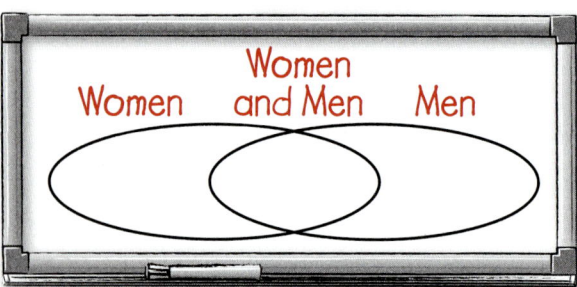

Women | Women and Men | Men

- Elicit something only women wear and write it on the diagram. Elicit something only men wear and write it on the diagram.

- Have students copy and complete the diagram in their notebooks.

- Elicit ideas and write the information on the diagram on the board.

C **Talk with a partner.**

- Go over the words in the box. Point out that all the nouns use an article except for *pants*.

- Model the activity with a more advanced student. Have the student say *May I help you?* Demonstrate how to substitute another word in your response (*Yes, I need a shirt*).

- Put the students in pairs to practice the conversation. Encourage students to practice several times and ask about different things.

- Have students switch roles.

D **Complete.**

- Direct students' attention to the pictures. Elicit the name of each item.

- Have students complete the sentences.

- Put students in pairs to compare answers.

- Ask for volunteers to give answers and make or ask for corrections as needed.

Answer Key 1. sweater; 2. belts

Expansion Activity: Pair Memory Dictation

- Put students in pairs. Designate one partner as the *teacher* and one as the *student*.

- Have the "teachers" come out to the hallway. Show them three character cards and say a sentence about what each character needs (*Sandy needs a dress. Ben needs a suit. Paul needs shoes.*).

- Have the "teachers" say the sentences to their partners. Have the "students" write the sentences on the board or a piece of paper.

- Have students switch roles and repeat with different characters and needs.

Objective
Identifying colors

Literacy Workbook pages 98–103
Workbook page 63

  A CD 2, TRACK 58 **Listen.**

- Have students look at the words.
- Play the audio or read the words.
- Play the audio or read the words again and have students repeat.

Literacy Development Activity:
Color Word Cards

- Give students nine index cards. Have students write one color word on each card.
- Have students put the cards in the same order as the colors in Activity A.
- Point to an object in the room. Elicit the color and have students hold up the word for that color.
- Continue with other objects and colors. When students know the words on the cards, point to objects and have students hold up the card without eliciting the color word first.

 B CD 2, TRACK 59 **Listen and circle.**

- Have students look at the first pair of pictures. Elicit the objects (*black shoes, yellow shoes*). Play the audio for the first item or read the first sentence in the listening script. Elicit that Leo has *white shoes*. Point out that the white shoes are circled.
- Play the audio or read the sentences in the script and have students circle what they hear.

- Put students in pairs to compare answers.
- Go over the answers with the class.

Listening Script
B. LISTEN AND CIRCLE.

1. Leo has black shoes.
2. Ben has a blue sweater.
3. Maria has a green blouse.
4. Isabel has a purple jacket.
5. Sandy has a pink bathing suit.
6. Tien has a black skirt.

Answer Key **1.** black shoes; **2.** blue sweater; **3.** green blouse; **4.** purple jacket; **5.** pink bathing suit; **6.** black skirt

  C CD 2, TRACK 60 **Listen.**

- Play the audio or read the conversation as students listen.
- Play the audio or read the conversation again and have students repeat.
- Put students in pairs. Designate one partner to be Sandy and the other to be Grace.
- Have students practice the conversation in pairs, then switch roles.

GRAMMAR Note

- Point out that we use *is* when asking about singular objects and *are* with plural objects.

Expansion Activity: **Ask Sandy.**

- Have students rewrite the conversation to ask Sandy what she is wearing.
- Put students in pairs to practice the new conversation.

D Talk with a partner about clothes.

- Model the activity with a more advanced student. Ask the student about his or her clothes.

- Put students in pairs to take turns asking about each other's clothing, using words in the box and other words they have learned.

- Call on students to tell the class what their partners are wearing.

Objective
Talking about what people are wearing

Literacy Workbook pages 98–103
Workbook page 63

  A CD 2, TRACK 61 **Listen.**

- Direct students' attention to the picture and ask *Who do you see? What are they wearing?*

- Have students look at the pictures and listen while you play the audio or read the sentences.

- Play the audio or read the sentences again. Pause and ask the students to repeat the sentences.

- Put students in pairs to practice the conversation.

GRAMMAR Note

- Tell students that we say the color and then the clothing (*blue dress*). This grammar point will be covered in Lessons 10 and 11.

B **Talk with 3 classmates.**

- Model the activity with a more advanced student. Have the student ask the question. Respond with what you are wearing.

- Have students talk to three classmates, asking and answering the question using words in the box and other ones they have learned.

- Call on students to say what one classmate is wearing.

Expansion Activity: **Chart it.**

- Copy the chart on the board.

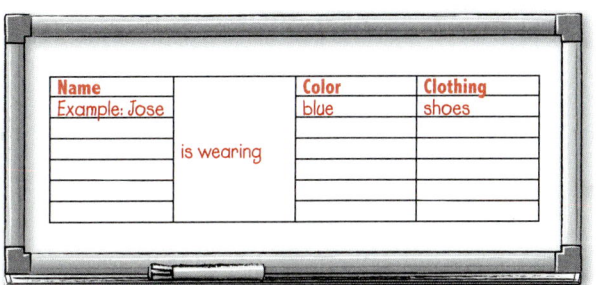

- Have students write the information in the chart as they talk to five classmates.

Expansion Activity: **Alphabetize.**

- Have students write the words from the word list box in alphabetical order.

- Pair a more advanced student with a less advanced student to compare lists.

- Have students write the words in order on the board.

C **Talk with a partner. Look at the picture on 86.**

- Have students look at the big picture on page 86 or put the transparency for this unit on the OHP.

- Ask a question: *What is Leo wearing?* Elicit the answer.

- Put students in pairs to take turns asking and answering questions about what the characters are wearing.

Expansion Activity:
Writing: Sentences About Clothes

- Have students look at the big picture on page 86 or put the transparency for this unit on the OHP.

- Have students write one sentence about each character in the big picture to tell what the character is wearing.

- Pair a more advanced student with a less advanced student to read their sentences aloud.

- Check the sentences for accuracy; then have volunteers write the sentences on the board.

Expansion Activity:
Memory Chain Game

- Call on a student and ask him or her to read a sentence from *My Life* (e.g., *I wear a suit to work*). Repeat the student's sentence (*Juan wears a suit to work*) and add your own sentence (e.g., *and I wear a dress to parties.*).

- Have the next student say both sentences and add his or her own. Continue around the class. In large classes, put the students in small groups to do the activity.

My Life

- Go over the directions and the example.

- Have students complete the sentences.

- Put students in groups to read their sentences aloud.

- Call on students to read their sentences to the class.

GRAMMAR Note

- Point out that we use *wear* to talk about clothing we wear in general, and *is wearing* to talk about what we have on today.

Objective
Talking about clothing and favorite colors

Literacy Workbook pages 98–103
Workbook page 64

  A CD 2, TRACK 62 **Listen.**

- Have students look at the pictures as you play the audio or read the conversation.

- Play the audio or read the conversation again and have students repeat.

- Have students practice the conversation in pairs.

GRAMMAR Note

- It is also correct to ask *And yours?*

B Talk with a partner.

- Model the activity with a more advanced student.

- Put students in pairs to practice the conversation.

- Call on students to tell the class about their partner's favorite color.

Expansion Activity:
Guessing Game

- Model the activity. Choose something in the classroom that is one color (e.g., *brown*) and say *I see something brown*.

- Tell students they must ask three questions about the object before they can guess what it is (e.g., *Is it something a student has? Is it something for the classroom? Is someone wearing it?*). Elicit guesses.

- Call on students to choose objects and elicit guesses.

C Ask classmates.

- Go over the sample conversation.

- Have students stand and walk around the classroom to ask classmates the question and complete the chart if possible.

- Have students tell one of their results.

Expansion Activity:
Stand up, sit down.

- Have students choose two colors. Tell students that you will tell a story. When they hear one of their colors they should stand up. When they hear the second color, they should sit down.

- Create a story, or read the one below. If everyone stands and sits by the end of the story, they have heard their two colors. If not, read the story again.

    Grace has a purple dress. Purple is her favorite color. Ben likes blue. He wears a blue shirt to school every Monday. Leo's favorite color is brown. He wears brown pants to work. Nadira likes orange. Orange makes her feel happy. Isabel likes green. It is one of her favorite colors. Maria's favorite color is pink, but she also likes red. Carlos likes every color. He wears black pants and a white shirt to parties. Paul wears yellow shoes to work.

Objective
Identifying clothing sizes

Vocabulary

small   medium   large

**Literacy Workbook pages 98–103
Workbook page 65**

  A   CD 2, TRACK 63   **Listen.**

- Direct students' attention to the pictures at the top of the page. Ask *What do you see? What colors do you see?*

- Play the first part of the audio or read the sentences in the script as students follow along silently.

- Play the rest of the audio or read the list of words and have students repeat.

- Put students in pairs to practice the conversation. Have students switch roles.

······ **Listening Script**

A. LISTEN.

1. Small. The red shirt is small.
2. Medium. The blue shirt is medium.
3. Large. The green shirt is large.

LISTEN AND REPEAT.

1. small
2. medium
3. large

VOCABULARY Notes

- Point out the abbreviations for *small, medium,* and *large.* Tell students that clothing tags often use these abbreviations.

- Tell them about other related sizes: *extra small (XS)* and *extra large (XL).*

 B   CD 2, TRACK 64   **Listen and circle.**

- Play the audio for the first sentence or read the first sentence. Point out that *large* has been circled.

- Play the rest of the audio or read the sentences and have students circle the size they hear.

- Put students in pairs to compare answers. Play the audio or read the sentences again if necessary.

- Go over the answers with the class.

······ **Listening Script**

B. LISTEN AND CIRCLE.

1. The pink sweater is large.
2. The black socks are small.
3. The white shirt is small.
4. The red skirt is medium.
5. Grace's yellow blouse is small.
6. Paul's blue pants are large.
7. My purple jacket is medium.
8. Tien's yellow bathing suit is small.

Answer Key   **1.** large; **2.** small; **3.** small; **4.** medium; **5.** small; **6.** large; **7.** medium; **8.** small

Expansion Activity:
Class Dictation

- Have students write a sentence in which they use their favorite color, their size, and an article of clothing (e.g., *My blue shirt is large*).

- Walk around the room and provide help as needed.

- Call on students to dictate their sentences to the class, or collect the sentences and dictate to the class.

- Have volunteers write the sentences on the board.

 C CD 2, TRACK 65 **Listen.**

- Direct students' attention to the picture. Ask *Who do you see? What is he doing? What is he wearing?*

> **Who do you see? What is he doing?**

- Play the audio or read the conversation with a student volunteer as students follow along silently.

- Play the audio or read the conversation again and have students repeat.

D **Talk with 5 classmates.**

- Model the activity with a more advanced student.

- Have students talk to five classmates and practice the conversation.

Literacy Development Activity:
Tally by size.

- Have students write the capital letters *S, M,* and *L* on separate lines in their notebooks.

- As students ask and answer questions in Activity D, have students make tally marks next to the appropriate letter to count the sizes they hear.

- Call on students to report their findings to the class (*Three people wear a large*).

CULTURE Note

- In some cultures, people don't really like to talk about their size, especially if they are larger. Tell students they can say any size they want or say, "I'd rather not say."

VOCABULARY Note

- Tell students that they can also ask, *What size do you wear?* This option may be more acceptable to some students as they may be a medium, but wear a large. Point out that the answer would be *a small/a medium/a large*.

Expansion Activity:
Character Cards

- Give students a character card.
- Put students in pairs to practice the conversation as characters.

Objective

Talking about clothing problems

Expansion Activity:
What are they wearing?

- Use this expansion as a warm-up for Activity A. Point to the first picture in Activity A. Elicit what Paul is wearing—just the color and the clothing item (*Paul is wearing blue pants.*).

- Have students write sentences about each picture to describe what the character is wearing.

- Put students in pairs to compare sentences.

- Have volunteers write the sentences on the board.

> **Answer Key** **1.** Paul is wearing white pants.; **2.** Maria is wearing blue pants.; **3.** Tien is wearing a green jacket.; **4.** Carlos is wearing black pants.

  A CD 2, TRACK 66 **Listen.**

- Direct students' attention to the pictures.

- Have students listen and follow along in the book as you play the first part of the audio or read the sentences in the script.

- Play the rest of the audio or read the phrases and have students repeat.

- Play the rest of the audio or read the phrases again and have students repeat.

Listening Script

A. LISTEN.

1. Too short. The pants are too short.
2. Too long. The pants are too long.
3. Too small. The jacket is too small.
4. Too big. The shirt is too big.

LISTEN AND REPEAT.

1. too short
2. too long
3. too small
4. too big

VOCABULARY Note

- Make sure students understand we use *too* to describe a problem. Pantomime *too short*: If you are wearing pants or a long-sleeved shirt or jacket, pull a pant leg or sleeve up a bit, point to it, and say *too short*.

B **Look at Activity A. Match.**

- Go over the example.

- Have students write the letter on the line to match the problem to the article of clothing.

- Put students in pairs to compare answers.

- Go over the answers with the class.

> **Answer Key** **1.** b; **2.** d; **3.** a; **4.** c

Expansion Activity: False Sentences

- Dictate four sentences with incorrect information about the pictures in Activity A (e.g., *The pants are too small.*). Say each sentence three times.
- Have students write the sentences and then compare sentences with a partner.
- Go over the sentences with the class.
- Have students correct the sentences.

C   Write 3 sentences about Leo's clothes.

- Direct students' attention to the picture. Ask *What is the problem with Leo's clothes?*
- Have students write three sentences about Leo's clothes.
- Put students in pairs to compare sentences.
- Have volunteers write sentences on the board.

Answer Key   **1.** Leo's pants are too long.; **2.** His shirt is too small.; **3.** His hat is too big.

Expansion Activity: Personalize.

- Model the activity. Write three sentences about clothing problems you have (*My green shirt is too small. My blue shoes are too big. My red skirt is too short.*).

- Write on the board:

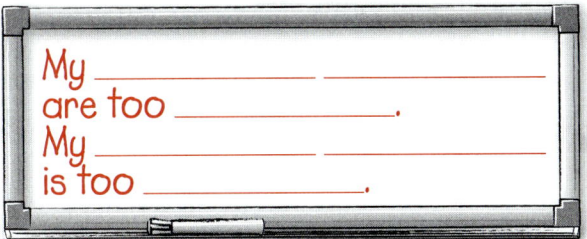

- Have students write three sentences about clothing problems they have using the sentence model.
- Put students in groups to read their sentences.
- Have volunteers write sentences on the board.
- **Variation for mixed level groups:** Put a more advanced student with a less proficient student. The more advanced student can write the sentences the partner dictates.

Extra Challenge
Old and New

- For added challenge, introduce old and new as clothing problems: *My shoes are too new (they hurt). My pants are too old (they have holes in them).*

Expansion Activity: Garage Sale

- Bring in old clothes, or have students bring old clothes to class.
- Have students practice asking for clothing items, saying their size, and then saying problems with various items.

Objective
Recognizing denominations of American money

Vocabulary

a penny	a dime	cent
a nickel	a quarter	dollar

Literacy Workbook pages 98–103
Workbook page 67

  A CD 2, TRACK 67 **Listen.**

- Have students look at the coins as you play the audio or read the amounts.

- Play the audio or read the amounts again and have students repeat.

- Read the numbers in random order and have students point to the correct coin.

  B CD 2, TRACK 68 **Listen.**

- Have students look at the bills as you play the audio or read the amounts.

- Play the audio or read the numbers again and have students repeat.

- Read the numbers in random order and have students point to the correct bill.

Expansion Activity: **Beanbag Toss**

- Call on a student and toss a beanbag or small ball. Say an amount of coins and elicit another way to say it. For example, if you say *a penny*, the student says *one cent*.

- Continue until everyone has a chance to participate.

- If you have the room in your classroom, you may want to have students stand in a circle for this activity. Otherwise, make sure students are paying attention if classmates are tossing the beanbag.

CULTURE/CIVICS Notes

- Point out the different sizes and illustrations on the coins and bills. The coins all have famous U.S. presidents. The penny has Abraham Lincoln on one side and the Lincoln Memorial on the other. The nickel has Thomas Jefferson on one side. The dime has Franklin D. Roosevelt, and the quarter has George Washington.

- The bills, or paper money, also have important Americans on one side. The name of the person is under his picture.

- Make sure students know to put the cent symbol after the money (e.g., *50¢*) and the dollar sign before the money (e.g., *$0.50, $2.00*).

C Write how much.

- Have students write the amounts.

- Put students in pairs to compare answers.

- Go over the answers with the class. Have students write the answers on the board.

Answer Key 1. $47.26

Expansion Activity: **Real Money**

- Bring in coins and bill denominations. You will need enough coins to distribute to pairs of students.

- Show students the coins and bills one at a time and elicit the amount. Students may need to come to your desk to see the coins and bills.

- Call on students as you say the name of a bill or coin. Have the student point.

- Put students in pairs. Give each pair of students examples of each type of coin.

- Call out the name of a coin or the amount (e.g., *five cents* or *nickel*) and have students point.

- Say amounts of money (e.g., *37 cents*) and have students work in pairs to put the amount of money together. Call on students to say what coins make that amount.

Objective
Writing checks

Literacy Workbook pages 98–103
Workbook page 68

A Read.

- Direct students' attention to the check.

- Ask comprehension questions: *Who writes the check? What is her address? What is the date? How much is the check? What is Isabel buying?*

CULTURE Notes

- Point out check-writing conventions such as how the amounts are written in the box vs. how they are written on the second line. Also point out that we usually write the purpose for the check on the memo line.

- Point out that many stores also require an ID when you pay by check. This ID usually must be a driver's license or a state ID card.

Expansion Activity: Parts of a Check

- Copy the check on the board or make an overhead transparency of Worksheet 24: *Blank Checks* (Teacher's Edition page 348).

- Point to the different parts of a check and have students say what they are. Include: address, signature line, memo line, check number (in upper right corner), date line, dollar sign, place where you must write the check amount using numbers, and place where you must write the check amount using letters.

- As an extension, say different dollar and cent amounts and have students practice writing the amounts, e.g., *$10.50; $76.89.* Point out the dollar sign.

B Write a check.

- Copy the check on the board or make an overhead transparency of Worksheet 24: *Blank Checks* (Teacher's Edition page 348).

- Model the activity. Complete the check for yourself.

- Have students complete the checks with their own information.

- Put students in pairs or small groups to talk about the information on their checks.

Expansion Activity: Blank Checks

- Photocopy and distribute Worksheet 23: *Blank Checks* (Teacher's Edition page 348).

- Bring in store circulars with clothing ads.

- Have students "go shopping" through the circulars.

- Ask students to pick an item and write a check for it.

- With more advanced classes, have students pick two items and write a check for the combined total.

Objective
Understanding nouns and adjectives

Literacy Workbook pages 98–103
Workbook page 69

  A CD 2, TRACK 69 **Listen and read.**

- Have students listen and read the chart as you play the audio or read the words and sentences.

- Play the audio or read the words and sentences again and have students repeat.

- Read each sentence in the chart and ask: *What is the adjective? What is the noun? Which is first, the adjective or the noun?*

GRAMMAR Note

- In this situation, *she has a white blouse* means the same as *she is wearing a white blouse.*

B **Look at the picture. Complete the sentences.**

- Direct students' attention to the picture. Ask questions: *Which boy is Andy? Which boy is Justin?* Remind or elicit from students that Justin and Andy are Sandy's sons.

- Read the first sentence. Point out that *white* is written on the line. Elicit that the boy with white shoes is Andy, and the other boy is Justin.

- Read each word in the box and have students repeat.

- Have students complete the sentences.

- Put students in pairs to compare answers.

- Go over the answers with the class.

Answer Key
1. white; **2.** long; **3.** blue; **4.** white; **5.** big

Literacy Development Activity: Adjective Cards

- Give each student five cards.

- Have students write the adjectives from the word box on the cards (one word per card).

- Say *Justin's pants* and have students hold up an appropriate card (*blue, long*).

- Continue with other articles of clothing in the picture.

- In a variation, give students more cards and have them write other adjectives on the cards.

- Say the name of a student and an article of clothing. Have students hold up the appropriate card.

C **Talk about a classmate.**

- Model the activity. Say a sentence about someone in the class using the sentence model (e.g., *Radek is wearing brown pants and a red jacket.*).

- Have students complete the sentence about a classmate.

- Call on students to read their sentences to the class.

Let's go shopping. 165

Extra Challenge

Write sentences.

- Have more advanced students write sentences to describe someone in the class using each word in the box from Activity B (e.g., *Tito is wearing a red shirt.*). Or, say an adjective as a prompt and have students write sentences.

- Put students in pairs to read their sentences.

- Call on students to read a sentence to the class.

Expansion Activity: Guess who.

- Have students read their sentences from Activity C to the class, saying *my classmate* instead of the person's name.

- Elicit guesses from the class.

Expansion Activity: Grammar: What are they wearing?

- Photocopy and distribute Worksheet 23: *What are they wearing?* (Teacher's Edition page 349)

- Put the transparency for Unit 6 on the OHP or have students look at page 86 in their books.

- Go over the directions.

- Have students complete the worksheet.

- Put students in pairs to compare answers.

- Go over the answers with the class.

Answer Key **1.** brown; **2.** cap; **3.** shirt; **4.** purple/white; **5.** purple sweater; **6.** green/gray pants; **7.** bathing suit

Objective
Using nouns and adjectives

Vocabulary
boots

Literacy Workbook pages 98–103
Workbook page 69

  A CD 2, TRACK 70 **Listen.**

- Have students look at the picture. Ask: *What do you see?* Elicit words and phrases and write them on the board.

- Play the audio or read the sentences as students look at the picture.

- Play the audio or read the sentences again and have students repeat.

- Ask comprehension questions: *What is on sale? When is the sale?*

> When is the sale?   The sale is today only.

Listening Script

A. LISTEN.

Big sale today only. Fifty percent off. A large hat, a brown jacket, black boots, a purple dress, yellow shoes, a green sweater, a blue men's suit, a pink blouse, a red skirt. It's a very big sale!

LISTEN AND REPEAT.

B **Read. Look at Activity A. Match.**

- Go over the example.

- Point to the new word *boots* in the picture and elicit the name.

- Have students write the letters to match the nouns to the adjectives.

- Put students in pairs to compare answers.

- Go over the answers with the class.

> **Answer Key** **1.** h; **2.** c; **3.** d; **4.** b; **5.** g; **6.** a; **7.** e; **8.** f; **9.** i

C **Look at Activity A. Write.**

- Have students write the words. Point out that more than one answer could be correct for each number. Remind students to use *a* and the *s* ending to choose which item to write on which lines.

- Put students in pairs to compare answers.

- Go over the answers with the class.

> **Answer Key** **1–7.** Any seven of the following phrases, in any order: a large hat; a brown jacket; a green sweater; a blue suit; a pink blouse; a red skirt; a purple dress; **8.** yellow shoes *or* black shoes

Expansion Activity:
Color and Clothing

- Call on a student and say a color (e.g., *brown*). Have the student respond with an article of clothing in the room that is that color (e.g., *Hugo's shoes*).

  brown   **Hugo's shoes**

- Continue the activity until everyone has had a chance to participate. As a variation, say the article of clothing (e.g., *Hugo's shoes*) and elicit the color (*brown*).

Extra Challenge
Write sentences.

- For extra writing and/or speaking practice, have students use the noun and matching adjective in a sentence, e.g., *A large hat is on sale.*

- Divide students into pairs to complete the activity.

- Call on pairs to read one of their sentences to the class or have them write it on the board so that all nine items have a sentence.

BIG PICTURE

Expansion Activity:
Reading: How much is it?

- Photocopy and distribute Worksheet 24: *How much is it?* (Teacher's Edition page 350)

- Put the transparency for Unit 6 on the OHP or have students look at the big picture in their books on page 86.

- Have students complete the worksheet.

- Put students in pairs to compare answers.

- Go over the answers with the class.

Answer Key 1. sweater/$29.95;
2. bathing suit/$20; **3.** watch/$20;
4. shirt/$32

Objective
Reading a catalog

Literacy Workbook pages 98–103
Workbook page 70

  A   CD 2, TRACK 71   **Listen and read.**

- Direct students' attention to the pictures and ask: *What do you see?* Elicit that they are from a clothing catalog. Have students listen and read along silently as you play the audio or read the catalog aloud.

- Play the audio or read the catalog aloud again and have students repeat.

- Put students in pairs to read the catalog aloud.

- Ask comprehension questions such as: *What is $18.75? How much are the sweaters? How much is a suit?*

Listening Script

A. LISTEN AND READ.

A. Children's pants. Sizes: small, medium, and large. Colors: blue, red, or brown. Price $18.75.
B. Women's sweaters and skirts. Women's sweaters. Sweater sizes: small, medium, large. Sweater colors: green or red. Price: $22. Women's skirts. Skirt sizes: small, medium, large. Skirt colors: brown, green, or blue. Price: $22.95.
C. Men's suits. Sizes: small, medium, large, extra large. Colors: brown, black, or blue. Price: $62.50.

B   Look at Activity A. Write the answers.

- Read each question and have students repeat.

- Go over the example.

- Have students write the answers.

- Put students in pairs to compare answers.

- Go over the answers with the class.

Answer Key

1. $62.50; **2.** green or red; **3.** small, medium, and large; **4.** $22.95; **5.** brown, black, or blue

Expansion Activity: **Add it up.**

- Write and read three different purchase orders from the catalog (e.g., *one pair of children's pants, two sweaters, one skirt*).

- Have students write the prices for each item in the order and then total the order.

- Put students in pairs to compare answers.

Expansion Activity: **Real World Catalogs**

- Bring in clothing catalogs, or go to an online catalog and print sample pages.

- Put students in pairs to ask and answer questions about the clothes.

Objective
Understanding a shopping list

Literacy Workbook pages 98–103
Workbook page 71

(A) Complete Sandy's shopping list.

- Direct students' attention to the picture. Ask: *Who do you see? What is she doing? What does Sandy want?*

- Go over the first item. Ask: *What does Justin need?* Elicit that he needs a blue baseball cap. Have students write blue on the line.

- Have students complete the list. Remind students to look at the catalog pictures to find the color. Point out that they also need to write two prices.

- Put students in pairs to compare answers.

- Go over the answers with the class.

Answer Key **1.** blue; **2.** shoes/$12.50; **3.** pink; **4.** jacket; **5.** red/$22.00

Expansion Activity: **Personalize.**

- Bring in catalogs or print pages from an online catalog (as in Lesson 12).

- Have students make lists of five items that they or people in their families need. Remind students to include the color, size, clothing item, and the price. Copy these categories on the board as a reminder.

- Put students in pairs to talk about their lists.

- Call on students to tell the class one thing on their lists and one thing on their partner's list.

- This activity can also be done without a catalog.

Literacy Development Activity: **Write the check.**

- Photocopy and distribute Worksheet 22: *Blank Checks* (Teacher's Edition page 348).

- Have students pretend they are Sandy and write a check for her order, signing her name (Sandy Johnson).

Objective
Review and assessment

  A CD 2, TRACK 72 **Listen and match.**

- Go over the directions and example.

- Point to each picture and elicit what it is.

- Play the audio or read the sentences as students write the number on the line. Stop after each sentence so students have time to write their answers.

- Put students in pairs to compare answers.

- Play the audio or read the sentences again and have students check their answers.

- Elicit the answers and write them on the board.

Listening Script

A. LISTEN AND MATCH.

1. I have a purple skirt with a white blouse.
2. I have blue pants, a green shirt, and white shoes.
3. I have a brown dress and a long scarf.
4. I have brown pants and a yellow T-shirt.

Answer Key **1.** Tien; **2.** Leo; **3.** Isabel; **4.** Ben

  B CD 2, TRACK 73 **Listen and fill in.**

- Go over the directions.

- Play the audio for the first sentence or read the first sentence. Point out that B is filled in.

- Have students look at each pair of answers.

- Continue to play the audio or read the sentences as students mark the answers. Stop after each sentence so students have time to mark their answers.

- Put students in pairs to compare answers.

- Play the audio or read the sentences again and have students check their answers.

- Elicit the answers and write them on the board.

Listening Script

B. LISTEN AND FILL IN.

1. I'm a medium.
2. He's wearing shoes.
3. It's a black suit.
4. It's thirty dollars and twenty-five cents.

Answer Key **1.** B; **2.** B; **3.** A; **4.** B

C **Talk about a classmate. Say, "Guess who."**

- Go over the example by reading one part and having a student volunteer read the other part.

- Model the activity. Describe someone in the class and say *Guess who*.

- Have students describe classmates. Have the class guess who it is.

D **Write about you.**

- Read the questions and have students repeat.

- Have students write answers to the questions.

- Put students in pairs to ask and answer the questions.

- Call on students and ask the questions.

E Read.

- Direct students' attention to the picture. Elicit what Carlos is wearing. Read the sentence.

- Point out that your favorite clothes are the ones you love to wear.

- Have students complete the sentence.

- Put students in pairs to read the sentence.

- Call on students to read their sentences to the class.

F Learning Log

- Go over the directions.

- Have students check the words they know.

- Put students in pairs to compare lists and review the words.

- Elicit words that students do not know and review their meanings.

- Have students write words they don't remember in a vocabulary notebook. Encourage students to write sentences using the difficult words.

LOOKING BACK

- Go over the directions.

- Put students in pairs to talk about what they see in the big picture on page 86.

- Walk around to monitor the activity.

- Call on students to talk about the picture.

Expansion Activity:
Listening/Speaking: Confirming Information About People's Clothes

- Divide the class into two teams.

- Have each team member write a sentence about the big picture on page 86 in their books. Tell them the sentences can be right or wrong. Write an example of a correct sentence on the board (e.g., *Isabel is wearing a green dress.*). Nod your head and say, *Yes, Isabel is wearing a green dress.* Write, *Leo is wearing blue pants.* Nod your head and ask, *yes?* Then shake your head and ask, *no?* Elicit that Leo is not wearing blue pants; he's wearing brown pants.

- Give the students a few minutes to write down their sentences. Circulate to help them, reminding them that some sentences should be wrong. If necessary, provide more examples: *Maria is wearing a blue dress.*

- Have the teams line up facing each other. They can check the transparency on the OHP if needed. Student 1 from Team A will read his or her sentence. Student 1 from Team B must say *yes* or *no*. Each correct answer earns the team a point. Repeat so that each team member reads a sentence and responds.

Objective
Review of singular and plural nouns
Review of simple present

A Circle the plural nouns.
- Review the information in the chart.
- Elicit additional examples of singular and plural nouns. Elicit examples of plural nouns with the noted endings that take *-es*.
- Go over the directions and the example.
- Have students read the story and circle the plural nouns.
- Put students in pairs to compare answers.
- Elicit answers from students. Provide or elicit corrections as needed.

Answer Key chairs, dresses, coats, watches, rooms, bedrooms, bathrooms

B Complete.
- Review the information in the chart.
- Read the sentences and have the students repeat. Listen for the final *-s* for *he/she/it*.
- Go over the directions and the example.
- Have students write the correct form of the verbs on the lines.
- Put students in pairs to compare answers.
- Go over the answers with the class.

Answer Key 1. read; 2. works; 3. play; 4. eats; 5. cook; 6. talks; 7. need; 8. sleep; 9. speak; 10. lives

C Match.
- Go over the example.
- Have students write the letters on the line that matches the answers with the questions.
- Put students in pairs to read their sentences aloud.
- Elicit answers from the class.

Answer Key 1. c; 2. e; 3. d; 4. a; 5. f; 6. b

D Read.
- Go over the directions and read the sentences about Maria.
- Have students review the checkout page.
- Ask comprehension questions: *Who is buying a sweater and shirts? Is she shopping in a store? How much is the total? How many shirts is Maria buying?*

E Check *Yes* or *No*.
- Have students check *yes* or *no* for each sentence.
- Call on students to provide answers. Provide or elicit corrections as needed.

Answer Key 1. Yes; 2. Yes; 3. No; 4. No; 5. Yes

Our Cultures
Homes

A **Circle the types of houses.
Underline the countries.**

- Tell students that this culture topic is *homes*.

- Read each photo caption and have students repeat.

- Read each photo caption in random order and have students point to the correct picture.

- Ask students about their countries, e.g., *What kind of home do you have in Mexico?*

- Put students in pairs to talk about the homes they have in their countries.

Answer Key Left to right, top to bottom:

Circle *pole house,* underline *Myanmar*; circle *adobe,* underline *Morroco*; circle *apartment building,* underline *Japan*; circle *Victorian,* underline *USA*; circle *yurt,* underline *Mongolia*; circle *palazzo*; underline *Italy*

B **Think about it. Complete the chart. What is your home like?**

- Go over the examples in the chart.

- Have students add information to the chart. They can cross out what is written there if it's not true for them.

C **Talk in groups.**

- Direct students' attention to the picture and ask: *Who do you see? What is Paul's home like in his native country? What is his home like in the US?*

- Put students in small groups to talk about their homes in their countries and here. Tell them to refer to what they wrote in their chart in Activity B.

- Call on students to tell the class about their homes.

UNIT OVERVIEW

Lesson	Objective	Student Book Page
1. We need eggs.	Talking about the food you need	p. 107
2. Do we need some fish?	Asking about what food you need	p. 108
3. I'm looking for some apples.	Categorizing and asking for food in a supermarket	p. 109
4. I eat three meals a day.	Talking about breakfast, lunch, and dinner	p. 110
5. Let's have lunch.	Talking about breakfast, lunch, and dinner	p. 111
6. A tuna sandwich, please.	Ordering food in a restaurant	p. 112
7. Do you have eggs for lunch?	Asking what people have for different meals	p. 113
8. Containers	Identifying and using words for food containers	p. 114
9. A Potluck Dinner	Talking about a potluck dinner	p. 115
10. Grammar: Count Nouns	Using count nouns	p. 116
11. Grammar: Non-count Nouns	Using non-count nouns	p. 117
12. Read: Supermarket Coupons	Reading supermarket coupons	p. 118
13. Write: A Shopping List	Writing a shopping list	p. 119
What do you know?	Review and assessment	p. 120

Big Picture Expansion Activities

Focus	Activity	Suggested Use
Reading	Grouping Food Words	Lesson 3
Grammar	At the Store	Lesson 11
Writing/ Vocabulary	Letter Lists	Lesson 8
Listening/ Speaking	What else does he need?	Lesson 13
Vocabulary	Sort by color and section.	What do you know?

Worksheets

Worksheet #/ Focus	Title	Teacher's Edition Page
25. Grammar	At the Store	p. 351
26. Speaking/ Writing	Class Party	p. 352
27. Listening/ Speaking	What else does he need?	p. 353
28. Vocabulary/ Reading	Color and Section	p. 354

Unit Opener

- Put the transparency for Unit 7 on the overhead projector (OHP) or have students look at the big picture on page 106. Ask: *Where is Carlos? Where are the people?*

- Point to each word as you ask the question at the bottom of the page: *What food do you see?*

- Elicit the words the students know and write them on the board.

Objective
Talking about the food you need

Literacy Workbook pages 104–109
Workbook page 74

Vocabulary

apples	carrots	milk
bananas	eggs	potatoes
beef	ice cream	rice

  A CD 3, TRACK 2 **Listen.**

- Have students look at the pictures and listen while you play the first part of the audio or read the sentences in the listening script.

- Play the rest of the audio or read the list of words. Have students listen and repeat.

- Play or read the list of words again. Have students repeat the words as you point to the pictures.

- Call on students. Read one of the words and have students repeat.

- Have students work in pairs and take turns reading the words in random order as their partner points to the picture.

Listening Script

A. LISTEN.

1. Eggs. We need some eggs.
2. Ice cream. We need some ice cream.
3. Carrots. We need some carrots.
4. Apples. We need some apples.
5. Potatoes. We need some potatoes.
6. Milk. We need some milk.
7. Rice. We need some rice.
8. Beef. We need some beef.
9. Bananas. We need some bananas.

LISTEN AND REPEAT.

1. eggs
2. ice cream
3. carrots
4. apples
5. potatoes
6. milk
7. rice
8. beef
9. bananas

Expansion Activity: Chart it.

- Write two headings on the board: *Words ending in* s and *Words without* s.

Words ending in s   Words without s

- Have students copy the headings on a piece of paper.

- Put students in pairs to write the nine words under the correct headings.

Extra Challenge

Write sentences.

- Play the audio for Activity A again or read the sentences from the script.

- Have advanced students write the sentences they hear.

- Put students in pairs to correct their sentences. Play the audio or read the sentences again if necessary.

 B CD 3, TRACK 3 **Listen.**

- Play the audio or read the conversation with a student volunteer as students listen.

- Play the audio or read the conversation again and have students repeat.

- Put students in pairs. Designate one partner to be Carlos and the other to be Antonio.

- Have students practice the conversation in pairs, then switch roles and/or partners.

Expansion Activity: **Spell it!**

- Give students a minute to study the words in Activity A.

- Call on a student, toss a beanbag or small ball, and say a word (e.g., *eggs*). Elicit how the word is spelled.

    eggs   **e-g-g-s**

- Continue until everyone has had a chance to participate.

- As a variation, have students toss the beanbag to a classmate.

- If you have the room in your classroom, you may want to have students stand in a circle for this activity. Otherwise, make sure students are paying attention if classmates are tossing the beanbag.

Literacy Development Activity: **Spell it!**

- For students with low literacy skills, allow students to look at the words as they spell them.

C **Talk with 5 classmates.**

- Go over the words in the box.

- Model the activity with a more advanced student.

- Divide students into groups of five and have them practice the conversation with different vocabulary words. Point out that they can also use words from Activity A.

Expansion Activity: **Mingle.**

- Write each word from Activity A on a separate index card. Make enough so that each student will get a word.

- Distribute the cards to students.

- Model the activity with a more advanced student. Hold up a card so students can see (*apples*). Have the student choose a card (*eggs*). Say *We need some apples.* and elicit *That's right. We need some eggs, too.* Then switch roles.

- Have students stand and walk around the room, practicing the conversation with the word on their cards.

Objective

Asking about what food you need

Vocabulary

beans	cheese	oranges
bread	chicken	pasta
butter	fish	
cake	lettuce	

**Literacy Workbook pages 104–109
Workbook page 75**

  A CD 3, TRACK 4 **Listen.**

- Have students look at the pictures and listen while you play the first part of the audio or read the sentences in the script below.

- Play the rest of the audio or read the list of words. Ask the students to repeat each word and point to it in their book.

- Play the audio again and have students repeat the list of words. Then have students work in pairs and take turns reading the word as their partner points to the word.

CULTURE Note

- Some cultures may not use butter. Point out that butter is made from milk, whereas margarine is made from vegetable oil. People often use butter in the United States while people in other cultures might use an oil such as olive oil.

······· **Listening Script**

A. LISTEN.

1. Cake. Do we need some cake?
2. Bread. Do we need some bread?
3. Fish. Do we need some fish?
4. Chicken. Do we need some chicken?
5. Lettuce. Do we need some lettuce?
6. Oranges. Do we need some oranges?
7. Butter. Do we need some butter?
8. Cheese. Do we need some cheese?
9. Pasta. Do we need some pasta?
10. Beans. Do we need some beans?

LISTEN AND REPEAT.

1. cake
2. bread
3. fish
4. chicken
5. lettuce
6. oranges
7. butter
8. cheese
9. pasta
10. beans

Literacy Development Activity: Noticing Blends and Digraphs

- Make sure students' books are closed. Write the first letter of each word from Activity A on the board followed by the appropriate number of blank lines to indicate each letter. If the word begins with a blend (*br*) or a digraph (*ch*), write both letters on the board.

- Have students write the words in their notebooks.
- Call volunteers to the front of the room to complete the words.
- Read each word, emphasizing the beginning sound.

Extra Challenge

Alphabetize.

- Have more advanced students write the food words from Lessons 1 and 2 in alphabetical order.
- Put students in pairs to compare lists.
- Go over the answers with the class.

Answer Key   apples, bananas, beans, beef, bread, butter, cake, carrots, cheese, chicken, eggs, fish, ice cream, lettuce, milk, oranges, pasta, potatoes, rice

  B   CD 3, TRACK 5   **Listen.**

- Play the audio or read the conversation with a student volunteer as students listen.
- Play the audio or read the conversation again and have students repeat.
- Put students in pairs. Designate one partner to be Grace and the other to be Ben.
- Have students practice the conversation in pairs, then switch roles.

Expansion Activity: **Draw It!**

- Divide the class into two teams.
- Call an "artist" to the board from each team.
- Whisper the same food word from Lesson 1 or 2 to each artist.
- Have the artists draw a picture of the food on the board and elicit guesses from the class. The first team to guess the word earns a point.
- Continue with other artists and other words.

C   **Talk with 5 classmates.**

- Go over the words in the box.
- Model the activity with a more advanced student. Ask: *Do we need some milk?* Elicit the appropriate response (*Yes, we do.*). Point out that students can decide if they need the food item or not.
- Have students walk around the room to practice the conversation with five classmates. Encourage students to ask about different things.

Objective

Categorizing and asking for food in a supermarket

Vocabulary

aisle	fruits	produce
bakery	meat	vegetables
dairy		

Literacy Workbook pages 104–109
Workbook page 75

  A CD 3, TRACK 6 **Listen.**

- Have students look at the picture. Ask:

  Who do you see? Where is she?

- Play the audio or read the conversation. Make sure students understand what an *aisle* is; point to one in the picture or ask a student to do so.

- Play the audio or read the conversation again and have students repeat.

GRAMMAR Note

- Students will learn more about count and non-count nouns in Lessons 10 and 11. Point out that if the word ends in an *s*, they should use *are*, and if not, they should use *is*.

Literacy Development Activity: Concentration

- Have students copy the food words from Lessons 1 and 2 on index cards (one word per card).

- Bring in magazine photos or circulars. Have students cut out pictures of the food words and tape or glue them to another set of index cards. Prepare enough sets so every

pair of students has a set of word cards and a matching set of picture cards.

- Put students in pairs.

- Have students shuffle the cards and turn them face down.

- Have students take turns trying to find a match between a word and a picture. They can only turn over two cards on each turn. If they don't find a match, they should turn the cards face down again.

  B CD 3, TRACK 7 **Listen and complete the chart.**

- Have students look at the picture in Activity A. Go over the chart with them, making sure they understand each aisle category.

- Play the audio and stop after Item 1, or read the first sentence in the listening script. Ask: *Where are the apples?* Elicit that apples are in aisle 1 and point to the checkmark.

- Play the rest of the audio or read the rest of the sentences and have students check what they hear.

- Put students in pairs to compare answers.

- Call on different students to provide answers.

Listening Script

B. LISTEN AND COMPLETE THE CHART.

1. Apples are in aisle 1.
2. Beef is in aisle 2.
3. Chicken is in aisle 2.
4. Cheese is in aisle 4.
5. Cake is in aisle 3.
6. Milk is in aisle 4.
7. Lettuce is in aisle 1.

Answer Key

Food	Aisle 1 Fruits/ Vegetables	Aisle 2 Meat	Aisle 3 Bakery	Aisle 4 Dairy
1. apples	✓			
2. beef		✓		
3. chicken		✓		
4. cheese				✓
5. cake			✓	
6. milk				✓
7. lettuce	✓			

Expansion Activity: Scribe

• Write the headings of the chart from Activity B on the board.

• Elicit other food items from the students and write them on the board.

• Have a student come to the board. Read each item and elicit the aisle/section. Have the student check the appropriate column.

C **Talk with a partner. Use the chart in Activity B.**

• Model the activity with a more advanced student. Say what you are looking for using the list of food in Activity B and elicit the correct aisle.

• Put students in pairs to practice talking about food and locations in the store.

• Call on students, name a food you are looking for, and elicit the correct aisle.

BIG PICTURE

Expansion Activity: Reading: Grouping Food Words

Before class: Bring to class pictures of foods from magazines or store circulars, or plastic food realia. Also make paper signs for each section in a store (dairy, produce, meat, and bakery).

1. Put the transparency for Unit 7 on the OHP or have students look at the big picture on page 106 in their books. Ask students what the picture shows. Elicit that it is a *grocery store* or *supermarket,* a place to buy food.

2. Point to each of the section headings (the signs in the store). As you point, say the name (e.g., *bakery*). Have the students repeat. Point to the words again in random order and have students read the names.

3. Tell students that most food is found in a particular section of the grocery store and point to the names of the sections again. Write on the board *Bananas are in the produce section.* Underline _the produce section_. Point to the bananas and the produce sign and repeat the sentence.

4. Tape the section headings on the wall in different parts of the room. Give each student a food picture or realia. Have them stand up and go to the appropriate section.

5. After students have grouped themselves, have them show their foods.

Option: Mix up the pictures/realia and redistribute. Have students repeat the activity.

Objective
Talking about breakfast, lunch, and dinner

Vocabulary

breakfast	dinner	meal
cereal	lunch	

**Literacy Workbook pages 104–109
Workbook page 76**

  A CD 3, TRACK 8 **Listen.**

• Direct students' attention to the pictures and ask *What do you see?* Elicit the foods in each picture. Make sure students understand what *meal* means.

• Have students look at the pictures and listen while you play the first part of the audio or read the sentences in the listening script.

• Play the rest of the audio or read the list of words. Ask the students to repeat.

• Play the audio or read the list again and have students repeat, focusing on pronunciation.

········ **Listening Script**

A. LISTEN.

1. Breakfast. At 7:00, I eat breakfast.
2. Lunch. At 12:30, I eat lunch.
3. Dinner. At 6:45, I eat dinner.

LISTEN AND REPEAT.

1. breakfast
2. lunch
3. dinner

Expansion Activity: Dictation

• Play the first part of the audio again and have students write the sentences.

• Put students in pairs to compare sentences.

• Have volunteers write them on the board.

Answer Key   **1.** At 7:00, I eat breakfast.; **2.** At 12:30, I eat lunch.; **3.** At 6:45, I eat dinner.

Expansion Activity: What time?

• Model the activity. Say, *Breakfast. I eat breakfast at 6:30*.

• Call on a student and say *Breakfast*. Elicit a sentence (*I eat breakfast at _____*.).

• Continue calling on students and prompting them with the name of a meal.

• As a variation, record answers on a chart, on the board, or OHP.

  B CD 3, TRACK 9 **Listen.**

• Have students look at the chart. Make sure students know what *cereal* is. Point out the box. Elicit what Ben eats for breakfast each day.

• Play the audio and have students read the conversation silently.

• Put students in pairs to practice the conversation.

GRAMMAR Note

• Make sure students understand the difference between *usually* and *sometimes*. Point out that *usually* is about 80 percent of the time, whereas *sometimes* is less than half the time.

C Talk with 5 classmates.

• Model the activity with a more advanced student. Have the student ask the question. Cue the student to substitute a meal word. Respond with what you usually and sometimes eat. Switch roles or call on another student and model the activity again, playing the other role.

• Have students talk to five classmates, asking and answering the question.

• Call on students to say what one classmate usually eats.

Objective
Talking about breakfast, lunch, and dinner

Vocabulary

hamburger	soup	taco
hungry	sushi	tomatoes
sandwich		

**Literacy Workbook pages 104–109
Workbook page 76**

 A CD 3, TRACK 10 **Listen.**

- Have students look at the pictures as you play the audio or read the conversation.

- Play the audio or read the conversation again and have students repeat.

- Have students practice the conversation in pairs, playing both roles.

VOCABULARY Note

- Write the new words from the conversation and the box on the board (*hamburger, sandwich, soup, sushi, taco, tomatoes*).

> hamburger, sandwich, soup,
> sushi, taco, tomatoes.

- Go over the meanings.

B **Talk with 3 classmates.**

- Copy the conversation on the board or on a transparency. Elicit that a time goes in the first slot, a meal in the second, and two foods in the third and fourth.

- Model the activity with a more advanced student.

- Put students in pairs to practice the conversation.

- Call on pairs to read their conversations.

Expansion Activity:
Inside/Outside Circles

- Divide the class in half. Have one group form a circle facing out. Have the second group form an outside circle facing in. Each student should be facing a classmate.

- Have students on the inside circle say A's lines and the students on the outside circle say B's lines, providing the missing information.

- After 30 seconds, cue the outside circle to move one place to the right (to face a new classmate). Have students repeat the conversation, substituting new information if they want.

- After 20-30 seconds switch again. Repeat several more times, making sure to keep the activity fast-paced. Students should be able to say the conversation much more fluently by the end.

C   **Complete. Read to your group.**

- Go over the example.

- Have students complete the sentences.

- Put students in pairs or small groups to read their sentences aloud.

- Call on students to read their sentences to the class.

Expansion Activity: Lineups

- Say *breakfast* and have students line up in order of the time at which they eat breakfast. Make sure the earliest times are on one side of the room and the latest are on the other.

- Start with the earliest time and have people say, *I usually eat breakfast at ____.* and complete the sentence. Continue down the line.

- Repeat with the other two meals.

My Life

- Go over the directions and the example.

- Have students complete the chart.

- Put students in groups to talk about their charts. Circulate and help with unfamiliar vocabulary as needed.

- Call on students to tell the class what they usually eat for each meal.

Objective
Ordering food in a restaurant

Vocabulary

coffee	soda
drink	tea
pizza	tuna sandwich

Literacy Workbook pages 104–109
Workbook page 77

 A CD 3, TRACK 11 **Listen.**

- Direct students' attention to the picture at the top of the page. Ask: *What do you see? Where is Paul?*

- Play the audio or read the conversation as students follow along silently.

- Play the audio or read the conversation again and have students repeat.

- Put students in pairs to practice the conversation. Have students switch roles.

B **Ask 4 classmates.**

- Go over the words in the box.

- Model the activity with a more advanced student. Have the student read A's lines and demonstrate how to make substitutions with the words from the box.

- Divide the class into groups and have students practice the conversation with their group members.

Expansion Activity: **Role-Play**

- Role-play a restaurant situation in the same groups of five students as in Activity B.

- Have students take turns playing the waiter and writing down the group's orders.

C **Circle what's in the sandwich.**

- Direct students' attention to the picture. Ask: *Is there bread in the sandwich?* Point out that *bread* is circled.

- Have students look at the picture and circle the words.

- Put students in pairs to compare answers.

- Go over the answers with the class.

Answer Key bread; cheese; lettuce; tomatoes

CULTURE Note

- We usually identify the type of sandwich by the meat or protein source. So, this would be a cheese sandwich, rather than a lettuce sandwich.

Expansion Activity:
What's like a sandwich?

- Explain that a sandwich is usually made with two pieces of bread and some kind of filling.

- Put students in groups to talk about what food is like a sandwich in their culture.

- Call on students to explain their culture's "sandwich" to the class.

Objective
Asking what people have for different meals

Literacy Workbook pages 104–109
Workbook page 78

  A   **CD 3, TRACK 12**   **Listen.**

- Direct students' attention to the pictures.

- Have students listen and follow along in the book as you play the audio or read the conversation.

- Play the audio or read the conversation a second time and have students repeat.

- Put students in groups of three to practice the conversation. Tell them to switch roles twice.

- Call on a volunteer group to read their conversation to the class.

B   **Talk with 6 classmates.**

- Go over the words in the box.

- Go over the four possible responses.

- Model the activity with a more advanced student. Ask a question (*Do you have pasta for breakfast?*) and elicit an appropriate response.

- Have students stand and walk around the class to practice the conversation with six classmates. Remind students to play both roles.

- Call on students to tell the class about a classmate's answer.

Expansion Activity: Frequency Lineup

- Have students stand. Point to one side of the room and say *always*. Point to the other side of the room and say, *No, I don't*. Point to places in between to indicate *usually* and *sometimes*. Write the words on signs and post if necessary.

- Make sure students understand that *No, I don't* means zero times.

- Ask questions (e.g., *Do you have eggs for lunch? Do you have cereal for dinner? Do you have rice for breakfast?*) and have students move to stand in the appropriate place to indicate their answer.

C   **Write 3 questions.**

- Have students write three questions about foods for different meals. Encourage students to use the words in the box or other words that they know for food. Point out the multiple write-on lines in Items 2 and 3.

- Put students in pairs to ask and answer their questions.

- Call on students to ask a classmate a question.

My Life

- Review the meanings of *always* and *sometimes*.

- Model the activity. Write three sentences on the board about your eating habits following the models.

- Have students complete the sentences.

- Put students in groups to read their sentences aloud.

Objective
Identifying and using words for food containers

Vocabulary/Numeracy

a bag	a can	container
a bottle	a carton	a jar
a box		

Literacy Workbook pages 104–109
Workbook page 79

  A CD 3, TRACK 13 **Listen.**

- Elicit or explain what a *container* is.

- Have students look at the containers as you play the first part of the audio or read the sentences in the script below.

- Play the rest of the audio or read the list of words and have students repeat.

- Read the names of the containers in random order and have students point.

- Put students in pairs to take turns reading the names of the containers as their partner points to the picture.

········· **Listening Script**

A. LISTEN.

1. A bottle. This is a bottle of oil.
2. A can. This is a can of tomato soup.
3. A bag. This is a bag of rice.
4. A box. This is a box of cereal.
5. A carton. This is a carton of milk.
6. A jar. This is a jar of peanut butter.

LISTEN AND REPEAT.

1. a bottle	4. a box
2. a can	5. a carton
3. a bag	6. a jar

Extra Challenge
A bottle of what?

- Play the audio from Activity A or read the sentences from the script again. Have students write the container and the food (*a bottle of oil*).

- Put students in pairs to take turns saying the kind of container and responding with the food, or saying the food and responding with the container.

  B CD 3, TRACK 14 **Listen and circle.**

- Play the audio and stop after the first item or read the first sentence in the listening script and elicit the name of the container. Point out that *a box* is circled.

- Play the rest of the audio or read the rest of the sentences and have students circle the container they hear.

- Put students in pairs to compare answers.

- Go over the answers with the class.

······ **Listening Script**

B. LISTEN AND CIRCLE.

1. I need a box of cereal.
2. We need a bag of rice.
3. Do we need a can of soup?
4. They need a carton of milk.
5. She needs a jar of peanut butter.
6. Paul needs a bottle of oil.

Answer Key **1.** a box; **2.** a bag; **3.** a can; **4.** a carton; **5.** a jar; **6.** a bottle

Literacy Development Activity: Realia

- Bring in one example of each type of container.

- Cut out pictures of each type of food from this unit.

- Call on a student and show the picture of the food as you say its name.

- Have the student come to the front of the room, say the food, and choose the container they buy it in. Cue the student to say, *I buy _____ in a _____.*

- Continue the activity with other students and foods.

C **Look at the picture. Complete the shopping list.**

- Direct students' attention to the picture and ask: *What is in the shopping cart?*

- Have students complete the shopping list.

- Put students in pairs to compare lists.

- Go over the answers with the class. If there are any incorrect answers, elicit the correct answer.

Answer Key a box of cereal, a bottle of apple juice, a carton of milk, a bag of potatoes, two cans of tuna fish, a jar of tomatoes, a box of pasta

Expansion Activity: **Personalize.**

- Have students put a checkmark next to the things on the list they always buy.

- Have students add three things to the list.

- Put students in pairs to talk about which of the items on the list they buy.

BIG PICTURE **Expansion Activity: Writing/Vocabulary: Letter Lists**

- Put the transparency for Unit 7 on the OHP or have students look at the big picture on page 106 in their books.

- Put students in pairs or small groups.

- Give students five minutes to list as many nouns as they see in the picture.

- After five minutes, ask how many words each group has on the list.

- Elicit ideas and write them on the board.

- As a variation, add foods to the list that students have learned but are not in the picture, e.g, *hamburgers*.

- For extra practice, have students alphabetize their lists.

Objective
Talking about a potluck dinner

**Literacy Workbook pages 104–109
Workbook page 80**

  A CD 3, TRACK 15 **Listen and read.**

- Direct students' attention to the picture. Ask questions: *Who do you see? What are they doing?*

- Play the audio or read the story as students follow along silently.

- Ask comprehension questions: *What is a potluck dinner? What does Sandy bring? What do the students bring? What does Carlos bring?*

- Put students in pairs to read the story aloud.

CULTURE Notes

- Explain or elicit that potluck dinners are meals that everyone brings something to. They are popular in the United States. Churches, schools, and clubs often have potluck dinners.

- Ask students if there is something like a potluck in their cultures.

Expansion Activity: Story Strips

- Photocopy the sentences from the story and cut them into strips. Mix the strips up.

- Give each pair of students a set of strips and have them recreate the story.

- Call on students to read the sentences in order.

- As a variation, put students in groups of eight. Give each student a strip.

- Have students memorize their strips and then line up in order of the sentences in the story to recite the story.

B Check *True* or *False*.

- Read each sentence aloud and have students repeat.

- Read the first sentence and elicit if it is true or false. Point out that *True* is checked.

- Have students check *True* or *False* for each sentence.

- Put students in pairs to compare answers.

- Go over the answers with the class.

Answer Key 1. True; 2. False;
3. False; 4. True; 5. True; 6. True

Expansion Activity: **Make it true.**

- Have students rewrite the false statements to make them true.

- Have students write their new sentences on the board.

Answer Key

2. Sandy brings coffee, milk, and tea to the potluck dinners.
3. The students bring different foods (Carlos brings dessert.).

Literacy Development Activity: Key Words

- Write each sentence from Activity B on the board. Make sure to leave space between each word so word breaks are easily identified.

- Write the key words or phrases in a different color (1. *once a month*; 2. *soda*; 3. *desserts*; 4. *cake*; 5. *their countries*; 6. *lunches*).

- Read each word and point to it. When you read each key word or phrase, elicit if it is true or false. If students say *false,* elicit the correct word. Write the correct word in place of the original.

- Have students copy the sentences in their notebooks.

Expansion Activity: Character Cards

- Give each student a character card. Have the students find out about foods from that character's country. Students can ask other students or instructors for ideas.

- Have students choose one food that character might bring to a potluck dinner.

- Put students in small groups to tell their classmates about the food.

C Write about you.

- Read the sentence aloud.

- Model the activity. Write what you bring on the board.

- Have students write what they bring.

- Put students in pairs to talk about their ideas.

- Call on students to share their ideas with the class.

- As a variation, organize a potluck with your class, if possible.

Objective
Using count nouns

Literacy Workbook pages 104–109
Workbook page 81

  A CD 3, TRACK 16 **Listen.**

- Have students look at the pictures. Ask: *What do you see? How many do you see?*

- Have students listen and read the chart as you play the audio or read the words and phrases.

- Play the audio or read the words and phrases again and have students repeat.

GRAMMAR Notes

- Point out that count nouns can be counted, and so can be singular or plural. Give an example, e.g., *one egg, two eggs*. Elicit other examples.

- Point out that we add *-es* to plural nouns that end in *s, x, ch, sh,* and *z*. Elicit or provide examples, e.g., *sandwiches, boxes,* etc.

  B CD 3, TRACK 17 **Listen and circle.**

- Go over the yellow note. Provide some examples.

- Play the audio for the first sentence or read the first sentence from the listening script. Elicit that *orange* is correct. Point out that *orange* is circled.

- Play the rest of the audio or read the rest of the sentences and have students circle the words they hear.

- Put students in pairs to compare answers.

- Call on volunteers to give the answers to the class. Elicit or provide corrections as needed.

Listening Script

B. LISTEN AND CIRCLE.

1. Grace has an orange.
2. Please get a bag of potatoes.
3. I need six bananas.
4. There are two desserts for lunch today.
5. Paul has two boxes of cereal.
6. Leo always has an apple for breakfast.
7. Do you want some cherry pie?
8. Maria makes three lunches for her children.

Answer Key **1.** orange; **2.** potatoes; **3.** bananas; **4.** desserts; **5.** boxes; **6.** apple; **7.** pie; **8.** lunches

Literacy Development Activity: Say and point.

- Put students in pairs to take turns saying one of the words from an item in Activity B as their partner points to the word.

- As a variation or for spelling practice, have students spell the word.

Extra Challenge

Dictation

- Play the audio from Activity B or read the sentences again and have students write the sentences they hear. Play the audio as many times as necessary, or see the option below.

- Put students in pairs to compare answers.

- Have students write the sentences on the board.

- As a variation, play the sentences just two times.

- Have students work in groups to decide on the correct sentence.

- Have representatives from each group write their sentences on the board. Elicit the correct version from the class.

Answer Key 1. egg; 2. boxes; 3. bananas; 4. lunch; 5. oranges; 6. carton

Expansion Activity: Rewrite it another way.

- Put students in pairs.

- Have students rewrite the sentences to make the other completion correct. For example, Sentence 1 could be *These are eggs.* or *This is a carton of eggs.*

- Have volunteers write sentences on the board. Provide or elicit corrections as needed.

Answer Key Same as audioscript for Activity B.

C   Circle.

- Read the first sentence and elicit the correct answer (*egg*). Point out that *egg* is circled.

- Elicit the clues for singular or plural (*a* or *an* for singular; *some,* other numbers, *a bag of,* for plurals).

- Have students circle the correct words.

- Put students in pairs to compare answers.

- Go over the answers with the class.

Objective
Using non-count nouns

Literacy Workbook pages 104–109
Workbook page 81

  A CD 3, TRACK 18 **Listen and read.**

- Have students look at the chart. Point out the title. Ask: *What do you see?*

- Play the audio or read the sentences as students look at the chart.

- Play the audio or read the sentences again and have students repeat.

GRAMMAR Note

- Read the yellow note. Point out that while count nouns can be singular or plural, non-count nouns cannot be counted and so are *always* singular in form, e.g., *milk, rice.* Singular count nouns require an article, e.g., *an egg, a potato,* while non-count nouns do not have an article, e.g., *milk, bread.*

B **Read and check.**

- Go over the example.

- Have students check *count* or *non-count* for the bold-faced noun in each sentence.

- Put students in pairs to compare answers.

- Go over the answers with the class.

Answer Key **1.** non-count; **2.** count;
3. non-count; **4.** non-count; **5.** non-count;
6. count

C **Check. Write the plural for count nouns.**

- Go over the directions and the example.

- Have students check count or non-count and then make the count nouns plural.

- Put students in pairs to compare answers.

- Elicit answers from the class. Point out that some nouns can be both count and non-count. Read the example of *lunch* as a non-count noun from the answer key below.

Answer Key

Noun	Count	Non-count
box	✔ boxes	
coffee		✔
lunch	✔ lunches	✔
oil		✔
pasta		✔

Expansion Activity: Team Challenge

- Divide the class into two teams. Alternate calling on a member of each team and saying a food noun. Elicit a sentence from the team member using the food noun correctly.

- Each correct sentence earns the team a point.

- Continue the activity until everyone has had a chance to participate.

Expansion Activity:
Grammar: At the Store

- Photocopy and distribute Worksheet 25: *At the Store* (Teacher's Edition page 351).

- Put the transparency for Unit 7 on the OHP or have students look at page 106 in their books.

- Go over the directions.

- Have students complete the worksheet.

- Put students in pairs to compare answers.

- Go over the answers with the class.

Answer Key 1. cheese; 2. cartons; 3. eggs; 4. cakes, bread; 5. chicken, fish, beef; 6. apples; 7. bananas; 8. oranges and carrots; 9. lettuce

Objective

Reading supermarket coupons

Vocabulary

coupon

Literacy Workbook pages 104–109
Workbook page 82

  A CD 3, TRACK 19 **Listen and read.**

- Direct students' attention to the pictures and ask: *What do you see?*

- Have students listen and read along silently as you play the audio or read the sentences.

- Play the audio or read the sentences again and have students repeat.

- Ask comprehension questions: *Why does Maria use coupons? How much is the coupon for the cereal? How many cents off are the beans?*

- Put students in pairs to read the information aloud.

B **Write.**

- Have students write the answers.

- Put students in pairs to compare answers.

- Go over the answers with the class.

Answer Key

Cereal	Apple Juice	Beans
Price: $4.29	Price: $.99	Price: $2.50
Coupon: $1.00	Coupon: $.50	Coupon: $.40
Cost: $3.29	Cost: $.49	Cost: $2.10

Objective
Writing a shopping list

**Literacy Workbook pages 104–109
Workbook page 83**

A CD 3, TRACK 20 **Listen and read.**

- Direct students' attention to the picture. Ask questions: *Who do you see? What is he doing? What does he need at the store?*

- Have students follow along silently as you play the audio or read the sentences.

B **Write a shopping list for a dinner party.**

- Brainstorm foods students want to have at a party. Write ideas on the board.

- Have students write shopping lists for the food they want.

- Put students in groups to share their ideas.

- Call on students to tell the class what is on their lists.

Expansion Activity: Class Party

- Photocopy and distribute Worksheet 26: *Class Party* (Teacher's Edition page 352).

- Put students in groups of four. Tell them that they should plan a party for the class.

- If possible, bring in supermarket circulars for students to get prices for their items. If not, have students estimate the prices of their items and write them on the list.

- Have students write checks for their total amounts.

BIG PICTURE

Expansion Activity:
Listening/Speaking: What else does he need?

- Photocopy and distribute Worksheet 27: *What else does he need*? (Teacher's Edition page 353).

- Put the transparency for Unit 7 on the OHP or have students look at the big picture on page 106 in their books.

- Go over the directions.

- Read the script below and have students check each item that they hear.

Script:
Carlos is shopping at the store. Ice cream is his favorite dessert. He needs three cartons of ice cream. Carlos also needs some fish and beef for dinners this week. He needs carrots and tomatoes. He also needs eggs for breakfast. For lunch, Carlos eats a sandwich and fruit. He needs bread for his sandwiches and apples and bananas. He drinks milk with every meal.

- Put students in pairs to compare answers. Read the script again if necessary. Have students work together to list the things Carlos needs that aren't in the shopping cart.

- Go over the answers with the class.

Answer Key
A. Check: apples, bananas, beef, bread, carrots, eggs, fish, ice cream, milk, tomatoes **B. List:** apples, bananas, beef, tomatoes

Objective
Review and assessment

 A CD 3, TRACK 21 **Listen and fill in the answer sheet.**

- Go over the directions.
- Point to each word and elicit what it is.
- Point out that students will fill in the answer sheet to the right of the activity.
- Play the audio or read the sentences in the listening script as students fill in the bubbles. Play it again if students need to complete the activity.
- Put students in pairs to compare answers.
- Play the audio or read the sentences again and have students check their answers.
- Elicit the answers and write them on the board.

······ **Listening Script**

A. LISTEN AND FILL IN THE ANSWER SHEET.

1. I need to buy chicken.
2. I need milk for breakfast.
3. I need apples for lunch.
4. I need oranges, too.
5. I need cheese.

Answer Key **1.** A; **2.** B; **3.** A; **4.** A; **5.** B

 B CD 3, TRACK 22 **Listen and fill in the answer sheet.**

- Go over the directions.
- Play the audio and stop after the first sentence or read the first sentence.
- Have students look at each pair of answers.
- Continue to play the audio or read the sentences as students mark the answers.
- Play it again if students need more time to complete the activity.
- Put students in pairs to compare answers.
- Play the audio or read the sentences again and have students check their answers.
- Elicit the answers and write them on the board.

······ **Listening Script**

B. LISTEN AND FILL IN THE ANSWER SHEET.

1. Let's have hamburgers.
2. Do we need fish?
3. What about you?
4. Excuse me.
5. Anything to drink today?
6. Do we need two boxes of cereal?

Answer Key **1.** B; **2.** B; **3.** A; **4.** A; **5.** B; **6.** A

C Ask 5 classmates.

- Go over the conversation and the example.

- Model the activity. Ask a student: *What is your favorite food?* Elicit the answer (e.g., *pizza*).

> **Teacher: What is your favorite food?**
>
> **Student: Pizza**

- Have students talk to their classmates to complete the chart.

- Call on students to tell the class about someone's favorite food.

D Look at the picture. Tell a partner what food you need.

- Direct students' attention to the picture. Ask questions: *Do you need sugar? Do you need tea?*

- Go over the example. Point out that there is very little sugar in the container, so you say, *I need sugar.*

- Put students in pairs to take turns saying what they need. Remind students to use the picture.

- Call on students to say what they need.

> **Answer Key** I need: sugar, tea, bread, oil

E Learning Log

- Go over the directions.

- Have students check the words they know.

- Put students in pairs to compare lists and review the words.

- Elicit words that students do not know and review their meanings.

- Have students write words they don't remember in a vocabulary notebook.

- Encourage students to write sentences using the difficult words and review the sentences for accuracy.

LOOKING BACK

- Go over the directions.

- Put students in pairs to talk about the big picture on page 106.

- Walk around to monitor the activity.

- Call on students to talk about the picture. Encourage them to use the grammar and vocabulary from the unit.

Expansion Activity:
Vocabulary: Color and Section.

Before class: Make copies of Worksheet 28: *Color and Section* (Teacher's Edition page 354).

- This first part of the activity is a warm-up showing how to sort by particular categories.

	Young (under 30)	Not Young (over 30)
Tall		
Short		

  Draw a four square chart on the board like the one above.

- Point to the upper left square (*tall* and *young*). Ask students to raise their hands if they are tall. Make sure all the tall students have their hands raised. Ask them to put hands down if they are over 30 years old. Write the names of the students who are both tall and young in the square. If you have a large class, just write examples.

- Repeat with the other three squares. Make sure students understand that they are looking at two qualities at the same time (age and height).

- Pass out Worksheet 28. Put the Unit 7 transparency on the OHP or have students look at the big picture on page 106 in their books. Tell students to refer to it as they complete the worksheet.

- Go over the worksheet directions. Tell students to write the foods in the list in the correct squares. Point out that in the example, *cheese* is both *yellow* and found in the *dairy* section, so it is written in the top left square.

- Have students check their answers with a partner.

- For added challenge, have students create another chart with categories of their choice, such as healthy/not healthy, dairy, and bakery.

Answer Key

	Yellow	Not yellow
Dairy	butter cheese	milk eggs
Produce	bananas	apples oranges carrots

UNIT OVERVIEW

Lesson	Objective	Student Book Page
1. It's raining.	Talking about the weather	p. 123
2. It's hot!	Identifying different kinds of weather	p. 124
3. What season do you like?	Talking about the seasons	p. 125
4. I'm dancing.	Talking about what people are doing	p. 126
5. What's Paul doing?	Talking about what people are doing	p. 127
6. What do you like doing in the spring?	Talking about what you like to do in different seasons	p. 128
7. It's hot and dry.	Talking and writing about the weather	p. 129
8. What's the temperature?	Talking and writing about temperatures	p. 130
9. A Weather Map	Reading a weather map	p. 131
10. Grammar: Present Continuous Tense	Understanding and using present continuous	p. 132
11. Grammar: Contractions	Using contractions with the present continuous	p. 133
12. Read: An Email	Reading emails	p. 134
13. Write: A Letter	Writing a letter	p. 135
What do you know?	Review and assessment	p. 136

Big Picture Expansion Activities

Focus	Activity	Suggested Use
Reading	Reviewing Descriptive Vocabulary	**Unit Opener**
Grammar	What are they doing?	**Lesson 10**
Writing	Two Weather Reports	**Lesson 9**
Vocabulary	Weather Opposites	**What do you know?**
Listening/ Speaking	Letter Dictation	**Lesson 13**

Worksheets

Worksheet #/ Focus	Title	Teacher's Edition Page
29. Reading	Reviewing Descriptive Vocabulary	p. 355
30. Listening/ Reading	Today's Weather	p. 356
31. Grammar	What are they doing?	p. 357
32. Listening	Letter Dictation	p. 358

Unit Opener

- Put the transparency for Unit 8 on the overhead projector (OHP) or have students look at the big picture on page 122.

- Point to each word as you ask the questions at the bottom of the page: *Where's Carlos? Where's Tien?*

- Elicit the words the students know and write them on the board.

Expansion Activity: Reading: Reviewing Descriptive Vocabulary

- **Before class:** Photocopy and cut up the sentences on Worksheet 29: *Reviewing Descriptive Vocabulary* (Teacher's Edition page 355).

- Put the Unit 8 transparency on the OHP or have students look at the big picture on page 122 in their books.

- Hold up the piece of paper that says *Tien is wearing*. Have students read it aloud. Elicit an ending to the sentence (*a purple sweater*). Hold up the piece of paper that says *a purple sweater*. Put the two pieces of paper side by side so students can see how they form a complete sentence.

- Give each student a strip. Tell them that each piece of paper has half of a sentence. Tell them to find the student that has the other half of the sentence.

- Have the students stand up and walk around reading the strips until they find a match. They should stand with their new partner.

- When all the students have found a match, have the partners read the sentences aloud. Use the original worksheet to check the matches.

- **Option:** Copy and cut up enough sentence strips so that each pair of students has a set. Mix the strips up before giving to students. Have them work in pairs to match all the sentences.

Objective
Talking about the weather

Vocabulary

cold	hot	raining
snowing	sunny	windy

Literacy Workbook pages 110–115
Workbook page 86

  A   CD 3, TRACK 24 **Listen.**

- Have students look at the pictures and listen while you play the first part of the audio or read the sentences in the listening script.

- Play the rest of the audio or read the sentences in the second part of the listening script. Pause and have the students repeat.

- Call on students. Read one of the vocabulary words and have students repeat.

- Have students work in pairs and take turns reading the words in random order as their partner points to the correct picture.

Listening Script

A. LISTEN.

1. Sunny. It's sunny.
2. Snowing. It's snowing.
3. Hot. It's hot.
4. Cold. It's cold.
5. Windy. It's windy.
6. Raining. It's raining.

LISTEN AND REPEAT.

1. It's sunny.
2. It's snowing.
3. It's hot.
4. It's cold.
5. It's windy.
6. It's raining.

GRAMMAR/VOCABULARY Note

- Students will learn about the present continuous later in the unit (Lessons 10 and 11). For now, point out that two expressions end in *-ing*, and two end in *-y*.

  B   CD 3, TRACK 25 **Listen.**

- Play the audio or read the conversation as students listen.

- Play the audio or read the conversation again and have students repeat.

- Put students in pairs. Designate one partner to be Carlos and the other to be Tien.

- Have students practice the conversation in pairs, then switch roles.

Expansion Activity: **Spell it!**

- Give students a minute to study the words from Activity A.

- Call on a student, toss a beanbag or small ball, and say a word (e.g., *sunny*). Elicit how the word is spelled. Have the student toss the ball back to you or to another student.

- Continue until everyone has had a chance to participate.

- If you have the room in your classroom, you may want to have students stand in a circle for this activity. Otherwise, make sure students are paying attention if classmates are tossing the beanbag.

Literacy Development Activity: **Spell it!**

- For literacy students, have them look at the words as they spell them.

C **Look at Activity A. Talk with 6 classmates about the pictures.**

- Review the words in Activity A.

- Model the activity with a more advanced student. Point to a picture and ask: *How's the weather?*

> **How's the weather?**
>
> **It's sunny.**

- Have students practice the conversation with six classmates either in a group or by walking around the room. Encourage students to practice with all of the words in Activity A.

Objective
Identifying different kinds of weather

Vocabulary

cold	hot	raining
snowing	sunny	windy

Literacy Workbook pages 110–115
Workbook page 86

  A CD 3, TRACK 26 **Listen and circle.**

- Point to each picture and elicit the correct sentence to describe it.

- Have students look at the pictures and listen while you play the audio for the first item or read the first sentence. Elicit the answer (*It's raining.*). Point out that the second picture is circled.

- Play the rest of the audio or read the rest of the sentences. Pause after each sentence and ask the students to repeat the word and circle the correct picture.

······ **Listening Script**

A. LISTEN AND CIRCLE.

1. It's raining.   3. It's cold.
2. It's hot.   4. It's windy.

Expansion Activity:
More Speaking Practice

- Have students work in pairs and take turns talking about the weather as their partner points to each of the pictures.

Extra Challenge
Write sentences.

- Play the audio for Activity A and have more advanced students write the sentences they hear.

- Have students check their answers by looking at Lesson 1.

Answer Key 1. It's raining. 2. It's hot.
3. It's cold. 4. It's windy.

B **Complete.**

- Point to the first picture. Elicit the sentence. Point out that *cold* is written on the line and crossed out in the word box.

- Have students complete the sentences.

- Put students in pairs to compare answers.

- Go over the answers with the class.

LITERACY Note

- Students from pre-literate cultures may have difficulty interpreting different kinds of images and seeing them as representing the same concepts. Point out that these pictures are similar to the symbols students might see in a newspaper.

Answer Key 1. cold; 2. sunny;
3. raining; 4. windy; 5. hot; 6. snowing

Objective

Talking about the seasons

Vocabulary

fall	**season**	**spring**
summer	**winter**	

**Literacy Workbook pages 110–115
Workbook page 87**

  A CD 3, TRACK 27 **Listen.**

- Have students look at the pictures. Ask: *What do you see?*
- Play the first part of the audio or read the sentences.
- Play the rest of the audio or read the words and have students repeat.

········ **Listening Script**

A. LISTEN.

1. Winter. It's winter.
2. Spring. It's spring.
3. Summer. It's summer.
4. Fall. It's fall.

LISTEN AND REPEAT.

1. winter
2. spring
3. summer
4. fall

CULTURE Notes

- Students may come from countries that don't have four seasons, just as some states do not have four dramatic seasons. Point out that in most parts of the United States there are four seasons.
- Tell students the start and end dates of each season in the United States: spring 3/21–6/20, summer 6/21–9/22, fall 9/23–12/21, winter 12/22–3/20.

Expansion Activity: **Calendar**

- Have students create a grid with three columns and four rows.
- Have students write the name of each month in one of the squares, in order from January to December.
- Create the same grid on the board. Ask students to come to the board and fill in the months.
- Using colored chalk or markers, block off the seasons on the chart. For example, all of January, February, and 3/4 of March would be in one color to represent winter (also, the end of December).
- Have students block off the seasons on their charts.

B CD 3, TRACK 28 **Listen.**

- Play the audio or read the conversation with a student as students listen.

- Play the audio or read the conversation again and have students repeat.

- Put students in pairs. Designate one partner to be Leo and the other to be Grace.

- Have students practice the conversation in pairs, then switch roles.

- If time permits, have them switch partners and practice the conversation again.

C **Talk with 4 classmates.**

- Go over the words in the box.

- Model the activity with a more advanced student. Have the student read A's questions. Respond.

> **What season do you like?**

> **Spring.**

- Have students practice the conversation with four classmates.

My Life

- Model the activity. Prompt a student to ask you what season you like. Say what season you like (e.g., *I like summer.*). Give a reason based on one of the weather words (*It's hot.*).

- Put students in small groups to answer the questions.

- Call on students to tell the class a season they like and don't like in their native country and why.

Expansion Activity:
Dates by Seasons

- Dictate ten dates to the class (e.g., *April 5th*).

- Have students write the season next to the date (e.g., *spring*).

- Put students in pairs to compare answers.

- Elicit answers from volunteers.

Objective
Talking about what people are doing

Vocabulary

cooking	reading
dancing	swimming
listening to music	walking
playing soccer	watching TV

Literacy Workbook pages 110–115
Workbook page 88

  A   CD 3, TRACK 29   **Listen.**

- Direct students' attention to the pictures and ask: *What do you see?*

- Have students look at the pictures and listen while you play the first part of the audio or read the sentences in the listening script.

- Play the rest of the audio or read the list of words. Pause and ask the students to repeat the words.

- Play or read the second part of the audio again and have students repeat.

Listening Script

A. LISTEN.

1. Walking. She's walking.
2. Playing soccer. He's playing soccer.
3. Dancing. They're dancing.
4. Reading. She's reading.
5. Swimming. He's swimming.
6. Listening to music. She's listening to music.
7. Cooking. He's cooking.
8. Watching TV. She's watching TV.

LISTEN AND REPEAT.

1. walking
2. playing soccer
3. dancing
4. reading
5. swimming
6. listening to music
7. cooking
8. watching TV

Expansion Activity: **Charades**

- Write activities on slips of paper.
- Have a volunteer come to the front of the room and choose a slip.
- Have the student act out the activity on the slip.
- Elicit the verb from the class.
- Continue until all the verbs have been used.

How's the weather? 209

 CD 3, TRACK 30 **Listen.**

- Have students look at the picture. Elicit what Leo and Nadira are doing.

- Play the audio or read the conversation with a student and have students read the conversation silently.

- Play the audio or read the conversation again and have students repeat.

- Put students in pairs to practice both roles in the conversation.

PRONUNCIATION Notes

- Students may have trouble with the *ing* sound. Point out that the *ng* sound is made with a closed back of the throat and an open mouth. The sound is not made by saying the *n* and the *g* separately.

- Point out that in relaxed speech, speakers may drop the *g* sound altogether.

C   Talk with 7 classmates.

- Go over the words and phrases in the box.

- Model the activity with a more advanced student. Have the student ask the question. Mime one of the activities in the box. Respond by saying the activity from the box that you are doing, then ask the student the second question.

- Have students talk to seven classmates, asking and answering the questions.

Expansion Activity: Beanbag Toss

- Call on a student, toss a beanbag or small ball, and mime an activity. Elicit the appropriate sentence (e.g., *You're swimming.*).

- Continue with other students and activities until everyone has had a chance to participate. Make sure students answer in a complete sentence.

- Remember, if this is hard logistically, have students stand, or eliminate the beanbag and just have students call on classmates.

Literacy Development Activity: Flashcards

- Have students create flashcards for the new vocabulary in this lesson. They should write a phrase on one side of each card, and draw a picture on the other side. If students are having difficulty with fine motor skills, photocopy the pictures from Activity A and have students cut them out and glue them to the flashcards.

- Put students in pairs to practice reading the words as their partner displays the picture and confirms the phrase by reading it on the back of the card.

- Have students save the flashcards for use in Lesson 6.

Objective
Talking about what people are doing

Vocabulary
playing basketball

**Literacy Workbook pages 110–115
Workbook page 88**

  A CD 3, TRACK 31 **Listen and circle.**

- Have students look at the first pair of pictures as you play the audio for the first item or read the first sentence in the listening script. Stop and elicit which picture shows the sentence they heard. Point out that the answer is circled.

- Have students circle the pictures as you play the rest of the audio or read the rest of the sentences in the script.

- Put students in pairs to compare answers.

- Go over the answers with the class.

Listening Script

A. LISTEN AND CIRCLE.

1. He's cooking breakfast.
2. She's reading.
3. They're dancing.
4. He's swimming.

Answer Key **1.** He's cooking breakfast. **2.** She's reading. **3.** They're dancing. **4.** He's swimming.

Expansion Activity: Say and point.

- Elicit what people are doing in each picture.
- Write the sentences on the board.
- Say each sentence and have students repeat.
- Put students in pairs to take turns reading sentences as their partner points to the picture.

  B CD 3, TRACK 32 **Listen.**

- Direct students' attention to the picture and ask: *Who do you see? What are they doing?*

- Play the audio or read the conversation.

- Play the audio or read the conversation again and have students repeat.

- Put students in pairs to practice the conversation.

C **Talk with 4 classmates.**

- Go over the words in the box.

- Model the activity with a student.

- Divide students into groups of five and have them practice the conversation.

- Call on students and ask about one of the characters in the box.

Extra Challenge
Write sentences.

- Have students write sentences for all of the pictures in Activity A.

- Ask students to write their sentences on the board.

Objective

Talking about what you like to do in different seasons

Literacy Workbook pages 110–115
Workbook page 89

 A   CD 3, TRACK 33   **Listen.**

- Play the audio or read the conversation with a student as students follow along silently.

- Play the audio or read the conversation again and have students repeat.

- Ask comprehension questions: *What does Grace like doing in the spring? What does she like doing in the winter?*

- Put students in pairs to practice the conversation. Have students switch roles.

GRAMMAR Note

- The *-ing* form practiced on this page is really a gerund, not part of the present continuous, but students don't need to understand the differences at this level. Focus on the words and phrases as indicators of activities.

B   **Talk to a partner.**

- Model the activity with a more advanced student. Have the student read A's lines and ask about a season. Answer with an activity. Suggest students refer to Lesson 4 to review the activities if necessary.

- Have students practice the conversation in pairs.

Expansion Activity: Inside/Outside Circles

- Divide the class in half. Have one group form a circle facing out. Have the second group form an outside circle facing in. Each student should be facing a classmate.

- Have students on the inside circle say A's lines and the students on the outside circle say B's lines.

- After 30 seconds, cue the outside circle to move one place to the right (to face a new classmate). Have students repeat the conversation, substituting new information if they want.

- After 20–30 seconds switch again. Repeat several more times, making sure to keep the activity fast-paced. Students should be able to say the conversation much more fluently by the end.

C   **Ask 8 classmates.**

- Have students stand and walk around the classroom to ask the question and complete the chart.

- Put students in pairs to compare charts.

- Call on students to tell the class about a classmate (e.g., *Carlos likes playing soccer in the spring.*).

Expansion Activity: Character Cards

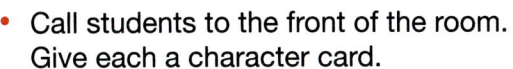

- Call students to the front of the room. Give each a character card.

- Ask the "characters" to say what they like doing in different seasons.

- Call on other students and ask about the character.

> **What does Carlos like doing in the spring?**

> **Carlos likes playing soccer in the spring.**

Expansion Activity: Tally the results.

- Write each season on the board.

- Go around the room and elicit an answer to the question from Activity C. Have a student write a tally mark next to the season and activity each student likes best.

	Spring	Summer	Fall	Winter
playing soccer	1			
walking				
dancing				
reading				
cooking				

Extra Challenge
Write sentences.

- Have students write sentences from the information in Activity C (e.g., *Carlos likes playing soccer in the spring.*).

- Put students in pairs to read their sentences aloud.

Literacy Development Activity: Flashcards and Seasons

- Have students get out their flashcards from the Literacy Expansion Activity in Lesson 4.

- Say a season. Have students find the correct card that expresses the activity they like doing in that season and hold the card up.

- Call on students and ask them to say the activity they like and hold up the correct card.

- Repeat with all the seasons.

Objective
Talking and writing about the weather

Vocabulary

cool	dry	warm

Literacy Workbook pages 110–115
Workbook page 90

  A CD 3, TRACK 34 **Listen and read.**

- Direct students' attention to the pictures.

- Have students listen and follow along in the book as you play the audio or read the sentences.

- Play the audio or read the sentences a second time and have students repeat.

- Call on students to read the sentences to the class.

Expansion Activity:
Call and Response

- Say, *It's summer.* Cue the students to respond *It's hot and dry.*

- Continue with the other seasons in random order. Say the weather (*It's snowing.*) and cue students to say the season (*It's winter.*).

B **Write.**

- Read the first sentence. Elicit words that could go on the lines (*cold* and *snowing*).

- Point out that different words may be used in different parts of the country.

- Have students complete the sentences.

- Call on students to read their sentences.

Answer Key Answers may vary but may include:

1. cold/snowing; **2.** sunny/cool;
3. hot/dry; **4.** warm/windy

My Life

- Go over the example.

- Put a chart on the board like the one below.

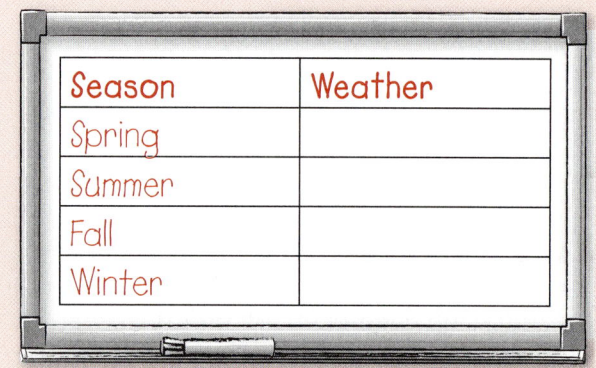

Season	Weather
Spring	
Summer	
Fall	
Winter	

- Have students copy the chart in their notebooks.

- Have students complete the chart with information from their countries.

- Put students in groups to talk about their charts.

Expansion Activity:
Character Card Research

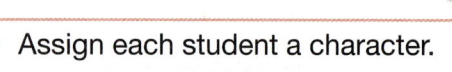

- Assign each student a character.

- Have students research the weather of the character's native country in different seasons.

- Call on students to tell the class about the weather in each character's native country.

Objective
Talking and writing about temperatures

Vocabulary/Numeracy

Celsius   temperature
Fahrenheit   thermometer

Literacy Workbook pages 110–115
Workbook page 91

  A CD 3, TRACK 35 **Listen and write the numbers.**

- Have students look at the thermometer and elicit what it is. Point to the abbreviations for Celsius and Fahrenheit on the yellow note.

- Tell students that in the USA, Fahrenheit thermometer readings are used.

- Have students look at the pictures and ask: *Who do you see? What are they doing? Is it hot?*

- Have students write the temperatures as you play the audio or read the sentences.

- Put students in pairs to compare answers.

- Go over the answers with the class.

Listening Script

A. LISTEN AND WRITE THE NUMBERS.

1. It's very hot. It's 105 degrees Fahrenheit. It's 41 degrees Celsius.
2. It's hot. It's 85 degrees Fahrenheit. It's 29 degrees Celsius.
3. It's warm. It's 70 degrees Fahrenheit. It's 21 degrees Celsius.
4. It's cool. It's 50 degrees Fahrenheit. It's 10 degrees Celsius.
5. It's cold. It's 27 degrees Fahrenheit. It's −3 degrees Celsius.

Answer Key
1. 105/41; 2. 85/29; 3. 70/21; 4. 50/10; 5. 27/−3

Extra Challenge
Conversions

- Outside of class, have advanced students search for temperature conversions on the computer.

- Have students convert temperatures from Fahrenheit to Celsius: 60° F, 25° F, 32° F, 40° F.

- Put students in pairs to compare answers.

Answer Key
60° F = 16° C; 25° F = −4° C; 32° F = 0° C; 40° F = 4° C

Literacy Development Activity: Match numbers to descriptions.

- Give each student five index cards and have students write one word on each card: *very hot, hot, warm, cool, cold.*

- Say a temperature in Fahrenheit. Have students find it on the thermometer and hold up the appropriate card. At first, use the temperatures in Activity A, but after some more practice, add temperatures above or below the ones they already know.

Objective
Reading a weather map

Vocabulary

| cloudy | raining | snowing |

Literacy Workbook pages 110–115
Workbook page 92

  A CD 3, TRACK 36 **Listen and read the weather map.**

- Direct students' attention to the map. Go over the meanings of *cloudy, raining, snowing.*

- Ask comprehension questions: *What is the weather like in Seattle? Where is it snowing? Where is it sunny?*

- Have students look at the map as you play the audio or describe the map.

Listening Script

A. LISTEN.

How is the weather around the nation today? It's a cloudy day in Seattle, and the temperature is 40 degrees Fahrenheit. It's raining in Los Angeles, but the temperature is hot—80 degrees. In Dallas, it's 82 degrees. It's a hot, sunny day. It's raining in Chicago, and the temperature is 25 degrees. In Denver, it's 20 degrees Fahrenheit, and it's snowing. New York is cool and cloudy at 40 degrees. And in Miami it's 75 degrees—sunny and hot!

B **Complete the chart.**

- Have students find Seattle on the weather map. Ask: *What's the temperature?* Elicit that it is 40° F. Point out that the temperature is written on the chart. Ask if it is sunny, raining, snowing, or cloudy. Have students check *cloudy* on the chart.

- Have students complete the chart.

- Put students in pairs to compare answers.

- Go over the answers with the class.

Expansion Activity:
Talk about the weather.

- Have students talk about the weather in each city by referring to the chart and the map and saying sentences about each city's weather.

Answer Key

City	Temperature	Sunny	Raining	Snowing	Cloudy
Seattle	40° F				✓
Los Angeles	80° F		✓		
Dallas	82° F	✓			
Chicago	25° F	✓			
Denver	20° F			✓	
New York	40° F				✓
Miami	75° F	✓			

Extra Challenge

Write sentences.

- Have more advanced students write sentences about the weather in each city on the chart.
- Put students in pairs to compare sentences.
- Have volunteers write sentences on the board.

C Write about the weather in your city.

- Read or have a student read the example.
- Have students write about the weather in your city. Tell students they can use the Celsius scale if they want.
- Put students in pairs to compare ideas.
- Have volunteers write their sentences on the board.

BIG PICTURE

Expansion Activity:
Writing: Two Weather Reports

- Put the transparency for Unit 8 on the OHP or have students look at the big picture on page 122 in their books.
- Have students write weather reports for Tien and Carlos. Encourage students to include a realistic temperature even though they can't see the exact temperature in the picture. It's okay if they use the Celsius scale for the temperatures.
- Put students in pairs to compare ideas.
- Call on students to share their ideas with the class.

Expansion Activity:
Today's Weather

- Photocopy and distribute Worksheet 30: *Today's Weather* (Teacher's Edition page 356).
- Bring in copies of the weather section of today's newspaper, or have students do this activity as an out-of-class assignment. If it is out of class, have students look in the newspaper or watch the news to get the weather.
- Have students complete as much of the chart as they can.
- Put students in small groups to compare information.
- Copy the chart on the board or make a transparency and have students fill in the information.

How's the weather? 217

Objective
Understanding and using present continuous

**Literacy Workbook pages 110–115
Workbook page 93**

  A CD 3, TRACK 37 **Listen and read.**

- Have students look at the picture. Ask: *Who do you see? What are they doing?*

- Have students listen and read the chart as you play the audio or read the sentences.

- Play the audio or read the sentences again and have students repeat.

GRAMMAR Notes

- Point out the present continuous has two parts: the verb *be* and the main verb with an *-ing* ending. Make sure students see that the verb *be* is the same here as it is when they are using *be* in the simple present.

- Point out that verbs that end in *-e* drop the *e* before adding *-ing*, e.g., *write → writing*.

B **Complete.**

- Go over the example. Point out that a form of the verb *be* must go right after the pronoun, as in the chart in Activity A.

- Have students look at the pictures and complete the sentences.

- Put students in pairs to compare answers.

- Go over the answers with the class.

Answer Key **1.** She <u>is</u> read<u>ing</u>. **2.** He <u>is</u> eat<u>ing</u>. **3.** They <u>are</u> listen<u>ing</u>.

Literacy Development Activity: Sentence Strips

- On separate index cards or strips, write each pronoun, each form of *be*, each main verb from Activity B, and *-ing*.

- Have a volunteer come to the front of the room. Dictate a sentence (e.g., *She is eating.*) and have the student form the sentence in a pocket chart or by taping it to the board.

- Continue with other students and sentences.

C **Write sentences.**

- Go over the example.

- Have students use the cues to write sentences.

- Put students in pairs to compare answers.

- Elicit answers from the class.

Answer Key **1.** Tien is walking to school. **2.** Sandy and I are playing soccer. **3.** You and Nadira are watching TV. **4.** I am studying English.

Expansion Activity:
Grammar: What are they doing?

- Photocopy and distribute Worksheet 31: *What are they doing?* (Teacher's Edition page 357)

- Put the transparency for Unit 8 on the OHP or have students look at the big picture on page 122 in their books.

- Go over the directions.

- Have students complete the worksheet.

- Put students in pairs to compare answers.

- Go over the answers with the class.

Answer Key   **1.** is sitting; **2.** is eating; **3.** is talking; **4.** is talking; **5.** is drinking; **6.** are walking; **7.** are wearing; **8.** is cooking

Objective
Using contractions with the present continuous

Literacy Workbook pages 110–115
Workbook page 93

  A CD 3, TRACK 38 **Listen and read.**

- Play the audio as students look at the chart, or read the sentences in the chart.

  B CD 3, TRACK 39 **Listen and complete.**

- Go over the example. Ask or elicit that Ben and Grace are studying. Point out that they are to write the contraction on the line: *They're studying.*

- Have students complete the sentences as you play the audio or read the sentences in the listening script.

- Play the audio or read the sentences again so students can check their answers.

- Put students in pairs to compare answers.

Listening Script

B. LISTEN AND COMPLETE.

1. They're studying.
2. She's reading.
3. She's pointing.

Answer Key 1. 're; 2. 's; 3. 's

Literacy Development Activity:
Practice with Contractions

- Write the full forms of the subject pronouns with the appropriate forms of *be*.

- Demonstrate how contractions are formed in each case. Cross out the appropriate letters and add apostrophes.

- Write sentences in the present continuous on the board (e.g., *I am studying. You are talking. He is reading.* etc.).

- Have students rewrite each sentence to use a contraction.

- Variation: Use a pocket chart. Write each word of each sentence on a separate card or strip. Write each part of *be* as a contraction. Show students how to substitute the contraction card for the part of *be*.

C **Write about your classmates.**

- Go over the directions and the example.

- Point to a student and ask: *What is he/she doing?* Elicit a sentence using the present continuous and a contraction.

- Have students write sentences, real or imagined, about four classmates.

- Have volunteers write sentences on the board.

Objective
Reading emails

**Literacy Workbook pages 110–115
Workbook page 94**

  A   CD 3, TRACK 40   **Listen and read.**

- Direct students' attention to the picture and ask: *What do you see? What is Leo doing? What is Nadira doing? What is the weather?*

- Direct students' attention to the email.

- Have students listen and read along silently as you play the audio program or read the email.

- Ask comprehension questions: *Who is writing the email? Who is the email to? How is the weather? Where is Tien? Is it cold?*

- Put students in pairs to take turns reading the email.

Expansion Activity:
Find the contractions and present continuous.

- Have students look at the email and circle the contractions and underline the present continuous.

- Write the sentences from the email on the board.

- Have volunteers circle the contractions and underline the present continuous.

B   **Complete. Add *-ing*.**

- Go over the directions and the example.

- Have students write the answers.

- Put students in pairs to compare answers.

- Go over the answers with the class.

Answer Key

1. eating; **2.** snowing; **3.** reading; **4.** drinking; **5.** watching/talking

Expansion Activity:
True or false?

- Put students in pairs. Try to pair a more advanced student with a less advanced student if possible.

- Have students work together to write three sentences about the email, some true and some false.

- Have each pair exchange sentences with another pair and write *true* or *false* after each.

- In a variation, collect the sentences and read them aloud. Elicit if each is true or false.

Extra Challenge
Write full forms.

- Put students in pairs to compare their rewritten sentences.

- Have students write the sentences on the board.

Objective
Writing a letter

Literacy Workbook pages 110–115
Workbook page 95

  A CD 3, TRACK 41 **Listen and read.**

- Direct students' attention to the picture. Ask questions: *Who do you see? What is he doing?*

- Have students follow along silently as you play the audio or read the letter.

- Ask comprehension questions: *Who is writing the letter? Where is he? What is the season?*

B **Write a letter to a classmate.**

- Put students in pairs.

- Have students write letters to their partners.

- Have students exchange letters.

- Call on students to read their letters to the class.

Expansion Activity: Cloze

- Write this cloze activity on the board:

January 20, 2010

Dear Tien,

    I'm in _____. My family is here, too. It's
_____. The weather is _____ and very _____.
Today we are _____ and having _____ at the beach.
    See you next week.

Your friend,
Carlos

- Have students look at the big picture on page 122 and complete the letter. Advanced students should do this activity looking at the big picture only. Allow literacy students to look at the completed letter on page 135 if needed.

Expansion Activity:
Listening/Speaking:
Letter Dictation

- Photocopy and distribute Worksheet 32: *Letter Dictation* (Teacher's Edition page 358).

- Put the transparency for Unit 8 on the OHP or have students look at the big picture on page 122 in their books.

- Go over the directions.

- Read the script below and have students write what they hear on the worksheet.

January 21, 2010

Dear Nadira,

    I'm in Miami. My family isn't here. They are in New York. The weather is sunny and cool. Today, I am reading the newspaper and listening to music.
    See you next week.

Your friend,
Carlos

- Have students complete Part B of the worksheet.

- Go over the answers with the class.

Answer Key

Part A: same as script; **Part B:** Answers may vary for the letter but may include:

In the picture	In the letter
1. It is very warm.	**1.** It is cool.
2. Carlos is sitting on the beach.	**2.** Carlos is reading the newspaper.
3. Carlos is talking on the phone.	**3.** Carlos is listening to music.

Objective
Review and assessment

  A CD 3, TRACK 42 **Listen and write.**

- Go over the directions and the example. Play the audio for the first item or read the first sentence in the script and point out the answer.

- Play the audio or read the sentences as students complete the sentences.

- Play the audio or read the sentences again if students need to hear it again.

- Put students in pairs to compare answers.

- Elicit and write answers on the board.

Listening Script

A. LISTEN AND WRITE.

1. How's the weather?
2. It's cold and windy.
3. My favorite season is spring.
4. I'm playing soccer.
5. What are you doing?
6. They like walking in the snow.

Answer Key 1. weather; 2. windy; 3. spring; 4. playing; 5. doing: 6. walking

  B CD 3, TRACK 43 **Listen and fill in the answer sheet.**

- Go over the directions. Have students look at each pair of answers.

- Play the audio and stop after the first sentence or read the first sentence in the listening script. Point out that A is filled in.

- Continue to play the audio or read the sentences as students mark the answers. Stop after each item so students have time to mark their answers.

- Put students in pairs to compare answers.

- Elicit and write answers on the board.

Listening Script

B. LISTEN AND FILL IN THE ANSWER SHEET.

1. They're dancing.
2. It's snowing in New York.
3. What do you like doing in the fall?
4. It's a windy day.
5. Carlos is listening to music.
6. How's the weather?

Answer Key 1. A; 2. B; 3. A; 4. A; 5. B; 6. A

  C CD 3, TRACK 44 **Listen and circle.**

- Play the audio or read the sentences and have students circle what they hear.

- Put students in pairs to compare answers.

- Go over the answers with the class.

····· **Listening Script**

C. LISTEN AND CIRCLE.

1. It's 60 degrees Fahrenheit.
2. Seattle is windy.
3. It's 55 degrees Fahrenheit in Miami.
4. Dallas is 40 degrees Fahrenheit.
5. It's cold in New York.
6. Los Angeles is sunny.

Answer Key **1.** 60° F; **2.** windy;
3. 55° F; **4.** 40° F; **5.** cold; **6.** sunny

D Write about you.

• Model the activity. Tell the class your favorite season and write the sentence on the board.

• Have students complete the sentences. Point out that the present continuous is used in the fourth sentence.

• Put students in pairs to read their sentences.

• Call on students to read their sentences to the class.

E Ask 4 classmates.

• Go over the sample conversation and example in the chart.

• Copy the chart on the board.

• Model the activity. Ask a more advanced student what he or she likes doing in each season. Write the answers on the chart.

> **What do you like doing in the winter?**
>
> **I like reading books.**

• Have students walk around the room to talk to four classmates and complete the chart.

• Call on students to talk about a classmate.

F Learning Log

• Have students check the words they know.

• Put students in pairs to compare lists and review the words.

• Have students write words they don't remember in a vocabulary notebook. Encourage students to write sentences using the difficult words.

🔍 LOOKING BACK

• Put students in pairs to talk about the big picture.

• Call on students to talk about the big picture.

BIG PICTURE

Expansion Activity: Vocabulary: Weather Opposites

• Introduce the concept of *opposite*. Tell students that *opposite* means "very different." Brainstorm a list of opposites from this unit (*hot/cold*, *summer/winter*). Include words from other units.

• Divide the class into teams. Team A lines up facing Team B. Team A talks about Carlos; Team B about Tien. Put the Unit 8 transparency on the OHP.

• Student 1 from Team A says something about Carlos or where he is (*It's hot.*). Student 1 from Team B responds with a sentence that uses an opposite about Tien or where she is (*It's cold.*).

Where's the post office?

UNIT OVERVIEW

Lesson	Objective	Student Book Page
1. Places Around Town	Talking about places in the community	p. 139
2. Neighborhood Map	Asking for and giving locations	p. 140
3. More Places in the Neighborhood	Talking about places in the neighborhood	p. 141
4. Where's the bank?	Asking and saying where people and places are	p. 142
5. It's across from the bus stop.	Saying where people and places are	p. 143
6. Do you live near a park?	Talking about places that are near or far	p. 144
7. Where do you buy stamps?	Talking about where you do different things	p. 145
8. A Deposit Slip	Making a deposit	p. 146
9. Using an ATM	Using an ATM	p. 147
10. Grammar: Prepositions of Place	Understanding prepositions of place	p. 148
11. Grammar: Preposition Practice	Using prepositions	p. 149
12. Read: Cashing a Check	Reading about cashing a check	p. 150
13. Write: An Application	Completing an application	p. 151
What do you know?	Review and assessment	p. 152

Big Picture Expansion Activities

Focus	Activity	Suggested Use
Reading	Nadira makes a withdrawal.	Lesson 9
Grammar	Where is the drugstore?	Lesson 11
Writing	Vocabulary Review	What do you know?
Listening/ Speaking	Dictation	Lesson 5

Worksheets

Worksheet #/ Focus	Title	Teacher's Edition Page
33. Writing/ speaking	Filling out Forms	p. 359
34. Reading	Nadira makes a withdrawal.	p. 360
35. Grammar	Where is the drugstore?	p. 361
36. Writing	Vocabulary Review	p. 362

Unit Opener

- Put the transparency for Unit 9 on the overhead projector (OHP) or have students look at the big picture on page 138.

- Point to each sign or place as you ask the question at the bottom of the page: *What places do you see?*

- Elicit the words the students know and write them on the board.

Objective
Talking about places in the community

Vocabulary

bank	hospital
drugstore	library
fire station	police station
gas station	post office

Literacy Workbook pages 116–121
Workbook page 98

  A CD 3, TRACK 46 **Listen. Look at page 138.**

- Have students look at the picture on page 138 and listen while you play the first part of the audio or read the sentences.

- Play the rest of the audio or read the list of words and have the students repeat.

- Call on students. Read one of the words and have students repeat.

- Have students work in pairs and take turns reading the words in random order as their partner points to the picture.

Listening Script

A. LISTEN. LOOK AT PAGE 138.

1. Police station. I'm going to the police station.
2. Bank. I'm going to the bank.
3. Drugstore. I'm going to the drugstore.
4. Hospital. I'm going to the hospital.
5. Fire station. I'm going to the fire station.
6. Gas station. I'm going to the gas station.
7. Library. I'm going to the library.
8. Post office. I'm going to the post office.

LISTEN AND REPEAT.

1. police station
2. bank
3. drugstore
4. hospital
5. fire station
6. gas station
7. library
8. post office

PRONUNCIATION Note

- Point out that in compound words (words or phrases formed by joining two words together) the stress is usually on the first word. For example, in *drugstore* we stress *drug,* and in *post office* we stress *post.*

Extra Challenge
Write the sentences.

- Play the audio for Activity A again or read the sentences in the script.
- Have students write the sentences.
- Check for accuracy.
- Ask volunteers to write the sentences on the board.

Literacy Development Activity:
Pick a card.

- Write all the places from Activity A on index cards, one to a card.
- Call students to the front of the room to pick a place card. Have students say the place and point to it in the picture or on the transparency.
- Continue with other students and cards.

 B CD 3, TRACK 47 **Listen.**

- Play the audio or read the conversation with an advanced student as students listen.
- Play the audio or read the conversation again and have students repeat.
- Put students in pairs. Designate one partner to be Maria and the other to be Nadira.
- Have students practice the conversation in pairs, then switch roles.

C Talk with 6 classmates.

- Go over the words in the box.
- Model the activity with a more advanced student. Point to a picture and ask: *Where are you going?* Elicit the appropriate response.

> **Where are you going?**
>
> **I'm going to the hospital. What about you?**

- Have students practice the conversation with six classmates. Make sure they get a chance to play both roles and use the words from the box.

GRAMMAR Note

- If your students are confused about using *the* vs. *a/an,* point out that we use *the* when we are referring to a specific place, or one that both speakers know about.

D Complete.

- Go over the example.
- Have students write the word on the line under the appropriate picture. Remind students they can only use each answer once, so they should look at all the pictures and words first.
- Put students in pairs to compare answers.
- Go over the answers with the class.

> **Answer Key** 1. drugstore; 2. post office; 3. fire station; 4. hospital

Objective
Asking for and giving locations

Literacy Workbook pages 116–121
Workbook page 99

A Write the places.

- Point out the title of the lesson and make sure students understand the word *neighborhood*.

Answer Key 1. fire station;
2. drugstore; 3. hospital; 4. gas station;
5. library

- Put students in pairs to compare answers.

- Call on volunteers to provide answers. Elicit or provide corrections as needed.

- Point to the place in the picture with *1* on it and ask: *What place is number 1?* Elicit that it is the fire station. Point out that *fire station* is written on Line 1.

- Have students write the other places in the picture on the correct lines.

B CD 3, TRACK 48 Listen.

- Play the audio or read the conversation with an advanced student as students listen.

- Play the audio or read the conversation again and have students repeat.

- Put students in pairs. Designate one partner to be the woman and the other to be Grace.

- Have students practice the conversation in pairs, then switch roles.

- If there is time, have them switch partners and practice the conversation again.

C Talk with 4 classmates.

- Go over the words in the box.

- Model the activity with a more advanced student. Have the student read A's questions. Respond.

> **Excuse me. Where's the gas station?**
>
> **It's on 20th Street.**

- Have students practice the conversation with four classmates, making sure they play both roles.

Extra Challenge

Write sentences.

- Write *The* _____ *is on*
_____. on the board.

The _____ is on _____.

- Have students write sentences about the places in the box.

- Put students in pairs to compare sentences.

- Have students write the sentences on the board.

Objective

Talking about places in the neighborhood

Vocabulary

bus stop	park
laundromat	restaurant
movie theater	supermarket

Literacy Workbook pages 116–121
Workbook page 100

  A CD 3, TRACK 49 **Listen.**

- Have students look at the pictures. Ask: *What do you see?*

- Play the first part of the audio or read the sentences in the script below.

- Play the rest of the audio or read the words and have students repeat.

···· **Listening Script**

A. LISTEN.

1. Laundromat. Wash your clothes at the laundromat.
2. Movie theater. I'm going to the movie theater.
3. Supermarket. I buy food at the supermarket.
4. Bus stop. Wait for the bus at the bus stop.
5. Park. My children play in the park.
6. Restaurant. Sometimes I eat at a restaurant.

LISTEN AND REPEAT.

1. laundromat
2. movie theater
3. supermarket
4. bus stop
5. park
6. restaurant

Expansion Activity: **Beanbag Toss**

- Call on a student, toss a beanbag or small ball, and say an action (*buy food*). Elicit the place (*supermarket*).

- Continue with other students and actions. Either have students toss the beanbag or ball back to you or have them toss it to another student and say an action.

- If you have the room in your classroom, you may want to have students stand in a circle for this activity. Otherwise, make sure students are paying attention if classmates are tossing the beanbag.

 **B** CD 3, TRACK 50 **Listen.**

- Play the audio or read the conversation as students listen. Read it with one or more advanced students if you wish.

- Play the audio or read the conversation again and have students repeat.

- Put students in groups of three. Designate one partner to be Leo, one Isabel, and one Maria.

- Have students practice the conversation in threes, then switch roles.

C **Talk with 7 classmates.**

- Go over the words in the box.

- Model the activity with a student. Point out the answers will be *yes* or *no*, depending on the question.

- Have students practice the conversation with seven classmates either in a group of eight or by walking around the room and talking to classmates.

Literacy Development Activity: Flashcards

- Have students draw a picture of one of the words from Lessons 1 and 3, one on each of 14 index cards. Or, you can bring in pictures and have students cut them out and glue them to cards.

- Have students write the words on the backs of the cards.

- Put students in pairs to practice saying the words as they look at the pictures.

Expansion Activity: Character Cards: Where is everyone?

- Write the names of places from Lessons 1 and 3 on signs and post them around the classroom.

- Call a group of students to the front of the class and give each a character card.

- Have the "characters" choose one of the places and go stand by the sign. Encourage students to spread out a bit.

- Call on other students and ask questions: *Where is Nadira? Where are Carlos and Ben?*

> **Where is Nadira?**

> **She's in the post office.**

Objective

Asking and saying where people and places are

Vocabulary

between   next to   on

Literacy Workbook pages 116–121
Workbook page 101

  A CD 3, TRACK 51 **Listen and read.**

- Direct students' attention to the picture and ask: *What do you see?*

- Have students follow along silently and listen while you play the audio or read the sentences.

- Ask comprehension questions: *Where's the bank? What's next to the bank?*

  B CD 3, TRACK 52 **Listen.**

- Play the audio or read the conversation and have students read the conversation silently.

- Play the audio or read the conversation again and have students repeat.

- Put students in pairs to practice both parts of the conversation.

Expansion Activity: Writing Practice

- Use the picture in Activity A.

- Write a sentence model on the board: *The _____ is _____.*

- Complete the sentence: *The <u>drugstore</u> is <u>next to the bank</u>.*

- Put students in pairs.

- Have students say then write sentences using the places in the art from Activity A, using *on, next to*, and *between*.

- Have volunteers write the sentences on the board. Provide or elicit corrections.

C **Look at Activity A. Talk with 5 classmates.**

- Model the activity with a more advanced student. Refer to the picture in Activity A.

- Have students talk to five classmates, asking and answering the question.

Expansion Activity: Question Whip

- Call on a student and ask about a place in the picture (*Where's the bank?*). Accept all correct responses.

- Go on to the next student and ask about a place. Continue around the room until everyone has had a chance to participate.

- As a variation, give students a specific preposition to use.

Objective
Saying where people and places are

Vocabulary
across from

Literacy Workbook pages 116–121
Workbook page 101

  A CD 3, TRACK 53 **Listen.**

- Direct students' attention to the picture and ask: *What do you see?*

- Play the audio or read the conversation with two advanced students. Make sure students understand the prepositional phrase *across from*.

- Play the audio or read the conversation again and have students repeat.

- Have students practice the conversation.

Literacy Development Activity:
Answer Cards

- Distribute index cards to students.

- Have students write each place from the map on a separate card. Have students also write *across from* and *next to* on cards.

- Ask a question (e.g., *Where's the bus station?*). Have students choose a preposition card and a place card to make an answer.

- Call on students and elicit possible answers. Continue with other questions.

B **Look at the map in Activity A. Talk with 4 classmates.**

- Go over the words in the map in Activity A and in the Word List box.

- Model the activity with a more advanced student.

- Have students practice the conversation with four classmates in a group of five.

- Call on students and ask about one of the places in the box.

> Where is the drugstore?
>
> It's across from the laundromat.

Expansion Activity:
Where's my classmate?

- Have students stand in a circle.

- Call on a student and ask about another student (e.g., *Where's Tina?*). Elicit an answer that uses a preposition (e.g., *She's next to Binh.* or *She's across from Yuri.*).

- Have that student call on a classmate and ask about another student.

- Continue until everyone has had a chance to participate.

  C CD 3, TRACK 54 **Listen and write.**

- Have students write the words they hear as you play the audio or read the complete sentences in the script.

- Put students in pairs to compare answers. Play the audio or read the complete sentences again if necessary.

- Elicit answers from class members, correcting pronunciation as needed.

- For extra pronunciation practice, have all students repeat the completed sentence as you go over the answers.

Listening Script

C. LISTEN AND WRITE.

1. The bus station is next to the supermarket.
2. The park is next to the post office.
3. The drugstore is across from the laundromat.
4. The post office is across from the bus stop.
5. The supermarket is between the drugstore and the bus stop.

Answer Key
1. next to; **2.** next to; **3.** across from; **4.** across from; **5.** between

My Life

- Direct students' attention to the picture and ask: *Who do you see? What is she doing?*

- Model the activity. Draw a map of your neighborhood on the board. Tell the class about the places and where they are.

- Go over the directions.

- Have students draw maps of their neighborhoods.

- Put students in groups to talk about the places in their neighborhoods.

Expansion Activity:
Ask and answer.

- Model the activity. Look at a student's map of his or her neighborhood. Elicit a question from the student (e.g., *Where's the library?*). Answer with information on the map (e.g., *It's next to the laundromat.*).

- Have students write three questions about places on their maps.

- Put students in pairs to take turns asking and answering questions about each other's maps.

BIG PICTURE

Expansion Activity:
Listening/Speaking: Dictation

- Put the transparency for Unit 9 on the OHP or have students look at the big picture on page 138 in their books.

- Dictate the following questions. Repeat as many times as necessary.
  Where is the bank?
  Where is the hospital?
  Where is the library?
  Where is the drugstore?
  Where is the gas station?

- Have volunteers write the questions on the board.

- Put students in pairs to practice asking and answering the questions using all the prepositions they have learned so far. Write the prepositions on the board if needed to remind students of them.

Objective

Talking about places that are near or far

Vocabulary

far from   near

Literacy Workbook pages 116–121
Workbook page 102

  A CD 3, TRACK 55 **Listen.**

- Have students look at the pictures and ask: *Who do you see?*

- Play the first part of the audio or read the sentences in the first part of the script as students follow along silently.

- Play the second part of the audio or read the second part of the script and have students repeat.

- Play the first part of the audio or read the first part of the audio again, focusing on the pronunciation of *near* and *far*.

⋯⋯ Listening Script

A. LISTEN.

1. Near. He's near the bus stop.
2. Far from. They're far from the bus stop.

LISTEN AND REPEAT.

1. near
2. far from

 B CD 3, TRACK 56 **Listen and circle.**

- Play the audio and stop after the first item or read the first sentence of the listening script and ask: *near* or *far from?* Elicit that the answer is *near.* Point out that *near* is circled.

- Have students circle the words they hear as you play the audio or read the sentences.

- Put students in pairs to compare answers. Play the audio or read the sentences again if necessary.

- Go over the answers with the class.

⋯⋯ Listening Script

B. LISTEN AND CIRCLE.

1. Leo lives near a bank.
2. Carlos lives near a bus stop.
3. Sandy lives far from the city.
4. Paul lives near a fire station.
5. We live far from a movie theater.
6. Tien lives near a post office.

Answer Key **1.** near; **2.** near; **3.** far from; **4.** near; **5.** far from; **6.** near

  C CD 3, TRACK 57 **Listen.**

- Have students follow along silently as you play the audio or read the sentences.

- Play the audio or read the sentences again and have students repeat.

- Model the conversation with students. Repeat the question until you hear both responses.

D **Ask 5 classmates.**

- Go over the example conversation. Point out that students have to ask about all five places on the chart. They can only have classmates sign the chart if they answer *yes*.

- Have students talk to five classmates and complete the chart if they can.

Expansion Activity: **Near or far?**

- Write *Near* and *Far* on opposite sides of the board, or write the words on pieces of paper and tape the signs to different sides of the room.

- Have students stand. Say a place (e.g., *police station*) and cue students to move to the sign that represents whether it is near or far from their homes.

- Call on a student from each group and ask where the place is and elicit the answer.

> **Where is the police station?**

> **The police station is far from my home.**

- Continue with other places. Keep the activity moving quickly.

Expansion Activity:
Ask more classmates.

- Have students ask each of ten classmates about all of the places in Activity D. Tell students to put a tally mark in the appropriate box for each *yes* answer.

- Put students in pairs to compare results.

- Call on students to tell the class about their results (e.g., *Five students live near a park.*).

Objective
Talking about where you do different things

Vocabulary

buy stamps	see a movie
cash a check	wash clothes

Literacy Workbook pages 116–121
Workbook page 102

 A CD 3, TRACK 58 Listen.

- Have students listen and follow along in the book as you play the first part of the audio or read the sentences in the script below.

- Play the rest of the audio or read the phrases and have students repeat.

Listening Script

A. LISTEN.

1. See a movie. Where do you see a movie?
2. Buy stamps. Where do you buy stamps?
3. Wash clothes. Where do you wash clothes?
4. Cash a check. Where do you cash a check?

LISTEN AND REPEAT.

1. see a movie	3. wash clothes
2. buy stamps	4. cash a check

Extra Challenge
Answer the question.

- Play the first part of the audio again and have students write the questions.

- Put students in pairs to ask and answer the questions.

B CD 3, TRACK 59 Listen.

- Have students follow along silently as you play the audio or read the conversation with a student.

- Play the audio or read the conversation again and have students repeat.

- Put students in pairs to practice the conversation.

C Talk with 4 classmates.

- Go over the words in the box.

- Model the activity with a more advanced student.

- Have students practice the conversation with four classmates.

- Call on students and ask about one of the places in the box.

My Life

- Go over the directions and the example.

- Have students complete the sentences.

- Put students in groups to read their sentences aloud.

- Call on students to read sentences to the class. For extra writing practice, have them write the sentences on the board.

Objective
Making a deposit

Vocabulary

deposit   savings account

Literacy Workbook pages 116–121
Workbook page 103

  A CD 3, TRACK 60 **Listen and read.**

- Have students follow along silently as you play the audio or read the sentences.

- Make sure students understand the terms *deposit, savings account,* and *deposit slip.*

- Have students look at the deposit slip. Ask comprehension questions: *Who is depositing money? What is the date? What is the total amount?*

Expansion Activity:
Choral Reading

- Read each sentence aloud and have students repeat.
- Cue the students to read the story aloud with you.
- Put students in pairs to take turns reading sentences from the story.
- Circulate and monitor pronunciation.

B **Write the numbers.**

- Go over the example. Have students write the numbers.
- Put students in pairs to compare answers.

Answer Key **1.** June 3, 2010;
2. 12-34565-43; **3.** $231.95; **4.** $42.95

C **Circle.**

- Go over the example. Students should cross out the wrong answer and write the correct answer on the line.

- Have students complete the sentences.

- Put students in pairs to compare answers.

- Elicit answers from the class.

Answer Key **1.** savings; **2.** one check;
3. $189.00; **4.** $231.95; **5.** sixth

Expansion Activity: **Realia**

- Photocopy and distribute copies of Worksheet 33: *Filling Out Forms* (Teacher's Edition page 359).

- Students will complete the first part of the worksheet—the deposit slip—for this activity.

- Dictate the following information:

  Carlos Avila puts money in his checking account every two weeks. He deposits his paycheck of $1,143.19. The date today is July 15, 2010. Carlos's account number is 01200967.

- Repeat the information if necessary. Have students fill in the missing information on the deposit slip.

- Put students in pairs to compare slips.

- Have students save the worksheet in their notebooks to finish in Lesson 13.

Objective
Using an ATM

Vocabulary

**ATM (automated teller machine)
pick
PIN (personal identification number)
slot
withdrawal**

Literacy Workbook pages 116–121
Workbook page 104

 A CD 3, TRACK 61 **Listen and read.**

- Direct students' attention to the pictures. Go over the yellow note.

- Have students follow along silently as you play the audio or read the sentences.

- Ask comprehension questions: *What do you do first? What do you get from an ATM? What is a PIN?*

PRONUNCIATION Note

- Tell students we pronounce *PIN* as a word *(pin)*, but when talking about an ATM, we say each letter *(A-T-M)*.

Expansion Activity: **Dictate steps.**

- Have students close their books.

- Dictate the four numbered sentences from Activity A in random order.

- Have students write numbers next to each step to put the steps in order.

- Put students in pairs to compare answers.

- Go over the answers with the class.

Extra Challenge
Play the teacher.

- Pair a more advanced student with a less advanced student.

- Have more advanced students dictate the sentences from Activity A to the less advanced partners. Suggest the advanced students spell words if necessary.

- Walk around the room. Check for proper pronunciation by the advanced student and understanding of the less advanced student.

CULTURE Note

- Point out or remind students that it is important to keep PIN numbers private. Otherwise it is easy for someone to steal money from your account. They should write their PIN down and keep it in a safe place.

Expansion Activity: ATM Field Trip

- For an out-of-class activity, take students to a nearby ATM.

- Model how to follow the steps. Make sure students know to take the cash, receipt, and card at the end of the transaction.

- If it isn't practical to take your class to an ATM, draw one on the board and model the steps.

B Look at Activity A. Circle.

- Go over the example.

- Have students circle the answers to complete the sentences.

- Put students in pairs to compare answers.

- Go over the answers with the class.

Answer Key 1. card; 2. 2-6-7-9; 3. withdrawal; 4. $100

BIG PICTURE

Expansion Activity: Reading: Nadira makes a withdrawal.

- Photocopy and distribute Worksheet 34: *Nadira makes a withdrawal* (Teacher's Edition page 360).

- Put the transparency for Unit 9 on the OHP or have students look at the picture on page 138 in their books.

- Go over the directions and example.

- Have students complete the worksheet.

- Put students in pairs to compare answers.

- Call on volunteers to provide answers.

Answer Key 1. park; 2. fire station; 3. restaurant; 4. police station; 5. bank; 6. hospital; 7. library; 8. post office; 9. gas station; 10. drugstore

Objective
Understanding prepositions of place

Literacy Workbook pages 116–121
Workbook page 105

  A   CD 3, TRACK 62   **Listen and read.**

- Have students look at the pictures. Ask: *What places do you see?*

- Have students listen and read the chart as you play the audio or read the sentences.

- Play the audio or read the sentences again and have students repeat.

- Ask questions: *Where is the restaurant? Where is the gas station?*

Expansion Activity:
More Questions

- Put students in pairs and have them ask more questions about the pictures.

- For added practice, have them cover up their books and answer locations from memory.

GRAMMAR Notes

- Point out that *next to* and *across from* always have two parts. Refer to the example in Activity A or elicit or provide another one.

- Point out that *between* is always used before two things. Refer to the example in Activity A or elicit or provide another one.

- Point out that we use *on* with streets (*on Bay Street*) and *in* with cities (*in Boston*).

Expansion Activity:
Magazine Photos

- Bring in photos from magazines that show outdoor scenes if possible.

- Put students in pairs.

- Have the students write sentences using prepositions about the places in the picture. Collect the sentences.

- Post the photos around the room.

  B   CD 3, TRACK 63   **Listen and check.**

- Go over the directions and the answer choices.

- Play the audio of the first item or read the first sentence of the listening script and point out that *on* is checked.

- Have students check the prepositions they hear as you play the audio or read the sentences.

- Go over the answers with the class.

······· **Listening Script**

B. LISTEN AND CHECK.

1. Isabel lives on Ocean Road.
2. Ocean Road is between 10th and 11th Streets.
3. Leo lives in Hill City.
4. His house is on Bay Street.
5. It is next to a school.
6. It is across from a park, too.

Answer Key   **1.** on; **2.** between; **3.** in; **4.** on; **5.** next to; **6.** across from

Objective
Using prepositions

Literacy Workbook pages 116–121
Workbook page 105

A Write *in* or *on*.

- Direct students' attention to the picture. Ask questions: *Who do you see? Where is he? What do you see in the picture?*

- Go over the example.

- Have students write *in* or *on* on the lines.

- Put students in pairs to compare answers.

- Go over the answers with the class.

Answer Key **1.** on; **2.** in; **3.** on; **4.** in; **5.** on; **6.** on

B Write *next to, between,* or *across from.*

- Direct students' attention to the picture. Ask questions: *What do you see? Where is the drugstore?*

- Go over the example.

- Have students write *next to, between,* or *across from* on the lines.

- Put students in pairs to compare answers.

- Call on student volunteers to read their answers to the class.

Answer Key **1.** next to; **2.** between; **3.** next to; **4.** across from; **5.** between; **6.** next to; **7.** across from; **8.** across from

Expansion Activity:
Preposition Practice

- Give pairs or small groups simple objects, or have them choose three things, e.g., a pen, book, and piece of paper.

- Have students position the objects in various ways and elicit statements about the position, e.g., *The pen is on the paper. The pen is next to the paper.*

- Circulate and assist as needed.

Literacy Development Activity:
Point to the preposition.

- Write the prepositions on the board.

- Call a student to the front of the room. Say a sentence (e.g., *The book is on the desk.*).

- Have the student point to the correct preposition.

- Continue with other students.

BIG PICTURE

Expansion Activity:
Grammar: Where is the drugstore?

- Photocopy and distribute Worksheet 35: *Where is the drugstore?* (Teacher's Edition page 361)

- Put the transparency for Unit 9 on the OHP or have students look at the big picture on page 138 in their books.

- Go over the directions.

- Have students compare answers.

Answer Key **1.** i; **2.** g; **3.** e; **4.** h; **5.** a; **6.** b; **7.** d; **8.** j; **9.** c; **10.** f

Objective
Reading about cashing a check

Literacy Workbook pages 116–121
Workbook page 106

  A   CD 3, TRACK 64   **Listen and read.**

- Direct students' attention to the pictures and ask: *Who do you see? Where is he? What is he doing?*

> Who do you see? Where is he? What is he doing?

- Have students listen and read along silently as you play the audio or read the sentences.

- Ask comprehension questions: *When does Ben get his paycheck? How much is his paycheck? What is the day today? Is the bank open?*

- Put students in pairs to take turns reading the sentences.

Expansion Activity: **Cloze**

- Photocopy or write on the board the cloze exercise below.

> Ben gets his paycheck _____
> Friday. His _____ is
> $154.85. He has a savings account
> _____ the bank. Usually
> _____ brings his check
> there. The teller gives _____
> $154.85. _____ is Saturday.
> The bank is _____.
> So Ben goes to a check cashing
> _____. The clerk
> _____ Ben's check. She gives
> him _____. She keeps $10.
> It costs $10 _____ the check
> cashing store. Ben is angry. He needs all
> the _____.

- Have advanced students write the missing information with books closed. Have less advanced students refer to the information in the book.

- Go over the answers with the class.

B   **Check.**

- Go over the directions.

- Have students check the sentence.

- Put students in pairs to compare answers.

- Elicit the answer from the class. Ask why the other choice is not correct and discuss.

Answer Key   **1.** Ben cashes a check.

C **Look at Activity A. Complete.**

• Go over the directions and the example.

• Have students complete the sentences.

• Put students in pairs to compare answers.

• Call on volunteers to provide answers.

Answer Key **1.** Saturday; **2.** $154.85;
3. $154.85; **4.** $144.85; **5.** bank; **6.** check cashing store

Extra Challenge

Write questions.

• Have more advanced students write questions for each sentence in Activity C. For example, the first question might be *Is the bank closed on Saturday?* Encourage students to write some *yes/no* questions with incorrect information, too.

• Walk around to monitor the activity and provide help as needed.

Literacy Development Activity: Answer questions.

• Pair literacy students with more advanced students to answer the questions from the Extra Challenge Activity above.

Objective

Completing an application

Vocabulary

card	pay	special

Literacy Workbook pages 116–121
Workbook page 107

A Read.

- Direct students' attention to the application. Ask questions: *Who is completing the application? What is the name of the supermarket?*
- Have students read the application.

CULTURE Note

- The information on applications should be printed, not written in cursive, and with blue or black ink. Point out that students should write neatly on all official forms to avoid mistakes.

Expansion Activity: Complete Sentences

- Write an example on the board: *Carlos's last name is _____.*

Carlos's last name is _____.

- Have students write three sentences about the application that need completion.

- Have volunteers write sentences on the board.
- Have the class copy and complete the sentences.
- Ask volunteers to complete the sentences on the board.

B Complete for you.

- Have students complete the application with their own information.
- Put students in pairs to talk about their applications.
- Call on students to tell the class one thing about their partner's application.

Expansion Activity: Pair Interview

- Photocopy and distribute Worksheet 33: *Filling out Forms,* or ask students to take the worksheet out of their notebooks if they saved it from Lesson 8.
- Put students in pairs to take turns interviewing their partners and completing the second part of the worksheet—the supermarket card application.
- Remind students to form questions beginning with *What is _____?* (e.g., *What is your first name? What is your zip code?*)
- Walk around to monitor the activity and provide help as needed.

Objective
Review and assessment

  A CD 3, TRACK 65 **Listen and write.**

- Go over the directions and the example.

- Play the audio or read the conversations in the listening script as students complete the sentences. There is a pause after each sentence so students have time to write their answers and cross out the word in the box. If students need more time for this part, play the audio again.

- Put students in pairs to compare answers.

- Play the audio again or read the conversations again and have students check their answers.

- Elicit the answers and write them on the board.

Listening Script

A. LISTEN AND WRITE.

1. **Sandy:** Do you live far from a bus stop?
   Tien: No, I don't.
   Sandy: Do you live near a park?
   Tien: Yes, I do.
2. **Isabel:** Excuse me. Where is the police station?
   Leo: It's on 54th Street, across from the park.
   Isabel: Thanks.

  B CD 3, TRACK 66 **Listen and fill in the answer sheet.**

- Go over the directions. Point out that students should completely fill in the correct answer on the answer sheet to the right.

- Play the audio and stop after the first sentence or read the first sentence of the listening script. Point out that B is filled in on the answer sheet.

- Have students look at each pair of answers.

- Continue to play the audio or read the sentences in the script as students mark the answers. There is a pause after each sentence so students have time to mark their answers.

- Play the audio or read the sentences again if students need more time to complete their answers.

- Put students in pairs to compare answers.

- Play the audio or read the sentences again and have students check their answers.

- Elicit the answers and write them on the board.

Listening Script

B. LISTEN AND FILL IN THE ANSWER SHEET.

1. I'm going to the hospital.
2. Where's the fire station?
3. The library is across from the post office.
4. Is there a movie theater in your neighborhood?
5. Where do you wash clothes?
6. Grace is making a deposit.

> **Answer Key** **1.** B; **2.** B; **3.** B; **4.** A; **5.** A; **6.** B

  **C** CD 3, TRACK 67 **Listen and fill in the answer sheet.**

- Go over the directions. Explain that students will hear six conversations that show where the people are.

- Play the audio and stop after the first conversation or read the first conversation in the script below. Ask: *Where are they?* Elicit that they are in a restaurant. Point out that B is filled in.

- Have students look at each pair of answers.

- Continue to play the audio or read the conversations as students mark the answers. There is a pause after each conversation so students have time to mark their answers.

- Play the audio or read the conversations again if students need more time to mark their answers.

- Put students in pairs to compare answers.

- Play the audio or read the conversations again and have students check their answers.

- Elicit the answers and write them on the board.

Listening Script

C. LISTEN AND FILL IN THE ANSWER SHEET.

1. Waiter: Can I help you?
   Sandy: Yes. A hamburger, please.
2. Leo: This is a good movie.
   Paul: Yes, it is.
3. Teller: May I help you?
   Grace: I want to make a deposit.
4. Clerk: Good morning.
   Ben: Good morning. I want to buy some stamps.
5. Grace: I have eight quarters.
   Ben: Good. We can wash the clothes.
6. Carlos: Excuse me, I'm looking for bread.
   Clerk: Bread is in aisle 12.

> **Answer Key** **1.** B; **2.** A; **3.** B; **4.** A; **5.** A; **6.** B

D Write about you.

- Point out the synonyms for *street* in Item 1.

- Model the activity. Say what street you live on. You can make one up, if you prefer.

- Have students complete the sentences.

- Put students in pairs to read their sentences.

- Call on students to read their sentences.

E Complete.

- Go over the words in the list.

- Read the first two sentences. Point out that *on* is written on the line in Sentence 2.

- Have students complete the paragraph.

- Put students in pairs to compare answers.

Answer Key Leo lives in an apartment building. It is ___on___ Water Street. His building is near a ___gas___ station. Leo lives across ___from___ a laundromat. He ___washes___ his clothes there. Leo likes his ___neighborhood___.

F Learning Log

- Go over the directions.

- Put students in pairs to compare lists and review the words.

- Elicit words that students do not know and review their meanings.

- Have students write words they don't remember in a vocabulary notebook.

- Encourage students to write sentences using the difficult words. Review them with the students for accuracy and to ensure comprehension.

LOOKING BACK

- Put students in pairs to talk about the big picture on page 138. Walk around to monitor the activity.

- Call on students to talk about the big picture using vocabulary and grammar from this unit.

BIG PICTURE
Expansion Activity:
Writing: Vocabulary Review

- **Before class:** Make student copies of Worksheet 36: *Vocabulary Review* (Teacher's Edition page 362).

- Put the transparency for Unit 9 on the OHP or have students look at the big picture on page 138 in their books.

- Draw a 3-column chart on the board. Write *19th Street* in the first column, *20th Street* in the second column, and *South Avenue* in the third.

- Ask the students to look at the big picture and tell you what places are on 19th Street. Write the places they say on the chart. Then repeat for 20th Street and South Avenue.

- Pass out copies of Worksheet 36. Copy the T-chart on the board.

- Read the heading for the first column, *Places I go every week*. Ask a few students to say a place they go every week. Write their answers in Column 1. Read the heading for the second column, *Places I do not go every week*. Ask a few students to say a place they don't go every week. Write their answers in the second column.

- Tell the students to fill out the chart for themselves, using the places shown in the big picture. For extra practice, have them list places not included in the picture that they do or don't go to, e.g., *laundromat*.

- Have the students share their T-charts with a partner.

Objective
Review of contractions with *be* and the present continuous

A Write the contractions: *'m*, *'s*, or *'re*.

- Review the information in the chart.
- Read the sentences and ask students to repeat, or call on individual students to read them.
- Go over the directions and the example.
- Have students write contractions on the lines.
- Put students in pairs to compare answers.
- Go over the answers with the class.

Answer Key 1. I'<u>m</u>; 2. You'<u>re</u>; 3. They'<u>re</u>; 4. She'<u>s</u>; 5. We'<u>re</u>; 6. I'm

B Complete. Use the present continuous tense.

- Review the information in the chart.
- Read the sentences and ask students to repeat.
- Go over the directions and the example.
- Have students write the correct form of the verb on the lines.
- Put students in pairs to compare answers.
- Call on individual students to provide answers.

Answer Key 1. He is walking; 2. They are eating; 3. She is withdrawing; 4. You are reading; 5. I am buying; 6. We are washing

C Talk in groups.

- Put students in groups.
- Have them answer the question.
- Call on students to tell what they are doing. Encourage students to do different things or mime different activities so they can practice the present continuous.

D CD 3, TRACK 68 Listen and circle.

- Play the audio for the first item or read the first conversation in the listening script. Point out that *It's raining* has been circled.
- Tell students to circle the sentence that corresponds to the picture.
- Play the rest of the audio or read the rest of the listening script.
- Put students in pairs to compare answers. Play or read the audio again if students want to check their work.
- Go over the answers with the class.

Listening Script

D. LISTEN AND CIRCLE.

1. **Mother:** Hello?
   Maria: Hi Mother. It's Maria. How are you?
   Mother: I'm fine. How's the weather in Los Angeles?
   Maria: It's raining.
2. **Grace:** Hi, Isabel.
   Isabel: Hi, Grace.
   Grace: What are Carlos and Tien doing?
   Isabel: They're playing soccer.
3. **Ben:** Hello?
   Leo: Hi, Ben. It's Leo.
   Ben: Hi, Leo. How's the weather in Chicago?
   Leo: It's cloudy today.
4. **Paul:** Hi, Tien. It's Paul.
   Tien: Hi, Paul.
   Paul: Do you know where Nadira is?
   Tien: She's swimming at the beach.

Answer Key 1. carton; 2. jar; 3. aisle 3; 4. laundromat; 5. milk; 6. summer; 7. bank

Answer Key 1. It's raining. 2. They're playing soccer. 3. It's cloudy. 4. She's swimming.

E Complete.

- Go over the words in the box.
- Go over the example.
- Have students complete the sentences with words from the box.
- Put students in pairs to compare answers.
- Elicit answers from individual students. Provide or elicit corrections as needed.

Our Cultures
Marketplaces

A Circle the types of marketplaces. Underline the countries.

- Tell students that this culture topic is *marketplaces.*

- Read each photo caption and have students repeat.

- Read the photo captions in random order and have students point to the correct picture.

- Ask students about their countries, e.g., *What kind of marketplaces do you have in Thailand?*

- Put students in pairs to talk about the markets they have in their countries.

Answer Key Left to right, top to bottom:

Circle *farmstand*, underline the *US*; circle *street market*, underline *Grenada*; circle *fish market*, underline *Japan*; circle *floating market*, underline *Thailand*; circle *night market*, underline *Taiwan*; circle *supermarket*, underline *Canada*

B Think about it. Complete the chart. Where do you get food?

- Go over the example in the chart.

- Have students complete the chart.

- Have students discuss their answers in pairs or discuss answers as a class.

C Talk in groups.

- Direct students' attention to the picture and ask: *Who do you see? Where does Carlos buy fish in his native country? Where does he buy fish in the U.S.?*

- Put students in small groups to talk about where they buy food in their countries and here.

- Call on students to tell the class about where they buy food. Tell them to refer to what they wrote in their chart in Activity B. If you have time, make a bar graph of the various responses.

- As a variation, write the Activity B chart on the board leaving a lot of room in the middle column for a variety of answers. Tally student answers and discuss the results.

UNIT OVERVIEW

Lesson	Objective	Student Book Page
1. What's the matter?	Identifying health problems	p. 159
2. His hand hurts.	Identifying parts of the body	p. 160
3. My daughter is sick.	Talking about symptoms and making a doctor's appointment	p. 161
4. Health Problems and Remedies	Talking about health problems and remedies	p. 162
5. She needs a bandage.	Talking about health problems and remedies	p. 163
6. I exercise.	Recognizing healthy habits	p. 164
7. Home Remedies	Talking about home remedies	p. 165
8. Taking Medicine	Understanding instructions for taking medicine	p. 166
9. Health Insurance	Filling out an insurance form	p. 167
10. Grammar: Action Verbs	Using action verbs	p. 168
11. Grammar: Negatives	Using negative forms	p. 169
12. Read: The Goldman Sisters	Reading about people with healthy habits	p. 170
13. Write: A Health Plan	Writing a health plan	p. 171
What do you know?	Review and assessment	p. 172

Big Picture Expansion Activities

Focus	Activity	Suggested Use
Reading	A Day at the Doctor's	Lesson 12
Grammar	Using the Negative	Lesson 11
Listening/ Writing	What to Do at the Doctor's Office	Unit Opener
Vocabulary	Creating Conversations	What do you know?
Listening/ Speaking	Yes or no?	Lesson 5

Worksheets

Worksheet #/ Focus	Title	Teacher's Edition Page
37. Listening/ Writing	What to Do at the Doctor's Office	p. 363
38. Listening	Insurance Form	p. 364
39. Grammar	Using the Negative	p. 365
40. Reading	A Day at the Doctor's	p. 366

Unit Opener

- Put the transparency for Unit 10 on the overhead projector (OHP) or have students look at the big picture on page 158.

- Point to each word as you ask the questions at the bottom of the page: *Where are the people? What do you see?*

- Elicit the words the students know and write them on the board.

Expansion Activity:
Listening/Writing: What to Do at the Doctor's Office

- Make student copies of Worksheet 37: *What to Do at the Doctor's Office* (Teacher's Edition page 363) and pass them out.

- Tell students you are going to read some sentences. The sentences tell people what to do when they go to the hospital or doctor's office. As you read the sentences, the students should write down what you say.

- Read the dictation sentences below two or three times, and pantomime the action. If needed, dictate the spelling of each word (*s-a-y*). Dictation sentences:

  Say goodbye.   *Come in.*
  See the doctor.   *Sit down.*
  Sign your name.

- Correct the sentences by having volunteers write them on the board. Check comprehension by reading the sentences again and having the students perform each action.

- Put the transparency for Unit 10 on the OHP or have students look at the big picture on page 158. Ask questions about the picture: *How many people do you see in the picture? Where are they?*

- Tell students that when people go to a hospital or doctor's office, they do things in a certain order. Have them look at their dictation sentences. Say the sentences are five things you do at a hospital or doctor's office. Ask which thing you do first. Elicit that *Come in* is the first thing.

- Point to *Come in.* in the first box of the flow chart.

- Have students work in pairs to complete the chart. Check answers as a class.

Answer Key **B.** Come in. Sign your name. Sit down. See the doctor. Say goodbye.

Objective
Identifying health problems

Vocabulary

a backache	a headache
a broken arm	a sore throat
a cold	a stomachache
an earache	a toothache

Literacy Workbook pages 122–127
Workbook page 110

 A CD 4, TRACK 2 **Listen.**

- Make sure students understand the question in the lesson title.

- Have students look at the pictures and listen while you play the first part of the audio or read the phrases and sentences.

- Play or read the first part of the audio. Pause and have the students repeat.

- Play the second part of the audio or read the phrases. Pause after each phrase and have the students repeat again.

- Call on students. Say one of the phrases and have students repeat.

- Have students work in pairs and take turns reading the phrases in random order as their partner points to the corresponding picture.

Listening Script

A. LISTEN.

1. An earache.
   Ana: I have an earache.
2. A sore throat.
   Will: I have a sore throat.
3. A headache.
   Maria: I have a headache.
4. A broken arm.
   Paul: I have a broken arm.
5. A toothache.
   Carlos: I have a toothache.
6. A stomachache.
   Nadira: I have a stomachache.
7. A backache.
   Ben: I have a backache.
8. A cold.
   Isabel: I have a cold.

LISTEN AND REPEAT.

1. an earache
2. a sore throat
3. a headache
4. a broken arm
5. a toothache
6. a stomachache
7. a backache
8. a cold

PRONUNCIATION Note

- Point out that *ache* is pronounced /āk/ and that the stress is always on the first syllable. Model the pronunciation, e.g., *headache, toothache.*

Expansion Activity: Character Cards

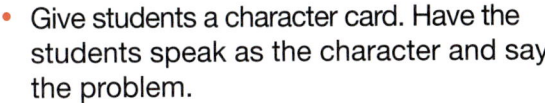

- Give students a character card. Have the students speak as the character and say the problem.

- Call on other students and ask about the character's problem.

> **What does Nadira have?**
>
> **She has a stomachache.**

Tell students to use *has* to talk about the characters.

 B CD 4, TRACK 3 **Listen.**

- Play the audio or read the conversation with a student as students listen.

- Play the audio or read the conversation again and have students repeat.

- Put students in pairs. Designate one partner to be Maria and the other to be the nurse.

- Have students practice the conversation in pairs, then switch roles.

C **Talk with 6 classmates.**

- Go over the words in the box.

- Model the activity with a more advanced student. Have the student ask the question. Answer with a problem in the box.

- Have students practice the conversation with six classmates. Remind students to use *a* before the problem.

Expansion Activity: **Mime.**

- Model the activity. Mime each problem and elicit what it is.

- Do the reverse by saying a problem and having the class mime it.

- Call on individual students, say a problem, and have the student mime it.

- Do the reverse by miming the problem and eliciting the words.

Literacy Development Activity: Alphabetical Order

- Review the alphabet if necessary.

- Have students look at the initial letter of the words in the box to write the words in alphabetical order.

- Have students write the words in order on the board.

You need to see a doctor. 255

Objective
Identifying parts of the body

Vocabulary

arm	foot	nose
chest	hand	stomach
eye	head	
finger	leg	

Literacy Workbook pages 122–127
Workbook page 110

  A CD 4, TRACK 4 **Listen.**

- Have students look at the picture and listen while you play the audio or read the words.

- Play the audio or read the words again. Pause after each word and have the students repeat.

- Call on students. Say one of the words and have students repeat.

- Have students work in pairs and take turns saying the words in random order as their partner points to the picture.

Expansion Activity:
Touch your head.

- Model the activity. Say, *Touch your head.* and touch your head. Wait until everyone has touched their head.

- Continue with the other body parts. Say the parts in random order and have students touch the part.

- Call on individual students and say, *Touch your _____.*

  B CD 4, TRACK 5 **Listen.**

- Direct students' attention to the picture and ask: *Who do you see? Who are they talking about?*

- Play the audio or read the conversation with a student as students listen.

- Play the audio or read the conversation again and have students repeat.

- Put students in pairs. Designate one partner to be Sandy and the other to be Leo.

- Have students practice the conversation in pairs, then switch roles.

C Talk with a partner.

- Go over the words in the box.

- Model the activity with a more advanced student. Have the student read A's question and substitute a name from the box. Respond with the correct possessive pronoun.

> **What's the matter with Tien?**
> **Her ear hurts.**

- Have students practice the conversation with four classmates. Point out that they need to respond with the correct possessive pronoun.

Extra Challenge
ACTIVITY: Write it another way.

- Write *ear, stomach, head, throat* on the board.

- Model the activity. Write, *My ear hurts.* and *I have an earache.* on the board.

- Have students write two sentences about the other three words.

Objective
Talking about symptoms and making a doctor's appointment

Literacy Workbook pages 122–127
Workbook page 111

  A CD 4, TRACK 6 **Listen.**

- Have students look at the picture. Ask: *Who do you see? What's the matter?*

- Play the audio or read the conversation with a student as students listen.

- Play the audio or read the conversation again and have students repeat.

- Put students in pairs. Designate one partner to be Ana and the other to be Maria.

- Have students practice the conversation in pairs, then switch roles.

VOCABULARY Note

- Point out that when you feel sick, you can say *I feel bad,* as is said in Activity A, or *I feel sick.*

Expansion Activity: **Word Cards**

- Write each word from Activity A on an index card. There are 12 words/cards in each set. Make enough sets so every student gets a card. Shuffle the cards.

- Give each student a card.

- Have students stand and recreate the conversation by standing in order and reading each word in order.

B **Talk with a partner.**

- Go over the words in the box.

- Model the activity with a student.

- Have students practice the conversation with a partner. Encourage students to practice the conversation with each word from the box. Have students switch roles.

  C CD 4, TRACK 7 **Listen.**

- Play the audio or read the conversation with a student as students listen.

- Play the audio again and have students repeat.

- Put students in pairs. Have students practice the conversation, then switch roles.

Literacy Development Activity: **Sentence Strips**

- Write each sentence on strips of paper.

- Give a set to each pair of students.

- Have students put the sentences in order.

My Life

- Model the activity. Pretend to call the doctor's office and make an appointment for someone. Point out the question in A's last line: *Today at ___?* Stress the importance of confirming appointment times to avoid confusion and mistakes.

- Have students use Activity C as a model and complete the conversation. Make sure they match the pronoun in B's sentence to the person who is sick.

- Put students in pairs to practice their conversations.

Objective
Talking about health problems and remedies

Vocabulary

an antibiotic	a cough	a fever
aspirin	cough syrup	an infection
a bandage	a cut	remedy

Literacy Workbook pages 122–127
Workbook page 112

  A CD 4, TRACK 8 **Listen to the health problems.**

• Direct students' attention to the pictures and ask: *What do you see?*

• Have students follow along silently and listen while you play the audio or read the words.

• Play the audio or read the words again and have students repeat.

  B CD 4, TRACK 9 **Listen to the health remedies.**

• Direct students' attention to the pictures and ask: *What do you see?* Make sure students understand the word *remedy* and see that each remedy is under the problem it treats.

• Have students follow along silently and listen while you play the audio or read the words.

• Play the audio or read the words again and have students repeat.

Expansion Activity: Pronunciation

• Write the words that can be sounded out phonetically on the board: *antibiotic, aspirin, bandage, cut, fever, infection, remedy.*

• Underline the second *i* in *antibiotic* and the first *e* in *fever.* Point out that these are long vowel sounds, i.e., they say their names (*I, E*).

• Circle the *ge* in *bandage.* Point out that this is a soft *g* sound and that the *e* is silent.

• Box the *ti* in *infection*. Point out that this is a *sh* sound.

• Read each word and have students repeat. Call on students and point to a word. Have students sound it out.

• Go over the pronunciation of *cough* and *cough syrup*. Have students practice saying the words and phrases.

CULTURE Notes

• Point out that *pharmacy* can be another word for *drugstore,* or a drugstore can have a special section that is the pharmacy. In that case, the pharmacy usually dispenses the prescription medicines, and the over-the-counter medications are found in the aisles of the drugstore.

• Point out or elicit that people can get the remedies listed in Activity A at the drugstore/ pharmacy. Antibiotics require a prescription from the doctor.

C CD 4, TRACK 10 **Listen and check.**

- Play the audio and stop after the first conversation or read the first conversation in the listening script. Ask: *What is wrong with Isabel?* Elicit that she has a cut on her hand.

  > **What is wrong with Isabel?**

  > **She has a cut on her hand.**

  Point out that *a cut* and *a bandage* are checked.

- Play the audio or read the conversations and have students check the appropriate problem for each person. Point out that the numbers of the conversation are written above each column, next to each person's name.

- Put students in pairs to compare answers. Play or read the audio again if students need to hear it again.

- Go over the answers with the class. Elicit that two students have the same problem.

Answer Key
1. cut/a bandage;
2. fever/aspirin; **3.** infection/an antibiotic;
4. fever/aspirin; **5.** cough/cough syrup

Expansion Activity: Beanbag Toss

- Call on a student, toss a beanbag or small ball, and say a problem (e.g., *I have a cut on my leg.*). Elicit a remedy (e.g., *You need a bandage.*).

- Continue with other students and health problems until everyone has had a chance to participate.

- If you have the room in your classroom, you may want to have students stand in a circle for this activity. Otherwise, make sure students are paying attention if classmates are tossing the beanbag.

Listening Script

C. LISTEN AND CHECK.

1. Isabel: Ow! I have a cut on my hand.
   Dr. Brown: Oh, no. You need a bandage.
2. Carlos: I have a fever.
   Dr. Brown: Oh, no. You need aspirin.
3. Don: Ow! My foot hurts. I have an infection.
   Dr. Brown: Oh, no. You need an antibiotic.
4. Leo: Oh, my head is hot. I feel bad. I have a fever.
   Dr. Brown: Oh, no. You need aspirin.
5. Nadira: I have a cough.
   Dr. Brown: Oh, no. You need cough syrup.

Objective
Talking about health problems and remedies

Literacy Workbook pages 122–127
Workbook page 112

  A CD 4, TRACK 11 **Listen.**

- Direct students' attention to the picture and ask: *Who do you see? What's wrong?*

- Play the audio or read the conversation as students follow along silently.

- Play the audio or read the conversation again and have students repeat.

- Put students in pairs to practice the conversation.

B **Talk with 5 classmates.**

- Go over the words in the box.

- Model the activity with a more advanced student.

- Have students practice the conversation with five classmates.

- Call on students and say a problem. Elicit the remedy.

> Leo has a cough.

> That's too bad. He needs cough syrup.

Expansion Activity:
Rewrite the conversation.

- Direct students' attention to Activity B.

- Have students rewrite the conversation in Activity A to follow the model in Activity B.

- Have volunteers write the conversation on the board.

  C CD 4, TRACK 12 **Listen. Complete the chart.**

- Play the audio for the first item or read the first conversation in the listening script. Point out the answers written in the chart. Go over the directions and answer any questions.

- Have students write the words they hear as you play the rest of the audio or read the conversations in the script.

- Put students in pairs to compare answers. Play the audio or read the conversations again if necessary.

- Elicit answers from the class. Ask for or provide corrections as needed.

······ **Listening Script**

C. LISTEN. COMPLETE THE CHART.

1. **Grace:** What's the matter, Leo?
   Leo: I have a cough and a sore throat.
   Grace: That's too bad. You need some cough syrup.
2. **Carlos:** What's the matter, Isabel?
   Isabel: I have a headache. My head hurts.
   Carlos: That's too bad. You need aspirin.
3. **Isabel:** What's the matter, Carlos?
   Carlos: I hurt my hand.
   Isabel: That's too bad. You need to see a doctor.
4. **Grace:** What's the matter, Nadira?
   Nadira: I have a cut finger.
   Grace: That's too bad. You need a bandage.

Answer Key

Name	Health Problem	Body Part	Health Remedy
1. Leo	cough	throat	cough syrup
2. Isabel	headache	head	aspirin
3. Carlos	hurt	hand	see a doctor
4. Nadira	cut	finger	a bandage

Expansion Activity:
Listening/Speaking:
Yes or *no*?

- Put the transparency for Unit 10 on the OHP or have students look at the big picture on page 158 in their books.

- Give students two cards — one for *yes*, one for *no*.

- Say a true or false sentence about the big picture (e.g., *A woman has a hurt finger.*) and have students hold up the correct card (*no*).

- Continue with other sentences. Create your own, or use the ones below.

  A woman has a cold.
  Maria has a headache.
  A boy has a broken leg.
  Someone needs an aspirin.
  Someone has a cough.

Objective
Recognizing healthy habits

Vocabulary

drink water	exercise
eat healthy food	get enough sleep
eat junk food (don't)	smoke (don't)

**Literacy Workbook pages 122–127
Workbook page 113**

  A CD 4, TRACK 13 **Listen.**

- Have students look at the pictures and ask: *What do you see?*

- Play the first part of the audio or read the first part of the listening script as students follow along silently.

- Play the rest of the audio or read the list of words and phrases and have students repeat and point to the correct picture.

- Play the audio or read the script again and have students repeat, focusing on proper pronunciation.

······ Listening Script

A. LISTEN.

1. Exercise. I exercise.
2. Drink water. I drink water.
3. Don't smoke. I don't smoke.
4. Get enough sleep. I get enough sleep.
5. Eat healthy food. I eat healthy food.
6. Don't eat junk food. I don't eat junk food.

LISTEN AND REPEAT.

1. Exercise.
2. Drink water.
3. Don't smoke.
4. Get enough sleep.
5. Eat healthy food.
6. Don't eat junk food.

GRAMMAR Note

- Make sure students understand that *don't* is the negative form of the verb *do: do + not = don't.* See if you can elicit that *does + not = doesn't.*

Expansion Activity:
Healthy or junk?

- Write two headings on the board: *Healthy Food* and *Junk Food.*

Healthy Food   Junk Food

- Put students in pairs to list as many foods as they can for both categories. Brainstorm a list of foods first if needed. Refer students back to Unit 7, page 121, for a list of food words.

- Set a time limit of three minutes.

- At the end of three minutes, elicit the foods and write them on the board.

B   Check what you do.

- Model the activity. Copy the sentences on the board or make a transparency and use the OHP. Check what you do.

- Erase your checkmarks. Have students check the sentences that are true for them.

C   Look at your answers in Activity B. Talk with 7 classmates.

- Direct students' attention to the picture and ask: *Who do you see? What does Grace do? What does Paul do?*

- Have students stand and walk around the room to practice saying what they do and don't do to seven classmates.

Expansion Activity:
Tally class results.

- Ask questions about what students do or don't do. Have students raise their hands. Tally the results on the board.

Exercise every day ✓ ✓ ✓ ✓ ✓ ✓ ✓

- Call on students to make statements about the results (e.g., *Seven students exercise every day.*).

Extra Challenge
Write sentences.

- Have students write sentences about the results of the Expansion Activity.

- Have volunteers write the sentences on the board.

Expansion Activity:
Character Cards

- Have two students come to the front of the class.

- Give each student a character card. Have the students say two things each character does. Encourage students to think about the character and what he or she would be likely to do. For example, Grace is going to have a baby, so she probably doesn't smoke.

- Have the class listen to what the character does and doesn't do. Then ask questions about each character.

Objective
Talking about home remedies

Vocabulary

drink hot water	rest
drink orange juice	take a shower

Literacy Workbook pages 122–127
Workbook page 114

  A CD 4, TRACK 14 **Listen.**

- Direct students' attention to the pictures.
- Have students listen and follow along in their books as you play the audio or read the sentences.
- Play the audio or read the sentences a second time and have students repeat.
- Call on students to read the sentences to the class. Correct pronunciation as needed.

CULTURE Note

- Elicit or point out why these remedies are considered home remedies (because no medicine is used and no doctor consulted).

  B CD 4, TRACK 15 **Listen.**

- Have students follow along silently as you play the audio or read the conversation with two students.
- Play the audio or read the conversation again and have students repeat.
- Put students in groups of three to practice the conversation.

C Talk with 4 classmates.

- Go over the words in the box.
- Model the activity with more advanced students.
- Have students practice the conversation with four classmates.
- Call on students and say a problem. Elicit a remedy from the box.

Expansion Activity: Role play

- Call on groups of students to role play their conversations for the class.
- Have them practice first, focusing on speaking clearly.

My Life

- Go over the directions.
- Have students complete the activity on their own.
- Put students in groups to share their ideas.
- Call on students to tell the class about a home remedy.

Expansion Activity: *Yes/No* Cards

- Have students get out their *Yes/No* cards. (See Worksheet 5—Teacher's Edition page 331.)
- Say sentences about the health problems and remedies listed in the My Life chart (e.g., *I drink orange juice for a cold.*) and have students hold up either the *yes* card or the *no* card.

Objective
Understanding instructions for taking medicine

Vocabulary

a capsule
drops
once
a pill

a teaspoon of medicine
three times
twice

Literacy Workbook pages 122–127
Workbook page 115

  A CD 4, TRACK 16 **Listen.**

- Direct students' attention to the pictures and ask *What do you see?*

- Have students follow along silently as you play the audio or read the words.

- Play the audio or read the words a second time and have students repeat.

- Read the words in random order and have students point.

VOCABULARY Note

- *Pill* is the older, more generic term for this form of medication. Now packaging often refers to a *tablet*, *capsule*, or *caplet*. If possible, bring in samples to show students.

  B CD 4, TRACK 17 **Listen.**

- Have students follow along silently as you play the audio or read the words.

- Play the audio or read the words a second time and have students repeat.

- Read the words in random order and have students point to the word and symbol.

VOCABULARY Note

- Point out that after *twice*, when indicating frequency, we say the number plus the word *times*, e.g., *three times, four times, ten times,* etc.

Expansion Activity: What do you take?

- Write three headings on the board: *Problem, Remedy, Form.*

- Model the activity. Write *cough* under *Problem*. Elicit remedies and medicines and write the ideas under *Remedy* (e.g., *cough syrup*). Under *Form*, elicit the form the medicine would come in (e.g., *a teaspoon*).

- Put students in groups to complete the chart for other health problems.

C Circle the answers in the chart.

- Direct students' attention to the labels and ask: *Who has medicine? What does Carlos take? How many times a day?*

- Have students read the labels and circle the answers.

- Put students in pairs to compare answers.

Answer Key Carlos: pill, 3x; Leo: capsule, 2x; Isabel: drops, 1x

Objective
Filling out an insurance form

Vocabulary

co-payment   insurance

Literacy Workbook pages 122–127
Workbook page 116

  A CD 4, TRACK 18 **Listen and read.**

- Direct students' attention to the health insurance card. Elicit what it is.

- Go over the yellow note. Make sure students understand the term *co-payment*.

- Have students follow along silently as you play the audio or read the word on the insurance card.

- Ask comprehension questions: *Who is the card for? What does D.O.B. stand for? How much does Grace have to pay to see the doctor?*

CULTURE Note

- Co-pays, or co-payments, usually range from $10 up to $30, depending on the specific insurance policy.

Expansion Activity: **Information**

- Write each type of information included on the health insurance card on a separate card or slip of paper (*name of patient, DOB, co-pay, ID number, type of plan, name of insured, name of employee*).

- Call on students to come to the board and draw a card.

- Have the student say the type of information on their card and write the information from Grace's form in Activity A on the board. Let students refer to the book to see how to write the information correctly.

- As a variation, when all of the information is on the board, call on students and point to information. Elicit the type of information.

B Complete the form for Grace.

- Have students complete the form using Grace's information.

- Put students in pairs to compare forms.

- Copy the form on the board. Have volunteers complete items on the form.

Expansion Activity: **Interview**

- Photocopy and distribute Worksheet 38: *Insurance Form.*

- Have the less advanced student pretend to be Grace. Have the more advanced student interview Grace to fill out the form. The less advanced student will answer according to the information in Activity A.

- Have volunteers act out the interview.

Answer Key WESTON Health Center

Patient's Name: Grace Lee
Today's Date: (will vary)
Date of Birth: 03/ 16 / 1980
Name of Employee: Ben Lee
Type of Plan: (circle one)
individual (family) **ID #:** 90933MC
Co-payment: $ 15

Objective
Using action verbs

Vocabulary

lift (weights)	swim
play (soccer)	walk
run	

**Literacy Workbook pages 122–127
Workbook page 117**

  A CD 4, TRACK 19 Listen and read.

- Have students look at the picture. Ask: *Who do you see? What is he doing? Where is he?*

- Have students listen and read the sentences in the chart as you play the audio or read the sentences.

- Play the audio or read the sentences in the chart again and have students repeat.

Extra Challenge
Other Verbs

- Tell advanced students to write all the forms for the verbs *walk* and *eat*. Suggest they follow the models in the chart.

- Have students write the forms on the board.

GRAMMAR Note

- Make sure students notice the *s* ending on verbs for *he, she,* and *it.*

B Look at the picture. Write the verbs in the correct form.

- Direct students attention to the picture. Ask: *What do Ben and Paul do every day?*

- Go over the words in the box. Play the audio for the first item or read the first sentence in the listening script.

- Have students complete the sentences using the words or phrases in the box as you play the rest of the audio or read the sentences in the listening script.

- Put students in pairs to compare answers.

- Call on class members to provide answers.

Answer Key 1. Ben and Paul run.
2. Leo lifts weights. 3. Nadira and Grace walk. 4. Isabel swims. 5. Carlos plays soccer. 6. The dog runs.

Expansion Activity: Mime.

- Write all the actions on slips of paper. You can include verbs from earlier units if you want.

- Call a student to the front of the room to draw a slip of paper and mime the action. Elicit the verb from the class.

Objective
Using negative forms

Literacy Workbook pages 122–127
Workbook page 117

  A CD 4, TRACK 20 **Listen and read.**

- Direct students' attention to the picture. Ask questions: *Who do you see? Where are they? What do you see in the picture?*

- Have students read the chart silently as you play the audio or read the sentences in the chart.

- Play the audio or read the sentences again and have students repeat.

Literacy Development Activity:
Make it negative.

- Use strips, pieces of paper, or index cards to write the following. Make sure the third person *s* card can fit snugly next to the verb.

I	don't	swim	
You	don't	swim	
We	don't	swim	
They	don't	swim	
He	doesn't	swim	s
She	doesn't	swim	s
It	doesn't	swim	s

- Use a pocket chart or tape the words to the board to form affirmative sentences (e.g. *I swim.*). Call a student to the board to make it negative.

- If necessary, cue the student to put a *don't* or *doesn't* card between the subject and the verb. Remind students to use the *s* ending in the affirmative but not in the negative.

- Continue with other students and subject pronouns.

GRAMMAR Notes

- Make sure students notice that we use *don't* with *I, you, we,* and *they,* and that we use *doesn't* with *he, she,* and *it.*

- Point out that *do + not = don't* and *does + not = doesn't.*

  B CD 4, TRACK 21 **Listen and write the number.**

- Have students read the sentences silently as you play the audio or read the sentences.

- Direct students' attention to the pictures and elicit what is happening in each picture.

- Play the audio or read the sentences again and have students write the number of the sentence below the correct picture.

- Put students in pairs to compare answers.

- Elicit answers from the class.

········ **Listening Script**

B. LISTEN AND WRITE THE NUMBER.

1. I run. I don't swim.
2. He walks. He doesn't run.
3. We drink water. We don't smoke.
4. They dance. They don't lift weights.

Answer Key **a.** 3; **b.** 2; **c.** 4; **d.** 1

Extra Challenge
Write the opposite.

• Model the activity. Write, *I don't run. I swim.* on the board.

• Have the students rewrite the sentences in Activity B so that the affirmative statements are negative and the negative statements are affirmative.

• Have volunteers write the sentences on the board.

BIG PICTURE
Expansion Activity:
Grammar: Using the Negative

• Photocopy and distribute Worksheet 39: *Using the Negative* (Teacher's Edition page 365).

• Put the transparency for Unit 10 on the OHP or have students look at the big picture on page 158 in their books.

• Go over the directions.

• Have students complete the worksheet.

• Put students in pairs to compare answers.

• Go over the answers with the class.

Answer Key   **1.** doesn't have; **2.** looks; **3.** answers; **4.** sit; **5.** don't walk; **6.** doesn't have; **7.** don't smoke; **8.** don't have; **9.** has; **10.** has

C Complete. Write the negative.

• Go over the directions and the example.

• Have students complete the sentences with the correct negative form.

• Have volunteers write the sentences on the board.

• Put students in pairs to talk about what they do and don't do in Activity C.

Answer Key   **1.** doesn't eat; **2.** doesn't swim; **3.** don't lift; **4.** don't dance

Objective
Reading about people with healthy habits

Literacy Workbook pages 122–127
Workbook page 118

  A CD 4, TRACK 22 **Listen and read.**

- Direct students' attention to the picture and ask: *Who do you see? What are they doing?*

- Direct students' attention to the information.

- Have students listen and read along silently as you play the audio or read the reading.

- Ask comprehension questions: *What are their names? Are they healthy? How old are they? What do they do?*

Literacy Development Activity: Sentence Strips

- Photocopy the story reproduced below and cut it into strips.

- Have students read the story a few times.

- Give each student a strip. Have students stand and walk around the room, reading their sentence so they can recreate the story in order.

- When students are standing in order, have each read or recite their sentence to the class.

  Frances and Eleanor Goldman are sisters.

  They are healthy.

  Eleanor is 81 years old.

  Frances is 83.

  They exercise and eat healthy food every day.

  Frances likes apples.

Eleanor likes oranges.

They drink water.

They get enough sleep.

They don't smoke.

Eleanor likes to walk her white dog.

Frances likes to walk, too.

She has a big dog.

Frances says, "Be healthy. Get a dog."

Eleanor says, "Be healthy. Don't eat junk food."

Expansion Activity: Chain Reading

- Read the first sentence. Point to a student on one side of the room to cue the student to read the second sentence. Cue the next student to read the third sentence, and so on.

- Continue around the room with students reading one sentence at a time, until everyone has read at least once. This may mean reading through the story several times. Remind students to follow along so they always know what sentence the class is on.

B **Complete.**

- Go over the words and phrases in the box.

- Go over the examples. Make sure students understand to put the things both Frances and Eleanor do in the center section.

- Have students complete the Venn diagram.

- Put students in pairs to compare answers.

- Elicit answers from class members.

Answer Key   **Eleanor:** 81, likes oranges, has a white dog

Eleanor and Frances: healthy, exercise, don't smoke, drink water, get enough sleep, walk a lot, eat healthy food

Frances: 83, likes apples, has a big dog

Expansion Activity:
Reading: A Day at the Doctor's

- Photocopy and distribute Worksheet 40: *A Day at the Doctor's* (Teacher's Edition page 366).

- Put the transparency for Unit 10 on the OHP or have students look at page 158 in their books.

- Have students write *he* or *she* on the lines.

- Go over the answers with the class.

Answer Key   I am a doctor. Today is a busy day. One child has a headache. _She_ needs aspirin. One person has a cut finger and an infection. _He_ needs a bandage and an antibiotic. Another person has a cold. _She_ needs to drink orange juice and rest. Someone has a sore throat. _He_ needs an antibiotic. A child has an earache. _She_ needs an antibiotic for an ear infection. Another patient has a hurt leg. _He_ needs aspirin. Someone has a toothache. _He_ needs aspirin. _He_ also needs to go to the dentist. Another person has a stomachache. _She_ needs to rest and drink hot water.

Objective
Writing a health plan

Literacy Workbook pages 122–127
Workbook page 119

  A **CD 4, TRACK 23** **Listen to and read Tien's health plan.**

- Direct students' attention to the picture and ask: *Who do you see? Where is she? What is the doctor giving Tien?*

- Have students follow along silently as you play the audio or read Tien's health plan.

- Ask comprehension questions: *What does Tien need to drink? What does Tien need to do every day?*

B **Write your health plan.**

- Go over the words in the box.

- Model the activity. Tell the class what your health plan is. Be specific (*Drink eight glasses of water every day.*).

- Have students write their own health plans. Encourage students to use the words in the box and to be specific. Tell them to use the negative at least once.

- Tell them they don't have to write six items if they can only think of fewer health plan points. Circulate around the room and help as needed.

- Put students in groups to talk about their health plans.

- Call on students to tell the class one thing about their partner's health plan.

Expansion Activity:
What's most important?

- Model the activity. Write Tien's plan on the board without the numbers. Point to the one that is most important to you. Write *1* next it. Then point to the second most important to you and write *2* next to it.

- Have students rewrite the sentences in order of their importance to them.

- Put students in pairs to talk about their rankings.

- Call on students to tell the class about what is most important to them and to their partners.

Expansion Activity:
Complete the diagram.

- Have students copy the Venn diagram from Lesson 12 on a piece of paper, substituting their own names and the names of their partners.

- Have students complete the diagram to compare and contrast the items on the two health plans.

> **Objective**
> Review and assessment

A Write.

- Go over the directions and the example.

- Have students write the problem under each picture.

- Put students in pairs to compare answers.

- Elict answers from the pairs. Provide or elicit correction as needed.

> **Answer Key** **1.** a toothache; **2.** a stomachache; **3.** a headache; **4.** a sore throat; **5.** a cold; **6.** a cut

 B CD 4, TRACK 24 **Listen and fill in the answer sheet.**

- Go over the directions.

- Play the audio and stop after the first conversation or read the first conversation in the listening script and elicit the answer. Point out that *A* is filled in.

- Have students look at each pair of answers.

- Continue to play the audio or read the rest of the conversations as students mark the answers. Stop after each conversation so students have time to mark their answers.

- Put students in pairs to compare answers.

- Play the audio or read the conversations again and have students check their answers.

- Elicit the answers and write them on the board.

····· Listening Script

B. LISTEN AND FILL IN.

1. **A:** What's the matter?
   B: I have a headache.
2. **A:** Can Dr. Wall see me today?
   B: Yes. Dr. Wall can see you at 3:00.
3. **A:** I have a stomachache.
   B: Drink hot water.
4. **A:** What's the matter with Sandy?
   B: Her ear hurts.
5. **A:** Are you healthy?
   B: Yes, I exercise and walk every day.

> **Answer Key** **1.** A; **2.** B; **3.** A; **4.** A; **5.** B

C Write.

- Have students complete the conversation. If necessary, remind students to write a problem on the first line and a remedy on the second. They will need a verb like *need* to complete the second line.

- Put students in pairs to compare ideas.

- Call on students to read their conversations to the class.

D **Read each health problem. Write a remedy.**

- Go over the directions and the example.

- Have students write remedies for each problem.

- Put students in pairs to compare answers.

- Elicit answers from the class. Accept all correct answers.

Answer Key Answers may vary.
1. Take some aspirin. 2. Take cough syrup.
3. Drink hot water. 4. Drink orange juice.
5. Take some aspirin.

E **Learning Log**

- Go over the directions.

- Have students check the words they know.

- Put students in pairs to compare lists and review the words.

- Elicit words that students do not know and review their meanings.

- Have students write words they don't remember in a vocabulary notebook. Encourage students to write sentences using the difficult words.

LOOKING BACK

- Go over the directions.

- Put students in pairs to talk about the big picture on page 158 using vocabulary and grammar from the unit.

- Walk around to monitor the activity.

- Call on students to talk about the big picture.

BIG PICTURE

Expansion Activity:
Vocabulary: Creating Conversations

- Put the transparency for Unit 10 on the OHP or have students look at the big picture on page 158 in their books.

- Point to Maria. Ask: *What is the matter with Nadira?* Elicit that *Nadira has a stomachache.* Ask: *What does Nadira say?* Elicit *I have a stomachache.* Point to all the patients in the picture and elicit what they would say.

- Point to the receptionist and then to yourself. Point to Isabel and ask for a volunteer to come to the front of the class (or point to Leo for a male volunteer). Model a conversation between the receptionist and Isabel or Leo. You play the receptionist. Say *Can I help you?* If necessary, prompt the volunteer with *What's the matter?*

- Put the students in pairs. Walk around the room. As you pass each pair of students, point to two people in the picture and tell them to create a conversation for those two people.

- Have volunteers read the conversations out loud. The other students must guess who is having the conversation.

UNIT OVERVIEW

Lesson	Objective	Student Book Page
1. What do you do?	Talking about what you do	**p. 175**
2. A cook uses pots and pans.	Identifying things that people use on the job	**p. 176**
3. Do you like to work outdoors?	Understanding and talking about job environments	**p. 177**
4. I can use a computer.	Understanding and talking about job skills	**p. 178**
5. Yes, I can.	Asking and answering questions about job skills	**p. 179**
6. Reading Want Ads	Understanding and using want ads	**p. 180**
7. I was a cashier.	Talking about past jobs	**p. 181**
8. A Paycheck	Reading and understanding information on a paycheck	**p. 182**
9. Safety Signs	Understanding safety signs	**p. 183**
10. Grammar: Simple Past of *Be*	Using the simple past of *be*	**p. 184**
11. Grammar: *Can/Can't*	Using *can* and *can't*	**p. 185**
12. Read: A Job Application	Understanding a job application	**p. 186**
13. Write: A Telephone Conversation	Writing a telephone conversation	**p. 187**
What do you know?	Review and assessment	**p. 188**

Big Picture Expansion Activities

Focus	Activity	Suggested Use
Listening/ Speaking	*Can* vs. *can't*	**Lesson 5**
Reading	Who is it?	**Lesson 12**
Grammar	Can she use a computer?	**Lesson 11**
Writing	Idea Map	**What do you know?**
Conversation/ Vocabulary	Matching Descriptions of Workers	**Unit Opener**

Worksheets

Worksheet #/ Focus	Title	Teacher's Edition Page
41. Grammar	Can she use a computer?	**p. 367**
42. Reading	Who is it?	**p. 368**
43. Writing/ Speaking	Job Application	**p. 369**
44. Writing	Idea Map	**p. 370**

Unit Opener

**Expansion Activity: Conversation/
Vocabulary: Matching Descriptions**

Before class: Copy and enlarge the list below; cut each section into slips of paper.

I am wearing a purple dress. I am wearing a purple scarf. I am tall.	I am wearing a blue shirt and pants. I have long brown hair. I am working.
I am sitting in a chair. I am talking on the phone. I am wearing a red jacket.	I am sitting in a chair. I am writing and talking on the phone. I am wearing a white shirt.
I wear a cap. I am sitting. I am drinking coffee.	I am buying a newspaper. I am wearing a white shirt. I am wearing black boots.
I am wearing a green shirt. I am standing on the street. I have brown pants.	I am wearing blue pants. I have brown hair. I am young.
I am reading a newspaper. I have brown hair. I am drinking coffee.	I am wearing white. I am cooking eggs. I have brown hair.
I am wearing a cap. I have a white shirt. I have blue pants.	I am walking. I work in a restaurant. I am wearing a white cap.
I have white hair. I am wearing a red jacket. I am walking.	I have gray hair. I am paying for my breakfast. I am wearing a blue shirt.

- Put the transparency for Unit 11 on the OHP or have students look at the big picture on page 174 in their books.

- Pass out the slips of paper, one to each student or pair.

- Ask students to read the descriptions aloud, and have the other students guess who it is.

Objective

Talking about what you do

Vocabulary

- a cashier
- a computer programmer
- a construction worker
- a cook
- a delivery person
- a health aide
- a sales clerk
- a taxi driver
- a waiter

Literacy Workbook pages 128–133
Workbook page 122

  A   CD 4, TRACK 26   **Listen. Look at page 174.**

- Play the first part of the audio or read the sentences in the listening script as students look at the list of jobs in the book.
- Play the rest of the audio or read the list of jobs. Have students repeat.
- Say the job titles in random order and have students point.

Listening Script

A. LISTEN. LOOK AT PAGE 174.

1. A sales clerk. He's a sales clerk.
2. A taxi driver. Leo is a taxi driver.
3. A health aide. Nadira's a health aide.
4. A waiter. He's a waiter.
5. A cook. He's a cook.
6. A cashier. She's a cashier.
7. A construction worker. Ben's a construction worker.
8. A delivery person. Tien's a delivery person.
9. An office worker. Isabel's an office worker.
10. A computer programmer. Paul's a computer programmer.

LISTEN AND REPEAT.

1. a sales clerk
2. a taxi driver
3. a health aide
4. a waiter
5. a cook
6. a cashier
7. a construction worker
8. a delivery person
9. an office worker
10. a computer programmer

Literacy Development Activity: Alphabetize.

- Have students write the job titles in alphabetical order.
- Put students in pairs to compare lists.
- Have students write the job titles in alphabetical order on the board.

B CD 4, TRACK 27 **Listen. Look at page 174.**

- Direct students' attention to the picture and ask: *Who do you see? What jobs do they have?*

- Play the audio or read the conversation as students follow along silently.

- Play the audio or read the conversation again and have students repeat.

- Put students in pairs to practice the conversation.

C **Talk with a partner.**

- Model the activity with a more advanced student. Cue the student to ask the question. Respond with your job. Elicit the student's job.

> I'm a teacher. And you?
>
> I'm a construction worker.

- Have students practice the conversation in pairs.

- Walk around the room to monitor the activity and provide job titles and other help.

CULTURE Notes

- Point out that in the United States people often say they are students if they aren't working but are taking classes.

- Point out that Americans consider *homemaker* to be an occupation if the man or woman is staying home and taking care of the house and/or children. *Housewife* is a term that is no longer really used.

D **Look at the picture on page 174. Complete.**

- Go over the directions and the example.

- Have students complete the sentences.

- Put students in pairs to compare answers.

- Elicit answers from pairs. Provide or elicit correction as needed.

> **Answer Key** **1.** a construction worker; **2.** a taxi driver; **3.** a health aide; **4.** an office worker; **5.** a computer programmer; **6.** a delivery person

Expansion Activity: Character Cards

- Give each student a character card. If there aren't enough, write the names of the characters on index cards and pass them out.

- Have students walk around the classroom as their character and practice the conversation in Activity C. Remind students to look at Lesson 1, page 175, if they need help remembering the character's job.

- Walk around the room to monitor the activity. Remind students to answer with the job of the character.

- As a variation, hand out the character cards and have students take turns performing conversations for the class.

Objective

Identifying things that people use on the job

Vocabulary

a cash register	pots and pans
a computer	a taxi cab
an order pad	tools

Literacy Workbook pages 128–133
Workbook page 123

  A CD 4, TRACK 28 **Listen.**

• Direct students' attention to the pictures.

• Play the first part of the audio or read the sentences in the listening script.

• Play the rest of the audio or read the list of words and phrases and have students repeat and point to the correct pictures.

• Read the words and phrases in random order and have students point to them. Check for accuracy.

Listening Script

A. LISTEN.

1. A taxicab. A taxi driver drives a taxicab.
2. An order pad. A waiter writes an order on an order pad.
3. Pots and pans. A cook uses pots and pans.
4. A computer. An office worker types on a computer.
5. A cash register. A cashier uses a cash register.
6. Tools. A construction worker works with tools.

LISTEN AND REPEAT.

1. a taxicab
2. an order pad
3. pots and pans
4. a computer
5. a cash register
6. tools

Expansion Activity: Pair Work

• Put students in pairs.

• Have students take turns reading the words and phrases from Activity A as their partners point to each picture.

• Walk around to monitor the activity and provide help as needed.

B Match.

• Go over the example.

• Have students match the items needed to do a job in the right column to the job in the left column.

• Put students in pairs to compare answers. Each pair should have a more advanced and a less advanced student if possible.

• Call on volunteer pairs to provide answers. Ask for or provide corrections as needed.

Answer Key 1. e; 2. f; 3. c; 4. d; 5. a; 6. b

Expansion Activity: Beanbag Toss

• Call on a student and say a job as you toss a beanbag or small ball. Elicit something you use in that job.

- Have the student call on or toss the beanbag to a classmate and say a job, eliciting something used for that job. If you have the room in your classroom, you may want to have students stand in a circle for this activity. Otherwise, make sure students are paying attention if classmates are tossing a beanbag.

- Continue until everyone has had a chance to play.

Extra Challenge
Write sentences.

- Direct students' attention to the title of the lesson (*A cook uses pots and pans.*).

- Have students write sentences with the information in Activity B. Remind students to follow the model *(A _____ uses _____).*

- Put students in pairs to compare sentences.

- Have volunteers write sentences on the board.

🎧 **C** CD 4, TRACK 29 **Listen and circle.**

- Play the first part of the audio or read the first item in the listening scripts. Stop and elicit the answer. Point out that *office worker* is circled.

- Play the rest of the audio or read the rest of the sentences. Have students circle the job they hear.

- Put students in pairs to compare answers.

- Play the audio or read the sentences again so students can check their work.

- Go over the answers with the class.

········ **Listening Script**

C. LISTEN AND CIRCLE.

1. **Woman:** I am an office worker. I use a computer.
2. **Man:** I am a construction worker. I use tools.
3. **Man:** I am a taxi driver. I drive a taxicab.
4. **Woman:** I am a cashier. I use a cash register.
5. **Woman:** I am a cook. I use pots and pans.
6. **Man:** I am a waiter. I use an order pad.

Answer Key **1.** office worker;
2. construction worker; **3.** taxi driver;
4. cashier; **5.** cook; **6.** waiter

Objective

Understanding and talking about job environments

Vocabulary

indoors	with machines
outdoors	with people

**Literacy Workbook pages 128–133
Workbook page 123**

  A CD 4, TRACK 30 **Listen.**

- Direct students' attention to the pictures. Ask: *What do you see?*

- Play the first part of the audio or read the sentences in the listening script as students look at the pictures.

- Play the rest of the audio or read the words and phrases and have students repeat and point to the pictures.

- Read the words and phrases in random order and have students point to them.

Listening Script

A. LISTEN.

1. Indoors. Do you like to work indoors?
2. Outdoors. Do you like to work outdoors?
3. With people. Do you like to work with people?
4. With machines. Do you like to work with machines?

LISTEN AND REPEAT.

1. indoors
2. outdoors
3. with people
4. with machines

B Check.

- Go over the example, pointing out what is checked. Elicit or point out that a construction worker usually works outdoors and with machines.

- Have students check the appropriate boxes for each job. Point out that students should focus on where the person usually works and who or what he or she usually works with.

- Put students in pairs to compare answers.

- Elicit answers from class members.

Answer Key

Some jobs may fit into several categories.

Jobs	Indoors	Outdoors	With People	With Machines
construction worker		✔		✔
waiter	✔		✔	
sales clerk	✔		✔	
delivery person	✔	✔	✔	✔

  C CD 4, TRACK 31 **Listen.**

- Play the audio or read the conversation as students follow along silently.

- Play the audio again and have students repeat.

- Put students in pairs to practice the conversation, then have them switch partners.

D **Talk with 5 classmates.**

- Go over the words in the box.

- Model the activity with a more advanced student.

- Have students stand and walk around the room to talk to five classmates.

- Call on students to tell the class about a classmate.

Expansion Activity: **Survey**

- Tell students that in this activity they must choose between working indoors and outdoors, and between working with people and machines.

- Copy the chart on the board.

	Likes indoors	Likes outdoors
Likes to work with machines		
Likes to work with people		

- Model the activity. Call on several students and ask: *Do you like to work indoors or outdoors? Do you like to work with machines or with people?* Put a tally mark in the appropriate square.

- Have students ask ten classmates where they would like to work and if they'd prefer to work with people or machines. Remind students to put a tally mark in one of the four squares for each student's response.

- Talk about the results with the class.

Expansion Activity: **Pair Dictation**

- Put students in pairs. Try to match a more advanced student with a less advanced student.

- Model the activity with an advanced student. Say a word and have the student spell it. Focus on the vocabulary from the first three lessons. As the student spells it aloud, write the letters he or she says on the board.

- Have the less advanced students say the words and write the letters that the more advanced students says.

Objective
Understanding and talking about job skills

Vocabulary

cook	**drive**	**sell**
deliver	**fix**	**use**

Literacy Workbook pages 128–133
Workbook page 124

  A   CD 4, TRACK 32   **Listen.**

- Have students look at the pictures.

- Play the first part of the audio or read the sentences in the listening script as students look at the words and pictures.

- Play the rest of the audio or read the list of words and have students repeat the words and point to the pictures.

·········· Listening Script

A. LISTEN.

1. Drive. I can drive a car.
2. Fix. I can fix things.
3. Sell. I can sell things.
4. Cook. I can cook food.
5. Use. I can use a computer.
6. Deliver. I can deliver packages.

LISTEN AND REPEAT.

1. drive
2. fix
3. sell
4. cook
5. use
6. deliver

Expansion Activity: **Speed Lists**

- Write these sentence starters on the board:

  I can drive _____.

  I can fix _____.

  I can sell _____.

  I can cook _____.

  I can use _____.

  I can deliver _____.

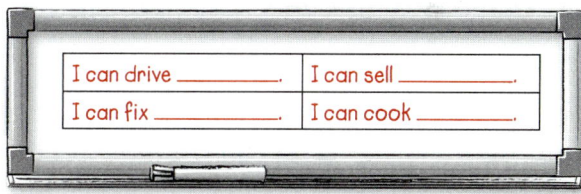

- Put students in pairs to list as many completions as they can for each sentence. Set a time limit of five minutes. Point out that the completions don't have to be true for them, but they do need to be logical completions.

- After five minutes, find out how many completions they had for each sentence.

Expansion Activity: **Beanbag Toss**

- Call on a student, toss a beanbag or small ball, and say, *I can drive _____.* Elicit a completion (*a car*). Point out that there could be other appropriate completions.

- Have the student say a student's name, throw the beanbag to that classmate, and start a different sentence (*I can fix _____.*), eliciting a completion. Remember, if this is hard logistically, have students stand, or eliminate the beanbag and just have students call on classmates.

- Continue until everyone has had a chance to participate.

B CD 4, TRACK 33 Listen.

- Play the audio or read the conversation as students follow along silently.

- Play the audio or read the conversation again and have students repeat.

- Put students in pairs to practice the conversation.

C Talk with 6 classmates.

- Model the activity with a more advanced student.

- Have students stand and walk around the room to practice the conversation with six classmates. Remind students to practice both roles.

- Walk around to monitor the activity and provide help as needed.

Expansion Activity:
Inside/Outside Circles

- Divide the students into two groups. Have one group form a circle facing out; have the other group form a concentric circle facing in.

- Designate the inside circle as A, the outside as B.

- Have students practice the conversation. After a few seconds, cue the outside circle to shift one place to the right.

- Continue until students have talked to at least five partners.

My Life

- Model the activity. Say your job and things you use (e.g., *I am a teacher. I use a board, books, and an overhead projector.*).

- Put students in groups to talk about their jobs and what they use at work. Remind them that being a student or staying at home caring for children or the home is a job. Provide vocabulary as needed.

- Call on students to tell the class about a classmate.

Expansion Activity:
Character Cards

- Have students come to the front of the class.

- Give each student a character card. Students know the jobs for Ben, Sandy, Leo, Nadira, Isabel, Paul, Maria, and Carlos. Remind students to look at Lesson 1, page 175, if they need help remembering the character's job.

- Have the class ask the character questions about his or her job.

Objective
Asking and answering questions about job skills

Literacy Workbook pages 128–133
Workbook page 124

  A   CD 4, TRACK 34   **Listen.**

- Have students look at the picture. Ask: *Who do you see? What is she doing?*

- Play the audio or read the conversation as students follow along silently.

- Play the audio or read the conversation again and have students repeat.

- Put students in pairs to practice the conversation.

PRONUNCIATION Note

- Point out that *can* and *can't* sound very similar in the short answers, but that the vowel sound is a little different in statements. Tell students that the affirmative *can* often has a short vowel sound and is made with a relaxed somewhat open mouth. *Can't* is pronounced with a longer vowel sound, and the mouth is stretched wider.

Expansion Activity: *Can* or *can't?*

- Have students use their *Yes* and *No* cards from Unit 2, Worksheet 5. (Teacher's Edition page 331).

- Remind students of the differences in pronunciation between *can* and *can't*.

- Say sentences with either *can* or *can't* (e.g., *I can cook meals. She can help people. We can't use a computer.*). After each sentence, have students hold up a *Yes* (for *can*) or *No* (for *can't*) card to show they can hear the difference in pronunciation.

B   Talk with 6 classmates.

- Go over the phrases in the box.

- Model the activity with a more advanced student.

- Have students stand and walk around the room to practice the conversation with six classmates. Remind students to practice both roles.

- Walk around to monitor the activity and provide help as needed.

Extra Challenge
Write questions.

- Have students write four questions about other skills that are not in the box (*drive a car, fix a refrigerator*).

- Put students in pairs to practice asking and answering their questions.

What's your job? 285

Expansion Activity: Listening/Speaking: *Can vs. Can't*

- Put the color transparency for Unit 11 on the OHP or have students look at the big picture on page 174 in their books.

- Dictate questions about the picture using can.

    Can Tien deliver boxes?
    Can Ben use tools?
    Can Isabel drive a taxi?
    Can Paul use a computer?

- Have students answer the questions with short answers.

Expansion Activity: **Take a stand.**

- Have students stand. Point to one side of the room and say *can*, or write it on a piece of paper and tape it to the wall. Point to the other side of the room and say *can't*.

- Say a skill (e.g., *drive a car*) and have students move to the side of the room that indicates their response.

- Continue with other skills. Keep the activity fast-paced.

C Write about you.

- Direct students' attention to the picture and ask: *Who do you see? What can Ben do? What can't Ben do?*

- Go over the directions.

- Model the activity. Say two things you can do and two things you can't.

- Have students complete the activity by writing two things they can do and two things they can't do.

- Put students in pairs to talk about their sentences.

Objective
Understanding and using want ads

Literacy Workbook pages 128–133
Workbook page 125

A Read the want ads. Circle the jobs.

- Have students read the ads and circle the jobs.
- Elicit the jobs (*cashiers, waiter, health aide*).
- Ask questions: *Where do they need cashiers? What place needs a waiter? Is the health aide job at a hospital?*

Literacy Development Activity: Abbreviations

- Write the abbreviations on the board: *Tues., Fri.*
- Have students write the complete word.
- As a variation, add other abbreviations students have learned in this book.

B Match.

- Go over the example.
- Put students in pairs to compare answers.
- Have students practice asking and answering the questions in pairs.

Answer Key 1. c; 2. d; 3. e; 4. f; 5. b; 6. a

C CD 4, TRACK 35 Listen and check the ad from Activity A.

- Play the first item of the audio or read the first sentence in the script. Elicit the answer.
- Play the audio or read the rest of the listening script and have students check the ads.
- Put students in pairs to compare answers.

Listening Script

C. LISTEN AND CHECK THE AD. . .

1. Hi, I'm Lina. I'm interested in a cashier job.
2. Hi, I'm Carlos Avila. I like to work with people. I can be a waiter.
3. Hello, Mr. Howard. My name is Pavel Asimov. I work as a cashier at my school cafeteria.
4. Good afternoon, Mrs. Flores. My name is Nadira Shaheed. I am a health care aide. Is the job still open?
5. Hello. My name is Betty Wong. I saw your sign. Do you still need a waiter?
6. Hello. I'm Pablo Ruiz. I can work evenings as your health care aide.

Answer Key 1. Lina: Ad #1; 2. Carlos: Ad #2; 3. Pavel: Ad #1; 4. Nadira: Ad #3; 5. Betty: Ad #2; 6. Pablo: Ad #3

Expansion Activity: Create a Conversation.

- Put students in pairs to create a telephone conversation in which one person calls and asks about a job.
- Have volunteers perform their conversations.

Objective
Talking about past jobs

Literacy Workbook pages 128–133
Workbook page 126

A   CD 4, TRACK 36   **Listen.**

- Direct students' attention to the pictures and ask: *Who do you see? What year is it?* Make sure students understand the concept of *before* or *past*. Gesture over your shoulder behind you.

- Play the audio or read the conversation as students follow along silently.

- Play the audio or read the conversation again and have students repeat.

- Put students in pairs to practice the conversation.

GRAMMAR Note

- Make sure students understand the meanings of *was* and *were*. Write the headings *Now* and *Before* on the board. Under *Now*, write *am, is,* and *are*. Under *Before*, write *was* and *were*.

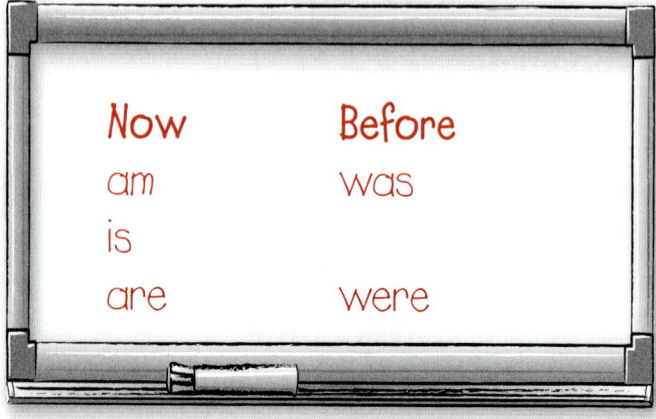

B   **Talk with a partner.**

- Model the activity with a more advanced student.

- Put students in pairs to practice asking and answering the question.

> **What did you do before?**
>
> **I was a cashier in Mexico.**

- Call on students to tell the class about their partner (e.g., *Maria was a cashier in Mexico.*).

C   **Complete the chart. Ask 7 classmates.**

- Go over the directions and the example.

- Have students stand and walk around the room, asking and answering the question from Activity B. Remind students to complete the chart as they talk to their classmates.

Expansion Activity:
Discuss the chart.

- Copy the first two columns of the chart on the board.

- Have students volunteer information about a classmate. Make sure all the students are listed on the board. Write the names next to the job.

- Discuss the results (e.g., *Five people were cashiers.*).

Objective

Reading and understanding information on a paycheck

**Literacy Workbook pages 128–133
Workbook page 127**

 A CD 4, TRACK 37 **Listen and read.**

- Play the audio or read the information as students look and read.

- Ask comprehension questions: *What is Isabel's job? Where does she work? How much does she make an hour? How many hours does she work?*

- Play the audio or read the information again and have students repeat.

- Go over any unfamiliar vocabulary in the check.

- Put students in pairs to practice reading aloud.

CULTURE Notes

- Point out that before a paycheck is cashed or deposited, the pay stub should be removed.

- Point out that sometimes the pay stub is attached to the *top or bottom* of the check, not to the side as in the art on this page. It is a good idea to hold onto a pay stub.

- Some companies use direct deposit, meaning that the check is deposited directly into the employee's bank account. Employees should still receive and keep their pay stubs with direct deposit.

Literacy Development Activity: Cloze

- Photocopy the text below.

   Isabel is an office _____. She works at _____. Isabel makes _____ an hour. She usually works _____ hours a week. She _____ $80 a week.

   Isabel has to pay _____. She pays _____ in federal taxes. She pays $2.95 in state _____. Isabel pays other taxes, too. Her _____ is $66.61. That is her _____ pay.

- Give each student a copy.

- Have students fill in the missing information. Encourage less advanced students to look at the text in the book.

- Go over the answers with the class.

Extra Challenge

Cloze

- Have more advanced students try to complete the above cloze activity from memory, without looking at the reading in the book.

B Circle.

• Go over the example.

• Have students circle the correct completion.

• Call on volunteers to read their answers to the class. Provide or elicit corrections as needed.

Answer Key 1. Isabel Lopez; 2. $10 an hour; 3. 8 hours a week; 4. $7.09; 5. $2.95; 6. $66.61

C Write.

• Have students complete the sentences. Point out that this information is new.

• Put students in pairs to compare answers.

• Call on random pairs to provide answers. Work out the answers on the board if students find that helpful.

Answer Key 1. $100; 2. $86.61

Objective
Understanding safety signs

Vocabulary

caution	keep out
emergency exit	no smoking
fire extinguisher	wash hands
high voltage	

Literacy Workbook pages 128–133
Workbook page 128

  A CD 4, TRACK 38 **Listen and read.**

- Direct students' attention to the signs. Elicit the ones they recognize.

- Play the audio or read the signs as students follow along silently.

- Play the audio or read the signs again and have students practice correct pronunciation.

- Ask questions about where these signs are usually seen.

> **Where do you see "Emergency Exit"?**
> **Where do you see "Wash hands"?**

- Read the signs in random order and have students point. Make sure students understand what *high voltage* means.

Expansion Activity:
Complete the sign.

- Call on a student and say the beginning of one of the signs (e.g., *Caution*). Elicit the completion (*Work Area*).

> **Caution**   **Work Area**

- Have the student call on a classmate and say the beginning of another sign.

- Continue until everyone has had a chance to participate.

B **Look at Activity A. Match.**

- Go over the directions and the example.

- Have students write the letter of the sign on the line next to its meaning.

- Put students in pairs to compare answers.

- Elicit answers from the class.

> **Answer Key**   **1.** c; **2.** e; **3.** d; **4.** a; **5.** f; **6.** b

C **Make a safety sign for work or school. Tell a partner.**

- Direct students' attention to the picture. Ask: *Who do you see? What does the sign mean?*

- Put students in pairs to brainstorm ideas.

- Distribute paper, or have students take a page out of their notebooks. Have students make safety signs for their work or school. Encourage them to make signs with a picture only, no words.

- Walk around and provide help as needed.

- Have pairs tell the class about their signs.

Expansion Activity: Gallery

- Post the signs around the room to create a gallery. Number each sign.

- Have students write the number of the sign and its meaning in their notebooks.

Objective
Using the simple past of *be*

Literacy Workbook pages 128–133
Workbook page 129

  A CD 4, TRACK 39 **Listen and read.**

- Direct students' attention to the picture and ask: *Who do you see? Now or before? What does she look like?*

- Read the sentence above the chart (*Sandy was a student in 1978.*).

- Play the audio or read the chart as students look at the chart.

- Play the audio or read the chart again and have students repeat.

- Read the pronouns in random order and elicit the past form of *be*.

  B CD 4, TRACK 40 **Listen and circle.**

- Go over the Post-it Note and the example. Play the first item of the audio or read the first sentence in the listening script. Elicit if it is past or present. Point out that *present* is circled.

- Play the rest of the audio or read the rest of the sentences and have students circle *present* or *past*.

- Put students in pairs to compare answers.

- Go over the answers with the class.

Listening Script

B. LISTEN AND CIRCLE.

1. Sandy is a teacher.
2. Maria was a health aide a long time ago.
3. Last year Paul was a student in Haiti.
4. Leo was a taxi driver in Russia.
5. He is a taxi driver now, too.
6. Isabel is an office worker.

Answer Key **1.** present; **2.** past; **3.** past; **4.** past; **5.** present; **6.** present

Extra Challenge
Dictation

- Play the audio or read the sentences from the script for Activity B three times.

- Have students write the sentences they hear.

- Put students in pairs to compare sentences.

- Have volunteers write the sentences on the board.

- As an extension, after the yellow note is reviewed, have advanced students rewrite these sentences using a word/ expression from the yellow note.

C **Complete. Write *was* or *were*.**

- Go over the example and point out or elicit that *2 years ago* is an example of a past expression.

- Have students write *was* or *were* on the lines.

- Put students in pairs to compare answers.

- Elicit answers from the class.

Answer Key **1.** was; **2.** were; **3.** was; **4.** were; **5.** were; **6.** was

D Write about you.

- Model the activity. Write the two sentence starters on the board and complete them using your own information.

- Have students complete the sentences using *was* or *were*. Refer them to Activity C if they need ideas for completing the sentences.

- Put students in pairs to read their sentences.

- Call on students to read their sentences to the class.

Expansion Activity: Timelines

- Write a timeline for yourself on the board. Include years, places, and/or occupations. Write at least five entries on your timeline.

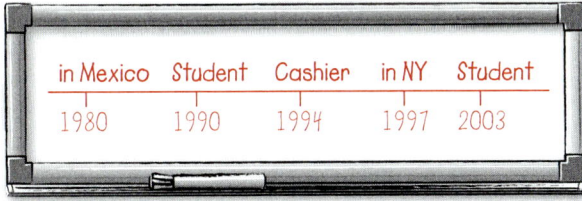

in Mexico	Student	Cashier	in NY	Student
1980	1990	1994	1997	2003

- Tell the class about your timeline (e.g., *In 1997, I was in New York.*).

- Have students create timelines to show places and jobs in their own lives.

- Put students in pairs to share their timelines.

Objective
Using *can* and *can't*

Literacy Workbook pages 128–133
Workbook page 129

A Write *can* or *can't*.

- Direct students' attention to the chart. Go over the information, making sure students understand how to make *yes/no* questions with *can* and short answers.

- Go over the example.

- Have students write *can* or *can't* on the lines.

- Put students in pairs to compare answers.

- Go over the answers with the class.

Answer Key 1. can; 2. can't; 3. can; 4. can; 5. can't; 6. can't

Expansion Activity: Questions

- Put students in pairs to write *yes/no* questions about the items in Activity A using *can* (e.g., *Can Paul use a computer?*).

- Have each pair join another pair to take turns asking and answering their questions.

B Ask 8 classmates.

- Go over the example conversation.

- Have students stand and walk around the room, taking turns asking the questions to complete the chart.

- Call on students to tell the class about a classmate.

BIG PICTURE

Expansion Activity:
Grammar: Can she use a computer?

- Have students look at the big picture on page 174 in their books, or put the transparency for Unit 11 on the OHP.

- Photocopy and distribute Worksheet 41: *Can she use a computer?* (Teacher's Edition page 367)

- Have students answer the questions.

- Elicit answers from the class.

Answer Key 1. A; 2. B; 3. A; 4. B; 5. B; 6. A; 7. A; 8. A

Objective
Understanding a job application

Literacy Workbook pages 128–133
Workbook page 130

A Read.

- Read the sentences about Leo's application aloud. Go over the Post-it Note.

- Have students read the application.

- Ask comprehension questions: *What was Leo's full name in Russia? Where was his school? Where does Leo work? How long was Leo a delivery person?*

CULTURE Note

- Point out or elicit that Leo's first and last name are different in the present. Elicit reasons why that might be. Tell students that sometimes people simplify their name to make it easier to spell and pronounce when they move to another country where a different language is spoken. In the United States, you have to pay a fee and go to court to change your name legally.

B Write the answers.

- Read the first question. Elicit the answer. Make sure students see where the information is on the application.

- Have students answer the questions.

- Call on volunteer students to provide answers. Provide or ask for corrections as needed.

Answer Key
1. 17 Water Street, Los Angeles, CA; **2.** Moscow Secondary School; **3.** taxi driver; **4.** delivery person; **5.** No, he can't. **6.** Yes, he can.

Expansion Activity: Reading: Who is it?

- Have students look at the big picture on page 174 in their books, or put the transparency for Unit 11 on the overhead projector (OHP).

- Photocopy and distribute Worksheet 42: *Who is it?* (Teacher's Edition page 368)

- Have students answer the questions.

- Put students in pairs to compare answers.

- Elicit answers from volunteers and provide or elicit corrections as needed.

Answer Key
(top down) Leo, Isabel, Paul, Nadira, Tien, Ben

Objective
Writing a telephone conversation

Literacy Workbook pages 128–133
Workbook page 131

  A   CD 4, TRACK 41   **Read and Listen.**

- Play the audio or read the conversation as students follow along silently.

- Ask comprehension questions: *Who is having a conversation? What are they talking about? What can Maria do? When can she work?*

- Put students in pairs. Have one student read Maria's lines and the other read Mr. Brand's, and then switch roles.

Expansion Activity: Sentence Strips

- Photocopy the conversation from Activity A and cut it into strips.

- Put students in pairs. Give each pair a set of strips.

- With books closed, have students put the conversation in order.

- **Option:** Have literacy students put the sentences from the conversation in order. Have more advanced students read and confirm their classmates' work.

B   Write a conversation for a job you want.

- Model the content of this activity. Have a student read Mr. Brand's lines. Demonstrate how to substitute your own information.

- Have students complete the conversation.

- Walk around and provide help as needed.

- Put students in pairs to take turns practicing their conversations.

CULTURE Note

- Point out that it can be very helpful to write down questions and information before having a telephone conversation, especially in a second language.

Expansion Activity: Role-Play

- Write *fast, slow, soft, loud* on the board. Model each word as you speak, demonstrating how to speak too fast, too slowly, and so on.

- Have volunteers perform the conversation from Activity B in front of the class.

- Ask the class for feedback after each performance *(Can you understand the speakers? Are they too soft or too loud?)*.

Expansion Activity: Job Application

- Photocopy and distribute Worksheet 43: *Job Application* (Teacher's Edition page 369).

- Put students in pairs.

- Have students take turns asking and answering questions to complete the application with their partner's information.

- Provide help as needed.

Objective
Review and assessment

A Write the job.

- Go over the directions, the words in the box, and the example.

- Have students look at the pictures and write the correct job from the box.

- Put students in pairs to compare answers.

- Go over the answers with the class.

Answer Key 1. delivery person;
2. office worker; 3. cook; 4. taxi driver;
5. waiter; 6. cashier

B CD 4, TRACK 42 Listen and fill in the answer sheet.

- Go over the directions.

- Play the first item of the audio or read the first sentence in the listening script. Stop and elicit that *A* is correct. Point out that *A* is filled in.

- Play the rest of the audio or read the rest of the sentences from the script. Have students fill in the answers.

- Put students in pairs to compare answers.

- Call on random pairs to provide answers. Provide or ask for corrections as needed.

Listening Script

B. LISTEN AND FILL IN THE ANSWER SHEET.

1. I'm a construction worker.
2. A waiter writes on an order pad.
3. What did you do before?
4. I was a health aide.
5. **A:** Can you cook a meal?
   B: No, I can't.

Answer Key 1. A; 2. A; 3. B; 4. B;
5. B

C Find a want ad. Look in a newspaper or online. Complete.

- Bring in want ads, or have students bring them in.

- Go over the directions.

- Have students write the information they find on the lines.

- Put students in pairs to talk about their ads.

- Call on students to tell the class about their ads.

D Complete the form.

- Have students complete the form with their own information. Point out that for the first two lines of information, they should write the information (*Last Name*, etc.) on the lines *above* the prompts.

- Put students in pairs to talk about the information on their forms.

- Call on students to tell the class about something on their forms.

E Learning Log

- Read each word aloud. Have students check the words they know.

Expansion Activity: Draw it!

- Divide the class into two teams.
- Have a volunteer from each team come to the board. Whisper the same word from the Learning Log to each person. Pick words that lend themselves best to this activity, e.g., *computer, taxicab, safety signs,* etc., though for added difficulty, some of the other words could be tried, too.
- Have the students at the board draw the word and elicit guesses from the class.
- Award one point to the team whose member guesses the word first.

LOOKING BACK

- Go over the directions.
- Put students in pairs to talk about the big picture on page 174 using grammar and vocabulary from the unit.
- Walk around to monitor the activity.
- Call on students to talk about the picture.

Expansion Activity: Writing: Idea Map

- Put the transparency for Unit 11 on the OHP or have students look at the big picture on page 174.
- Photocopy and distribute Worksheet 44: *Idea Map* (Teacher's Edition page 370).
- Copy the idea map on the board or onto a transparency and put it on the OHP. Point to the circle *Outdoor jobs,* and ask *Who works outdoors?* Point to the two people outside the building in the big picture. Elicit *taxi driver.* Point out that *taxi driver* is written in the circle. Have students write the word on their worksheets.
- Point to each of the other circles on the worksheet and read the titles. Have students repeat the titles after you.
- Have students work in pairs to complete the idea map.

Answer Key **Outdoor jobs:** taxi driver, construction worker, delivery person; **Driving jobs:** taxi driver, delivery person; **Job at a desk:** computer programmer, office worker; **Jobs in a restaurant:** waiter, cook; **Jobs working with people:** waiter, cashier, health aide, sales clerk; **Indoor jobs:** sales clerk, waiter, health aide, construction worker, office worker, computer programmer

UNIT OVERVIEW

Lesson	Objective	Student Book Page
1. I take a bus.	Asking and answering questions about modes of transportation	p. 191
2. It's on the left.	Understanding, asking for, and giving directions	p. 192
3. It's next to the market.	Asking for and giving directions	p. 193
4. How do I get to the airport?	Asking for and giving directions	p. 194
5. When does the next train leave?	Asking and answering questions about departure times	p. 195
6. Getting a Learner's Permit	Applying for a learner's permit	p. 196
7. Road Signs	Understanding and reading road signs	p. 197
8. How often does the train leave?	Understanding and asking about departure schedules	p. 198
9. A Bus Schedule	Reading a bus schedule	p. 199
10. Grammar: Questions with *Be*	Using *wh-* questions with *be*	p. 200
11. Grammar: Questions with *Do/Does*	Using *wh-* questions with *do/does*	p. 201
12. Read: A New Baby	Reading about car safety	p. 202
13. Write: Getting to School	Writing about transportation	p. 203
What do you know?	Review and assessment	p. 204

Big Picture Expansion Activities

Focus	Activity	Suggested Use
Listening/ Speaking	Confirming Visual Information	**Unit Opener**
Reading	Safety Tips	**Lesson 12**
Grammar	*Wh-* Questions	**Lesson 11**
Writing	Modes of Transportation	**Lesson 13**
Conversation/ Vocabulary	On the Road Bingo	**What do you know?**

Worksheets

Worksheet #/ Focus	Title	Teacher's Edition Page
45. Realia	Getting a Learner's Permit	p. 371
46. Grammar	*Wh-* Questions	p. 372
47. Reading	Safety Tips	p. 373
48. Vocabulary	On the Road Bingo	p. 374

Unit Opener

- Put the transparency for Unit 12 on the OHP (overhead projector) or have students look at the big picture on page 190.

- Point to the picture as you ask the question at the bottom of the page: *What do you see?*

- Elicit any vocabulary words the students know and write them on the board.

Expansion Activity:
Listening/Speaking: Confirming Visual Information

1. Divide the class into two teams.

2. Tell the students that you are going to read some sentences. When you call on a team member, that student will tell you if the sentence is right or wrong. If the sentence is wrong, the student will change it to make it right. The team will get a point for each correct response.

3. Put the transparency for Unit 12 on the OHP or have students look at the big picture on page 190. Do an example with the class. Say *I can see 17 people in the picture.* Ask if that sentence is right or wrong (*wrong*). Elicit the correct sentence (*I see 22 people in the picture.*). If necessary cue the students by pointing to people in the picture and counting.

4. Using your own sentences or sentences from the list below, call on a student from Team A, then one from Team B, and so on, alternating teams. Each team member should answer at least one time, but they may confer with their teammates before answering. Set a time limit of 15 seconds. Keep track of the points on the board.

   Sample sentences: *The bus stop is on 81st Street. There are four people at the bus stop. A woman with white hair is talking to a man with blue pants. There is a woman in a red car. A woman is driving a taxi. There are two taxis. The bus is the M-15. There is a man wearing a suit. There is a woman with glasses. There is a man in a blue shirt. There is a woman in a purple dress. Maria is in a car. Sandy is not in the picture.*

Objective
Asking and answering questions about modes of transportation

Vocabulary

drive a car	take a bus	take a taxi
ride a bike	take a subway	walk

Literacy Workbook pages 134–139
Workbook page 134

  A CD 4, TRACK 44 **Listen.**

- Play the first part of the audio or read the sentences in the first part of the listening script as students look at the words in the book.

- Play the rest of the audio or read the list of words. Have students repeat.

- Read the phrases in random order and have students point.

- Elicit any other ways that students get to school or work (e.g., *get a ride*).

······· **Listening Script**

A. LISTEN

1. Take a bus. I take a bus to school.
2. Take a subway. I take a subway to school.
3. Ride a bike. I ride a bike to school.
4. Drive a car. I drive a car to school.
5. Walk. I walk to school.
6. Take a taxi. I take a taxi to school.

LISTEN AND REPEAT.

1. take a bus
2. take a subway
3. ride a bike
4. drive a car
5. walk
6. take a taxi

Expansion Activity: Number Patterns

- Write the following number patterns on the board: *513, 416, 414, 413, 4.*

- Have students copy the patterns into their notebooks.

- Tell students that the numbers represent the number of letters in each word of the phrases in Activity A. For example, *513* would represent a phrase in which the first word has five letters; the second, one letter; the third, three letters.

- Have students write the phrases next to each number pattern.

- Go over the answers with the class.

Answer Key **513:** drive a car; **416:** take a subway; **414:** take a taxi, ride a bike; **413:** take a bus; **4:** walk

B **Ask 8 classmates.**

- Go over the example conversation.

- Have students stand and walk around the classroom talking to eight classmates. Remind students to have classmates sign their names under the appropriate form of transportation.

- Call on students to tell the class about a classmate (e.g., *Ming rides a bike to work.*).

Expansion Activity: Category Sort

- Have students stand. Ask: *How do you get to school*? Remind students to sort themselves by response. Ask someone from each group how they get to school.

- Repeat with other questions: *How do you get to work? How do you get to the grocery store? How do you get to the beach?*

- As a variation, have students tally the results. After you ask each question, have a representative from the group tally the number on the board to complete the chart below.

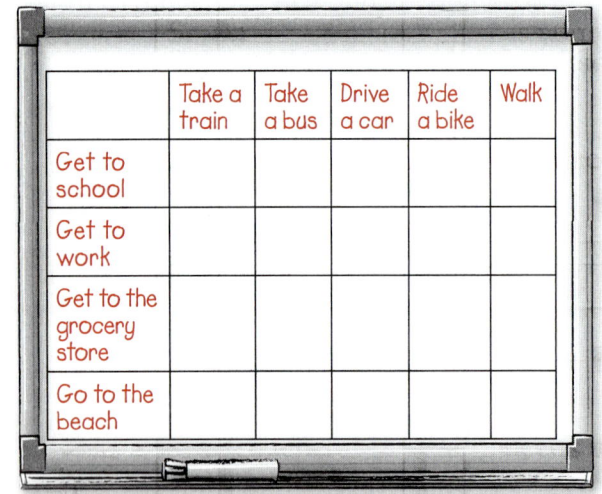

	Take a train	Take a bus	Drive a car	Ride a bike	Walk
Get to school					
Get to work					
Get to the grocery store					
Go to the beach					

Objective

Understanding, asking for, and giving directions

Vocabulary

on the left	straight ahead
on the right	

**Literacy Workbook pages 134–139
Workbook page 135**

 A CD 4, TRACK 45 **Listen.**

- Direct students' attention to the picture and ask: *Who do you see? What places do you see?*

- Play the first part of the audio or read the sentences in the listening script as students follow along.

- Play the rest of the audio or read the second part of the listening script and have students repeat.

- Read the phrases in random order and have students point to them. Check for accuracy.

Expansion Activity: Follow the arrow.

- Draw arrows on the board to point to the three directions in Activity A.

- Point to the arrows in random order and have students say the direction.

- Call on students and point and have students say the directions.

- Call individual students to the board. Say a direction and have students point.

Listening Script

A. LISTEN

1. On the left. The movie theater is on the left.
2. Straight ahead. The post office is straight ahead.
3. On the right. The bank is on the right.

LISTEN AND REPEAT.

1. on the left
2. straight ahead
3. on the right

GRAMMAR Note

- Make sure students understand that they must use *on* with *the right* and *the left* but not with *straight ahead*.

 B CD 4, TRACK 46 **Listen.**

- Play the audio or read the conversation with a student as students follow along silently.

- Play the audio or read the conversation again and have students repeat.

- Put the students in pairs to practice the conversation. Have students switch roles.

C **Look at the picture in Activity A. Talk with 3 classmates.**

• Go over the places in Activity A.

• Model the activity with a more advanced student. Have the student ask you about a place in Activity A. Answer appropriately.

• Have students walk around the room to practice asking and answering about the places in Activity A with three classmates.

D CD 4, TRACK 47 **Listen and circle.**

• Play the first sentence of the audio or read the first sentence of the listening script. Stop and elicit the answer. Point out that *on the right* is circled.

• Play the rest of the audio or read the rest of the sentences in the listening script. Have students circle the location they hear.

• Put students in pairs to compare answers.

• Elicit answers from the class.

········ **Listening Script**

D. LISTEN AND CIRCLE.

1. The bank is on the right.
2. The post office is straight ahead.
3. The movie theater is on the left.
4. The drugstore is on the right.

Answer Key **1.** on the right;
2. straight ahead; **3.** on the left; **4.** on the right

**Expansion Activity:
Who's on your right?**

• Model the activity with a more advanced student. Ask and elicit answers to these questions: *Who is on your right? Who is on your left? Who is straight ahead?* Point to each student as you ask the questions.

• Call on a student, and ask: *Who is on your right?*

> Who is on your right?

Elicit the name of the classmate to the student's right.

• Have the student call on a classmate and ask one of the three questions.

• Continue until everyone has had a chance to participate.

• As a variation, have students stand and form a circle. Now the person facing the student on the circle is straight ahead.

**Expansion Activity:
Character Cards**

• Give students a character card.

• Have students stand in front of the class holding the character card in front. Make sure students are oriented in the same way.

• Call on students and ask questions: *Who is on Carlos's right? Who is on Nadira's left? Is Isabel on the left of Ben?*

Objective
Asking for and giving directions

Vocabulary

across from	near
behind	next to
between	on the corner of

**Literacy Workbook pages 134–139
Workbook page 135**

  A   CD 4, TRACK 48   **Listen.**

- Direct students' attention to the picture. Ask: *What places do you see?*

- Play the first part of the audio or read the first part of the listening script as students follow along silently.

- Play the rest of the audio or read the rest of the listening script and have students repeat the phrases.

- Read the phrases in random order and have students point to them.

······ Listening Script

A. LISTEN.

1. On the corner of. The bank is on the corner of 22nd Street and Pond Street.
2. Next to. The laundromat is next to the bank.
3. Between. The market is between the bank and the post office.
4. Behind. The parking lot is behind the post office.
5. Across from. The bakery is across from the market.
6. Near. The green truck is near 22nd Street.

LISTEN AND REPEAT.

1. on the corner of
2. next to
3. between
4. behind
5. across from
6. near

Literacy Development Activity:
Point to the places.

- Read each sentence of the listening script for Activity A slowly and have students point to the places as you say them.

Extra Challenge
Write sentences.

- Play the audio or read the sentences in the first part of the listening script again as many times as necessary. Have students write the sentences they hear.

- Have volunteers write the sentences on the board.

  B   CD 4, TRACK 49   **Listen.**

- Play the audio or read the conversation with a student as students follow along silently.

- Play the audio or read the conversation again and have students repeat.

- Put students in pairs to practice the conversation.

C   **Look at the picture in Activity A. Talk with 5 classmates.**

- Say each place in the picture in Activity A and have students repeat.

How do you get to school? 305

- Model the activity with a more advanced student. Have the student ask about one of the places. Respond appropriately.

> **Where is the laundromat?**
>
> **It's next to the bank.**

- Have students stand and walk around the room to talk to five classmates, or divide them into groups of six. Encourage students to ask about a different place each time.

- Call on students to tell where one place is.

Expansion Activity: **Place Cards**

- Give each student seven index cards and have students write one of the places from Activity A on each card (*bank, laundromat, market, post office, parking lot, bakery*).

- Copy the streets from Activity A on the board. Do not put in any buildings.

- Have students copy the map onto big pieces of plain paper.

- Call a student to the board with their cards. Tell the student where one place is, giving it a new location (e.g., *The bank is on the corner of Lake and 22nd*.). Point out that the buildings are in different places now. Have the student tape the correct card to the place on the board.

- Call another student to the board and give the location of a different place (e.g., *The laundromat is across 22nd Street from the bank*.). Have the student tape that card to the board in place.

- Continue until the board is filled in.

- Put students in pairs to take turns telling their partners where places are as their partners place the cards on their paper maps.

Expansion Activity: **Draw a map.**

- Have students draw a map of their neighborhoods, labeling the places.

- Put students in pairs to talk about their maps.

Objective
Asking for and giving directions

Vocabulary

airport   line   train

**Literacy Workbook pages 134–139
Workbook page 136**

A Match.

- Have students look at the pictures of buses and trains.

- Make sure students understand the meanings of the words *airport*, *line,* and *train*.

- Go over the example. Have students write the letter next to the mode of transportation.

- Put students in pairs to compare answers.

- Go over the answers with the class.

Answer Key   **1.** c; **2.** d; **3.** b; **4.** a

B   CD 4, TRACK 50   Listen.

- Play the audio or read the conversation with a student as students follow along silently.

- Play the audio or read the conversation again and have students repeat.

- Put students in pairs to practice the conversation.

Literacy Development Activity:
Letters and Numbers

- Give each student ten cards or slips of paper.

- Have each student write one different uppercase letter on each of five cards, and one number between 1 and 100 on each of the other five cards.

- Collect all of the cards.

- Call a student to the front of the room to draw one letter and one number card.

- Have the student show the two cards to the class, first the letter, then the number. Tell the class it is the bus number.

- Elicit the bus letter and number from the class (*It's the M53 bus.*).

- Continue until students seem comfortable with reading "bus signs."

C   Talk with 6 classmates.

- Model the activity with a more advanced student. Have the student ask about one of the places in Activity A. Answer with the correct form of transportation.

- Have students walk around the room to practice both roles of the conversation.

- Walk around and provide help as needed.

Expansion Activity: **Real Life**

- Have students bring in maps for the form of public transportation they take at least sometimes. If students have trouble getting route maps, go online and print the route maps.

- Have students practice asking and answering questions about how to get to different places on the maps.

- Walk around and provide help as needed.

Objective

Asking and answering questions about departure times

Vocabulary

Boston	Newark	San Antonio
Chicago	Newtown	San Diego
Cincinnati	New York	Santa Fe
Dallas	Oakland	Tempe
Los Angeles	Orlando	Tucson
Miami	Riverside	

Literacy Workbook pages 134–139
Workbook page 136

  A CD 4, TRACK 51 **Listen.**

• Have students look at the picture. Ask *Who do you see? What is he doing?*

• Play the audio or read the conversation as students follow along silently.

• Play the audio or read the conversation again and have students repeat.

• Put students in pairs to practice the conversation.

GRAMMAR Note

• Point out that we use *at* before we say the times on a clock.

PRONUNCIATION Note

• Point out that the first *o* sound in *o'clock* is an unaccented schwa sound. We say it the same way we say *a clock*.

B **Talk to 4 classmates.**

• Go over the places and times in the box.

• Model the activity with a more advanced student. Ask the student about one of the places in the box. Elicit the time.

• Have students stand and walk around the room to practice the conversation with four classmates. Remind students to practice both roles.

• Walk around to monitor the activity and provide help as needed.

  C CD 4, TRACK 52 **Listen and circle.**

• Read each of the cities in Activity C and have students repeat.

• Play the audio and stop after the first item or read the first conversation in the listening script. Elicit the place and the time. Point out that *Chicago* and *6:14* are circled.

• Play the audio or read the conversations in the listening script and have students circle the places and times they hear.

• Put students in pairs to compare answers.

• Go over the answers with the class.

Listening Script

C. LISTEN AND CIRCLE.

1. **Man:** When does the next train to Chicago leave?
   Clerk: It leaves at six fourteen.
   Man: At six fourteen? Thanks.

2. **Man:** When does the next train to Los Angeles leave?
   Clerk: It leaves at ten o'clock.
   Man: At ten o'clock? Thanks.

3. **Woman:** When does the next train to Tempe leave?
   Clerk: It leaves at twelve o'clock.
   Woman: At twelve o'clock? Thanks.

4. **Woman:** When does the next train to Newark leave?
   Clerk: It leaves at 10:02.
   Woman: At 10:02? Thanks.

5. **Man:** When does the next train to Boston leave?
   Clerk: It leaves at 8:30.
   Man: At 8:30? Thanks.

6. **Woman:** When does the next train to Miami leave?
   Clerk: It leaves at 5:15.
   Woman: At 5:15? Thanks.

7. **Woman:** When does the next train to San Antonio leave?
   Clerk: It leaves at 2:30.
   Woman: At 2:30? Thanks.

8. **Woman:** When does the next train to San Diego leave?
   Clerk: It leaves at 11:03.
   Woman: At 11:03? Thanks.

Answer Key 1. Chicago/6:14;
2. Los Angeles/10:00; 3. Tempe/12:00;
4. Newark/10:02; 5. Boston/8:30;
6. Miami/5:15; 7. San Antonio/2:30;
8. San Diego/11:03

Literacy Expansion Activity: Alphabetical Order

- Have literacy students alphabetize the cities in the first column of Activity C.
- Have volunteers write the cities on the board in alphabetical order.

Extra Challenge
Alphabetical Order

- Have more advanced students alphabetize all the cities in Activity C.
- Have volunteers write the words in alphabetical order on the board.

Expansion Activity: Ask about the others.

- Model the activity. Ask about the next train to Cincinnati. Cue student to respond with the time that is not circled in number 1 of Activity C.
- Put students in pairs to take turns asking and answering questions about the other places and times in Activity C. Remind students that the city and the time they should use are the uncircled items.
- Call on students and ask about the next train to one of the cities. Elicit the time.

Objective
Applying for a learner's permit

Vocabulary
driver's education classes
female
learner's permit
male

Literacy Workbook pages 134–139
Workbook page 137

  A   CD 4, TRACK 53   **Listen and read.**

- Direct students' attention to the picture and ask: *Who do you see? What is she doing?*

- Play the audio or read the story as students follow along silently.

- Ask comprehension questions: *What does Nadira want to do? What does she do first? Then what does she do? How does she make an appointment? How much does the test cost?*

- Say each sentence aloud and have students repeat.

- Put students in pairs to take turns reading the information aloud.

Expansion Activity:
Find the match.

- Photocopy the following sentence strips and cut along the lines.

Nadira wants	to drive to school.
She needs	a learner's permit.
First, she takes	the driver's education classes.
Then she needs to take	a test to get the learner's permit.
She calls	to make an appointment.
She can take	the test on Thursday.
The test	is $26.
Leo can teach Nadira	to drive after the test.

- Give each student a strip.

- Have students first find the match to complete their sentences. Remind students to use uppercase letters and periods as clues to sort sentence beginnings and endings.

- Then, as an added challenge, have students recreate the story.

B   Circle.

- Read the first sentence. Elicit the completion. Make sure students circle *a learner's permit.*

- Have students circle the completion to each sentence.

- Put students in pairs to compare answers.

- Call on students to provide the answers.

Answer Key 1. a learner's permit;
2. appointment; 3. Thursday; 4. $26

C **Complete the learner's permit form about you.**

- Go over the information on the learner's permit application. Make sure students understand what *male* and *female* mean.

- Direct students' attention to the form and elicit the information it requires.

- Have students complete the form.

- Walk around to monitor the activity and provide help as needed.

- Point to the last question, *Glasses?* Ask students why they think this question is included on the application.

Expansion Activity: Pair Interview

- Photocopy and distribute Worksheet 45: *Getting a Learner's Permit* (Teacher's Edition page 371).

- Have students interview a classmate, family member, or friend, and complete the form.

Objective
Understanding and reading road signs

Literacy Workbook pages 134–139
Workbook page 138

 A   CD 4, TRACK 54   Listen.

- Direct students' attention to the pictures and ask: *What signs do you see?*

- Play the audio or read the signs as students follow along silently.

- Play the audio or read the signs again and have students repeat.

- Read the signs in random order and have students point to the sign.

Expansion Activity:
Which sign is it?

- Tell students you are going to say what each sign means in random order.

- Say, *The hospital is here* and elicit the number of the sign (5).

- Continue with other sentences. Create your own or use the ones below.

    You need to stop at the corner.
    Don't park your car here.
    Don't drive more than 35 miles an hour.
    Wait for the bus here.
    You can't drive both ways on this street.

B   Circle the problem.

- Point out that road signs tell drivers what they can and can't do. For each sign in Activity B, one of the two pictures shows a violation. Point to each picture and ask: *right or wrong?*

- Have students look at the signs then circle the picture that does *not* follow the instructions on the road sign.

- Put students in pairs to compare answers.

- Elicit answers from the class. Elicit what violation the picture of the wrong answer shows.

Answer Key   **1.** b; **2.** b

My Life

- Go over the directions. Provide an example of a sign.

- Have students copy or draw a road sign in their neighborhood.

- Put students in groups to talk about their signs.

Expansion Activity:
Draw the problem.

- Have students draw a picture of someone not following the directions on the sign they made.

- Post the pictures and signs around the classroom.

Objective
Understanding and asking about departure schedules

Literacy Workbook pages 134–139
Workbook page 139

  A CD 4, TRACK 55 **Listen.**

- Direct students' attention to the picture and ask: *Who do you see? Where are they?*

- Play the audio or read the conversation as students follow along silently.

- Play the audio or read the conversation again and have students repeat.

- Put students in pairs to practice the conversations; then have them switch partners and practice.

Literacy Development Activity: Give examples.

- Write three headings on the board: *Every Hour, Every Half Hour, Every 15 Minutes*

> Every Hour, Every Half Hour,
> Every 15 Minutes

Under *Every Hour*, write 4:00, 5:00, 6:00.
Under *Every Half Hour*, write 12:00, 12:30, 1:00. Under *Every 15 Minutes*, write 10:15, 10:30, 10:45.

- Put students in pairs. Assign each pair one of the headings on the board to write two groups of times for their category. Encourage students to use other times on the clock for each category. For example, one group for every hour might be 3:15, 4:15, and 5:15.

- Call on students to say one of their groups (e.g., the students who were assigned *Every Half Hour* might say, *7:30, 8:00, 8:30*). Do not have students say the heading. Elicit the expression that matches the group from the class (e.g., *every half hour*).

> **7:30, 8:00, 8:30.**   **Every half hour**

B Match.

- Have students write the letters to match the expression to the times.

- Put students in pairs to compare answers.

Answer Key 1. c; 2. b; 3. a

Extra Challenge
Create a conversation.

- Put students in pairs to create a conversation following the model in Activity A. Have students substitute the information from Activity A.

- Have volunteers perform the conversation in front of the class.

C Talk with 3 classmates.

- Model the activity with a more advanced student. You read A's lines and elicit the appropriate substitution from the student.

- Have students ask and answer questions about schedules with three classmates.

Objective
Reading a bus schedule

Literacy Workbook pages 134–139
Workbook page 140

  A CD 4, TRACK 56 **Listen and read.**

- Direct students' attention to the picture. Ask questions: *What do you see? Where is the schedule? Where is the bus stop? What time is it?*

- Play the audio or read the sentences as students follow along silently.

- Ask questions: *How often does the bus leave Pond Street? Where does it go after Westside Park? What is the last stop?*

- Read each sentence aloud and have students repeat.

- Put students in pairs to take turns reading the paragraph aloud.

Expansion Activity: **Cloze**

- Photocopy and distribute the following paragraph.

     This is a bus _____ for the K-52 Bus. It leaves Pond Street every _____ minutes. The bus goes to Westside Park, City Library, _____, and Midway Airport. It's _____. The next bus _____ Pond Street at 4:45.

- Give students two minutes to read the paragraphs in their books again.

- Have students fill in the missing information. Suggest that more advanced students complete the paragraph from memory. Encourage less advanced students to refer to the book if necessary.

- Call on students to write completed answers on the board. Correct spelling as needed.

B Look at the bus schedule. Answer the questions.

- Direct students' attention to the bus schedule. Make sure students know how to read it. Ask questions: *What is the first stop? What is the third stop? What is the number of this bus?*

- Go over the directions and the example.

- Have students answer the questions.

- Put students in pairs to compare answers.

- Go over the answers with the class.

Answer Key 1. 4:30, 4:45, 5:00, 5:15, and 5:30; 2. 5:15, 5:30, 5:45, 6:00, 6:15; 3. 4:30, 4. 4:45, 5. 5:15; 6. 5:30; 7. 6:45; 8. 5:45

Expansion Activity: **Write questions.**

- Put students in pairs to write three more questions about the schedule. If possible, pair a more advanced student with a less advanced student.

- Have each student pair exchange questions with another pair.

- Have students answer the questions.

- Call on students to read a question to a classmate. Elicit the answer.

Objective
Using *wh-* questions with *be*

Literacy Workbook pages 134–139
Workbook page 141

  A CD 4, TRACK 57 **Listen and read.**

- Play the audio or read the questions and answers in the chart as students look at the chart.

- Play the audio or read the questions and answers in the chart again and have students repeat.

- Call on students and ask a question from the chart. Have them find and provide the answer from the chart.

Literacy Development Activity:
Ask and answer.

- Put students in pairs to take turns asking and answering the questions in the chart.

Extra Challenge
Write long answers.

- Have more advanced students write long answers to each question in the chart (e.g., *The name of my school is City College.*).

- Put students in pairs to compare sentences.

- Have volunteers write sentences on the board.

  B CD 4, TRACK 58 **Listen and complete.**

- Go over the question words in the box.

- Go over the example. Play the audio for the first item or read the first item in the listening script and elicit the question word. Point out that *Where* is written on the line.

- Play the audio or read the questions and answers in the listening script and have students write the question word they hear. Remind students to look at the answers to help determine which question word is correct.

- Put students in pairs to compare answers.

- Go over the answers with the class.

- Put students in pairs to practice asking and answering the questions.

········ **Listening Script**

B. LISTEN AND COMPLETE.

1. **A:** Where is the school?
   B: Newark.
2. **A:** What is your classmate's name?
   B: Yuri.
3. **A:** Who is your teacher?
   B: John Friedman.
4. **A:** When is the class?
   B: On Wednesday at 3:00.

Answer Key **1.** Where; **2.** What;
3. Who; **4.** When

Expansion Activity:
Answer for yourself.

- Put students in pairs to practice asking and answering the questions from Activity B. Remind students to answer the questions with their own information.

- Call on students and ask a question. Elicit the answer.

> Where is the school?
>
> Newark.

Expansion Activity:
Character Card Memory Challenge

- Put students in pairs. Give each pair a character card.

- Have students write three questions with a question word + *be* about their character (*Where is Grace from? What is her last name?*).

- Call on students to ask a question of a classmate.

- In a variation, divide the class into two teams. Give each team half the character cards to write questions about. Alternate calling on each team to pose questions of the other. Each correct answer earns a point.

C Complete.

- Have students write a question word on the lines.

- Put students in pairs to compare answers.

- Go over the answers with the class. Provide or elicit correction as needed.

Answer Key **1.** What; **2.** When;
3. Where; **4.** Who

Objective
Using *wh-* questions with *do/does*

Literacy Workbook pages 134–139
Workbook page 141

  A CD 4, TRACK 59 **Listen and read.**

- Direct students' attention to the chart. Go over the information, making sure students understand how to make *wh-* questions and give short answers.

- Play the audio or read the questions and answers as students follow along silently.

- Play the audio or read the questions and answers again and have students repeat.

- Put students in pairs to practice asking and answering the questions in the chart.

- Call on students and ask a question from the chart.

GRAMMAR Notes

- Point out that we can answer these questions with a short or long answer. People usually use short answers, but long answers are also correct.

- Point out that when giving a short answer to describe how we get someplace, we usually use *by (by train)* rather than just say *a train*.

Extra Challenge
Write long answers.

- Have more advanced students write long answers to each question in the chart (e.g., *I take the train.* instead of *By train.*).

- Put students in pairs to compare sentences.

- Have volunteers write sentences on the board.

B **Match.**

- Go over the example.

- Have students write the letters to match the answer to the question.

- Put students in pairs to compare answers.

- Go over the answers with the class. Elicit or provide corrections as needed.

- Have students practice asking and answering the questions with their partners.

Answer Key **1.** b; **2.** a; **3.** c; **4.** d

Literacy Development Activity: Card Scramble

- Have students write the questions from Activity B on index cards, one word on each card.

- Have students shuffle the cards.

- With books closed, have students unscramble the cards to recreate the questions.

BIG PICTURE

Expansion Activity: Grammar: *Wh-* Questions

- Have students look at the big picture on page 190 in their books, or put the transparency for Unit 12 on the OHP.

- Photocopy and distribute Worksheet 46: *Wh-* Questions (Teacher's Edition page 372).

- Have students answer the questions.

- Put students in pairs to compare answers.

- Go over the answers with the class.

Answer Key **1.** It's on the corner of West End Avenue and 81st Street. *or* It's next to the bank.; **2.** Maria; **3.** She is using the ATM.; **4.** It is arriving now.; **5.** Maria; **6.** He is taking the subway.; **7.** Leo; **8.** It's in the window.

C Complete.

- Go over the example. Point out that the answer is crossed out in the list of words. Encourage students to cross out the answers as they go.

- Have students complete the activity on their own then check their answers with a partner.

Answer Key **1.** What time; **2.** When; **3.** How; **4.** Where

Objective
Reading about car safety

Literacy Workbook pages 134–139
Workbook page 142

  A CD 4, TRACK 60 **Listen and read.**

- Direct students' attention to each picture and ask: *Who do you see? What are they doing?*

- Play the audio or read the story and have students follow along silently.

- Ask comprehension questions: *Where were Ben and Grace? Who is Adam? What do Ben and Grace use to keep Adam safe? What do Ben and Grace use to keep themselves safe?*

Expansion Activity: **Reading Cloze**

- Read the story about Ben and Grace. As you read each sentence, stop before the last word and elicit the completion (e.g., *Ben and Grace were at the hospital last _____*).

> Ben and Grace were at the hospital last _____.

- Have more advanced students complete the sentences from memory. Have literacy students follow along and read the missing word.

B **Check.**

- Read the questions and answers.

- Elicit the answer.

- Make sure students check *a*.

Answer Key   **1.** Use Car Seats and Belts

C **Answer the questions.**

- Go over the example.

- Have students answer the questions.

- Put students in pairs to compare answers. Have them take turns reading the questions.

- Go over the answers with the class.

Answer Key   **1.** last night; **2.** home; **3.** a baby car seat; **4.** their friends; **5.** always

Extra Challenge
Write more questions.

- Have advanced students write three more *wh-* questions about the reading in Activity A.

- Walk around to monitor the activity and provide help as needed.

Literacy Development Activity: Answer questions.

- Pair an advanced student from the challenge activity above with a less advanced student.

- Have the advanced students ask the questions as their partners read them.

- Have the less advanced students answer the questions.

Expansion Activity: Reading: Safety Tips

- Have students look at the big picture on page 190 in their books, or put the transparency for Unit 12 on the OHP.

- Photocopy and distribute Worksheet 47: *Safety Tips* (Teacher's Edition page 373).

- Have students answer the questions.

- Put students in pairs to compare answers.

- Go over the answers with the class.

Answer Key **1.** car; **2.** motorcycle, bicycle; **3.** roller skating; **4.** subway, bus; **5.** subway; **6.** walking; **7.** car, taxicab; **8.** walking, bus, car, taxicab

Objective

Writing about transportation

Literacy Workbook pages 134–139
Workbook page 143

  A CD 4, TRACK 61 **Listen and read.**

- Direct students' attention to the picture and ask: *Who do you see? What bus is he taking?*

- Play the audio or read the story.

- Ask comprehension questions: *How does Paul usually go to school in his country? How does he go to school now? How do his classmates go to school?*

- Put students in pairs. Have students take turns reading the story aloud.

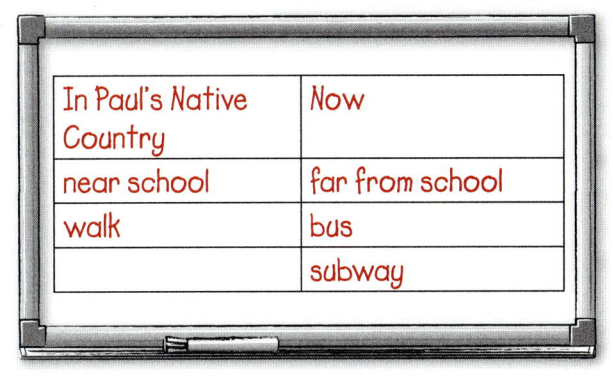

In Paul's Native Country	Now
near school	far from school
walk	bus
	subway

Expansion Activity: **Chain Reading**

- Start on one side of the room and have a student read the first sentence of Paul's story. Continue moving around the room with each student reading the next sentence. Encourage students to follow along silently so they know where they are in the story.

Expansion Activity: **Compare.**

- Write a chart on the board like the one on the whiteboard.

- Elicit ideas for each part of the chart and write them on the board.

- Have students create a similar chart to write their ideas for Activity B.

B **Write about you.**

- Ask the questions. Write answers on the board.

- Have students write sentences about how they get to school in their native countries and how they get to school now.

- Walk around to monitor the activity.

- Put students in pairs to read their sentences.

BIG PICTURE **Expansion Activity:**
Writing: Modes of Transportation

- Put the transparency for Unit 12 on the OHP or have students look at page 190.

- Model the activity. Choose a person in the picture and write a sentence starter on the board (e.g., *The woman with glasses is _____.*) and elicit the completion *(driving a car)*.

- Have students write sentences about people in the picture and the modes of transportation they are taking.

- Have volunteers come to the board and write their sentence on the board.

Objective
Reviewing the unit

  A CD 4, TRACK 62 **Listen and write.**

- Play the audio or read the conversation and have students write the words they hear. Play the audio or read the conversation again if needed.

- Put students in pairs to compare answers.

Listening Script

A. LISTEN AND WRITE.

A: Excuse me. Where is the drugstore?
B: It's on the left, next to the movie theater.

Answer Key **1.** Where; **2.** left

  B CD 4, TRACK 63 **Listen and fill in the answer sheet.**

- Go over the directions.

- Play the audio for the first item or read the first sentence in the listening script. Stop and elicit that *B* is correct. Point out that *B* is filled in.

- Play the audio or read the sentences. Have students fill in the answers.

- Go over the answers with the class.

Listening Script

B. LISTEN AND FILL IN THE ANSWER SHEET.

1. I take the subway to work.
2. How do you get to school?
3. When does the next bus to Portland leave?
4. Excuse me. Where is the Blue Line?

5. Central Park is straight ahead.
6. A: How often does the train leave?
   B: It leaves every 15 minutes.

Answer Key **1.** B; **2.** A; **3.** A; **4.** A; **5.** B; **6.** A

C **Complete the road signs. Write what they mean.**

- Go over the directions.

- Have students write the name of the road sign under the picture.

- Go over the answers with the class.

Answer Key **1.** Go one way; **2.** Stop; **3.** No Parking; **4.** Hospital

D **Write 4 questions. Ask a partner.**

- Have students write four questions in the chart.

- Have students stand and walk around the room to practice asking and answering the questions. Remind students to ask a different question of each classmate and write the answer.

- Reconvene as a class and call on student volunteers to tell the question they asked one classmate and his/her answer.

E Learning Log

- Read each word or phrase in the list aloud. Have students check the ones they know.

Expansion Activity: Draw it!

- Divide the class into two teams.
- Have a volunteer from each team come to the board. Whisper the same word from the Learning Log to each person.
- Have the students at the board draw the word and elicit guesses from the class.
- Award one point to the team whose member guesses the word first.
- Continue until everyone gets a turn to draw a word or until the time limit you set (e.g., 5 minutes) has been reached.

LOOKING BACK

- Put students in pairs to talk about the big picture on page 190.
- Call on students to talk about the picture.

BIG PICTURE

Expansion Activity: Conversation Vocabulary: On the Road Bingo

- Make copies of Worksheet 48: *On the Road Bingo* (Teacher's Edition page 374). Pass out the worksheet.
- Put the Unit 12 transparency on the OHP or have students look at page 190.
- Tell the students to choose three colors (e.g., *yellow*), three types of transportation (e.g., *subway*), and three

signs (e.g., *one way*) that they can see in the picture. Tell them the signs can be any type. Tell them to write one word in each square on the worksheet. Model the activity by drawing a bingo card on the board and filling it in.

- Walk around and make sure students have completed the bingo sheet.
- Next say you are going to tell a story. They should mark the box if they hear that word in the story. Model how to mark a box with the card on the board. Tell the students that if they have three marked boxes in a row, they should say *Bingo*.
- Tell a story that uses at least three signs, colors, and forms of transportation. Create your own or tell the following one. Repeat it if necessary.

  Leo is having a bad day. He is driving his yellow taxicab down a one way street. He doesn't see the red car. The red car stops at the corner of West Avenue and 81st Street. Leo turns to the left and hits a garbage truck. He can't drive anymore. At the same time, Isabel is getting money at the ATM at the bank. Maria and her daughter are buying a newspaper. A boy with brown hair is running with his parents. An old man and an old woman are watching Leo.

Objective
Review of the simple past of *be* and *can/can't*

A Write *was* or *were*.

- Review the information in the chart.
- Have students repeat the sentences after you, or call on individual students to read a sentence.
- Go over the directions and the example.
- Have students write *was* or *were* on the lines.
- Put students in pairs to compare answers.
- Go over the answers with the class.

Answer Key 1. was; 2. was; 3. were; 4. were; 5. were; 6. was; 7. was/Answers will vary.

B Write *can* or *can't*.

- Review *can/can't*. Remind students that *can/can't* must be followed by another verb.
- Go over the directions and the example.
- Have students write *can* or *can't* on the lines.
- Call on volunteers to give the answers. Provide or elicit corrections as needed.

Answer Key 1. can; 2. can't; 3. can; 4. can't; 5. can't; 6. can't; 7. can; 8. can

C Talk in groups.

- Put students in groups.
- Have students answer the questions.

- Call on students to tell what they can and can't do.

D Match.

- Go over the directions and the example.
- Have students write the letters to match the answers to the questions.
- Put students in pairs to compare answers.
- Go over the answers with the class.
- For extra practice, put students in pairs to practice asking and answering the questions.

Answer Key 1. c; 2. d; 3. b; 4. a; 5. g; 6. h; 7. e; 8. f

E CD 4, TRACK 64 Listen. Complete. Write the time.

- Go over the directions.
- Play the audio for the first item or read the first conversation in the listening script. Point out the example answers.
- Go over the words in the box.
- Play the rest of the audio or read the rest of the conversations in the listening script and have students write the problem in the middle column and the appointment time in the right column.
- Put students in pairs to compare answers. Play the audio or read the script again if students want to hear it again.
- Call on volunteer pairs to write the answers on the board. Elicit or provide correction as needed.

········· **Listening Script**

E. LISTEN. COMPLETE. WRITE THE TIME.

1. **Grace:** Hello. This is Grace Lee. I have a cold. Can Dr. Brown see me today?
   Man: Dr. Brown can see you at eleven o'clock.
   Grace: At eleven o'clock? That's fine. Thank you.

2. **Paul:** This is Paul Lemat. I have a headache. Can the doctor see me today?
   Woman: Yes. Dr. Black can see you at three thirty this afternoon.
   Paul: At three thirty? Thank you.

3. **Tien:** Hello. This is Tien Lam. I have a toothache. Can I see Dr. Green today?
   Man: Dr. Gray can see you at twelve thirty.
   Tien: At twelve thirty? Fine.

4. **Carlos:** This is Carlos Avila. I have an infection. Can I see Dr. Brown today?
   Woman: Can you come at four fifteen?
   Carlos: Four fifteen? Yes, I can be there at four fifteen.

5. **Maria:** Hello. This is Maria Cruz. I have a backache. Can I see Dr. Brown today?
   Man: Dr. Brown can see you at one forty-five.
   Maria: At one forty-five? That's fine. Thank you.

6. **Isabel:** This is Isabel Lopez. I need to see the doctor. I have a sore throat.
   Man: Dr. White can see you at 5:15.
   Isabel: At 5:15? I'll be there. Thanks.

7. **Sandy:** This is Sandy Johnson. My daughter Jane has a fever. Can Dr. Red see her today?
   Man: I'm sorry to hear that. Dr. Red can see Jane at 9:45.
   Sandy: At 9:45? That's great. Thank you.

Answer Key **1.** a cold/11:00;
2. headache/3:30; **3.** toothache/12:30;
4. infection/4:15; **5.** backache/1:45;
6. sore throat/5:15; **7.** fever/9:45

Our Cultures
Transportation

A **Circle the types of transportation. Underline the country.**

- Tell students that this culture topic is *transportation.*

- Read each phrase and have students repeat.

- Read the phrases in random order and have students point to the correct picture.

- Ask students about their countries, e.g., *What kind of transportation do you have in Brazil?*

- Put students in pairs to talk about the transportation they have in their countries.

Answer Key Top to bottom, left to right:

Circle *scooters*, underline *Italy*; circle *subway*, underline *Japan*; circle *tuk-tuk*, underline *Laos*; circle *taxicab*, underline the *US*, circle *bicycles*, underline *China*; circle *bus*, underline *India*

B **Think about it. Complete the chart. What transportation do you use to go to the places in the box?**

- Go over the words and phrases in the box.

- Go over the example in the chart.

- Copy the chart on the board.

- Have students complete the chart. Remind students to write about different activities they use transportation for, not just going to and from school.

- Elicit student ideas and write them on the chart on the board.

C **Talk in groups.**

- Direct students' attention to the picture and ask: *Who do you see? How does she go to school?*

- Put students in small groups to talk about the forms of transportation they take to do different things. Tell them to refer to what they wrote in their chart in Activity B.

- Call on students to tell the class about the forms of transportation they take to do different things.

Name: _____ Date: _____

Grace Lee

Directions: Look at the big picture for Unit 1 on page 2. Read the story. Complete the form.

Grace Lee is a student. She is in Sandy's English class. Grace's telephone number is (831) 555-9021. Grace's address is 4020 Board Street. Ben Lee is a student, too. Ben's telephone number is (831) 555-9021. Ben's address is 4020 Board Street.

SANTA CRUZ COMMUNITY SCHOOL

Your Name: **Grace** _____
　　　　　　First Name　　　　　　　Last Name

IN AN EMERGENCY:

Please Call: **Ben** _____
　　　　　　First Name　　　　　　　Last Name

_____
Phone Number

Name: _____   Date: _____

I'm, It's, What's

Directions: Look at the big picture for Unit 1 on page 2. Complete the sentences with *I'm, It's,* or *What's.* Then write the character name.

1. Nice to meet you. _____ from Somalia.

   Character: _____

2. My name is Isabel. _____ your name?

   Character: _____

3. I listen and write. _____ my homework.

   Character: _____

4. Hello, students. _____ the teacher.

   Character: _____

5. I circle the letter. _____ the letter *n.*

   Character: _____

6. My first name is P–A–U–L. _____ your name?

   Character: _____

7. _____ a computer.

   Character: _____

Name: _____   Date: _____

Interview

Directions: Interview a classmate and complete the form about your classmate.

SANTA CRUZ COMMUNITY SCHOOL

Your Name: _____

First Name   Last Name

IN AN EMERGENCY:

Please Call: _____

First Name   Last Name

_____

Phone Number

Name: _____ Date: _____

Count the objects.

Directions: Look at the big picture on page 2. Count the objects. Make tally marks for each one.

student	✝✝✝✝ ✝✝✝✝ ||||
chair	
book	
door	
backpack	
notebook	
board	
computer	

Name: _____   Date: _____

Yes / No Cards

Directions: Cut along the black lines and hand out to students. Save for future activities.

Yes

No

Name: _____　Date: _____

Three in a Row

Directions: Write the words your teacher says.

Name: _____   Date: _____

Be or *Have?*

Directions: Look at the big picture on page 18. Write *am/is/are* or *have/has* on the lines. Who is it? Write the name.

Description	Name
1. She is from the USA. She _____ red hair.	**1.** _____
2. They _____ from China.	**2.** _____
3. He _____ gray hair.	**3.** _____
4. She is from Vietnam. She _____ glasses.	**4.** _____
5. He _____ black hair. He _____ from Haiti.	**5.** _____
6. He _____ brown eyes. He is from Brazil.	**6.** _____
7. She _____ blond hair and blue eyes.	**7.** _____

Name: _____   Date: _____

Using a Bar Graph

Directions: Look at the big picture on page 18. Count the number of students pictured with gray hair (1 student). Color in one block in the *Gray hair* column on the graph below. Continue counting the hair color of the people in the picture.

Gray	Red	Blond	Brown	Black

Number of people

Name: _____ Date: _____

Sandy's Form

Directions: Look at the big picture on page 34. Complete the form for Sandy Johnson.

Family Form

Your name: <u>Sandy Johnson</u>

Mr./Mrs./Ms. First and Last Name	Relative
	husband
	son
	son
	daughter
	father
	mother
	brother

Name: _____ Date: _____

Possessives

Directions: Look at the big picture on page 34. Read the conversation between Sandy and Leo. Complete the sentences with the correct possessive (*my, his, her, your, their*).

1. **Sandy:** _____ mother's name is Ann.

2. **Leo:** What is _____ father's name?

3. **Sandy:** _____ name is Arthur.

4. **Leo:** Who is John?

   Sandy: _____ brother. _____ wife's name is Tomiko.

5. **Leo:** What are _____ children's names?

6. **Sandy:** _____ names are Andy, Justin, and Jane.

7. **Leo:** Does your brother have a daughter?

   Sandy: Yes. _____ name is Sara. _____ brother's name is Miles.

8. **Leo:** _____ family is very nice.

Name: _____ Date: _____

Sandy's Family

Directions: Look at the big picture on page 34. Complete the story for Sandy Johnson.

Andy	children	daughter	eleven
Jane	Justin	Sandy Johnson	sons
the USA	young		

Her name is _____. She is from

_____.

She has three _____. She has one

_____ and two _____.

Their names are _____ _____, _____, and

_____.

Her children are _____. She has

_____ people in her family.

Name: _____ Date: _____

Vocabulary Review

Person A:	A and B	Person B:
_____ (Name)		_____ (Name)

Name: _____   Date: _____

Rooms in a House

Directions: A. Write the words your teacher says.

1. <u>grandmother</u> _____

2. _____

3. _____

4. _____

5. _____

6. _____

7. _____

B. Write the words from Activity A in the correct box below.

bathroom	bedroom
kitchen	dining room
yard grandmother	

Name: _____ Date: _____

What does Sandy have?

Directions: Look at the big picture on page 54. Choose the correct word or phrase and write it on the line.

1. Sandy has _____ a table _____ (a table/tables) in the kitchen.

2. She has _____ (a chair/two chairs) in the kitchen.

3. There are _____ (a chair/five chairs) in the dining room.

4. There is _____ (a refrigerator/two refrigerators) in the kitchen.

5. There is _____ (a sofa/sofas) in the living room.

6. Sandy has _____ (a tub/tubs) in the bathroom.

7. There are _____ (a lamp/three lamps) in the house.

8. There is _____ (a dresser/dressers) in the bedroom.

9. Sandy and Will have _____ (a fireplace/fireplaces) in their house.

10. They have _____ (a closet/closets) in the bedroom.

Name: _____ Date: _____

John's House

Directions: Look at the big picture on page 54. Read about John's house. Complete the chart below.

John is Sandy's brother. John and his wife Tomiko live in a house, too. Their house is in a city. They don't have a yard or a garage. They have a balcony. There is a kitchen, two bathrooms, two bedrooms, and a living room. They don't have a dining room. They eat in the kitchen.

There is	John's house	Sandy's house
a bathroom	✔	✔
a kitchen		
a living room		
a yard		
a garage		
a dining room		
a bedroom		
a balcony		

Name: _____   Date: _____

Word Map

Directions: Look at the big picture on page 54. Write the rooms in the big circles below. Write the furniture words for each room in the small circles.

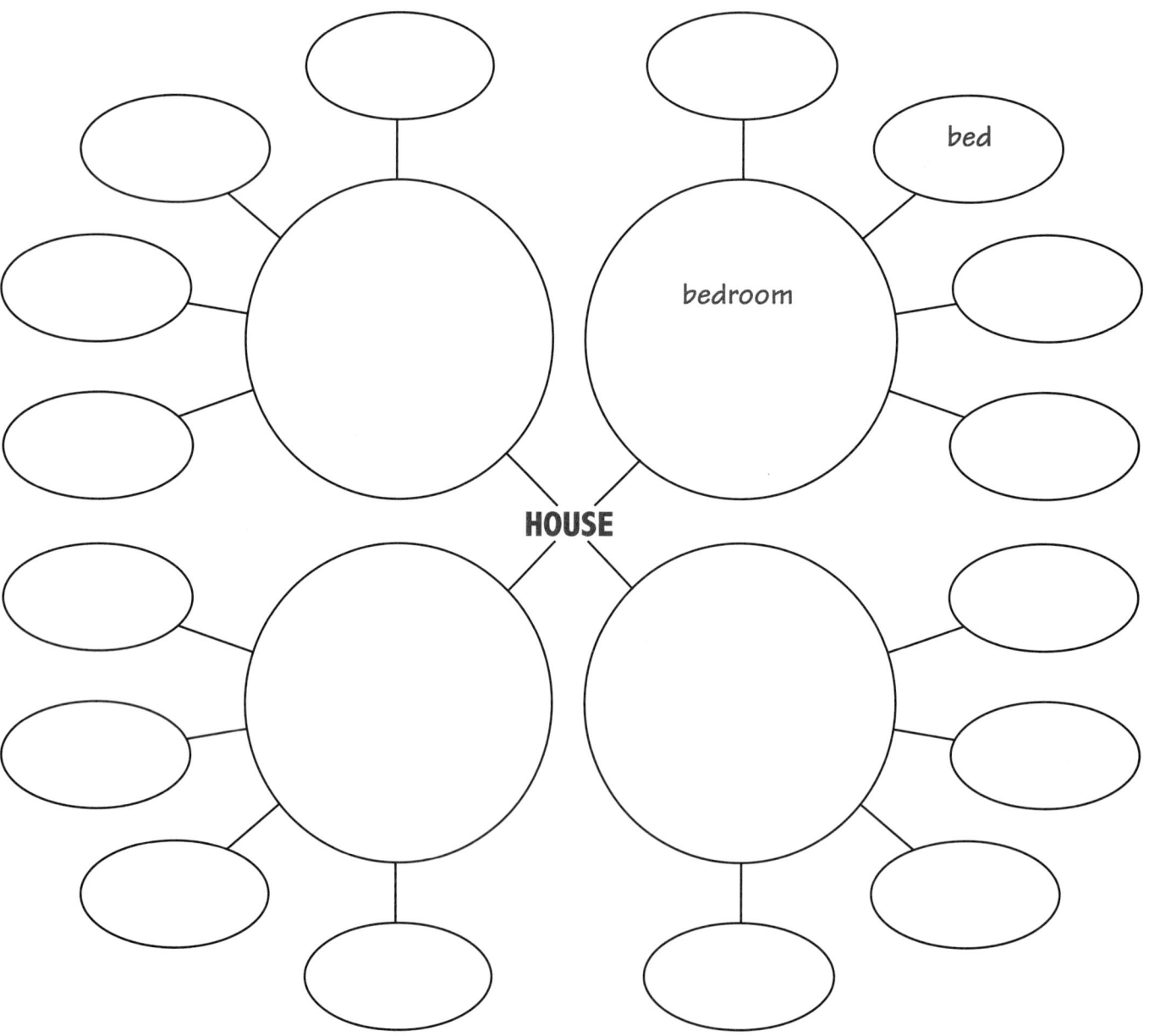

Name: _____ Date: _____

Medical Form

Directions: A. Work with a partner. Complete the form with your partner's information.

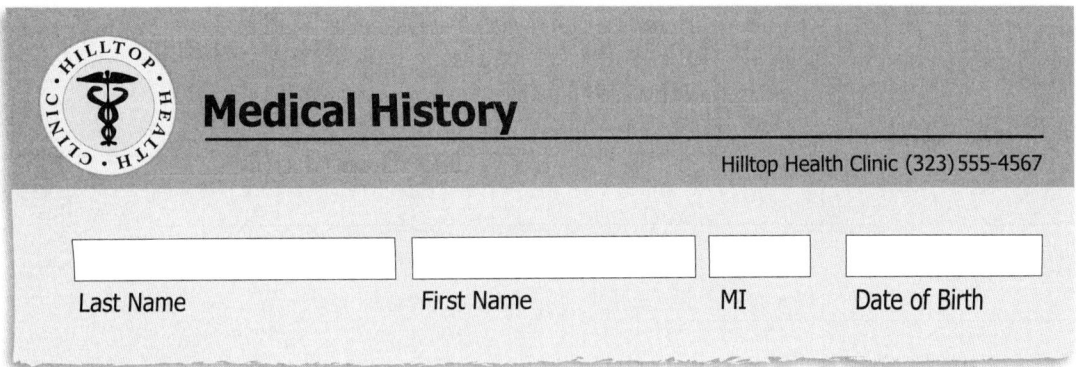

Directions: B. Copy the information from the form above. Write one letter or one number on each line.

Medical History

Hilltop Health Clinic (323) 555-4567

_ _ _ _ _ _ _ _ _ _ _ _ _   _ _ _ _ _ _ _ _ _ _ _   _   _ _ _/_ _/_ _ _ _

Last Name   First Name   MI   Date of Birth

Name: _____ Date: _____

Who does what?

Directions: Look at the big picture on page 70. Write the correct form of a verb from the box to complete the sentences. You may use some verbs more than once.

brush their teeth	comb their hair	eat breakfast
listen to music	read the newspaper	talk on the phone
work on the computer	be	

1. Leo _____ and _____ every day.

2. Carlos _____ every day.

3. Paul _____ every day.

4. Justin and Andy _____ and _____ every day.

5. Maria and her children _____ together every day.

6. Sandy and Will _____ married. They

   _____ once a day.

Name: _____   Date: _____

Whose birthday is it?

Directions: Look at the big picture on page 70. Read and complete.

Today is my birthday. I am 35 years old. In my country, we sing "Happy Birthday" in my language. We sing another song in my language, too. I am happy on my birthday. My children give me presents. We play together. My daughters clean the house. My son cooks special foods with me. Then we eat together.

1. The name of the birthday person is _____.

2. She has two _____ and one _____.

3. They sing _____.

4. They _____ special foods.

5. Today, she is _____ years old.

Name: _____ Date: _____

What time do you . . . ?

Directions: A. Look at the activities in the big picture on page 70. Write the time you do each activity (e.g., *I listen to music at 7:00*). Add three more sentences describing when you do other activities.

1. I eat breakfast at _____.

2. I work on the computer at _____.

3. I brush my teeth at _____.

4. I comb my hair at _____.

5. I listen to music at _____.

6. I read at _____.

7. I _____.

8. I _____.

9. I _____.

Directions B. Write the activities from Activity A above the correct time. Follow the example.

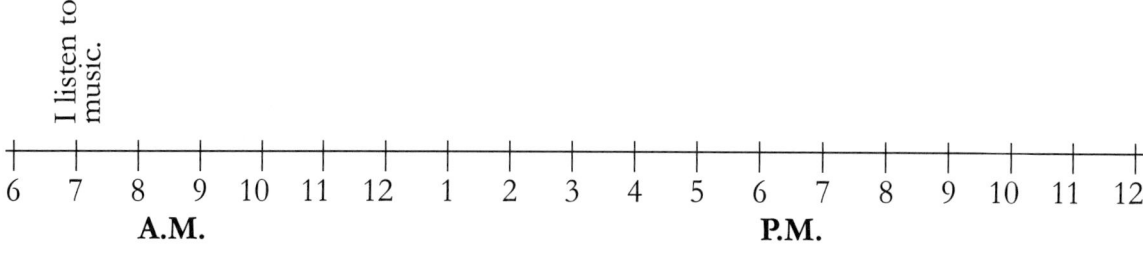

Name: _____ Date: _____

Taking Inventory

Directions: Look at the clothes in the big picture on page 86. Count how many are in the picture and write that number under *Number in picture*. Decide how many are left after customers buy some things. Write that number under *Number left*.

	Number in picture		Number left
Sweaters	4	Isabel buys 1 sweater.	3 (4 − 1 = 3)
Men's suits		Paul buys 5 suits.	
Women's coats		Maria buys 3 coats.	
Men's shirts		Ben buys 4 shirts.	

Name: _____ Date: _____

Blank Checks

Directions: Your teacher will tell you what information to use for the checks.

	1179
	DATE _____ 2-5654-1234

PAY TO THE ORDER OF _____ $ [   ]

_____ **DOLLARS**

Lakeland
City Bank

MEMO _____

⑃012345⑃ ⑃123456543⑃01234567⑃

	1180
	DATE _____ 2-5654-1234

PAY TO THE ORDER OF _____ $ [   ]

_____ **DOLLARS**

Lakeland
City Bank

MEMO _____

⑃012345⑃ ⑃123456543⑃01234567⑃

Name: _____   Date: _____

What are they wearing?

Directions: Look at the big picture on page 86. Complete the sentences with the correct word from the box. You may use some words more than once.

bathing suit	white	gray	brown	cap
sweater	green	pants	shirt	purple

1. Paul is holding a _____ suit.

2. A man is wearing a blue _____.

3. Ben is wearing a white _____.

4. Grace is wearing a _____ and

   _____ shirt.

5. Isabel is wearing a _____ _____.

6. Leo is wearing a _____ shirt and

   _____ _____.

7. Carlos is wearing a _____ _____.

Name: _____ Date: _____

How much is it?

Women's sweaters
Sweater sizes: S, M, L
Sweater colors: blue, purple, pink
Price: $29.95

Men's and women's watches
All sizes and styles
Price: $20.00

Men's bathing suits
Sizes: small, medium, large
Colors: blue, purple, green
Price: $20.00

Men's and boy's shirts
Sizes: men's S, M, L; boys' S, M, L
Price: $32.00

1. Isabel is looking at a _____. It is $ _____.

2. Carlos is looking at a _____. It is $ _____.

3. Leo is looking at a _____. It is $ _____.

4. Ben is looking at a _____. It is $ _____.

Name: _____   Date: _____

At the Store

Directions: Look at the big picture on page 106. Complete the sentences with a count or non-count noun.

Dairy

1. There is some _____.

2. There are six _____ of milk.

3. The _____ are in pink cartons.

Bakery

4. There are _____ and some _____.

Mcat

5. The _____, _____, and

_____ are in the meat section.

Produce: Fruits/Vegetables

6. There are four red _____.

7. The _____ are yellow.

8. _____ and _____ are orange.

9. _____ is green.

Name: _____ Date: _____

Class Party

Directions: A. Work with a small group to plan a class party. List everything you need. Write the prices for the foods (guess or look at a store flyer).

Shopping List

Directions: B. Write a check for your total amount. Make it out to *Big Store Foods*.

Name: _____   Date: _____

What else does he need?

Directions: A. Look at the big picture on page 106. Listen to your teacher read Carlos's list. Check the things he needs.

☐ apples

☐ bananas

☐ beef

☐ bread

☐ cake

☐ carrots

☐ eggs

☐ fish

☐ ice cream

☐ lettuce

☐ milk

☐ tomatoes

Directions: B. Work with a partner. Look in the shopping cart on page 106. What else does Carlos need? (He needs it if it's not in the cart.)

_____

_____

_____

_____

Name: _____   Date: _____

Color and Section

Directions: Write the words in the correct boxes below. Compare ideas with a partner.

cheese	apples	oranges	eggs
bananas	milk	carrots	butter

	Yellow	Not yellow
Dairy	cheese	
Produce		

Name: _____ Date: _____

Reviewing Descriptive Vocabulary

Directions: Photocopy and cut along the lines. Look at the big picture on page 122 and create matches.

Tien is wearing	a purple sweater.
Carlos is wearing	a bathing suit.
Tien is drinking	coffee.
Tien has long	brown hair.
Tien and Carlos are talking	on the telephone.
Tien needs	a coat.
Carlos is at	the beach.
Someone is cooking eggs	for breakfast.
There is a family with	Carlos.
The man on the street is wearing	a blue coat and hat.
The grandmother is wearing	a red and white dress.
Both Tien and Carlos are wearing	glasses.
Carlos and Tien are not	at school.

Name: _____ Date: _____

Today's Weather

Directions: Look at the weather in today's paper or listen to the news. Write the temperature and check the kind of weather in the chart.

City	Temperature	Sunny	Rainy	Snowy	Cloudy
Seattle	40° F				
Los Angeles					
Dallas					
Chicago					
Denver					
New York					
Miami					
Your city					

Name: _____   Date: _____

What are they doing?

Directions: Look at the big picture on page 122. Complete the sentences with a present continuous verb.

1. Carlos _____ in a chair.

2. His family _____ fruit.

3. Carlos _____ on the phone.

4. Tien _____ on the phone, too.

5. She _____ coffee.

6. Two people _____ _____ on the street.

7. They _____ _____ coats and hats.

8. A woman _____ eggs in the restaurant.

© McGraw-Hill

Name: _____ Date: _____

Letter Dictation

Directions: A. Listen and complete the letter.

_____ _____ , _____

Dear _____ ,

    I'm in _____. My _____ isn't here. They are in

_____. The weather is _____ and _____.

Today, I am _____ _____ _____ and

_____ _____ _____.

        See you next week. _____ _____,

                         Carlos

Directions: B. Look at the big picture on page 122. Complete the chart.

In the big picture	In the letter
1. It is very warm.	1. It is _____.
2.	2.
3.	3.

Name: _____   Date: _____

Filling Out Forms

Directions: Listen to your teacher. Complete the deposit slip.

DEPOSIT SLIP

	Dollars	Cents
CASH		
CHECK 1.		
2.		
3.		
TOTAL		

Deposit TO

THE ACCOUNT OF _____

ACCOUNT # _____ DATE _____

DEPOSITED TO: *(PLEASE CHECK ONE)*

❏ Checking   ❏ Savings

**First Bank
of Weston**

|012345| |123456543| |01200967|

Directions: Complete the form for your partner.

SUNNY SUPERMARKET
CLUB CARD APPLICATION

Last Name _____   First Name _____

Street Address _____   Apartment Number _____

City _____   State _____   Zip Code _____

Date of Birth (month/day/year)   Driver's License Number or State I.D. Number

_____   _____

Home Phone _____

Applicant's Signature _____   Date _____

Name: _____ Date: _____

Nadira makes a withdrawal.

Directions: A. Look at the big picture on page 138. Read the sentences below. Write the place from the big picture next to the sentence.

1. Justin and Andy go for a walk. _____park_____

2. It's across from the park. _____

3. Sandy's family goes out to eat. _____

4. It's next to the bank. _____

5. Nadira makes a withdrawal. _____

6. Ben sees the doctor. _____

7. Sandy takes out books and videos. _____

8. Grace buys stamps. _____

9. Leo buys gas. _____

10. Maria buys aspirin and a toothbrush. _____

Name: _____ Date: _____

Where is the drugstore?

1. Where is the drugstore? _____

2. Where is the bank? _____

3. Where is the police station? _____

4. Where is the post office? _____

5. Where is the library? _____

6. Where is the gas station? _____

7. Where is the fire station? _____

8. Where is the hospital? _____

9. Where is the restaurant? _____

10. Where is the ATM? _____

a. It's on 20th Street, next to the gas station.

b. It's on South Avenue, between the library and the hospital.

c. It's above the drugstore.

d. It's across from the park.

e. It's on 19th Street across from the hospital.

f. There's one outside the bank.

g. It's next to the police station.

h. It's across from the library.

i. It's near the fire station, across from the hospital.

j. It's across from the police station.

Name: _____ Date: _____

Vocabulary Review

Directions: Write the places from the big picture on page 138 in the correct places on the chart.

Places I go every week	Places I do not go every week
	police station

Name: _____   Date: _____

What to Do at the Doctor's Office

Directions: A. Write the sentences your teacher says.

1. _____

2. _____

3. _____

4. _____

5. _____

Directions: B. Write the sentences from Part A in the squares. First, you come into a doctor's office. Write the things that you do next in the correct order.

First Come in.	→		→	

	→	**Last**

© McGraw-Hill

Name: _____ Date: _____

Insurance Form

Directions: Work with a partner. Ask and answer questions to fill out the form for Grace. Use the information in Activity A on page 167.

WESTON Health Center

Patient's Name: _Grace Lee_____ Today's Date: _____

Date of Birth: _ _ / _ _ / _ _ _ _

Name of Employee: _____

Type of Plan: [circle one] **individual**   **family**   ID #: _____

Co-payment: $ _____

Name: _____ Date: _____

Using the Negative

Directions: Look at the big picture on page 158. Circle the answers.

1. Maria	has	doesn't have	a headache.
2. The doctor	looks	doesn't look	at the man's throat.
3. The office worker	answers	doesn't answer	the phone.
4. The people	sit	don't sit	in the waiting room.
5. The people	walk	don't walk	around the room.
6. Nadira	has	doesn't have	a cut arm.
7. People	smoke	don't smoke	at the doctor's office.
8. Leo and Carlos	have	don't have	stomachaches.
9. Isabel	has	doesn't have	a cold.
10. Leo	has	doesn't have	a hurt finger.

© McGraw-Hill

Name: _____ Date: _____

A Day at the Doctor's

Directions: Look at the big picture on page 158. Read the sentences. Write *he* or *she* on the lines.

I am a doctor. Today is a busy day. One child has a headache. _____

needs aspirin. One person has a cut finger and an infection. _____ needs a

bandage and an antibiotic. Another person has a cold. _____ needs to drink

orange juice and rest. Someone has a sore throat. _____ needs an antibiotic.

A child has an earache. _____ needs an antibiotic for an ear infection.

Another patient has a hurt leg. _____ needs aspirin. Someone has a toothache.

_____ needs aspirin. _____ also needs to go to the dentist. Another person

has a stomachache. _____ needs to rest and drink hot water.

Name: _____   Date: _____

Can she use a computer?

Directions: Look at the big picture on page 174. Circle the correct answer.

1. Can Leo drive a taxi?

   A. Yes, he can.   B. No, he can't.

2. Nadira doesn't have a driver's license. Can Nadira drive a taxi?

   A. Yes, she can.   B. No, she can't.

3. Can Ben use tools?

   A. Yes, he can.   B. No, he can't.

4. Can the waiter make soup?

   A. Yes, he can.   B. No, he can't.

5. Can Tien cook a meal for her job?

   A. Yes, she can.   B. No, she can't.

6. Can the sales clerk give correct change?

   A. Yes, he can.   B. No, he can't.

7. Can customers order coffee at the restaurant?

   A. Yes, they can.   B. No, they can't.

8. Can Isabel and Paul use computers?

   A. Yes, they can.   B. No, they can't.

Name: _____   Date: _____

Who is it?

Directions: Look at the big picture on page 174. Write the name of the character next to the job description.

Employer	Skills	Name
Swift Taxi, Inc.	Can drive a car Can drive a van Can speak Russian, Polish, Slovak, and English	Leo
ICM Computers	Can use a computer Can take phone messages Can speak Spanish and English	
ICM Computers	Can use a computer Can program computers Can speak English and French	
Home Health Helpers, Inc.	Can care for sick people Can speak Somali and English	
Quick Deliveries Service (QDS)	Can drive a car, van, truck Can speak Vietnamese and English	
New World Builders	Can use power tools Can drive a car and truck Can speak Chinese and English	

Name: _____ Date: _____

Job Application

Directions: Work with a partner. Ask questions and complete the application with your partner's information.

C.L.T. Human Resources Job Application

_____   _____   _____
LAST NAME   FIRST NAME   MI

_____
STREET ADDRESS

_____   _____   _____   _____
CITY   STATE   ZIP CODE

Telephone Number: (____ ____ ____) ____ ____ ____ — ____ ____ ____ ____

Last Job: _____   Dates: _____

Employer: _____

Name: _____ Date: _____

Idea Map

Directions: Look at the big picture on page 174. Write the jobs you see in the correct circle.

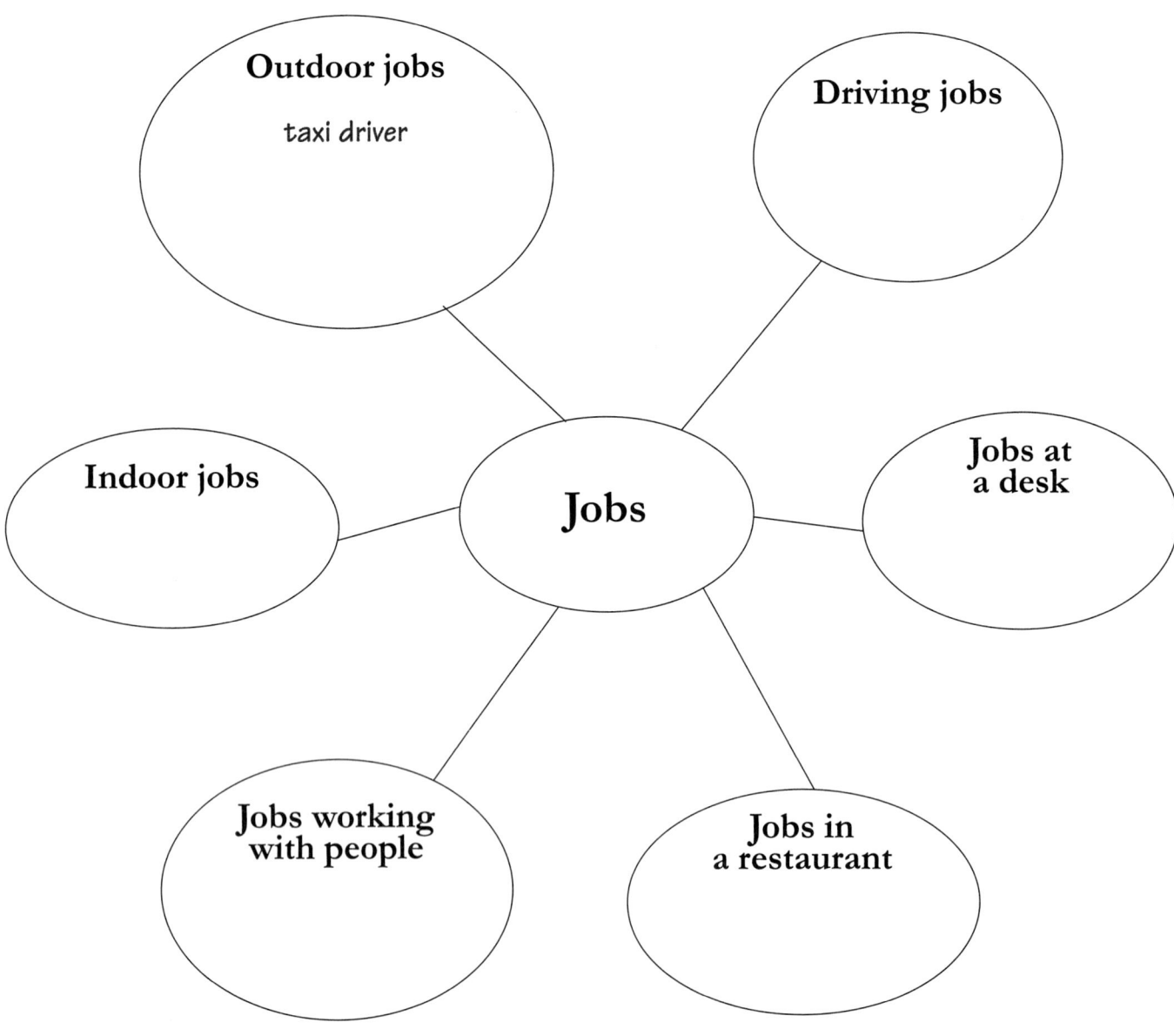

Outdoor jobs

taxi driver

Driving jobs

Indoor jobs

Jobs

Jobs at a desk

Jobs working with people

Jobs in a restaurant

Name: _____   Date: _____

Getting a Learner's Permit

Application for a Learner's Permit

Name:_____
      (Last)   (First)   (MI)

Address:_____
     (Street)   (City)   (State)   (ZIP)

Telephone Number: _____
      (Area code)

Date of birth: _____   _____   _____
    (MM/DD/YY)   male   female

Eye color: _____   Hair color: _____

Glasses? _____ yes   _____ no

                        _____
                               (Signature)

Name: _____   Date: _____

Wh- Questions

1. Where is the subway entrance?

   _____

2. Who is buying something at the magazine stand?

   _____

3. What is Isabel doing?

   _____

4. When is the next M-16 bus?

   _____

5. Who is with her daughter Ana?

   _____

6. How is the boy with red hair getting home?

   _____

7. Who is not driving his taxicab?

   _____

8. Where is the cat?

   _____

Name: _____ Date: _____

Safety Tips

Directions: Look at the big picture on page 190. Read the information below. Write the name of the kinds of transportation under the safety tip. You can write more than one answer.

1. Wear a seat belt.

   _____

2. Wear a helmet and follow traffic laws.

   _____

3. Wear a helmet and safety pads on your arms and legs.

   _____

4. Sit down or hold on to a safety bar or strap.

   _____

5. Walk, don't run down the stairs.

   _____

6. Cross the street at a light or crosswalk.

   _____

7. Don't talk on a cell phone.

   _____

8. Stop at traffic lights.

   _____

Name: _____   Date: _____

On the Road Bingo

Directions: Look at the big picture on page 190. Think of three colors, three types of transportation, and three signs that you see in the picture. Write one word in each box below in any order. Listen to the teacher's story. Cross off the words as you hear them. Raise your hand and say "Bingo" if you get three in a row.

Name: _____ Date: _____ Score: _____

🎧 **A**   **Listen and ✔ check the answer.**

1. _____ Hello, Maria. I'm Carlos.

   _____ Hello, Carlos. I'm Maria.

2. _____ Hi, Carlos. I'm Leo. Nice to meet you.

   _____ Hi. My name is Carlos. I'm from Brazil.

3. _____ I'm from Brazil.

   _____ My name is Maria Cruz.

4. _____ My first name is M-A-R-I-A.

   _____ My first name is Maria.

5. _____ I'm Isabel.

   _____ A desk.

B   **Fill in.**

1. My name is Paul. _____ from Brazil.

   (A) I'm   (B) What's   (C) It's

2. _____ your name?

   (A) I'm   (B) What's   (C) It's

3. _____ a pen.

   (A) I'm   (B) What's   (C) It's

4. _____ this?

   (A) I'm   (B) What's   (C) It's

5. _____ (704) 555-1212.

   (A) I'm   (B) What's   (C) It's

C Complete.

| backpack | book | chair | notebook | paper |

1. _____   2. _____   3. _____

 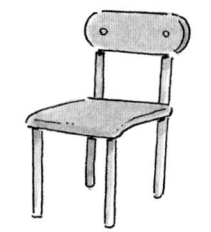

4. _____   5. _____

D Complete. Write the number.

| 1 | 4 | 7 | 8 | 10 |

1. _____ four

2. _____ seven

3. _____ one

4. _____ eight

5. _____ ten

Name: _____   Date: _____   Score: _____

A **Listen and ✔ check the answer.**

1. _____ I speak Chinese.

   _____ I'm from China.

2. _____ He speaks Russia.

   _____ He speaks Russian.

3. _____ I'm speak Spanish.

   _____ I'm from Somalia.

4. _____ I'm from Brazil.

   _____ My address is 142 Book Street.

5. _____ My zip code is 95945.

   _____ My address is 95 Pen Street.

B **Fill in.**

1. I _____ from China.

   Ⓐ am   Ⓑ is   Ⓒ are

2. They _____ from the US.

   Ⓐ am   Ⓑ is   Ⓒ are

3. He _____ brown eyes.

   Ⓐ is   Ⓑ has   Ⓒ have

4. We _____ black hair.

   Ⓐ have   Ⓑ doesn't have   Ⓒ has

5. You _____ average height.

   Ⓐ have   Ⓑ are   Ⓒ has

C Complete.

> average height   average height   short   tall   short

1. Leo is _____.

2. Paul is _____.

3. Carlos is _____.

4. Maria is _____.

5. Tien is _____.

D Match.

1. _____ fifteen   **a.** 12

2. _____ fourteen   **b.** 17

3. _____ twelve   **c.** 15

4. _____ seventeen   **d.** 11

5. _____ eleven   **e.** 14

Name: _____ Date: _____ Score: _____

A Listen and ✔ check the answer.

1. _____ I'm 22 years old.

_____ My grandfather is old.

2. _____ Her name is Ann.

_____ His name is John.

3. _____ Yes, I do.

_____ I am middle aged.

4. _____ Yes, I have two sons.

_____ She's 27 years old.

5. _____ Tom is 35 years old.

_____ Tom is Andy's brother.

B Fill in.

1. I'm short. _____ sister is tall. My brother is short.

Ⓐ Their   Ⓑ His   Ⓒ My

2. Do you have a brother? What is _____ name?

Ⓐ his   Ⓑ my   Ⓒ our

3. This is my sister. _____ name is Tina.

Ⓐ Our   Ⓑ His   Ⓒ Her

4. I have two brothers. _____ names are Tom and Dan.

Ⓐ Their   Ⓑ Our   Ⓒ Your

5. Ann and I are sisters. _____ family has four people in it.

Ⓐ Their   Ⓑ Our   Ⓒ Your

C Complete.

| Mrs. | middle-aged | Mr. | old | young |

1. She is _____.

2. She is _____.

3. Ben's parents are
_____.

4. This is _____ Lemat.

5. This is _____ Johnson.

D Match.

1. _____ fifty   **a.** 30

2. _____ twenty-four   **b.** 100

3. _____ twenty   **c.** 24

4. _____ thirty   **d.** 50

5. _____ one hundred   **e.** 20

Name: _____   Date: _____   Score: _____

A Listen and circle.

1. 14   40
2. 18   80
3. 17   70
4. 16   60
5. 15   50

B Write.

1. one table   two _____

2. one _____   four books

3. one chair   three _____

4. one city   two _____

5. one _____   three windows

C Circle.

1. There's a tub in the _____.   bathroom   bedroom

2. There's a stove in the _____.   backyard   kitchen

3. There's a _____ in the bedroom.   refrigerator   bed

4. There's a sink in the _____.   kitchen   living room

5. There are _____ in the dining room.   tubs   windows

D Circle.

1. shower   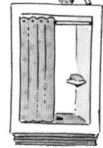

2. closet      

3. sink   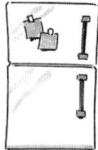   

4. microwave      

5. rug   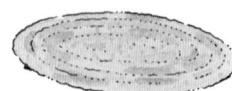

Name: _____ Date: _____ Score: _____

A   Listen and ✔ check the answer.

1. _____ January 12, 1971.

   _____ Friday at 10:30.

2. _____ Tuesday at 3:15.

   _____ It's in December.

3. _____ Wednesday at 8:15.

   _____ 8:15.

4. _____ Once a week.

   _____ In March.

5. _____ Saturday at 9:45? That's fine.

   _____ Saturday at 9:15? That's fine.

B   Complete.

comb	eat	get	open	take

1. I _____ my hair every morning.

2. He _____ a haircut once a month.

3. We _____ breakfast.

4. She _____ photos.

5. They _____ presents.

C ✔ Check the time.

1. _____ 2:30

_____ 2:00

2. _____ 7:00

_____ 7:15

3. _____ 4:45

_____ 4:15

4. _____ 8:45

_____ 8:15

5. _____ 12:30

_____ 12:00

D Match.

a.   b.   c.   d.   e.

1. _____ I work on my computer.

2. _____ I talk on the phone.

3. _____ I eat breakfast.

4. _____ I brush my teeth.

5. _____ I read the newspaper.

Name: _____   Date: _____   Score: _____

A Listen and ✔ check the answer.

1. _____ Yes, I'm looking for a sweater.   _____ Sweaters are over there.

2. _____ A blue coat.   _____ Blue.

3. _____ I'm wearing a red dress.   _____ It's purple.

4. _____ I'm looking for pants.   _____ They're black.

5. _____ I'm wearing sneakers.   _____ I'm a medium.

B Match.

1. _____ $5.50   a.

2. _____ $3.00   b.

3. _____ 75¢   c.

4. _____ $2.53   d.

5. _____ $7.05   e.

C Complete.

a blouse	a dress	shoes	a suit	a watch

1. Maria is looking for _____.

2. Grace is looking for _____.

3. Sandy is looking for _____.

4. Carlos is looking for _____.

5. Paul is looking for _____.

D Circle.

1. She has a _____ dress.   red   shoes

2. I am wearing a large _____.   shirt   medium

3. Justin has _____ pants.   blue   coat

4. The black _____ are on sale.   small   shoes

5. Your _____ is too small.   green dress   dress green

Name: _____ Date: _____ Score: _____

 A **Listen and circle.**

1. We need _____.   beef   bread

2. We need _____.   chicken   cheese

3. We need _____.   beef   bread

4. We need _____.   apples   oranges

5. We need _____.   cake   ice cream

B **Complete.**

┌───┐
│   bag   bottle   box   con   can   │
└───┘

1.   a _____ of tomato soup

2.   a _____ of milk

3.   a _____ of rice

4.   a _____ of oil

5.   a _____ of cereal

C **Complete.**

bread   butter   cheese   eggs   oranges

   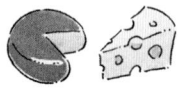   

1. _____   2. _____   3. _____

4. _____   5. _____

D ✔ **Check.**

1. bread   _____ count   _____ non-count

2. apple   _____ count   _____ non-count

3. egg   _____ count   _____ non-count

4. milk   _____ count   _____ non-count

5. rice   _____ count   _____ non-count

Name: _____ Date: _____ Score: _____

🎧 **A** **Listen and check the answer.**

1. _____ It's winter.

   _____ It's sunny.

2. _____ Fall.

   _____ It's rainy.

3. _____ I'm reading.

   _____ I like dancing.

4. _____ I like swimming.

   _____ I like soda.

5. _____ I'm listening to music.

   _____ She's listening to music.

B **Fill in.**

1. I _____ breakfast.

   Ⓐ am eating   Ⓑ is eating   Ⓒ are eating

2. He_____ basketball.

   Ⓐ 'm playing   Ⓑ 's playing   Ⓒ 're playing

3. We _____ TV.

   Ⓐ am watching   Ⓑ are watching   Ⓒ is watching

4. They're _____ for a test.

   Ⓐ are studying   Ⓑ studying   Ⓒ study

5. You're _____ brown shoes today.

   Ⓐ are wearing   Ⓑ is wearing   Ⓒ wearing

C Complete.

> cooking   dancing   listening to music   reading   watching TV

1. _____

2. _____

3. _____

4. _____

5. _____

D Complete.

> playing soccer   playing basketball   swimming   talking   walking

1. _____

2. _____

3. _____

4. _____

5. _____

Name: _____   Date: _____   Score: _____

A Listen and circle.

1. bank   post office

2. library   supermarket

3. fire department   drugstore

4. post office   bank

5. laundromat   restaurant

B Complete.

| between | between | in | next to | on |

1. The movie theater is _____ the restaurant.

2. The drugstore is _____ the bank and the park.

3. Paul is _____ the restaurant.

4. The restaurant is _____ Lake Avenue.

5. The restaurant is _____ the bank and the movie theater.

C **Complete.**

| bus stop | laundromat | supermarket | movie theater | restaurant |

1. _____   2. _____   3. _____

4. _____   5. _____

D **Complete with _in_, _on_, _next to_, or _between_.**

1. Ben is _____ the library.

2. He is sitting _____ Grace and Tien.

3. The book is _____ the table.

4. Tien is _____ Leo.

5. The library is _____ Second Avenue.

Name: _____ Date: _____ Score: _____

 A **Listen and circle.**

1.

4.

2.

5.

3.

B **Fill in.**

1. We _____ swim.

(A) don't   (B) doesn't

2. I _____ lift weights.

(A) don't   (B) doesn't

3. He _____ exercise.

(A) don't   (B) doesn't

4. They _____ work here.

(A) don't   (B) doesn't

5. She _____ live with her family.

(A) don't   (B) doesn't

C **Match.**

1. _____ foot

2. _____ hand

3. _____ head

4. _____ chest

5. _____ arm

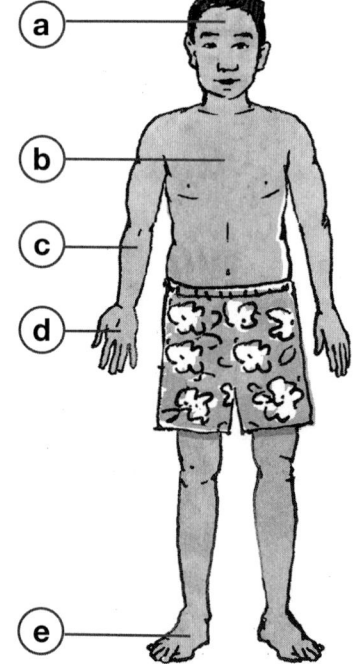

D **Match.**

1. _____ finger

2. _____ leg

3. _____ stomach

4. _____ eye

5. _____ nose

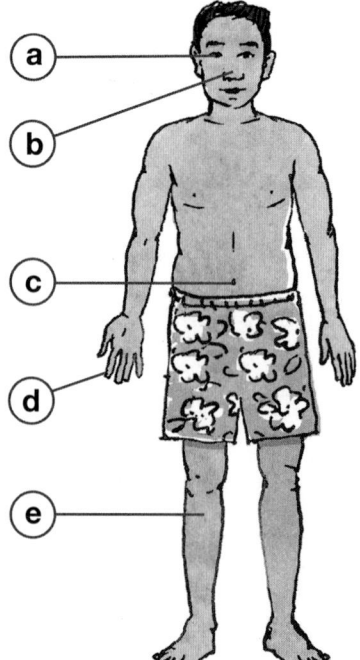

Name: _____ Date: _____ Score: _____

 A **Listen and circle.**

1.

2.

3.

4.

5.

B ✔ **Check.**

Jobs	Indoors	Outdoors	With People	With Machines
1. taxi driver				
2. construction worker				
3. cook				
4. health aide				
5. delivery person				

© McGraw-Hill

C Complete.

> a cashier   a delivery person   a cook   an office worker   a waiter

1. _____

2. _____

3. _____

4. _____

5. _____

D Fill in.

1. I _____ a waiter in 2001.

   Ⓐ am   Ⓑ was

2. We _____ in Brazil in 2003.

   Ⓐ was   Ⓑ were

3. She _____ a receptionist in 2006.

   Ⓐ was   Ⓑ were

4. They _____ speak Spanish. They are from China.

   Ⓐ can   Ⓑ can't

5. Can you drive a car? Yes, I _____.

   Ⓐ can   Ⓑ can't

Name: _____ Date: _____ Score: _____

A Listen and ✔ check the answer.

1. _____ I take a bus.   _____ It's on the left.

2. _____ Take the Blue Line.   _____ It's straight ahead.

3. _____ It leaves at 4:30.   _____ It leaves every fifteen minutes.

4. _____ Take the M Train.   _____ It's on the left.

5. _____ It leaves at 2:00.   _____ I take a taxi.

B Circle.

1. The laundromat is _____.   next to the bank   between

2. The library is _____.   straight ahead   on the corner

3. The bank is _____.   on the corner   next to the post office

4. The park is _____.   on the left   next to the police station

5. The market is _____.   next to the laundromat   between the bank and the post office

C Write.

1. **A:** _____ is the name of your school?
    B: John F. Kennedy.

2. **A:** _____ do you get to school?
    B: I take a bus.

3. **A:** _____ is the school?
    B: 1432 South Main Street.

4. **A:** _____ does your bus leave?
    B: At 4:00.

5. **A:** _____ is your teacher?
    B: Sandy Johnson.

D Write.

Bus	Parking	One	Limit	Stop

1. _____   2. _____   3. _____

4. _____   5. _____

Tests Listening Script

Unit 1

A. LISTEN AND CHECK THE ANSWER.

1. Hello, Maria. I'm Carlos.
2. Hi, my name is Carlos. I'm from Brazil.
3. My name is Maria Cruz.
4. My first name is M-A-R-I-A.
5. a desk.

Unit 2

A. LISTEN AND CHECK THE ANSWER.

1. What language do you speak?
2. Leo is from Russia. What language does he speak?
3. I'm from Mexico. Where are you from?
4. What's your address?
5. What's your zip code?

Unit 3

A. LISTEN AND CHECK THE ANSWER.

1. How old are you?
2. What's your father's name?
3. Do you have two daughters?
4. Do you have children?
5. Who is Tom?

Unit 4

A. LISTEN AND CIRCLE.

1. I'm 40 years old.
2. I have 80 dollars.
3. I need 17 pens.
4. My mother is 60 years old.
5. We have 15 chairs.

Unit 5

A. LISTEN AND CHECK THE ANSWER.

1. What is your date of birth?
2. When is your birthday?
3. What time is it?
4. How often do you cook dinner?
5. Can you come on Saturday at nine forty-five?

Unit 6

A. LISTEN AND CHECK THE ANSWER.

1. May I help you?
2. What's your favorite color?
3. What are you wearing to the party?
4. What color are your pants?
5. What size are you?

Unit 7

A. LISTEN AND CIRCLE.

1. We need bread.
2. We need cheese.
3. We need beef.
4. We need apples.
5. We need ice cream.

Unit 8

A. LISTEN AND CHECK THE ANSWER.

1. How's the weather?
2. What's your favorite season?
3. What are you doing?
4. What do you like doing in the summer?
5. What's Maria doing?

Unit 9

A. LISTEN AND CIRCLE.

1. You buy stamps at the post office.
2. You read at the library.
3. You buy aspirin at the drugstore.
4. You deposit money at the bank.
5. You wash clothes at the laundromat.

Unit 10

A. LISTEN AND CIRCLE.

1. I have a headache.
2. I have a stomachache.
3. I have a sore throat.
4. I have a fever.
5. I have a cut.

Unit 11

A. LISTEN AND CIRCLE.

1. I can drive a car.
2. I can fix things.
3. I can sell clothes.
4. I can use a computer.
5. I can use a cash register.

Unit 12

A. LISTEN AND CHECK THE ANSWER.

1. How do you get to school?
2. Excuse me. Where is the drugstore?
3. How often does the 5 Bus leave?
4. How do I get to the beach?
5. When does the next plane to New York leave?

Tests Answer Key

Unit 1

A. Listen and check the answer.
1. Hello, Maria. I'm Carlos.
2. Hi, My name is Carlos. I'm from Brazil.
3. My name is Maria Cruz.
4. My first name is M-A-R-I-A.
5. A desk.

B. Fill in.
1. a
2. b
3. c
4. b
5. c

C. Complete.
1. book
2. notebook
3. paper
4. backpack
5. chair

D. Complete. Write the number.
1. 4
2. 7
3. 1
4. 8
5. 10

Unit 2

A. Listen and check the answer.
1. I speak Chinese.
2. He speaks Russian.
3. I'm from Somalia.
4. My address is 142 Book Street.
5. My zip code is 95945.

B. Fill in.
1. a
2. c
3. b
4. a
5. b

C. Complete.
1. tall
2. average height
3. average height
4. short
5. short

D. Match.
1. c
2. e
3. a
4. b
5. d

Unit 3

A. Listen and check the answer.
1. I'm twenty-two years old.
2. His name is John.
3. Yes, I do.
4. Yes, I have two sons.
5. Tom is Andy's brother.

B. Fill in.
1. c
2. a
3. c
4. a
5. b

C. Complete.
1. young
2. old
3. middle-aged
4. Mr.
5. Mrs.

D. Match.
1. d
2. c
3. e
4. a
5. b

Unit 4

A. Listen and circle.
1. 40
2. 80
3. 17
4. 60
5. 15

B. Write.
1. tables
2. book
3. chairs
4. cities
5. window

C. Circle.
1. bathroom
2. kitchen
3. bed
4. kitchen
5. windows

D. Circle.
1. illustration on the left
2. illustration on the left
3. illustration on the right
4. illustration on the right
5. illustration on the left

Unit 5

A. Listen and check the answer.
1. January 12, 1971.
2. It's in December.
3. 8:15

4. Once a week.
5. Saturday at 9:45? That's fine.

B. Complete.

1. comb
2. gets
3. eat
4. takes
5. open

C. Check the time.

1. 2:00
2. 7:15
3. 4:45
4. 8:15
5. 12:30

D. Match.

1. d
2. c
3. a
4. b
5. e

Unit 6

A. Listen and check the answer.

1. Yes, I'm looking for a sweater.
2. Blue.
3. I'm wearing a red dress.
4. They're black.
5. I'm a medium.

B. Match.

1. b
2. d
3. e
4. c
5. a

C. Complete.

1. a watch
2. a dress
3. a blouse
4. a suit
5. shoes

D. Circle.

1. red
2. shirt
3. blue

4. shoes
5. green dress

Unit 7

A. Listen and circle.

1. bread
2. cheese
3. beef
4. apples
5. ice cream

B. Complete.

1. can
2. carton
3. bag
4. bottle
5. box

C. Complete.

1. oranges
2. cheese
3. eggs
4. bread
5. butter

D. Check.

1. non-count
2. count
3. count
4. non-count
5. non-count

Unit 8

A. Listen and check the answer.

1. It's sunny.
2. Fall.
3. I'm reading.
4. I like swimming.
5. She's listening to music.

B. Fill in.

1. a
2. b
3. b
4. b
5. c

C. Complete.

1. listening to music
2. cooking
3. watching TV
4. reading
5. dancing

D. Complete.

1. swimming
2. playing soccer
3. talking
4. walking
5. playing basketball

Unit 9

A. Listen and circle.

1. post office
2. library
3. drugstore
4. bank
5. laundromat

B. Complete.

1. next to
2. between
3. in
4. on
5. between

C. Complete.

1. bus stop
2. supermarket
3. laundromat
4. movie theater
5. restaurant

D. Complete with *in, on, next to*, or *between*.

1. in
2. between
3. on
4. next to
5. on

Unit 10

A. Listen and circle.

1. illustration on the left
2. illustration on the right
3. illustration on the left

4. illustration on the left

5. illustration on the right

B. Circle.

1. a

2. a

3. b

4. a

5. b

C. Match.

1. e

2. d

3. a

4. b

5. c

D. Match.

1. d

2. e

3. c

4. a

5. b

Unit 11

A. Listen and circle.

1. illustration on the left

2. illustration on the right

3. illustration on the left

4. illustration on the left

5. illustration on the left

B. Check.

1. taxi driver: Outdoors; With People

2. construction worker : Indoors; Outdoors; With Machines

3. cook: Indoors; With People; With Machines

4. health aide: Indoors; With People; With Machines

5. delivery person: Indoors; Outdoors; With Machines; With People

C. Complete.

1. a delivery person

2. a cook

3. a cashier

4. an office worker

5. a waiter

D. Fill in.

1. b

2. b

3. a

4. b

5. a

Unit 12

A. Listen and check the answer.

1. I take a bus.

2. It's straight ahead.

3. It leaves every fifteen minutes.

4. Take the M Train.

5. It leaves at 2:00.

B. Circle.

1. on the corner

2. next to the police station

3. next to the bank

4. on the corner

5. between the bank and the post office.

C. Write.

1. What

2. How often

3. Where

4. When

5. How long

D. Write.

1. Parking

2. Stop

3. Limit

4. One

5. Bus

Workbook Answer Key

Unit 1: Welcome to the classroom.

Page 2

A.

   Jane: Hello, I'm <u>Jane</u>.
   David: Hi, Jane. I'm David. Nice to <u>meet</u> you.
   Jane: <u>Nice</u> to meet you too, <u>David</u>.

B.

   Alex: <u>Hi</u>. I'm <u>Alex</u>. I'm <u>from</u> Mexico
   Mei: Hello. My name is Mei. <u>I'm</u> from <u>China</u>.

Page 3

A.

   <u>A B C D E F G H I J K L M</u>
   <u>a b c d e f g h i j k l m</u>

B.

   <u>A B C D E F G H I J K L M</u>
   <u>a b c d e f g h i j k l m</u>

C.

   1. A – a
      B – b
      C – c
      D – d
      E – e
      F – f
      G – g
   2. H – h
      I – i
      J – j
      K – k
      L – l
      M – m

Page 4

A.

   <u>N O P Q R S T U V W X Y Z</u>
   <u>n o p q r s t u v w x y z</u>

B.

   <u>N O P Q R S T U V W X Y Z</u>
   <u>n o p q r s t u v w x y z</u>

C.

   Eva: Hello. I'm Eva Martinez. <u>What's</u> your name?
   Ivan: My name is Ivan Stoli.
   Eva: <u>How</u> do you <u>spell</u> that?
   Ivan: My <u>first</u> name is I-V-A-N. My <u>last</u> name is S-T-O-L-I.

Page 5

A.

   1. backpack
   2. desk
   3. door
   4. student
   5. board
   6. pen
   7. book
   8. teacher
   9. chair
   10. computer
   11. notebook
   12. paper

Page 6

A. backpack

B. board

C. Answers will vary.

D. C

E.

   1. b   **2.** a

Page 7

A.

1.

2.

3.

4.

B.

   1. Close the door.
   2. Put away the paper.
   3. Take out the pen.

Page 8

A.

   one, two, three, four, five, six, seven, eight, nine

B.

   1. 1
   2. 7
   3. 2
   4. 9
   5. 4
   6. 5

C.

   1. phone number
   2. address
   3. email address

Page 9

B.

   ten numbers—Yes
   the alphabet—Yes
   a door—Yes

a board—Yes
a book—Yes
a computer—No
a desk—No
a student—Yes
a teacher—Yes
a teacher—Yes
a paper—Yes

Page 10

A.

1. I'm
2. It's
3. What is
4. It's
5. What's
6. I am
7. It's
8. I am
9. What is
10. It is

Page 12

A.

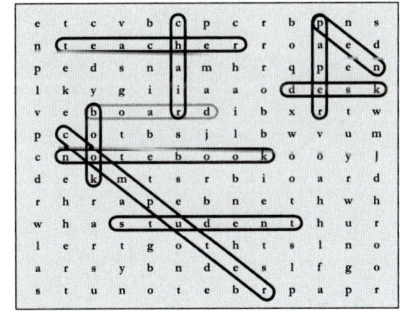

Unit 2: Where are you from?

Page 14

A.

Alex: I'm from Mexico. Where are you from?
Mei: I'm from China.

B.

Thomas: Where is Alex from?
Erik: He's from Mexico.
Thomas: Where is Mei from?
Erik: She's from China.

Page 15

A.

Ivan: I speak Russian. What do you speak?
David: I speak Vietnamese.

B.

Mei: I speak Chinese. What do you speak?
Marco: I speak Spanish.

Page 16

B.

1. **A:** Marco is from Colombia. What does he speak?
   B: He speaks Spanish.
2. **A:** Aziza is from Somalia. What does she speak?
   B: She speaks Somali.
3. **A:** Luna is from Brazil. What does she speak?
   B: She speaks Portuguese.
4. **A:** Alex is from Mexico. What does he speak?
   B: He speaks Spanish.
5. **A:** Mei is from China. What does she speak?
   B: She speaks Chinese.

Page 17

A.

1. married
2. divorced
3. widowed

B.

1. widowed
2. single
3. married
4. divorced

Page 18

A.

1. Lin is tall.
2. David is average height.
3. Alex is tall.
4. Mei is short.

B.

1. David has glasses.
2. Alex and Mei don't have glasses.

Page 19

A.

eleven, twelve, thirteen, fourteen, fifteen, sixteen, seventeen, eighteen, nineteen

B.

1. 11
2. 14
3. 15
4. 19
5. 16
6. 12

C.

Alex: What's your address?
Lin: My address is 324 Short Street.
Alex: What's your zip code?
Lin: My zip code is 92924.

Page 20

B.

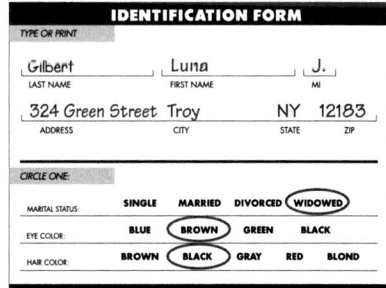

Page 21

A.

1. Mei is from China.
2. I am from Colombia.
3. Luna and Erik are from Brazil.
4. You are from Haiti.
5. Ivan is from Russia.

B.

1. Luna <u>has</u> black hair.
2. You <u>have</u> blue eyes.
3. Thomas <u>has</u> brown hair.
4. I <u>have</u> gray hair.
5. They <u>have</u> blond hair.

C.

1. David <u>is</u> from Vietnam.
2. Alex and Anita <u>are</u> from Mexico.
3. Jane and Ivan <u>have</u> green eyes.
4. Mei <u>has</u> black hair.
5. Luna <u>has</u> brown eyes.
6. We <u>are</u> from Vietnam.

Page 22

A.

1. Califonia
2. Texas
3. Florida
4. New York
5. Colorado
6. Illinois

Page 24

A.

Across
2. address
5. Chinese

Down
1. from
2. address
3. eleven
4. code

B.

1. Russian
2. Chinese
3. Portuguese
4. Spanish

Unit 3: This is my family.

Page 26

A.

1. Van
2. Tam
3. Loc
4. Bao

B.

1. brother
2. daughter
3. sister
4. wife

Page 27

A.

1. father
2. mother
3. brother

B.

1. B
2. A
3. A
4. A
5. A
6. B

Page 28

A.

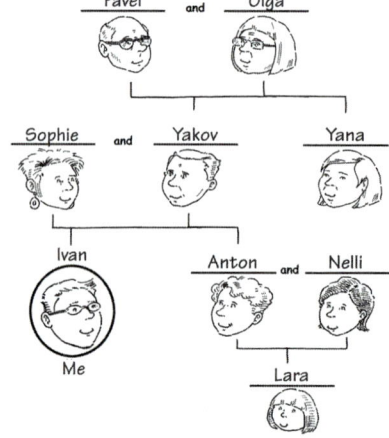

B.

1. young
2. old
3. middle-aged

Page 29

A.

1. <u>Mr.</u> Stoli
2. <u>Mr.</u> and <u>Mrs.</u> or <u>Ms.</u> Stoli
3. <u>Miss</u> or <u>Ms.</u> Stoli
4. <u>Miss</u> or <u>Ms.</u> Stoli
5. <u>Mrs.</u> or <u>Ms.</u> Stoli
6. <u>Mr.</u> Anton Stoli
7. <u>Mrs.</u> or <u>Ms.</u> Stoli

Page 30

A.

David: Do you have <u>children</u>?
Aziza: No, I <u>don't</u>.
Ly: Yes, I have a son and a <u>daughter</u>.
Alex: <u>Do</u> you have children?
Jane: <u>No</u>, I don't.
Luna: Yes, <u>I</u> have <u>three</u> sons.

Page 31

A.

1. 90
2. 22
3. 50
4. 70
5. 30
6. 40
7. 100
8. 50
9. 60
10. 80

B.

<u>20 30 40 50 60 70 80 90 100</u>

C.

Eva: How <u>old</u> are you?
Luna: I'm 52 <u>years</u> old. <u>How</u> old are <u>you</u>?
Eva: I'm <u>68</u> years old.

Page 32

B.

Census Form

Address: 178 Old Street

Troy		N.Y.	12183
City		State	Zip Code

List all the people at your address.

First Name	MI	Last Name	Age
1 Alex	J.	Reyes	48
2 Juan	M.	Reyes	70
3 Anita	S.	Reyes	70
4 Linda	F.	Reyes	46
5 Ana	T.	Santos	74
6 Lola	C.	Reyes	17
7 Ben	S.	Reyes	15

Page 33

A.

1. Yes, I do.
2. No, I don't.
3. Yes, I do.
4. No, I don't
5. Yes, I do.
6. Yes, I do.

B.

This is <u>my</u> mother. <u>Her</u> name is Sophie. This is my father. <u>His</u> name is Yakov. I have a brother. <u>His</u> name is Anton. He has a wife and a daughter. <u>Their</u> names <u>are</u> Nelli and Lara.

Page 34

B.

1. John is David's favorite relative.

C.

1. tall
2. black
3. Vietnam
4. one daughter
5. brother
6. brown
7. married
8. daughter

Page 35

A.

My <u>name</u> is Marco Chavez. My family is <u>from</u> Colombia. I <u>live</u> in the United States now.

I have four <u>children</u>. I have one <u>daughter</u> and three <u>sons</u>.

My children are <u>young</u>. <u>Their</u> names are Serena, Marco, Juan, and Miguel. I have five <u>people</u> in my family.

I have one <u>sister</u>. <u>Her</u> name is Clara. <u>She</u> lives in the United States, too. She has two <u>children</u>. <u>Their</u> names are Rosa and Pedro.

Page 36

A.

1. F A T H E R
2. D A U G H T E R
3. S O N
4. M O T H E R

B.

Y O U   A R E   S M A R T !

Unit 4: Welcome to our house.

Page 38

A.

1. kitchen
2. bathroom
3. bedroom
4. living room
5. garden
6. dining room

B.

1. kitchen
2. living room
3. bedroom
4. garden
5. dining room

Page 39

A.

Luna: Is <u>there</u> a <u>chair</u> in the living room?
Erik: <u>Yes</u>, there is.
Luna: Is there a lamp in the <u>kitchen</u>?
Erik: <u>No</u>, there isn't.

B.

1. Yes, there is.
2. No, there isn't.
3. Yes, there is.
4. Yes, there is.
5. No, there isn't.

Page 40

A.

1. kitchen
2. bedroom
3. kitchen
4. kitchen
5. bathroom
6. bedroom
7. bathroom

B.

1. apartment
2. house
3. rented room

C.

1. rented room
2. apartment
3. house

Page 41

B.

Eva: <u>What</u> do <u>you</u> need?
Mei: I <u>need</u> a bed.
Eva: Do you need a <u>desk</u>?
Mei: No, I don't. <u>Thanks</u>.

C.

Mei has: lamps, a desk, a sofa, a table, a bed
Mei needs: chairs, a dresser

Page 42

A.

1. **A:** Where do you <u>shower</u>?
   B: I shower in the <u>bathroom</u>.
2. **A:** Where do you <u>cook</u>?
   B: I cook in the <u>kitchen</u>.
3. **A:** Where do you <u>study</u>?
   B: I study in the <u>living room</u>.
4. **A:** Where do you <u>sleep</u>?
   B: I sleep in the <u>bedroom</u>.

B.

1. in the city
2. at the beach
3. in the country

Page 43

A.

1. 30
2. 12
3. 13
4. 20
5. 18
6. 90
7. 80
8. 19

B.

1. seventy
2. sixty
3. seventeen
4. fifty
5. sixteen
6. fifteen

C.

1. 20
2. 60
3. 18
4. 14
5. 12
6. 50
7. 17
8. 19

Page 44

A.

1. e
2. b
3. d
4. c
5. a

Page 45

A.

Plural Nouns: beaches,
daughters, bedrooms,
bathrooms, closets, sofas,
chairs, beds, dressers

Singular Nouns: house,
husband, house, living room,
kitchen, dining room, backyard,
living room, table, dining room,
house

B.

1. kitchens
2. tub
3. houses
4. closet
5. bathrooms
6. chair

C.

David lives in <u>an</u> apartment
in <u>a</u> city. His apartment has <u>a</u>
bedroom, <u>a</u> bathroom, <u>a</u> kitchen,
<u>a</u> living room, and <u>a</u> closet. It has
<u>an</u> air conditioner, <u>a</u> stove, and <u>a</u>
refrigerator.

Page 46

B.

2. Mei's apartment

C.

1. No
2. Yes
3. Yes
4. No
5. No
6. No
7. No

Page 47

A.

Dear Mrs. <u>Kim</u>,

I live at <u>456</u> White Street. I
live in apartment <u>412.</u> I have
a broken <u>refrigerator</u> in the
<u>kitchen</u>. Please fix the <u>door</u>. My
phone number is <u>(518) 555-2705</u>.

Thank you,

<u>Mei Wong</u>

Page 48

A.

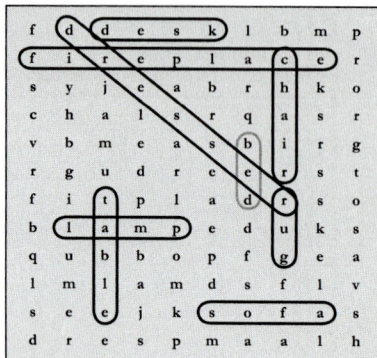

Unit 5: I talk on the phone.

Page 50

A.

1. c
2. e
3. a
4. f
5. d
6. b

B.

David: <u>What</u> <u>do</u> you do
every <u>day</u>?
Eva: I <u>brush</u> my teeth.

Page 51

A.

Sunday, Monday, Tuesday,
Wednesday, Thursday, Friday,
Saturday

B.

1. Sunday
2. Friday
3. Sunday and Tuesday
4. Monday and Wednesday

C.

1. August
2. February
3. March
4. December
5. January
6. October

Page 52

A.

1. b
2. c
3. a
4. d

B.

1. 6:30
2. 6:45
3. 7:15
4. 9:00

Page 53

A.

Alex: I'd like to make an appointment for a tune-up.
Man: Can you come on Monday at 7:00?
Alex: Monday at 7:00? That's fine.

B.

Eva: I'd like to make an appointment for a haircut.
Woman: Can you come on Friday at 3:45?
Eva: Friday at 3:45? That's fine.

Page 54

A.

Luna: What do you do once a week?
Erik: I get a haircut.
Luna: I go to garage sales.

B.

1. once a week
2. once a month
3. every day

Page 55

A.

1. j
2. g
3. i
4. h
5. b
6. d

7. e
8. c
9. a
10. f

B.

1. 9th
2. 3rd
3. 11th
4. 7th
5. 14th
6. 8th
7. 1st
8. 6th
9. 13th
10. 9th
11. 5th
12. 12th

Page 56

A.

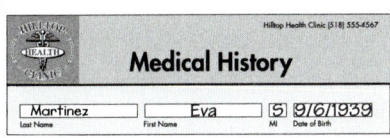

B.

1. Jover
2. H.
3. August 26, 1981

Page 57

A.

1. eat
2. cooks
3. plays
4. work
5. needs
6. shops
7. gets
8. study
9. sleep
10. talks

B.

1. am
2. is
3. are
4. is; are

Page 58

B.

1. It's June 17.
2. Marco is 42.
3. The party is in class.
4. Class is at 3:15.
5. Luna brings a cake.
6. David brings CDs.
7. Aziza takes photos.
8. The teacher is at the party.

Page 59

A.

Dear Juan,

These are photos of my classmates. They are very nice. Mei and I go to garage sales once a week. David is from Vietnam. David and I go to the movies once a month. Aziza is from Somalia. Aziza and I study on Saturdays.

Love, Marco

Page 60

A.

January	F e b r u a r y
March	April
M a y	J u n e
J u l y	A u g u s t
September	O c t o b e r
November	December

B.

W H E N I S Y O U R
B I R T H D A Y ?

Unit 6: Let's go shopping.

Page 62

A.

1. shoes
2. a coat
3. a suit
4. a watch
5. pants

6. a sweater
7. a dress
8. a skirt

B.

Luna: <u>Excuse</u> me, I'm <u>looking</u> for a <u>watch</u>.
Clerk: Follow <u>me</u>, please.
Luna: <u>Thank</u> you.

C.

Clerk: <u>May</u> I <u>help</u> you?
Juan: Yes, <u>I'm</u> looking for a <u>jacket</u>.

Page 63

A.

Kim: <u>What</u> are you <u>wearing</u> to the party?
David: <u>I'm</u> wearing black pants <u>and</u> a blue shirt. What <u>are</u> you wearing?
Kim: I'm wearing a purple <u>dress</u>.

B.

1. pants and a shirt
2. a sweater
3. a skirt
4. a blouse
5. a shirt
6. a suit

Page 64

A.

Thomas: <u>What</u> is your <u>favorite</u> color?
Marco: <u>My</u> favorite <u>color</u> is <u>blue</u>.

B.

Ivan: What color <u>is</u> your <u>dress</u>?
Aziza: Red.
Ivan: What <u>color</u> are <u>your</u> shoes?
Aziza: <u>Brown</u>.

Page 65

A.

1. medium
2. small
3. large

B.

Mei: What <u>size</u> are <u>you</u>?
Alex: I'm a <u>medium</u>. <u>What</u> size <u>are</u> you?
Mei: <u>I'm</u> a small.

Page 66

A.

1. too long
2. too short
3. too small
4. too big
5. too big
6. too long

B.

Answers will vary but may include:
Thomas's hat is too small.
Thomas's sweater is too big.
Thomas's pants are too short.
Thomas's shoes are too big.

Page 67

A.

1. 1 cent
2. a nickel
3. 10 cents
4. a quarter; 25¢

B.

1. $25.25
2. $16.11
3. $5.40
4. $2.00

Page 68

B.

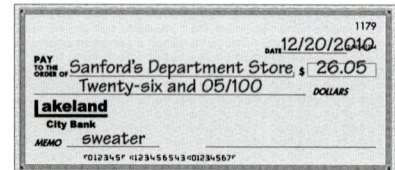

Page 69

A.

1. large
2. skirt
3. short

4. pants
5. scarf
6. large

Page 70

B.

1. $34.55
2. small, medium, large
3. black, brown, or blue
4. $22.50
5. white, black, red, or pink
6. $88.99

Page 71

A.

1. jacket
2. $14.75
3. shirt
4. belt
5. $17.95

Page 72

B.

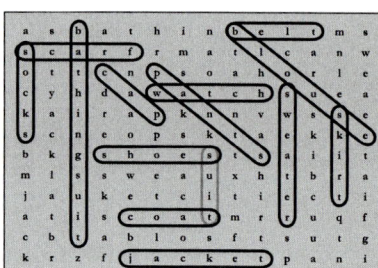

Unit 7: I'm so hungry!

Page 74

A.

1. carrots
2. eggs
3. potatoes
4. milk
5. apples
6. ice cream

B. Complete.

Alex: We <u>need</u> some apples.
Linda: That's <u>right</u>. We need <u>some</u> milk, too.
Alex: We need some <u>potatoes</u>.
Linda: <u>That's</u> right.

Page 75

A.

1. e
2. g
3. d
4. a
5. b
6. c
7. f

B.

Ivan: Excuse <u>me</u>. I'm looking for some lettuce.
Clerk: Lettuce is <u>in</u> aisle 1.
Ivan: I'm <u>looking</u> for <u>pasta</u>, too,
Clerk: Pasta is in <u>aisle</u> 5.

Page 76

A.

Aziza: What do you have for <u>breakfast</u>?
Eva: I usually have <u>eggs</u>. I sometimes have <u>cereal</u>.
Aziza: What <u>do</u> you have for lunch?
Eva: I always have a <u>sandwich</u>.
Aziza: What do you <u>have</u> for dinner?
Eva: I usually have <u>fish</u>. I sometimes have chicken.
Answers may vary.

B.

1. b
2. a
3. c

Page 77

A.

1. pizza
2. hamburger
3. sandwich
4. coffee
5. soda
6. pie

B.

Server: <u>May</u> I help you?
David: Yes, A <u>hamburger</u>, please.

Server: Anything to <u>drink</u> today?
David: Yes, <u>thanks</u>. Some <u>soda</u>, please.

Page 78

A.

Ivan: Do <u>you</u> have hamburgers for dinner?
Thomas: No, I <u>don't</u>.
Ivan: Do you <u>have</u> pizza <u>for</u> dinner?
Thomas: Yes, I <u>do</u>.

B.

Thomas: Do you have eggs for <u>breakfast</u>?
Ivan: Yes, I do. Do you have <u>chicken</u> for <u>lunch</u>?
Thomas: Yes, I do.

Page 79

A.

1. bottle
2. bag
3. box
4. carton
5. can
6. jar

B.

1. bottle
2. carton
3. jar
4. can
5. bag
6. box

Page 80

B.

1. True
2. True
3. False
4. True
5. False

Page 81

A.

1. Non-count
2. Non-count

3. Count
4. Non-count
5. Count
6. Count
7. Non-count
8. Non-count
9. Non-count
10. Count

B.

Count Nouns: bananas, carrots, sandwich, oranges
Non-count Nouns: pasta, cake, bread, rice, cereal, lettuce

Page 82

B.

Eggs: Price: $3.75
        Coupon: 50¢
        Cost: $3.25
Coffee: Price: $9.50
        Coupon: 60¢
        Cost: $8.90
Rice: Price: $7.10
        Coupon: 75¢
        Cost: $6.35

C.

1. 4
2. 2
3. Answers will vary. Total price of items should be less than $20.00.

Page 83

A.

Coffee, tea, cake, two cartons of milk, two boxes of pasta, chicken, three steaks, a bag of potatoes, a box of butter, cheese, a loaf of bread, lettuce, a bunch of carrots, ice cream, six cans of soda

A.

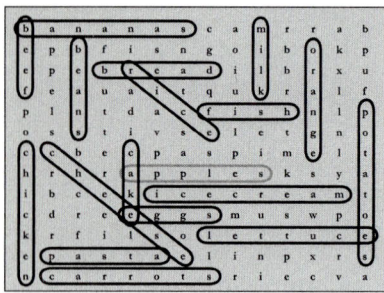

Unit 8: How's the weather?

Page 86

A.

1. sunny
2. raining
3. windy
4. hot
5. cold
6. snowing

B.

Luna: How's the weather in New York?
Alex: It's cold. How's the weather in Los Angeles?
Luna: It's hot.

Page 87

A.

1. It's summer.
2. It's winter.
3. It's fall.
4. It's spring.

B.

Eva: What season do you like?
Ly: Fall.
Eva: What season don't you like?
Ly: Spring.

Page 88

A.

1. playing soccer
2. watching TV
3. dancing
4. cooking
5. reading
6. walking

B.

1. dancing
2. talking on the phone
3. reading
4. playing soccer

Page 89

A.

Mei: What do you like doing in the summer?
Ivan: I like swimming.

B.

1. **Ly:** What do you like doing in the spring?
   Aziza: I like walking.
2. **Ly:** What do you like doing in the winter?
   Thomas: I like reading.
3. **Ly:** What do you like doing in the summer?
   Eva: I like swimming.
4. **Ly:** What do you like doing in the fall?
   Erik: I like cooking.

Page 90

A.

1. It's cold. It's snowing.
2. It's hot and sunny.
3. It's cold and cloudy.
4. It's raining and windy.

Page 91

A.

1. It's cold. It's 30° F. It's −1° C.
2. It's very hot! It's 103° F. It's 39° C.
3. It's warm today. It's 70° F. It's 21° C.
4. It's cool today. It's 50° F. It's 10° C.

Page 92

B.

City	Temp.*	Sunny	Raining	Snowing	Cloudy
Seattle	55° F		✔		
Los Angeles	75° F				✔
Dallas	80° F	✔			
Chicago	30° F			✔	
Miami	70° F	✔			

*Temp. = Temperature

Page 93

A.

1. I am eating.
2. He is talking.
3. We are reading.
4. They are singing.
5. She is listening.
6. You are studying.

B.

1. Aziza is studying in the kitchen.
2. David and Thomas are playing soccer.
3. Eva is buying milk.
4. Alex is cooking dinner.
5. Ly and Van are eating dinner.

C.

1. I'm watching TV.
2. We're buying food.
3. He's reading the newspaper.
4. They're playing basketball.
5. You're walking home.

Page 94

B.

1. Erik and his friends are drinking coffee.
2. It's cool and it's raining.
3. Eva is reading a book and eating a sandwich.
4. David is listening to music.
5. Lin is watching the rain.

Page 95

A.

Dear Erik,

I'm in San Diego. My sister is here, too. The weather here is sunny and very hot. Today we are <u>talking</u> and having <u>lunch</u> in the park.

Your friend,

Mei

Page 96

A.

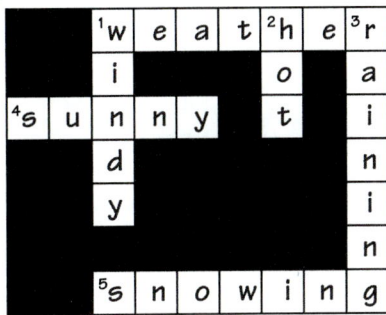

Unit 9: Where's the post office?

Page 98

A.

1. library
2. gas station
3. fire station
4. hospital
5. bank
6. policc station

B.

Thomas: <u>Where</u> are you <u>going</u>?
Erik: <u>I'm</u> going to the <u>bank</u>.
    What <u>about</u> you?
Thomas: I'm going <u>there</u>, too.
    Let's go <u>together</u>.

Page 99

A.

1. **Eva:** Excuse me. Where's the <u>post office</u>?
    Thomas: It's on Cherry Street.
    Eva: On <u>Cherry Street</u>? Thanks.
2. **Ivan:** Excuse me. Where's the <u>drugstore</u>?
    Mei: It's on Paper Street.

Ivan: On <u>Paper Street</u>?
    Thanks.
3. **Lin:** Excuse me. Where's the <u>police station</u>?
    Marco: It's on Cherry Street.
    Lin: On <u>Cherry Street</u>?
    Thanks.

Page 100

A.

1. restaurant
2. park
3. movie theater
4. bus stop
5. laundromat
6. supermarket

B.

Ly: Is <u>there</u> a restaurant in your neighborhood?
David: Yes, there is.
Ly: Is there a <u>library</u> in your neighborhood?
David: No, there <u>isn't</u>.

Page 101

A.

Aziza: Where's the <u>drugstore</u>?
Ly: It's <u>on</u> State Street.
Aziza: On State <u>Street</u>?
Ly: That's right. It's <u>between</u> the post office and the <u>restaurant</u>.
Aziza: Where's the laundromat?
Ly: It's <u>next to</u> the bank.

B.

1. between
2. next to
3. on

Page 102

A.

Eva: Do you <u>live</u> near a post office?
Aziza: Yes, I <u>do</u>.
Eva: Do <u>you</u> live <u>near</u> a bank?
Aziza: No, I <u>don't</u>.

B.

1. b
2. d
3. a
4. c

Page 103

B.

1. October 25, 2010
2. 123-6545
3. $695.75
4. savings
5. three

Page 104

B.

1. 1-2-5-6
2. withdrawal
3. checking
4. $200.00

Page 105

A.

1. in
2. on
3. on
4. on
5. on
6. in

B.

1. next to
2. between
3. next to
4. across from
5. between

Page 106

B.

2. Alex goes to the bank and the supermarket

C.

1. $472.38
2. $447.38
3. $25
4. week
5. food
6. $.65 or 65¢

Page 107

B.

Page 108

A.

1. M O V I E   T H E A T E R
2. L A U N D R O M A T
3. D R U G S T O R E
4. S U P E R M A R K E T

B.

W H A T S   Y O U R
F A V O R I T E   M O V I E ?

Unit 10: You need to see a doctor.

Page 110

A.

1. a sore throat
2. a stomachache
3. a cold

B.

1. hand
2. finger
3. leg
4. foot

C.

Mei: What's the <u>matter</u>?
Eva: I have a <u>headache</u>.
Mei: What's the matter <u>with</u> Marco?
Eva: His <u>arm</u> hurts.

Page 111

A.

Ben: I feel <u>bad</u>. My <u>stomach</u> hurts.
Alex: You <u>need</u> to see a <u>doctor</u>.

B.

Alex: Hello. <u>This</u> is Alex Reyes. My son is <u>sick</u>. Can Dr. Black see him today?

Woman: Yes. Dr. Black can <u>see</u> him at 8:30.
Alex: <u>Today</u> at 8:30? That's <u>fine</u>. Thank you.

C.

Ben's <u>stomach</u> hurts. He has an appointment to see Dr. <u>Black</u>. He will see the doctor <u>today</u> at <u>8:30</u>.

Page 112

A.

1. a fever
2. a cough
3. a cut
4. an infection

B.

1. aspirin
2. an antibiotic
3. cough syrup
4. a bandage

C.

David: Luna <u>has</u> a cut on her leg.
Eva: That's too <u>bad</u>. She <u>needs</u> a <u>bandage</u>.

Page 113

A.

1. c
2. a
3. e
4. b
5. d

Page 114

A.

Marco: I <u>have</u> a <u>cold</u>.
Lin: <u>Drink</u> orange juice.
Ivan: <u>Rest</u>.

B.

Eva: I have a <u>cough</u>.
Thomas: <u>Take</u> a hot <u>shower</u>.
Aziza: Drink <u>hot</u> water.

C.

David: <u>I</u> have a <u>stomachache</u>.
Luna: Rest.
Mei: <u>Drink</u> hot <u>water</u>.

Page 115

B.

Ivan: drops; 3x a day
Luna: a pill; 2x a day
Thomas: a capsule; 3x a day

Page 116

B.

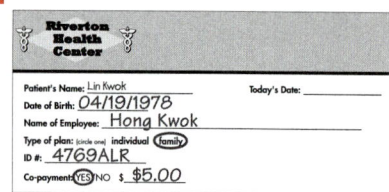

Page 117

A.

1. walks
2. play
3. read
4. swim
5. run
6. drinks
7. writes
8. lift weights
9. walk
10. runs

B.

1. doesn't like
2. don't play
3. don't eat
4. don't drink
5. don't dance
6. don't read
7. doesn't drink
8. don't like
9. doesn't play
10. don't eat

Page 118

B.

Lin: 44; plays soccer; likes carrots
Ping: 74; dances; likes apples
Lin and Ping: healthy; exercise every day; walk in the park; eat healthy food; don't eat junk food; don't smoke

Page 120

A.

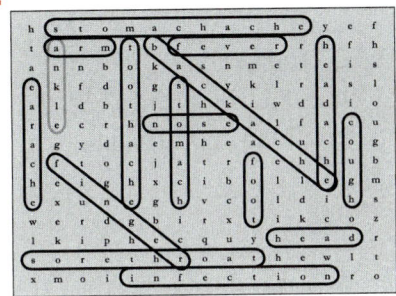

Unit 11: What's your job?

Page 122

A.

1. cashier
2. delivery person
3. waiter
4. health aide
5. computer programmer
6. sales clerk

B.

Erik: What <u>do</u> you do?
Mei: <u>I'm</u> a delivery <u>person</u>. And you?
Erik: I'm a <u>cook</u>.

Page 123

A.

1. e
2. d
3. a
4. b
5. c

B.

1. office worker
2. waiter
3. taxi driver
4. construction worker
5. computer programmer

C.

Jobs	Indoors	Outdoors	With People	With Machines
waiter	✔		✔	
sales clerk	✔		✔	
health aide	✔		✔	
delivery person	✔	✔	✔	
taxicab driver		✔	✔	✔

Page 124

A.

1. sell
2. drive
3. fix
4. use

B.

Aziza: <u>What</u> can <u>you</u> do?
Ly: I can <u>cook</u>. <u>And</u> you?
Aziza: I can use a <u>computer</u>.

C.

Marco: Can <u>you</u> drive a <u>car</u>?
Alex: <u>Yes</u>, I can. Can you <u>fix</u> things?
Marco: No, I <u>can't</u>.

Page 125

A.

1. taxi driver
2. computer programmer
3. cashier

B.

1. b
2. e
3. f
4. c
5. a
6. d

C.

1. Lin: 2
2. Eva: 3
3. Thomas: 1

Page 126

A.

Ivan: I <u>was</u> a salesclerk in Russia. What did you <u>do</u> before?
Marco: I was a waiter in Colombia.
David and Mei: We <u>were</u> cooks in Vietnam. What did you do <u>before</u>?
Thomas: I was a <u>taxi driver</u> in Haiti.

Page 127

B.

1. Ivan Stoli
2. Jake's Restaurant
3. 25 hours
4. $364.96
5. $21.90

C.

1. $364.96
2. $135.04

Page 128

A.

1. Caution Work Area
2. Fire Extinguisher
3. High Voltage KEEP OUT
4. No Smoking
5. Emergency Exit
6. Wash Hands

Page 129

A.

1. were
2. was
3. was
4. was
5. were
6. were
7. were
8. was
9. was
10. were

B.

1. can't
2. can
3. can
4. can't
5. can
6. can
7. can
8. can't
9. can't
10. can

Page 130

B.

1. 474 Jones Street, Troy, NY
2. (518) 555-6263
3. Sales clerk
4. Banana Computers
5. No, she can't.
6. Yes, she can.

Page 131

A.

Thomas: Good morning, Ms. Carter. I'm calling about the want ad for a delivery person. I work at Kane's Department Store now. <u>I deliver refrigerators and stoves.</u>

Ms. Carter: What did you do before?

Thomas: <u>I was a taxi driver in Haiti.</u> I can drive a car.

Ms. Carter: Can you drive a truck?

Thomas: <u>Yes, I can.</u>

Ms. Carter: When can you work?

Thomas: <u>I can work Tuesday to Saturday from 7:00 A.M. to 5:00 P.M.</u>

Ms. Carter: There is an opening from 7:00 A.M. to 2:00 P.M. Tuesday to Friday. Is that good for you?

Thomas: <u>Yes, it is. Thank you.</u>

Page 132

A.

Unit 12: How do you get to class?

Page 134

A.

1. drive a car
2. take a bus
3. ride a bike
4. take a subway
5. walk
6. take a taxicab

B.

Marco: How do you get to school?

Ivan: I <u>ride</u> a bike.

Thomas: I <u>drive</u> a car.

Lin: I don't have a car. I <u>walk</u>.

Alex: I <u>take</u> a bus.

Page 135

A.

David: Excuse <u>me</u>. Where is the <u>post office</u>?

Eva: It's straight <u>ahead</u>.

Thomas: Excuse me. <u>Where</u> is the restaurant?

Eva: It's <u>between</u> the drugstore and the library.

B.

1. It's across from the bank.
2. It's across from the restaurant.
3. It's between the hospital and the park.

Page 136

A.

1. d
2. c
3. a
4. b

B.

Aziza: How do I get to East Beach?

Thomas: Take the <u>12 Bus</u>.

Aziza: How do I get <u>to</u> Riverton Airport?

Thomas: Take the <u>J Train</u>.

C.

Aziza: When <u>does</u> the <u>next</u> train to Dallas leave?

Woman: It leaves at <u>7:30</u>.

Aziza: At 7:30? <u>Thanks</u>.

Page 137

B.

1. a learner's permit
2. Tuesday
3. 10:00
4. $34

C.

Page 138

A.

1. Hospital
2. Bus Stop
3. Stop
4. One Way
5. No Parking
6. Speed Limit

B.

1.
2.

Page 139

A.

Marco: How often <u>does</u> the D Train leave?

Woman: It leaves <u>every</u> half hour.

Marco: Oh good. At 2:00, 2:30, and 3:00.

Eva: <u>How</u> often does the subway leave?

Woman: It leaves every 15 <u>minutes</u>.

Eva: Oh good. At 12:00, 12:15, and 12:30.

Mei: How <u>often</u> does the bus <u>leave</u>?

Woman: It leaves every <u>hour</u>.

Mei: Oh good. At 6:00, 7:00, and 8:00.

B.

1. Every half hour
2. Every hour
3. Every half hour
4. Every 15 minutes
5. Every hour

Page 140

B.

1. 3:25
2. 6:15
3. 3:25
4. 4:10
5. 3:40
6. 3:25
7. 5:45
8. 3:10
9. 2:55
10. 4:25

Page 141

A.

1. When
2. Where
3. Who
4. What
5. What
6. What
7. Where
8. Who

B.

1. g
2. f
3. c
4. e
5. a
6. d
7. b

Page 142

B.

1. Jade's problem at school

C.

1. She takes the bus.
2. Her appointment is at 7:30.
3. Her class is at 8:00.
4. She talks to her classmates.
5. They want Jade to stop talking to her classmates when the teacher is talking.

Page 144

A.

1. Take
2. Ride
3. Drive
4. Take
5. Take
6. Walk